Titles by Anthony Horowitz

The Power of Five (Book One): *Raven's Gate*
The Power of Five (Book Two): *Evil Star*
The Power of Five (Book Three): *Nightrise*
The Power of Five (Book Four): *Necropolis*
The Power of Five (Book Five): *Oblivion*

The Alex Rider series:
Stormbreaker
Point Blanc
Skeleton Key
Eagle Strike
Scorpia
Ark Angel
Snakehead
Crocodile Tears
Scorpia Rising

The Devil and His Boy
Granny
Groosham Grange
Return to Groosham Grange
The Switch
More Bloody Horowitz

The Diamond Brothers books:
The Falcon's Malteser
Public Enemy Number Two
South by South East
Four of Diamonds

OBLIVION

OBLIVION

ANTHONY HOROWITZ

WALKER
INDIA

First published 2012 by Walker Books Ltd
87 Vauxhall Walk, London SE11 5HJ

This edition published 2012

2 4 6 8 10 9 7 5 3 1

This book has been typeset in Frutiger

Printed and bound in India

British Library Cataloguing in Publication Data:
a catalogue record for this book is
available from the British Library

ISBN 978-1-4063-4481-3

www.walker.co.uk

www.powerof5.co.uk

CONTENTS

THE VILLAGE

ONE

It was the week before my sixteenth birthday when the boy fell out of the door and everything changed. Is that a good start? Miss Keyland, who taught me at the village school, used to say that you have to reach out and grab the reader with the first sentence. If you waste time with descriptions of the sky or the weather or the smell of freshly cut grass or whatever, people may not bother to read on, and I've got a big story to tell. In fact, it's the biggest story in the world. The end of the world ... and stories don't get any bigger than that.

Maybe that's where I should have begun. All these different things were happening in Britain, in America, in the Middle East – and, of course, in Antarctica. That's where the armies were heading. There was going to be this huge battle in which the future of everything and everyone would be decided. And I didn't know anything about it. I didn't even realize how horrible everything had become.

Well, it's too late now. I've started so I might as well keep going. Me. The boy. The door. Let's take them one by one.

My name is Holly – at least, that's what everyone used to call me. I was christened Hermione but that was considered much too posh for the sort of girl I became, and anyway, Holly was easier to spell. Nobody ever used my family name. Like a lot of kids in the village, my parents were dead and everyone found it easier just to stick to first names. I expect you want to know what I look like. I'm not sure how to describe myself but I might as well say straight off that, back then, I wasn't pretty. I had straw-coloured hair and unfortunately it looked a bit like straw too, long and tangled like something falling out of a mattress. I had round cheeks and freckles and bright, blue eyes. I'd been working on the farm since I was old enough to push a wheelbarrow (which was actually very young indeed) so I was quite stocky. My nails were chipped and full of dirt. If I'd ever had nicer clothes, I might have looked all right, but the shirt and dungarees I always wore had been worn by several people before me and they didn't do me any favours.

I lived with my grandparents. Actually, they weren't related to me at all. We didn't have any shared blood. But that was how I thought of them. Their names were Rita and John and they must have been in their late seventies ... they were the sort of age that's so old you don't bother trying to guess any more. To be fair, they were both in pretty good shape; slow but they could get around and they were fully *compos mentis* (*compos* meaning "in command" and *mentis* meaning "of the mind", from the Latin. Miss Keyland taught me that). If I had a problem with them, it was that they didn't talk very much. They liked to keep themselves to themselves – which wasn't that easy once they'd adopted me and taken me into their house. They had been married for as long as anyone could remember and they would have been lost without each other.

There was a church in the middle of the village, St Botolph's, which dated back to the Normans. It stood at the crossroads next to the main square and it was a grim old place, bashed around by the centuries and rebuilt so often that it was a complete patchwork, as if a bulldozer had crashed into it at some time and they'd had to put it back together quickly before anyone noticed. It was full every Sunday, but then, nobody in the village would have thought of not going to Sunday service, and even Rita and John put on their best clothes and hobbled down there arm in arm. Personally, I hated the place. For a start, I didn't believe in God and often used to think that if there was a God, even He would get bored of the same hymns and prayers week after week. That didn't stop the vicar though. His sermons went on for hours and they never varied. *Pray for mercy. We're being punished for our sins. We're all doomed.* He may have had a point but I never believed the answer was to be found on my knees, on that hard stone floor.

The church was also used for village meetings every Wednesday, but we weren't allowed to go to them until we were sixteen. Until then, you weren't considered grown up enough to join in the discussion, even if you were grown up enough to slog your guts out from dawn to dusk. It was funny how it worked.

The door wasn't actually in the church. It was round the back. The church was surrounded by a cemetery full of wonky gravestones with a gravel path running through the middle, and I often used it as a short cut home. On the other side there was an even older church, or the remains of one that had originally stood on the site. Not much of it was left; just a couple of crumbling archways and a wall with two gaping holes that might once have been magnificent windows, stained glass and all the rest of it, and beneath them a wooden door.

There had always been something strange about the door because, first of all, it didn't go anywhere. There were a couple of tombstones in front of it and a small gravel yard behind, but it didn't lead into a sacristy or a cloister or any other part of the building. And there was a sort of question mark over the door itself. That is to say, who made it and when? The ruins were literally hundreds of years old ("pre-medieval," Miss Keyland said) and yet the door didn't look ancient at all. I mean, if it had been there for centuries, how come the wood hadn't rotted? Obviously, someone must have replaced it, but Rita, who had been born in the village, told me it hadn't happened in her lifetime and that must have been almost a century in itself. It was all very weird.

And one evening at the end of August, it suddenly opened and a boy fell out.

I was on my way home from the orchards, where I had been apple picking, one of my least favourite jobs, although to be honest anything to do with the growing and storing of food is hard work – boring and repetitive. The worst things about apple picking? Realizing that the overripe Golden Delicious you've just spent half an hour shaking off the branch is actually going to be neither golden nor delicious. Finding that a wasp has burrowed into its rotten core and getting a nasty sting on your palm as a result. Spiking yourself for the fiftieth time on a bramble that's been waiting a whole year to gouge into your flesh. Lugging the basket back to the collection point in the full heat of the afternoon, with blisters on your shoulders and worse ones on your fingers. And the endlessness of it. Mr Bantoft – farm manager, fruit division – had said there were fewer apples that year. He said the entire orchard was beginning to fail. But it didn't seem that way to me.

Anyway, I was tired and I was grubby and I wasn't thinking of very much when the door in the old wall opened and this boy staggered forward and crumpled onto the grass. He was quite skinny with long, very black hair cut straight across his forehead, and I was puzzled because I didn't recognize him at once. But then, one side of his face was streaked with blood. In fact, there were pints of the stuff pouring down the side of his cheek. It was dripping onto his shoulder and his shirt was soaked. I ran over to him and stopped with my heart pounding, biting on my knuckles, which is what I always do when I'm shocked by something. And here was the thing. I had never seen this boy. Impossible though it was, I knew at once.

He wasn't from the village.

He saw me and his eyes widened, reminding me of a rabbit just before you put an arrow through its throat. He wasn't as badly hurt as I had first thought. Something had whacked into the side of his head just above the temple and he had a nasty cut, but I didn't think his skull was fractured. He was wearing a shirt, jeans and trainers and they looked new. He was about as strange as a stranger could be. He didn't even look English. His eyes were as dark as his hair. And there was something about his nose and his cheekbones ... it was as if they'd been carved out of wood.

"Where am I?" he asked.

"You're at the church," I said. It was such an odd question. I wasn't sure how to answer.

"What church? Where is it?"

"The church is called St Botolph's. It's in the village."

The boy looked at me as if I didn't know what I was talking about. Then he gave up on me. "This isn't right," he said. "I have to go back."

"Back where?"

But he wasn't listening to me. He had already got up and gone back to the door. He closed it, then opened it again. I don't know what he was expecting to find on the other side but, like I've already explained, it opened into this little yard with just a few tufts of grass sprouting out of the gravel. The boy went through the door, shutting it behind him. I walked round so I could see him on the other side. He was standing there, breathing heavily. He seemed to have forgotten the wound on his head. Then he noticed me watching him. "It's broken," he said.

"What's broken?"

"The door. It should have sent me back."

"Whoa! Slow down." I stepped forward and almost grabbed hold of him, then thought better of it. "It's just a door. It opens and closes. What else is it meant to do?"

"I just told you. I want it to take me where I came from. I have to find my brother. I have to go back."

"Go back where?"

"Hong Kong."

I had been worried that the boy might need to see a doctor for the wound in his head, and that would cause all sorts of problems because he would have to explain how he'd arrived in the village and they'd probably beat him up and interrogate him before they even thought about treating him. But that was only half of it. It seemed that he was delirious. He said he had come from Hong Kong, which was on the other side of the world, and even if there had been any commercial planes flying, which there weren't, that would have been impossible.

And there was something else that I only noticed now. His accent. He certainly wasn't from the village or anywhere close by. He didn't even sound English.

I had more or less made up my mind by this point. It was time to be on my way. The boy was hurt, foreign, deranged and uninvited – all of which added up to serious trouble. But it didn't need to be my trouble. I would continue home and leave someone else to look after him. But even as I was about to make my move, he glanced up at me as if he had somehow read my mind and suddenly he looked so hopelessly lost and afraid that I knew I couldn't leave him.

"Hermione?" he asked.

I couldn't remember telling him that. "That is my name," I said. "But my friends call me Holly."

"Holly..." He looked dazed.

"How did you hurt yourself?" I asked.

He put his hand to his head, then examined the blood on his fingertips as if noticing it for the first time. "I don't know. I guess something must have hit me. The whole place was being torn down … this temple in Hong Kong. There was a typhoon. You must have seen it on TV."

"There is no TV. Not any more." There was something else that didn't add up. "When were you in Hong Kong?" I asked.

"Right now. Just a minute ago."

That was when I knew he was crazy and I would have been on my way except at that moment I heard voices: two men crossing the graveyard from the north side. I knew at once who they were – Mike Dolan and Simon Reade. They worked together on the outer perimeter and must have been on their way there now as they were both carrying guns. If they saw the boy, it would all be over. He was a stranger. He had no place here. They would blast him full of holes without even asking him his name – something that, incidentally, I hadn't yet done myself.

"You have to get out of sight," I whispered.

"What?"

"Just do it!" I shoved the boy away and he crouched down right in the corner, where the ancient wall jutted away from the church. It was dark there, out of the sun, and a shadow fell over him like a piece of tarpaulin. A second later, the two men saw me. "What are you doing out here, Holly?" Dolan asked. "Shouldn't you be at home?" That was typical of him. Just because he carried a gun he thought he had the right to boss everyone around. He was a big, thick-set man with a beard and dirty clothes. Well, we all had dirty clothes but his were worse than most. I'd never much liked him.

"I was just on my way," I said.

"What's that you've got on your hands? Have you hurt yourself?"

I looked down and saw the boy's blood. I must have got some on myself when I pushed him. "It's nothing," I said. "I cut myself."

"On an apple tree?" They both laughed.

Then Reade turned on me with laser eyes. He was the smaller of the two, thin and pale. He liked hanging around with Dolan because it made him feel important. He was suspicious of everything, like a dog always sniffing at your feet. "Did I hear you talking to someone?" he asked.

"No."

"I think I did."

I didn't know what to say. Out of the corner of my eye, I could see the boy scrunched up in the corner and I wondered why I was lying on his behalf. What could I possibly have been doing here that would make these two men leave me alone? My mind scrabbled for an answer and it was given to me by the church. "I was praying," I said.

The two of them nodded. They both had wives who could have been nuns if they weren't married ... the sort who crossed themselves ten times a day and actually cried when they read the Bible. There were a lot of people in the village like that. They even had prayer meetings on their afternoons off. I smiled and tried to look holy. Somehow, it worked.

"It's good to pray," Dolan said. "We need all the help we can get. But it'll be dark soon. You'd best be home."

"Absolutely, Mr Dolan."

They went on their way, the two of them chatting together with their guns slanting across their shoulder blades. I waited until they had gone, then hurried over to the boy. To my astonishment, he had fallen asleep – although it was more likely that shock and exhaustion had knocked him out. I shook him awake.

"Scott...?" he muttered.

"Who is Scott?" I asked.

"My brother..."

"Well, I'm afraid I'm not Scott. I'm Holly. How are you feeling?"

"I don't know. I'm confused."

"You haven't told me your name."

"You haven't asked."

"I'm asking now."

"It's Jamie. I'm Jamie Tyler..." He tried to get to his feet but he was too weak and dizzy. "You have to help me," he said.

"I've already helped you. I just stopped you from getting shot. And maybe I'll help you some more. But you have to tell me where you came from – where you really came from – and who you are. You don't understand how much trouble I could get into, even for talking to you."

"OK." He swallowed and I saw a wave of pain pass across his eyes. "Do you have any water?"

I reached for my backpack and opened it. I'd had a full bottle of water when I started work but now there wasn't much left. I handed it to him and he emptied it at once, as if he had no idea how valuable it was. The water seemed to revive him a little. He straightened up. The blood was drying in what was left of the afternoon sun. "What country is this?" he asked.

I shrugged. What sort of question was that? "What country do you think it is?" I exclaimed. "It's England. Where else would it be?"

"Are we near London?"

"I've never been to London. I've got no idea." I was rapidly losing my patience. "Tell me what I want to know or I'm going to be on my way and leave you here."

"No. Don't do that." He put out a hand, stopping me. "I'll tell you what I can. But it won't help you. You won't believe me."

"Try me." And you'd better get on with it, I wanted to add. The sun was dipping behind the steeple. The gravestones were throwing out shadows that reached ever further. I would already be expected home.

"Is there somewhere else we can talk? Can we go inside?"

"Tell me now."

But he never did … at least, not then. I hadn't heard the footsteps behind me. I hadn't realized that Mike Dolan and Simon Reade had come back until I turned round and saw them, saw them standing there, aiming at Jamie.

"There you are," Reade said. "I told you something was up."

"Who is he?" Dolan demanded, then, to Jamie, "Who are you?"

"I'm Jamie."

"How did you get here?"

Jamie hesitated. I could see him thinking what to say. "I took a bus," he said, finally.

It was the wrong answer. Almost lazily, Dolan swung his rifle so that the butt crashed into the side of Jamie's head and he went sprawling. It was the side that had been undamaged. Until that moment anyway. I shouted out but Reade stepped in front of me, blocking my way. Jamie lay still. Dolan stood over him. He turned to me. "You've got some explaining to do, Holly," he said. "But that can come later. Right now you'd better get home." He nodded at Simon. "Let's get this boy tied up and locked somewhere safe. And find the Reverend Johnstone. We're going to have to call an Assembly."

And that was it. I could only stand there and watch as the two men scooped up the boy and dragged him away.

TWO

Rita and John lived in a modern, three-bedroomed house next to the garage – not, of course, that there was any petrol. The two pumps stood next to each other like metal tombstones, the glass broken and the metal rusted, with Mr and Mrs Esso lying dead beneath. I ran straight past it and didn't stop until I got home.

I'm going to have to describe the village, or what happened later won't make any sense.

Basically, it was set on the side of a very slight hill, with the square and the church and the main hall in the middle so there was an upper and a lower village, which were actually quite different from each other. The bit where I lived was mainly modern, consisting of neat brick houses with picture windows and back gardens which had once been full of flowers but that were now planted with vegetables. The bottom half was much older. This was where all the weekenders had lived, but they were all gone now and their houses had been taken over. These were mainly thatched cottages, which caused all sorts of problems with grubs living in the thatch and leaks in the windows, but there were also a couple of rows of pretty terraces that almost vanished behind the wisteria and honeysuckle that still erupted every spring, even though nobody looked after them.

Walking down from the square, you came to a crossroads with the Queen's Head on one side. The Queen, as everyone called it, was white, half-timbered and still made its own beer. Known as Queen's Rot, it had been something of a joke in the county: weak, watery and wet was how the locals described it. Nobody had thought that, one day, it would be the only beer you could get. Turn right and you looped back on yourself, coming out on Ferry Lane behind the garage. Turn left and you passed about half a dozen houses before coming to open farmland and the orchards. The village grew wheat, potatoes and sugar beet, depending on the season, and there were pigs and chickens too. Everyone had their own allotment but the rule was that you had to share everything, even though this always led to arguments.

Follow the main road all the way down to the bottom and you came to a quay with a flagpole but no flag, and the river, a dead end in every sense because although the water had once been full of fish, it was now thick and oily and a five-minute swim would put you into hospital – if we had one, which we didn't – or more probably the grave. In The Queen there was a photograph of the river as it had once been, and even though it was a black-and-white picture it still looked more colourful than it did now. There was no other way out of the village and only one way in. That was its distinguishing feature. A single road ran through the thick woodland that surrounded us on three sides. Over the years, a ring of watchtowers had been constructed so that it was impossible to approach the village without being seen. Big signs warned people that they would be shot if they came too close and I did hear gunfire once or twice in the middle of the day, but as I never went to a village meeting I don't know how many people tried to get in, how many were turned back or how many died.

We villagers were allowed to come and go. We had passwords that changed every month and that were posted in the old bus shelter which stood as a reminder of the time when there had been buses. September's password was "samphire". There were still plenty of rabbits in the wood (although fewer in recent years) and we were encouraged to go out hunting, using bows and arrows to conserve bullets. I'd once brought down a wild deer with a single arrow through its neck and for about a week after that I was the village hero. Everyone had something nice to say about me. But then the last scrap of meat was eaten and the bones were boiled down to the last bowl of soup and things quickly went back to normal.

Anyway, there you have it. A village of about three hundred people with a dense wood at one end and a dead river at the other. We were isolated. And we all knew that was probably the reason we were still alive.

Rita was waiting for me on the other side of the front door and she knew immediately from my face that something was wrong. She was stick-thin with long, silver hair and eyes that had retreated into caves. When she was angry, she looked like a witch. Now she was just scared, although as usual she was doing her best not to show it. Rita kept her emotions locked up like her best china and only brought them out for special occasions.

"What is it, Hermione?" She was the only one who called me that. "What's happened? Why are you late?"

"I met someone..." I hesitated.

"Who did you meet?"

"It was a boy. But he wasn't from the village."

She stared at me. "What do you mean?

"He just appeared at the church. He said his name was Jamie. I'd never seen him before."

"So what did you do?"

"I didn't do anything. I talked to him."

Rita's shoulders sagged. It was a very deliberate movement. She did that to show she was annoyed. Then she turned on her heel and hurried into the kitchen, where John and the last member of our little household – George – were having their tea.

I don't need to tell you a lot about John. He never said very much. He was a small, white-haired man – shorter than Rita – who spent most of his time sitting there with a sort of half-dazed smile on his face. He wasn't stupid. I think he just didn't want to get involved. George was another matter. He was eighteen, three years older than me, and like me he had no parents. He worked at the village bakery and you could tell that just by looking at him because he was quite fleshy and he was always covered in a thin coating of flour. He had blond hair, which he never combed, and blue eyes. They were his best feature. Nobody thought George had very much to offer, but I knew him better than anyone and if I'd had to choose one person in the village to stick up for me, it would have been him.

The two of us had grown up as brother and sister, looked after by Rita and John. George was very shy and always seemed to be uncomfortable when I was around. I sometimes thought that when Rita and John died, we'd simply take over the house and end up living together ... and well we might have if things hadn't turned out the way they did.

"There's been a stranger in the village," Rita announced as I followed her into the room.

"A stranger?" John looked up from his porridge – or whatever slop he was eating.

"I found him in the churchyard," I said.

"Where did he come from?"

"I don't know. He was just there." I wasn't going to tell them about the door. That still didn't make any sense to me.

"So who was he?" George asked. "What was his name?"

"He said his name was Jamie. I didn't talk to him much. He was just a boy about the same age as me. And he had a funny accent. I don't think he was English."

"And you raised the alarm...?"

This was the big question. Everyone waited for me to answer.

"I didn't have a chance to. Simon Reade and Mike Dolan found us together. They grabbed Jamie and they sent me home."

"They found you talking together? And you hadn't raised the alarm?" Rita stared at me.

I nodded miserably.

"You don't realize how much trouble you're in. You broke the first rule of the village. The moment you saw him, you should have called for help."

"I know. But he was so young. And he was hurt. He was covered in blood."

"He'll be worse than that when the Council have finished with him."

"You shouldn't be angry with her," George said. He had a way of talking, slow and deliberate, that always made you feel he'd thought very carefully about what he was about to say. "Holly didn't help this boy come here and it wasn't her fault she saw him first. And if he was hurt, it was only right she should try to help him."

"Simon and Mike won't see it that way."

"They'll try to make trouble. They always do. It makes them feel important." George got up from the table and fetched the saucepan. "You'd better have something to eat," he said. "We left you some stew."

"I'm not hungry."

"You should eat anyway."

I did as I was told. It was getting dark and Rita nodded at George, who got out a couple of candles and lit them. I would have preferred an electric light. The little flames somehow emphasized the darkness rather than illuminating it. I could feel the world outside and all sorts of unnamed troubles pressing in on me. But there was no reason to waste a battery. They were only kept for emergencies.

There was a knock at the door. John went out and I expected him to return with Simon Reade or Mike Dolan, so I was relieved when it was Miss Keyland that he showed into the room.

Anne Keyland was one of those people you couldn't help liking. She was about sixty, but young with it, full of energy, striding around the place in her yellow wellington boots. She had lost a lot of weight recently and there were rumours that she was ill, but even if that had been the case, she would never have admitted it. She still ran the village school. She was also deputy chair of the Council. I guessed at once that was the reason she was here.

She gave me a hug. "Holly. Trust you to get into trouble! A stranger in the village and you have to be the one who finds him. You're going to have to tell me everything he said to you, my dear. How did he get past the watchtowers? What was he doing at the church? Where had he come from?"

"I'll tell you everything," I exclaimed. I was just glad it was her. Whatever rules I'd broken, I knew she'd be on my side.

"Not just me, I'm afraid. They've called a Council meeting. They're going to talk to the boy and decide what to do with him – and they want you there."

"At the Council?"

"Yes. You don't need to be scared. We just need to know the truth about what happened."

"What will they do to him?" George asked.

"That depends on where he came from and what he was hoping to do. If he was sent to spy on us…" She left the sentence unfinished.

"I want to come," said George. "I don't think Holly should go on her own."

"I'm afraid that's not possible, George. Rita will come as Holly's guardian. And I'll be there, so you don't need to worry."

"When is the Council meeting?" I asked. I expected it to be the following morning or maybe in the early evening, after work.

"They're already there," Miss Keyland replied. "They're waiting for you now."

Out of the corner of my eye, I saw Rita and John exchange a look. It was as if they'd just heard very bad news. People very rarely went out at night ... and certainly not without the light of a full moon. It was only now that I saw how serious this was.

"Well, we'd better go then," Rita said.

And that was it. She stood up. And we went.

THREE

They were waiting for us inside the church, arranged in a semi-circle, up near the altar with the cross and the stained-glass window showing the apostles St Peter and St Andrew fishing – although it was pretty much blank against the night sky. More candles and a couple of oil lamps had been lit so I could clearly see all the people who were waiting for me. I can't say any of them smiled as I came in, but even so I relaxed a little. They might call themselves the Council with a capital C but these were men and women I had known all my life. At the end of the day, I hadn't really done anything wrong. They weren't going to hurt me.

The vicar, Reverend Johnstone, was the first one I saw, with that long face he always pulled before one of his endless sermons. Mike Dolan and Simon Reade were next to him, enjoying their moment of glory. Then came Mr and Mrs Flint, a solid, ordinary couple in their fifties. They had the house at the bottom of the hill, overlooking the river, and although they had lost both their children, they always tried to be positive. Miss Keyland took her place next to them, sitting beside Sir Ian Ingram, universally known as "I. I." (though not to his face), the chairman of the Council and the oldest, wisest, most serious man in the village. Nobody knew why he had been knighted. Indeed, we only had his say-so that he ever had been. But nobody would have dreamt of arguing. When I say that his word was law, I mean it quite literally. He had once been a barrister and he had set down in writing a lot of the laws by which we now lived.

Jamie Tyler was sitting with his back to me, facing the altar. He was slumped in a chair; not tied to it, but looking too exhausted to move. He turned round as I came in and I saw that his face had been cleaned up and that someone had put a bandage on his forehead. They had also taken his shirt, and if he'd asked me when he'd get it back, I would have told him not to bother waiting. Once it had been washed, it would make a nice present for someone's teenage son because it was almost brand new and still had its colour and all of its buttons. He would just have to make do with the ill-fitting and worn-out T-shirt with HEINZ 57 written on the front – which was what he had been given in its place.

Our eyes met and for just a second I felt him trying to tell me something. I wanted to look away but somehow I found my gaze locked in place. George often did something quite similar at the dinner table – somehow signal to me not to repeat something he'd said or avoid telling Rita what we'd been up to during the day. But with Jamie it was much more than that. It was as if I could hear his voice whispering to me, right up against my ear.

Don't say anything...

It was the weirdest sensation I'd ever had, and as I sat down next to him (not good – two chairs facing the Council, two of us being accused) I had to work hard to persuade myself that I'd just imagined it, that he hadn't just trespassed inside my head. Examining him now, he looked so ordinary, so innocent. And yet I was beginning to realize that he was anything but.

Rita took her place in one of the pews, meaning that she was watching, rather than part of the Council. The session began.

To start with, Reade and Dolan gave their version of what had happened, each of them trying to outdo the other in being the centre of attention so that they ended up saying everything twice. They had seen me, they had asked me what I was doing, they had realized I was lying, they had come back and found me with the boy. Although they tried to dress it up and make it worse than it really was, that was about the sum of it.

Sir Ian glared at me. "Why did you not raise the alarm the moment you saw the boy?" he asked.

"I was going to," I said. "But I didn't have a chance."

"You lied to Mr Dolan and to Mr Reade."

"I don't know why I did that." It was certainly the truth. I must have been out of my mind. "I suppose it was because he was hurt."

"The safety of the village, our entire survival, rests on a single premise. We don't let anyone know we are here. We protect ourselves from the outside world – with force if need be. If this boy came and went and told others what we have here, it could all be over for us. Do you understand that? And yet you were prepared to let that happen."

"He didn't look like a spy," I said. My mouth had gone dry and I felt wretched.

Sir Ian turned his attention to Jamie. "Your name is Jamie Tyler," he said.

"Yes, sir."

"Where have you come from?"

"I've already told you." Jamie's voice had changed since I had found him an hour or two ago. It had lost the edge of panic. He sounded more assured. "I can't remember what happened to me. I woke up in the wood and someone had hit me on the head. There was a lot of blood. I didn't know which way to go so I just sort of stumbled forward and then I came upon this village. I was scared of being seen so I hid behind the church. That was where Holly found me."

He was lying. He hadn't told them about the door – or about the typhoon and Hong Kong … all the things he had told me. I was going to say something but there he was again, inside my head.

Please…

"How did you get past the watchtowers?" the vicar asked.

"I didn't see any watchtowers, sir. I didn't see anything until I reached the village and I didn't mean to come here. It was just where I arrived."

"And where had you come from?" Sir Ian repeated his question.

Jamie touched the bandage around his head. "I'm afraid I can't tell you that, sir. I don't remember. All I know is that I woke up in the forest. I guess I must have been dumped there."

"He's lying," Reade said.

"Nobody could have got past the watchtowers," Dolan agreed.

"Give us an hour alone with him," Reade continued. "We'll make him remember where he came from."

"We're not hurting children." I forget if it was Mr or Mrs Flint who said that, but both of them looked outraged. He and his wife looked very similar. They always agreed with each other.

"Is this what he told you?" Sir Ian had turned back to me.

This was the moment of truth. I was the only person in the church who knew for certain that Jamie was making everything up. He certainly hadn't had amnesia when he met me and even if he had been lying then, it was a different story from the one he was telling now. All my instincts were screaming at me to separate myself from him, to stand up and accuse him. But for some reason I couldn't do it. I had no idea who he was. I had barely spoken to him. But still I found myself speaking on his behalf. "He was very confused," I said. "He didn't make a lot of sense. He certainly didn't know where he was." All of which was true, sort of. It just wasn't completely true.

Sir Ian examined Jamie. "You have an American accent," he said.

"Yes, sir."

"But that's not possible. You couldn't possibly have come from America. Do you have any memories of being in a plane or a ship?"

"Sir, I wish I could help you. But I don't remember anything."

Sir Ian turned to his deputy. "Anne?"

Miss Keyland drew herself up in the way I had often seen her do in class. She had put her glasses on, but she was looking over them, not through them. "If the boy can't help us, then we're going to have to decide among ourselves what we're going to do with him," she said. "What are the choices? We know how we've dealt with intruders in the past."

"He's a child," Reverend Johnstone said, making the same point as the Flints.

"He's at least fifteen," Dolan countered. "And he knew what he was doing, coming here."

"We could give him a home and make him one of us," Miss Keyland went on. "We would have to watch him, of course. He wouldn't be allowed outside the perimeter. In normal circumstances, given his age, that is what I would recommend. But these are not normal circumstances, are they, Sir Ian?"

"Unfortunately not."

Sir Ian produced a large white envelope. Even the sight of it seemed to send a collective shudder among the members of the Council and I wondered what on earth it could be about and why it was relevant now. They all knew what was inside, even before he opened the envelope and took out a photograph. He flipped it round so that Jamie could see it – and so I saw it too. There were actually five photographs on a single sheet, the faces of four boys and a girl. And written underneath:

REWARD. £100,000 FOR INFORMATION LEADING TO THE ARREST OF ANY OF THESE FIVE CHILDREN. CALLS WILL BE TREATED IN THE STRICTEST CONFIDENCE. CONTACT THE POLICE ON 999 AT ANY TIME.

Jamie's face was one of them. No. I did a double-take. His face was actually *two* of them. There must have been some sort of mistake at the printers because two of the pictures were duplicates, one next to the other. Then I remembered. Before he'd contracted his fake amnesia, Jamie had talked to me about a brother. It must have been a twin brother. But who were the others? And how – and when – had the photographs arrived in the village? There hadn't been a mail delivery for as long as I could remember. And anyway, nobody used money any more. A hundred thousand pounds was worthless. It could be a million pounds and it would make no difference. I suddenly wished I was in my bed. I didn't understand any of this.

"This is not the boy in the photograph," Mrs Flint said.

"It's him," Dolan snapped.

"It can't be. The photograph was taken ten years ago and look at him! He hasn't grown up at all!"

"It's still him. It's identical."

"If the police are looking for him, they should be informed," Reade said, although I had no idea how he was going to manage that either. What was he going to do? Send them a carrier pigeon? "They can work out why he looks the same. "

"What will we do with the reward money?" Mr Flint asked.

"The reward may have changed," Reade said. "It could be food. Machinery. Seeds. It could be anything we want..."

"The reward is not the issue," Sir Ian cut in. "If the police are looking for the boy it's our duty to inform them. I propose that's what we do. We call the police and keep the boy in custody until they arrive. Shall we put it to the vote?"

Reade and Dolan raised their hands straight away. "I agree," Dolan said.

Mr Flint shook his head. "I'm not so sure..." he began. "Do we really want to get involved with the police – or with anyone outside the village?" He looked at Mrs Flint, who nodded her agreement. That was three for, two against.

"I think we should consider the issue further," the vicar muttered. That was typical of him. He never did anything in a hurry. He was the sort of man who could hum and haw for twenty minutes at a christening before he announced the name. "Yes," he agreed with himself. "We need to think about it more."

Three all. Miss Keyland had the casting vote. I saw her deliberating. She didn't look happy. But as it happened, she never got a chance to speak.

"You need your heads examined if you're going to call the police..."

The voice came from the back of the church. I twisted round to see who it was, noticing at the same time that all the members of the Council had reacted with outrage. Reade and Dolan were already on their feet. Miss Keyland was shocked, Sir Ian furious.

A figure moved out of the darkness.

It was the Traveller. Who else could it have been? And now I'm going to have to stop for a moment to tell you about him, the one man who had arrived in the village during my lifetime, the only outsider who'd been allowed to stay.

He had come seven years before, when I was eight, travelling down the river on a houseboat pulled by a black-and-white cross-shire horse. That makes him sound like some sort of gypsy, and he might well have been, but there was something more to him that he always kept concealed. He was about forty with dark, intelligent eyes that refused to meet your own and he had a habit of never being quite where you expected him to be. In many ways he reminded me of an actor. I had seen pictures of performers in the time of Shakespeare and he had that same look, the same confidence. He had the right voice for it too. When he spoke, you wanted to listen.

There were some who said he'd been in government, others said the army or the air force, but nobody knew for sure. He had come down the river on that houseboat of his – *Lady Jane* was its name – and of course he had been pulled out and arrested the moment he showed his face. Half the village wanted to expel him and the other half weren't a great deal more welcoming. There were plenty who would have liked to have strung him up from a tree in case he told anyone about us, how many of us there were, how many supplies we had. But the Traveller had used that voice of his to talk his way out of trouble. He had talked to the whole village and after that they had put it to the vote and decided to take him in.

How had he done it? Well, first of all there were all the supplies on the boat – the food and the medicine which he could have hidden upriver but which he chose instead to share. He even had a dozen bottles of whisky, which made him a lot of friends. And then there was his horse, which was put to work for a while but which quickly ended up providing fresh meat for most of the population. I don't like horse myself. It's tough and chewy and has a nasty smell – but after an almost non-stop diet of vegetables and herbs, anything with a bone in it is to be welcomed. The Traveller gave the village everything he had except his name. That he kept to himself. He moored his boat about a quarter of a mile down the river and lived there on his own. He never came to Assemblies. On the other hand, he was a good craftsman and helped mend the roofs that had been damaged in the storms of the winter before. Almost single-handedly, he rebuilt the wall at the bottom of the pig field. It had been in a state of collapse for years. People still didn't trust him completely, but he kept himself to himself and made no enemies and so they let him stay.

But what he had done now was against all the rules. He had been inside the church during a meeting of the Council and if eavesdropping wasn't bad enough, he had actually made himself known, joining in the discussion, giving his opinion where it wasn't wanted. And he was still at it, moving forward in that dark way of his, passing me and facing the Council members but at the same time examining Jamie Tyler out of the corner of his eye and smiling to himself, as if he'd been waiting to meet him and had come here expressly for that purpose.

"This is a disgrace," Sir Ian exclaimed in the sort of tone he might once have used in court. "Traveller, you have absolutely no right to be here..."

"He was spying on us!" Dolan said. Spying. Suddenly it was everyone's favourite word.

"And we did not ask for your opinion," Sir Ian went on.

"But you're going to get it anyway."

Reade and Dolan were already moving towards the Traveller with violence in their eyes. I had no doubt that they were going to grab hold of him and throw him out of the church – perhaps into prison too. There was a pit in the garage that was used for exactly that purpose, a square hole covered in wire mesh. It hadn't been used since Jack Hawes, the undertaker, had attacked his neighbour in a dispute over cabbages. He had been sent there for six weeks but he had been let out after three because Mrs Draper had suddenly died and nobody else could be bothered to dig her grave.

"Wait a minute!" Mr Flint had got to his feet and put himself between the three men. He was a small, neat man with wavy grey hair and if a fight had broken out he would have been squashed in an instant. But a fight was exactly what he was trying to avoid. "The Traveller is here," he said. "The damage is done. We might as well hear what he's got to say."

Reade and Dolan looked ugly – not difficult for them – but all eyes turned back to Sir Ian, awaiting his decision. Meanwhile, I glanced at Jamie. He had sat perfectly still through all this but I could see he was thinking hard, as if he had no idea what was going on here but was doing his best to work it out.

Sir Ian was still dithering. Whose side should he take? How could he get out of this without losing authority? In the end, Miss Keyland came to his rescue.

"I don't think it will hurt to let him speak, Sir Ian," she said. "After all, these are exceptional circumstances. And the Traveller came here just like the boy. I agree with Mr Flint. We should hear what he has to say."

"Very well." Now that someone else had made the decision for him, Sir Ian felt more comfortable. "But be brief, Traveller. Say what you have to and then leave."

Everyone took their places again. The Traveller had reached the open space in front of me and Jamie and stood there, surrounded by the Council members. Rita, wisely, had said nothing for the whole time. I knew she still had deep suspicions about the Traveller and her opinion hadn't changed in all the seven years he had been here. "There was nothing chance about the way he arrived, slipping in in the middle of the night," I'd once heard her say. "And what does he get up to on that boat of his? He says it won't move. He says it's stuck on a mudbank. But I wonder!"

"He doesn't have a horse any more," I'd reminded her. "And anyway, why would he want to move?"

"Why did he come in the first place? That's what I'd like to know!"

And here he was now, examining the Council with a glimmer in his eye, as if he knew a lot more than they did and a lot more than he was going to tell.

"It's very simple," he began. "You said it yourselves when you were examining the girl. The only reason that this village has survived as long as it has is because nobody knows it's here. You've got the forest and the river but there's more to it than that, isn't there? How many years is it since you took down all the road signs and dug up the road so nobody would find their way through? You've even got watchtowers. You've taken a lot of care to make sure that you're left alone – and quite right too."

"You found us," Reverend Johnstone muttered.

"I found you by chance, vicar," the Traveller agreed. "And you were one of those who voted to let me stay. I'll always be grateful to you for that. I like it here. I'm comfortable on the *Lady Jane* and I'm sure you'll agree that I pull my weight in the village. I'd say I'm pretty much one of you now – which is why I don't want you to spoil it. You contact the police, you'll be telling them about yourselves. Worse than that, you'll be inviting them here – and who's to say what will happen as a result? Of course, they'll take the boy. But are you so sure they'll be grateful to you? You really think you'll get their thanks?"

"They offered a reward," Dolan growled.

"That's easy enough to do, isn't it. A hundred thousand pounds that you don't need and that you can't spend. And for that you're willing to risk the life of every man, woman and child in this place?"

"Why should we be afraid of the police?" Sir Ian asked. He had been one of those who had voted to send Jamie away.

"Because if you're afraid of everyone – and you're right to be – you should be equally scared of the police." The Traveller ran a hand across his cheek. It was dark with stubble. He was still shaving, although with blades that he must have used hundreds of times. A lot of the men in the village had given up when they ran out of razors and now had shaggy beards. "When I travelled here seven years ago," he went on, "I passed through villages upriver, miles away. The buildings were still standing but there was nobody in them ... not a soul. I found houses stripped bare and empty fields with nothing growing except weeds. What happened to those people, do you suppose? Maybe one of them decided to get in touch with the police for some reason. Maybe someone found out where they were."

He let those last words, ice cold, hang in the air.

"The police could come here anyway," Miss Keyland said. "They could find the boy quite by chance. If we were harbouring him, we could all be punished."

"Why should the police come here unless we call them?" Mr Flint said. He was obviously taking the part of the Traveller.

"Even so, if the boy has committed some sort of crime..." Miss Keyland reached out and picked up the photograph. I was surprised that she could even consider turning Jamie in, but at the same time she was a teacher and so I supposed she had a greater respect for the law.

"I've done nothing wrong," Jamie said, quietly. It had been a while since he had spoken.

"How can you know that?" Dolan sneered. "I thought you'd lost your memory."

"I wouldn't do anything to hurt anyone. I didn't come here to hurt you."

"Then why are you in the photograph?" Miss Keyland asked. "Why do the police want you?"

"I don't know. And they're not telling you either. All they're doing is offering you money..."

"There's also the question of why the photograph appears to

be ten years out of date," Mrs Flint added.

"I agree with the Traveller," I said. "I don't think you should send him away. What's wrong with letting him stay?"

That was most definitely a mistake. Sir Ian turned on me with a withering look. "You are not here to vote, Holly," he intoned. "You are here because you are accused of breaking village law and helping to conceal a stranger. And we've heard enough from you too, Traveller, thank you very much. You will now leave this place and allow the Council to do its work and decide on the matter."

I thought the Traveller was going to answer back but he knew better than me and simply bowed his head, turned and left. I noticed he walked with a slight limp. Maybe the cold and the damp of the river had entered his bones. We waited until he had gone, his footsteps echoing on the stone floor. A door at the back of the church creaked open, then boomed shut. Once more we were alone.

"There is nothing more to be said," Sir Ian exclaimed. "We were about to have a vote. We have now heard certain representations. Let us make a decision."

"I think the Traveller was right," Mr Flint said. "Why put ourselves in danger? The boy can stay here, even if we have to keep him under lock and key. Let's leave the police out of this."

Not surprisingly, Mrs Flint agreed. The vicar nodded too. "He's a child. Maybe, if we look after him, his memory will return. Until then..." His voice trailed away.

Equally unsurprisingly, Dolan and Reade hadn't altered their position one jot. "Turn him in," Reade said.

"Get the reward," Dolan added.

"I don't know," Miss Keyland said. She was looking very old and tired. Her face was full of concern.

Before she went on, Sir Ian weighed in. "All in all, I think we need more time. I agree with Mr and Mrs Flint – and with

Reverend Johnstone. There may be more danger handing this boy back than there is in keeping him."

"Then why not just kill him?" Dolan said. "We have laws here. That's what we do to intruders..."

"Shame on you!" Rita had got to her feet and I had never seen her so angry. She had quite forgotten where she was. "He's a fifteen-year-old boy, young enough to be your son, and you talk about killing him as if he were no more than an animal. Well, maybe the village doesn't deserve to survive if that's what we've come to!" She drew a breath. "He can come and stay with me, if the Council will allow it. I'll vouch for him and I'll make sure he doesn't set foot outside the house ... at least until he's been before the Assembly. As for you, Michael Dolan, I remember you when you were his age." She nodded at Jamie. "You were cruel and spiteful then and it's a shame you haven't grown up to be any kinder. Now it's late and I want to get to bed. So what do you say?"

There was a bit more argument. Sir Ian was obviously annoyed that his precious Council had been interrupted a second time, but in the end it was agreed. Miss Keyland didn't even have to pass her vote.

And that was how Jamie Tyler came to live with us.

FOUR

There were three bedrooms in our house and now there were five of us living there, but Rita had already worked that out. She moved Jamie into the bathroom – it had been years since the bath or the toilet had worked – with cushions from the spare sofa spread out in the bath. It wasn't very pleasant but at least it was private and, as she said (so often that it was one of her favourite sayings), beggars can't be choosers and we were all beggars now.

It was a Wednesday when Jamie first appeared ... I think. Officially, we didn't really have days of the week any more because if you had days of the week you had weekends, and since the work never stopped that wasn't exactly helpful. Of course, everyone had a rough idea of the date. For example, I knew my birthday was coming up. But most of the time, things were kept deliberately vague.

Anyway, we had to wait four days until the next Assembly, which was different from the Council because everyone was expected to be there – and that was when Jamie would be presented to the entire village. Until then, he couldn't leave the house, which, for the rest of us, meant there was going to be no avoiding him. George and John reacted to the new guest in different ways. As usual, John said very little but I saw him glance at Rita once or twice and knew that he was questioning her judgement and that he was nervous about what might happen next, having a stranger living with us. As for George ... he disappointed me. When I first told him about Jamie, he seemed to be on my side but now that Jamie was living with us, he completely changed his opinion.

"The house isn't big enough."

"George – he won't be here for ever. As soon as the village has got used to him, he'll be given his own place to live. Anyway, he's sleeping in the bathroom! I thought you were glad I'd helped him."

"I was glad you didn't just walk away when he was hurt. And you were right not to turn him in to Mike Dolan and Simon Reade. I hate those two. But that didn't mean you had to bring him here."

"That wasn't me. That was Rita."

"Well, I'm surprised. Living in a place like this, you just have to keep your head down and get on with it. You don't want to do anything that upsets anyone. Everyone's going to be talking about us now and – you'll see – no good will come of it."

George was right, of course. For the next few days everything went on as sort of normal. George left for the bakery as soon as the sun was rising and I headed for the orchard. We had breakfast together but we never talked very much as we were too tired and the room was too cold. Winter wasn't that far away and the general feeling was that it was going to be a bad one. Meanwhile, Jamie stayed indoors, not doing very much as far as I could tell, mainly resting and regaining his strength.

I really wanted to talk to him, to find out more about him. I even went back to the church and walked through the door a couple of times to see what that had been all about. But it was impossible to have a proper conversation. The two of us were hardly ever on our own and Jamie was still sticking to his amnesia story, even though I was certain it wasn't true.

And then came the village Assembly. Practically everyone was there. Attendance was compulsory unless you were sick or on duty at the perimeter, but nobody would want to miss an Assembly. We were alone in a world that was dangerous and difficult to understand. Everyone was afraid more or less all the time. At the end of the day, we needed each other. We needed to be reassured.

The meeting began with the usual stuff. All the crops – from the wheat to the apples and even the wild blackberries on the hedgerows – were down and once again there would have to be cutbacks, although we'd still be able to survive. Old Mrs Brooke had finally died and nobody was going to miss her. She'd been suffering from dementia for some time, wandering in and out of The Queen and swearing at the top of her voice. Applications were now open for those wanting to move into her house. More volunteers were needed for the collection of winter firewood. It looked as if the snow was going to be worse than ever this year and stocks were low.

At last Reverend Johnstone climbed into the pulpit.

"My friends," he began. That was what he always called us, although at the end of one of his dreary sermons there were plenty of us who were anything but. "I do have one remarkable piece of news for you. Many of you will remember that it has been seven years since the Traveller arrived in the village and was welcomed by us. Well, another visitor has turned up out of the blue and presented himself to us, this time a young man of about fifteen. His name is Jamie Tyler and he came here through the wood after being badly injured. He has no memory and cannot tell us where he came from, but having taken account of his age and the fact that he is unarmed and alone, the Council has decided to let him stay."

That was the cue for Jamie to step out and present himself – which he did, quite nervously. I'd have been nervous myself. There was one of him and three hundred of us, staring at him with a mixture of fear, curiosity and disbelief. The one thing about life in the village was nothing new ever happened, nobody new ever came. Jamie's sudden appearance was totally unexpected, as if the clouds had turned green or the pigs had begun to talk. It was completely shocking. And it didn't matter that he was just a scrawny kid with long hair and a scar on the side of his head. He was a threat to everything the village stood for.

But the Council had agreed and although there was a lot of muttering, nobody was outright hostile. Jamie made a short speech. He thanked everyone for accepting him (although they hadn't, really) and promised to work hard in the village. I was looking at him as he spoke. Then I glanced sideways and noticed George, who was watching me while I was staring at Jamie. He didn't look pleased and when I heard that Jamie was going to work at the bakery, helping fuel and clean the ovens, I had a feeling it wasn't a good idea.

That wasn't quite the end of it. We all milled out of the church, people still talking to each other in low voices and more or less ignoring Jamie, who was now on his own, near the door. I was about to go over to him when suddenly I found the Traveller at my side. I don't think he'd spoken to me more than a few times in all the years he'd been here, but he spoke to me now.

"The boy is staying with you."

"That's right."

"Of course. You were the one who found him." The Traveller glanced in Jamie's direction. "Did he come through the door?" he asked.

I hesitated. "What do you mean?"

"You heard me."

"He was near the door – but I don't think he came through it." Why was I lying to the man? Why was I even having this conversation?

The Traveller looked at me curiously. I'd never been quite so close to him before and now saw that he was younger than I had thought – about thirty, and that if he had shaved properly and took a bit more care of himself, he might even have been handsome.

"Are you his friend?" he asked me.

The question took me aback. "Yes. I suppose so," I said.

"Then look after him, Holly. Watch out for him. He's important."

And then he turned and went, leaving me more confused than ever.

I tried to get to know Jamie a little better in the next couple of weeks but that wasn't easy. He was allowed to leave the house now. He could mingle with the other villagers. But that meant I saw less of him than I had before and somehow he was never on his own. We were both working so we were apart for most of the day, and he always seemed to come home earlier or later than me so we never got the chance to walk together. If I hadn't been so stupid, I'd have realized that he was doing it on purpose, that he didn't want to be alone with me. I was the only person who knew that he was lying ... about the amnesia anyway. Jamie was avoiding me because he didn't want me asking him questions. He didn't want to tell me the truth.

And that made me think of the Traveller and the weird conversation we'd had outside the church. The Traveller knew about the door, which meant he must know something about Jamie too. I was half-tempted to run down to the *Lady Jane* after work and confront him. But I had never been on that old canal boat. I don't think anyone had. It wasn't really part of the village ... it was outside. And if I did show up, I doubted that the Traveller would make me welcome.

I saw Jamie every night at supper and I tried to let him know that I was on his side, sitting next to him, being nice to him, whatever. To be honest, supper was never very easy. Once there had been television and newspapers and things you could talk about. Now there was just the village. I still had a PlayStation in my room and how I wished I could plug it in, turn it on and plug myself into it, but with no electricity it was just a useless piece of junk and I don't even know why I kept it. There was an electrical generator in the storeroom next to the town hall but it was only used in emergencies – like when Dr Robinson got sick and had to be nursed day and night ... although Miss Keyland had also been allowed to show it to us in class. The fact was that in my whole life I had only seen an electric light half a dozen times.

I was nice to Jamie. That's all. And then one evening as I was coming back from the orchard I saw Mr Christopher – who was the baker – and Mike Dolan leaving the house and I knew, with a sick feeling in my stomach, that something bad had happened. I hurried in and there was George, sitting in a chair with a black eye and a bloody nose, the blood dry now but standing out red-brown against the coating of flour on his skin. Jamie was sitting opposite with a cut on his lip and a torn shirt. Rita was standing over them, her arms crossed and her face filled with rage. John was hovering in a corner, dismayed.

Jamie and George had been in a fight.

Fighting was illegal in the village.

"What happened?" I asked.

"He started it," George said. He shot a glance at Jamie.

"That's not true," Jamie said, looking at me.

"It doesn't matter which one of you started it," Rita snapped. "Haven't you got that into your thick heads? Look at you! You're both covered in blood. You'll both be punished."

"I didn't start the fight," Jamie said. "George's been looking for an excuse – ever since I arrived."

"I wish you hadn't arrived," George muttered. "Nobody asked you to come here. And where did you come from anyway? We don't know anything about you."

"That's enough..." Rita began.

But Jamie was already on his feet. "You think I want to be here?" he demanded and suddenly there were tears in his eyes. "You have no idea what I've been through. I've lost my brother. I've lost my friends. I'd sooner be anywhere else but here." And before anyone could stop him, he stormed out of the room. We heard the front door slam.

More trouble. It would be dark in about half an hour. Nobody was allowed out after dark.

John and Rita were looking at me and somehow I knew what they expected me to say. "I'll go after him," I said.

"Holly..." George pleaded.

By then I was on my way. I went out of the front door and into the street. There was enough light left in the sky to see the village but already the colours were fading. There would be no moon tonight and we hardly ever saw any stars ... there was too much stuff in the atmosphere. I looked left and right. There was no sign of Jamie and no one around to ask if they'd seen him. That didn't matter. I had a good idea where he'd gone.

I hurried down to the graveyard, passing through the gate and following the path round the side of the church. And that was where I found him, standing by that wretched door of his, one hand resting on the handle. As I approached, I saw him close the door behind him and knew that he must have just walked through it again – but it hadn't taken him anywhere. He saw me coming and looked up.

"You have to come back to the house," I said. "No one's allowed out after dark and you're only going to get yourself into more trouble."

He nodded. "I'm sorry I hit your friend."

"You're my friend too." I didn't know what to say. "Did he really start it?"

"I suppose so. He's been needling me all week. But that's no excuse. He was upset because … I don't know. He thinks I'm some kind of threat to him."

"Are you?"

"No. I just want to go."

"Go where? Jamie – why don't you tell me the truth about yourself? Where did you come from? What is this thing with the door?"

He thought for a moment. "You wouldn't believe me."

"You hardly know me. How can you say that?"

"Nobody would believe me. I'm not even sure I understand it myself."

"Tell me!"

He didn't want to tell me. I could see that. But at the same time, it was going to help him – putting it into words. And if he didn't share what had happened to him, he was always going to be on his own.

"There were five of us," he said. "Me. My brother, Scott. A boy called Matt. Pedro. And a girl. Her name is Scarlett. We didn't know each other. We lived thousands of miles apart. Matt was in England. Pedro was in Peru. Scarlett wound up in Hong Kong. That's where I was before I came here.

"How can I explain it to you, Holly? Where do I even begin? Scott and I were on our own in a place called Reno, which is in Nevada, America. We're twins and from the time we were very small we knew we were special. You don't have to believe me if you don't want to but I'm telling you the truth. We had this ability to read each other's minds. Telepathy, I'd guess you'd call it. And we had this sort of uncle who was making money out of us, putting us on the stage. That's what we were doing night after night. Cheap magic tricks that people thought were just tricks but that really were, in a way, magic. We weren't having a good life but at least we had each other. We dreamed that one day we'd turn eighteen and then we could run away and set up on our own. We used to talk about it all the time.

"All that changed when these people came after us. The Nightrise Corporation. That's what they called themselves. They were just business executives ... at least, that's what they looked like. Men in suits. But they represented something totally different, which is to say they were working for these ... creatures. They were monsters. They were totally evil. They weren't from this world."

"You mean ... they were aliens?"

"No. Not aliens. I suppose you'd say they were more like ... demons."

He must have seen my face fall because he stopped and turned away. "I said you wouldn't believe me."

"No. Go on," I said. "I might as well hear all of it."

He nodded. "The creatures were called the Old Ones," he said. "All they wanted to do was destroy everything. In a way they were like cancer. When cancer invades a body it kills it, even though in the long run it will end up killing itself. There is no reason. It's just what it does. The Old Ones invaded the planet and they set out to kill everyone and everything on it. They wouldn't be happy until there was nothing left."

"What do they look like, the Old Ones?" I asked.

"They're all different. There are shape-changers who are human one minute and then change into freaks. There are fly-soldiers and horsemen. But they don't like to be seen. They like to hide behind human beings who do their work for them. And this whole process, this destruction, it has to be as slow as possible because that's what gives them pleasure. They feed on pain. They create it. They inspire it.

"A very long time ago, maybe ten thousand years, they came very close to wiping out the human race. There were just a few survivors but the ones that were left came together and formed an army. And the strange thing is, the leaders of the army weren't adults. They were kids. Four boys and a girl."

"You!" I exclaimed.

"Not us. Not exactly. There were five of us then at the very beginning and there were five of us again, ten thousand years later. It was as if we had been born again, on the other side of time, sent back into the world to finish the job that we'd begun.

"You see, Holly, there was this great battle and the Old Ones were defeated and thrown out of the world. I know it's a lot to take on board but this is how it was. Two gates were constructed to stop them coming back. The first one, Raven's Gate, was in a place called Yorkshire, here in England. The second one was in Nazca, in Peru. The gates stood there for thousands and thousands of years and the Old Ones kept on trying to find a way back, and in the end, of course, they succeeded. Matt tried to stop them but he wasn't strong enough on his own and they smashed through the second gate. Since then they've started all over again, destroying everything they can."

The darkness was almost total. The church loomed over us but although I could feel it, I could barely see its edges, its outline blurring into the night sky. If Jamie hadn't been so pale, he would have been invisible.

"Five had defeated them at the dawn of time and five would defeat them again," Jamie went on. "But first we had to find each other. You see, we all had powers. Scott and I were telepathic. Pedro was a healer. Scarlett could control the weather. And Matt ... well, he could do all sorts of stuff. But on our own, we were too weak. Matt found that out in Nazca and he was almost killed. It's only when we come together that we'll be strong enough to do what we have to, somehow build a new gate and get rid of the Old Ones once and for all.

"Do you still believe me? Are you glad you asked me about all this?"

"I'm still here," I said. "Tell me the rest of it."

"Aren't we supposed to be inside? I don't want your friends hanging us upside down by our feet or whatever it is they do."

"That's not fair, Jamie. They're just scared, that's all."

"OK. There's not much more to say. I could talk all night. I could tell you about the dreamworld. I could tell you about Flint and Sapling and the war that happened all those years ago. But I'm tired, Holly. And I'm scared too. I don't know what's going on any more. I'm not sure how I got here..."

He drew a breath.

"I was on the run from the Nightrise Corporation but I was helped by a secret organization called the Nexus. They were these rich people who knew about the Old Ones because of a diary written by an old monk. They knew the Old Ones were coming but they also knew about the Five. The whole point of the Nexus was that they were there to help us fight them.

"And there was something else. A long, long time ago, somebody built a series of doors all over the world and they were designed specially for us to get from place to place without taking planes or ships. There was a door beside Lake Tahoe in Nevada that took us all the way to Peru. There was another door in Hong Kong that brought me here." He pointed at the dark shadow just behind him. "This is one of the doors. I'd just come through it when you found me. It should be able to take me back. I don't understand why it's not working."

"A magic door," I said and the strange thing is that although

I'd meant to sound scornful, it all sort of made sense. After all, I'd seen Jamie arrive. He'd stepped out of nowhere, just like he'd said. And right now I couldn't think of any other explanation as to how he'd got here.

"I suppose you could say the doors are kind of magic," Jamie agreed. "That's why they're always found in churches or sacred places. Over the ages, people vaguely half-knew about them so they built sacred buildings around them. But they forgot about the Old Ones. And they didn't know anything about us."

I stumbled over to the door and opened it, then shut it again. "Why isn't it working?" I asked.

"I already told you. I don't know. We were in the Tai Shan Temple in Hong Kong ... all five of us. It was amazing ... just finding each other for the first time. And that should have been the end of it. That's what I thought anyway. But then everything went wrong. There was a typhoon blowing and the whole building would have been knocked down if it hadn't been for Scarlett. She was holding the weather back. But then Scarlett got shot. She was standing right beside me and I think the bullet was meant for me. Anyway, after that, everything happened very quickly. It was like being in the middle of a nuclear explosion. We had to get out fast and the only thing to do was to tumble through the door. I guess I must have got hurt by some of the debris and that explains why I was so bloody when you found me."

"Why did you come here?" I asked.

"I don't know." Jamie shook his head. "I've been thinking about that a lot and as far as I know, it works like this. The doors take you to places but you have to know where you want to go. We were in such a hurry to get out of there that we all just piled in so we've all been taken to different places. I ended up here." He couldn't keep the misery out of his voice. "We're back where we started," he went on. "Only worse. Scott and I were hardly ever apart and now I can't find him ... not even in the dreamworld. I can't find any of them. And the door doesn't work any more. I'm stuck here. And I'm on my own."

"There's something else," I said. I was thinking about the photograph now, the one that had been shown in church. It had been taken ten years ago but it had shown Jamie's face as it was now. In a nasty sort of way, things were slotting into place.

"What?"

"I know that Hong Kong was hit by a typhoon. Half the city was destroyed and thousands of people were killed. Miss Keyland told us about it in class. But that didn't happen two weeks ago, Jamie. It didn't happen the day you arrived. It happened ten years ago. Ten years..."

Both of us worked it out in silence. We didn't need to speak. I'd read enough books to be able to work out what had happened. When Jamie had escaped from the Tai Shan Temple in Hong Kong, he hadn't just crossed the world. He had taken a giant leap forward in time.

He had escaped from Hong Kong ten years ago and the whole world had changed while he'd been gone. And now he'd finally arrived.

But he'd left it far too late.

FIVE

Back to work. Everyone worked all the time, not just because we had to grow food and prepare for the winter but because if we stopped, we might notice that there was no real point in going on. We weren't living, really. We were surviving. But back then I was too young to notice the difference.

Jamie and George weren't punished. Maybe the Council had decided to make allowances because Jamie was a new arrival or maybe it just hadn't been serious enough to turn any heads. Boys will be boys and all that. There were a nervous few days while we waited for the knock on the door but it didn't come and soon the whole incident was forgotten ... at least on the face of it. Jamie and George patched things up and stopped fighting, but they didn't spend time together. When one entered the room, the other soon found an excuse to leave.

I tried to make up with George but it was no good. "You haven't been the same since he got here, Holly," he said, miserably. "I don't know why you're always on his side." This wasn't true, but from the moment Jamie had told me his story he had dragged me into his world, making me an accessory whether I liked it or not. I found that I couldn't stop thinking about the Old Ones. I had nightmares about them. I wondered if they were somehow responsible for the way we lived now.

It had become easier to talk to Jamie. Maybe it was because

I hadn't laughed at his story and he knew he could trust me. He told me that he was planning to leave. He was going to escape through the wood and head south to London, even though I did my best to talk him out of it. First he would have to get through the perimeter without being seen. Then he would have to survive out in the wood with nothing to eat or drink. All the fresh water in the village was supplied by a well and it still had to be boiled before it could be drunk. Outside, there was nothing. London was miles away. And although I'd seen pictures of it at school, I had no idea what it was like now. Nobody did.

"What else can I do, Holly?" Jamie insisted.

"You can stay here."

"And what about my brother? What about Matt and the others? Do you just want me to forget about them?"

"But how will going to London help?"

"There's another door. It's in a church called St Meredith's. If I can find it, it may still be working. I can use it to get back."

But get back where? Hong Kong wasn't there any more ... or not very much of it. And what about all the other cities with secret doors? A lot could have happened in ten years and at a guess, none of it would have been very nice.

I didn't know what to say but in the end it didn't matter anyway. As things turned out, Jamie's time in the village was almost over – and mine too.

There was a holiday. We did have days off now and then – and this was a bright, sunny afternoon when everyone seemed to be in a good mood. At least most of the village had turned out in the main square and a little band – they called themselves The Optimists – was playing, even though their guitars were out of tune and we'd heard all their songs a hundred times before. There was soup and sandwiches to eat and the bakery had even managed several trays of doughnuts, although they would have tasted better if we hadn't run out of sugar. Some of the smaller kids were playing football. All the adults, particularly the older ones, were dressed up in their best clothes. When I think back to the village, that's how I like to remember it. We had very little, but even so, every so often we were able to have a good time.

I was sitting with George on the edge of the square where the road curved round past the town hall and that was why I noticed Miss Keyland, not joining in but walking past, in a hurry to get somewhere.

I called out her name.

"Oh ... Holly!" She seemed out of breath. There were red pinpricks in her cheeks.

"Aren't you staying?" I asked.

"No, dear. I'm just on my way to Miss Tristram." Mary Tristram helped out at the school. She lived quite near us on the other side of the garage. "She's not well."

I glanced down. Miss Keyland was wearing heavy walking boots.

"I thought a walk might do her good," she explained.

She hurried away and the next thing I knew, Jamie was at my side. "Holly, I need to talk," he said.

George looked at him disdainfully. "I'll leave you two alone." He got up and walked in the direction of the band.

"George...!" I called after him, but he didn't even turn round. "What is it?" I asked Jamie, not even trying to disguise my irritation.

"We have to go after her," Jamie said. He was right next to me, talking in a low, urgent voice.

"Who?"

"Miss Keyland."

"Why?"

"She's made up her mind about me. She thinks it was a mistake not turning me in to the police. That's what she's going to do now. She's going to claim the reward for herself."

"No!" I shook my head. "I've known Miss Keyland all my life. She was my teacher … and my friend. She'd never do that."

"I'm telling you. She's on her way. We have to follow her. I can't go on my own. I've never been outside the perimeter."

"But how do you know she's going to betray you? You can't know that."

"I do know, Holly. I read her thoughts."

I still found it hard to believe. Jamie had told me about his powers and I'd had direct experience of them myself. But was it possible that dear old Miss Keyland could go against the wishes of the Council and put us all in danger? I thought about what she had just said – visiting a sick friend. I remembered the walking boots. "All right," I said. "Let's see where she goes."

I glanced in the direction of George but he had already disappeared into the crowd. What would he think when he got back and found me gone? But there was no time to worry about that. Jamie was already moving away from the square, keeping his distance behind Miss Keyland. I caught up with him and we followed her up through the village, past the modern houses – including our own. The road climbed a hill then dipped down steeply. At this point, the white lines faded out and a short while later the tarmac itself became chopped up and disappeared into the mud and the grass. The very edge of the village was marked by a yellow bus, which had once ferried passengers to the surrounding towns but now sat rotting on its side, the glass windows shattered and all the upholstery and engine parts long gone. Miss Keyland walked past it without giving it so much as a glance. I felt sad, seeing it. My mother had taken me on that bus – quite a few times, actually – and although it had been years since it had run, seeing it made me think of her.

The forest began almost at once, which was just as well as it would have been impossible to track Miss Keyland across open fields. I knew now, if I had ever doubted it, that Jamie was right. She certainly wasn't visiting any friends.

I had memories of the forest being a very beautiful place, full of bluebells in the spring, cool and scented in the summer, somehow welcoming even when the leaves had fallen and the snow had come. And you would have thought that, left on its own all these years, it would have grown into a perfect wildness, a haven for animals and birds. But that hadn't happened. The forest was dark and comfortless. Weeds, thistles and briars had taken over. As I knew from hours spent hunting, any signs of life were becoming increasingly rare, as if all the foxes, deer and rabbits had been swallowed up and suffocated. Even the leaves seemed to have changed colour. It had been such a slow process that it would have been hard to tell when exactly it had happened. But in the autumn they didn't turn gold any more. They just died.

"Stand where you are!"

I heard the shout and grabbed hold of Jamie, dragging him behind the thick trunk of a horse chestnut tree. We had already reached the perimeter and there, in front of us, a watchtower rose six feet above the ground. Made of wooden beams and platforms with a ladder up the side, it stood level with the tops of the trees and was painted brown and dark green so that it would blend in with its surroundings. I knew the guard who had given the order. His name was Tom Connor and he was only a couple of years older than me, not that you would have guessed it seeing him in his khaki uniform, already scrabbling for the rifle that was slung across his chest.

He hadn't seen the two of us. It was Miss Keyland who had caught his attention. Not so long ago, she had been teaching him. Now he was aiming a loaded gun at her.

"Hello, Miss Keyland!" he called out, more friendly once he saw who it was. "What are you doing?"

"I thought I'd try and find some mushrooms," Miss Keyland replied. Another lie.

"Mushrooms? You'll be lucky. But if you do find any, save some for me." He raised his wrist. All the guards at the perimeter had watches. "You've got an hour and a half more light."

"Thank you, Tom. I'll be back before then."

This was the tricky bit. We couldn't pass the observation tower without being seen and if we tried and were caught, Tom would be sure to raise the alarm ... he had a large bell attached to the roof just above his head. We had to wait long enough for Miss Keyland to have gone but not so long that she disappeared altogether. It was all a question of timing, and having judged the moment correctly – I hoped – I pushed Jamie forward and showed myself.

"Is that you, Tom?" I called out.

"Holly...?"

"Have you seen Miss Keyland?" I asked in my most innocent voice. "Reverend Johnstone sent us to look for her. He asked us to give her a message."

I just had to hope that Miss Keyland was far enough away not to hear me. At least Tom didn't question my story. "You just missed her," he said. He turned round and peered over the tree-tops. "There she goes!" He pointed. "I can call out to her if you like."

"No. We'll find her." Jamie and I hurried ahead. Tom smiled and waved.

The forest got thicker and more tangled. The leaves and the branches seemed to be tied together, as if they didn't want to let us through. We could hear Miss Keyland fighting her way ahead of us, but looking back, I realized that the observation tower was out of sight. We pressed on for about ten minutes. This was never the way I came when I went hunting and I just wanted to stop, to go home, to forget all about it. What did it matter what Miss Keyland did? If Jamie was right, if she really was calling the police, he would just have to leave. He had been planning that anyway. And what exactly was she doing, stuck out here in the middle of this wilderness? What made her think she would find anything here?

"There!"

Jamie had seen it first and we both crouched down behind a bush with sharp, spiny needles instead of leaves. It was in a clearing, which made it easier to see. And it was bright red, the colour vibrant against all these greens and browns. It was a rectangular box and even the straight lines seemed alien in the middle of a wood. I knew exactly what I was looking at. I had seen pictures in books.

It was an old-fashioned public telephone box, the sort that had been replaced by modern glass counterparts and then phased out altogether when people started carrying their own mobiles. What was it doing here? Of course, it would have once stood next to a road but the road had been carefully removed. The telephone box had been left behind and it was alien, like a visitor from a forgotten world. I had been in the forest loads of times and I was amazed that I had never seen it, but then, I had never come this way. How had Miss Keyland known it was there? Could it possibly be still connected?

We watched her go in. She opened and shut the heavy door behind her. Some of the little square panes of glass were broken but we were too far away to hear what she said. She dialled a number and began to talk. The conversation couldn't have lasted more than a couple of minutes and then she hung up and came out again, retracing her steps and passing so close to us that I was certain she would see us. But her thoughts must have been on what she had just done. She was inches away from us but she didn't look down or stop.

We waited until we were sure she had gone.

"I knew it," Jamie said. "She's told them I'm here."

"Told who?"

"The police. The Old Ones. It doesn't matter. They could be the same."

"What now?" I asked, although I already knew the answer.

"They'll come for me. Maybe tonight, maybe tomorrow. I can't stay in the village." He looked at me and I was shaken to see how scared he was. "They'll punish you for taking me in, Holly. You, Rita, John and George. They'll punish the whole village."

"We didn't do anything wrong."

"You don't know them." Jamie closed his eyes, suddenly tired. He opened them again. "I should go now."

"You can't!" I said. "You'll never find your way through the forest. Even in the day it's hard enough." I looked up. The sun was already dipping. Why did the days have to be so short? Already the treetops seemed to be closing in on us and if we didn't go back to the village soon, we'd be stuck out here ourselves.

"I don't want to bring trouble to you," Jamie said.

He sounded so sad that I made up my mind. "Wait here," I said.

"Where are you going?"

"We don't know that the telephone is connected. And if it is, how do we know she called the police? I'm not even sure there are any police any more."

"No, Holly!"

But he was too late. I had already got to my feet and was making my way over to the telephone box. I could feel my heart pounding. It was such an ordinary thing … or at least, it had been.

But at the same time there was something strange and horrible about it – the thick, mottled glass, the bright crimson paint. As I approached, it could have been a spaceship that had landed here and was waiting to swallow me up and carry me away.

I opened the door. It was even heavier than I had imagined. The floor was a slab of concrete. There was a black telephone clinging to a panel above a box with a narrow slot to take a credit card, the little pieces of plastic that people had once used instead of money. A thick wire curled down from the handset. I didn't want to touch any of it. I couldn't even remember the last time I had made a telephone call – if I ever had. All I wanted to do was see if the phone was working.

I picked up the receiver, solid and strange in my hand. One end for the ear, the other for the mouth. I held it against my head but there was no sound. What now? There were buttons marked one to nine with a zero beneath. Once there might have been instructions but someone had taken them away. I looked through the window and saw Jamie waiting for me anxiously. The glass twisted him out of focus. It was as if he were bleeding into the forest around him.

What number was I meant to dial? The receiver was still pressed against my ear. Of course … it was 999. Everyone knew that. But before I had a chance to do anything, a voice spoke to me … a woman's voice, not old, not young. She sounded almost bored.

"Hello?" There was a pause. "Who is this?"

I didn't know what to say. Already I was wishing that I had listened to Jamie and hadn't gone into the kiosk. I wanted to put the phone down and leave but I couldn't. I was rooted to the ground, no longer in control of my own movements. I could feel my hand trying to crush the plastic receiver beside my ear.

"We're on our way," the woman said. "We'll be with you very shortly."

But it wasn't just the woman's voice that I heard right then. I became aware of something else ... the sound of breathing. There was nothing human about it. At first I couldn't even tell if it was coming from the phone. It was as if it was underneath me, far below the ground, the rumble of an earthquake about to happen. And then, a second later, it was all around me, inside the kiosk, suffocating me. I tried to put the phone down but I couldn't.

I looked out through the windows but the forest had gone. It had simply been whipped away. Everything was white and, impossibly, it was snowing. Jamie had disappeared. Ahead of me, about a hundred metres away, I saw some sort of castle, built into the side of a mountain, enclosed by huge towers and walls. The clouds were racing past as if they had been speeded up. Everything was white and grey.

"Who is this?" the woman asked.

And then again, the breathing, and a single word – my name: "Holly". Spoken by something inside the mountain. Mocking me. Colder and crueller than any voice I had ever heard. I was holding the telephone so tightly that I was actually hurting myself, pressing it into the side of my head. But I couldn't let go.

I don't know what would have happened next but then the door was jerked open and Jamie grabbed hold of me, dragging me out. I shouted and dropped the telephone, watching it fall and dangle at the end of the wire. And then I was lying on the forest floor, almost in tears, more frightened than I had ever been in my life.

"What is it, Holly?" Jamie cried. "What happened?"

He was cradling me and now I really was sobbing. I couldn't stop myself. "I don't know," I said. "There was a woman. But then there was something else. I heard it. And I saw..."

"What did you see, Holly?"

"I can't tell you. A castle. Something..." I shook my head,

trying to get the vision out of my thoughts. "But they're coming, Jamie. She told me. They're on their way."

He held me, waiting for me to recover. Finally, when I was strong enough, he helped me to my feet and together we went home.

For the last time.

SIX

We ran back to the house. We didn't know where else to start. My first thought was to get Jamie out of the village and on his way to … it didn't matter where, he just had to go. But at the same time I knew that it was too late, that it would do no good. The voice on the phone had not been human. No person in this world would have been able to talk like that. And they had spoken my name, known it was me on the other end before I had said a word.

The Old Ones.

It had to be.

When Jamie had told me his story, that evening after the fight with George, I had believed every word he had said, even though common sense, everything I knew about the world, had told me not to. I hadn't doubted him for a second. Why was that? Perhaps it was because I had been the one who had found him, and from the moment the door had opened we had been inextricably linked. It was as if it was all meant to happen. But now I saw that he had unwittingly brought danger to the village, to the only people I cared about.

"We'll be with you very shortly."

It wasn't his fault, I had to remind myself. It was Miss Keyland. She had gone against what the Council had decided and in doing so she had sacrificed us all.

We got back just as Rita was preparing supper, already wondering where we were. John was standing by the table, laying out plates as if there was anything to put on them other than the usual bread and vegetable stew. Rita knew at once that something was wrong. I had torn my clothes stumbling out of the forest. My hair was wild. My eyes must have been shining with fear. Jamie was deathly pale, already blaming himself. I understood how he felt. Despite what I knew, part of me wanted to blame him too and wished that he had never arrived.

"What is it?" Rita asked.

"It was Miss Keyland," I gasped. "We followed her. There was a telephone in the forest. Why did you never tell me about it? She called the police. They're coming."

It had all come out in a breathless rush. Rita stared at me.

"Coming to the village?" George had appeared on the staircase, dressed in a crumpled white shirt with the sleeves rolled up. He had heard what I was saying and I thought he would be pleased. If the police came, they would take Jamie away. That was surely what he wanted. But I was wrong. He stood there and his face was aghast.

"Did you hear what Miss Keyland said?" Rita asked.

"No. But I picked up the phone and I heard them..." I felt tears stealing out of the corners of my eyes. I couldn't stop them. "They were horrible," I said. "They knew my name. They knew everything."

John glanced at Rita and I saw her shoulders slump, not in a gesture of defeat but of acceptance. It was as if she had been waiting for something like this to happen, and now that it had she was almost relieved. But when she spoke it was with quiet authority, the steel will that I had always known.

"George," she said. "Go to the church and sound the alarm. Three rings, three times – you know the code. We have to alert the village." George didn't move so she turned her head and snapped at him. "Go now."

George went. As he left the room our eyes met and I saw that he was worried about me and that he was apologizing, in his own way, for all the tension that there had been between us in the last few days. I tried to smile at him but I'm not sure what expression he saw on my face. Then he was gone.

Rita was already burrowing in a cupboard under the sink, pulling out a bundle wrapped in an old sack. "This is for you, Jamie," she said. "I know you've been saving your own supplies but I'm sure this will suit you better. There's water, bread, dried fruit and nuts. Enough to keep you going for a few days. Also a compass and a map. You have to leave the village at once – do you understand that? And I want you to take Holly with you."

"But, Rita—"

"Don't argue!" she said and I suddenly knew that she had been preparing for this, that the food and the compass had been there all along. How could she have known it was going to happen? She placed the bundle in my hands and just for one last moment we were close. "I always knew about the door," she said. "Do you think I could live in a village like this and not hear all the stories? My grandmother told me about it before I was your age. One day a boy would appear through the door and that would be the end of the village. That was what she said. But it wasn't all bad news. She also told me that it would be the start of a better future, a new life. Let's hope so." She kissed me very briefly. "Go back through the forest. The telephone box used to be on a road and if you continue north, you'll find it. If you can't see it, feel it under your feet. Whatever you do, don't stop. Don't come back."

"But what about you?"

"There's nothing you can do for us."

"I'm sorry," Jamie said, miserably. They were the only two words he'd spoken.

"Don't be sorry. Be strong. And take care of Holly. That's all we ask."

Jamie nodded. We hurried out of the room and the last I saw of Rita and John was the two of them standing together. John had gone over to her and she had laid her head on his shoulder. It was more affection than she had ever shown in the whole time I had been with them.

As we left the house, the church bell began to ring – three peals, then a pause, then three more, then three again. About a minute later, something extraordinary happened. The village lit up. Of course there had always been lighting – street lights and arc lamps and bulbs hanging in porches – but I had never seen them all working at the same time and had assumed they were simply left overs that no one could be bothered to take away. But someone had started up the generator and thrown a switch and they had immediately flickered into life, casting a harsh white glow that made the church, the town hall and all the other buildings seem to leap out of the ground, and scattering the pathways with the deepest black shadows.

"What's happening?" I whispered or maybe I just thought it, but either way there was no time to stop and find out, no time to take in the marvel of what the world had once been like. We ran the other way, leaving the village square behind us, retracing the steps we had taken just a few minutes ago. Even the houses at the edge of the village were partly illuminated and I was aware of people hurrying out, pulling jerseys over their heads as they went. Perhaps if I had been allowed to attend meetings of the Council, I would have known about these emergency plans. Everyone was coming together. The guards at the perimeter would have heard the church bells too. Perhaps they would have been told to defend themselves to the last bullet. Maybe they would fall back and help the village. I just hoped somebody would know what to do.

We passed the broken-down bus, with the forest very black, a seemingly impassable barrier, ahead of us. We ran into the trees, Jamie still not speaking. And me...? I wanted to get away. But even more, I wanted to see George. Perhaps I could have persuaded him to come with us. At the same time, I wished I could find Miss Keyland and confront her with what she had done. I wondered if we might not find somewhere to hide after all and come back in an hour or so when everything had quietened down. I looked over my shoulder and saw the church steeple silhouetted against a white glow that spread out like a fan in the sky. This was the village. This was my whole life. I couldn't just abandon it, could I?

"Holly..."

"What?"

Jamie had grabbed my arm, stumbling to a halt. He had heard something. What was it? It was a thudding sound, in the sky above us. I looked up and saw what I thought were three stars – two green ones and a red one – moving across the darkness, incredibly fast. Then I felt a gust of wind across my cheek and knew that I was looking at some sort of flying machine. That was incredible. It was impossible. A helicopter or something had come out of nowhere. It was very low and it was heading for the village.

It made my skin crawl. I had seen planes before – maybe four or five times. I knew there were people who still flew. But the planes had always been tiny specks above the horizon, barely more than a glint of silver in the otherwise empty sky, soundless, belonging to that other world. This ... helicopter ... was landing right here. It was invading us.

It also reminded me, if I needed reminding, that time was running out. The police had already arrived. We had to get away.

With a new sense of urgency we plunged into the forest, letting it devour us, separating us from the village.

But we hadn't gone very far before Jamie stopped me again and this time I didn't need to ask him why.

There were specks of white light, electric again, moving towards us in a long line that curved all the way round the darkness in front of us so that no matter which direction we took, we would have to confront them. I could see the lights dancing between the trees like huge insects, fireflies, but I knew they were torches held by human hands. How many of them were there and how had they got here so quickly? Before I could even start counting, a voice called out and I recognized Tom Connor, who was still in his observation tower somewhere above us but invisible in the blackness of the treetops.

"Stop right there!"

It was the same command he had delivered to Miss Keyland but now he sounded terrified and the lights didn't hesitate, not for a second.

"I warn you," he shouted. "I'm armed."

There was a brief pause and then a tongue of flame unfurled itself from the darkness. It seemed very small at first, like someone lighting a match, but it grew monstrously, rolling forward, billowing out in a diagonal line from the ground to the top of the observation tower. Tom must have realized what was about to happen. For a few brief seconds I saw him, standing there in the middle of his useless wooden fortification, bringing up the useless gun that he had taken from his shoulder, bathed in orange. The fire rushed towards him, hissing through the night. Jamie grabbed hold of me and spun me round before it hit, but not before I saw Tom, a boy I had once played with, disappear in an all-consuming fireball and heard his single, unforgettable scream.

"We have to go," Jamie said. "We have to get back."

I looked round. The observation tower was on fire, the flames lighting up the forest all the way to the point where we were concealed. But for a dip in the ground, we would have been seen ourselves. The torches continued moving. Somebody – one of the other perimeter guards – shouted. There was a single shot, followed by a much louder, angrier stammer from a machine gun. Another pause. Then a body fell through the trees and hit the forest bed with a soft thump.

They were getting nearer. The police, the Old Ones, whatever they were. I wanted to cry out but I knew that to do so would be death. I allowed Jamie to pull me away and together we scrambled back the way we had come, running faster even than before, the path lit by a faint orange glow. There were more shots behind us and, as we went, another scream. I tried to block them out of my head. I wanted to find Rita and John again. I wanted to see George.

Normally, we wouldn't have been able to move so fast, not at night, but the village was still illuminated ahead of us. We ran past houses with open doors and gates; signs that the inhabitants had left in a hurry. The church bell was silent now and had remained so since the original alarm. But everyone in the village must have heard the gunfire. We heard a further burst even as we reached the garage, softer and less distinct but still unmistakeable. The petrol pumps watched us as we went past, two old soldiers who had been left on the sidelines. The white glow of the electric light was stronger right ahead of us. We allowed it to draw us in.

And so we came to the edge of the square, lingering in the shadows where we wouldn't be seen. I couldn't tell if all the villagers had assembled but certainly most of them were there, pushed back against the sides to make room for the helicopter which had landed right in the middle. I searched anxiously for my own family but couldn't see any of them. I noticed Mike Dolan and Simon Reade – together as always – and Dr Robinson and Sir

Ian Ingram were close by too. Their eyes were fixed on the helicopter. All of them looked small and afraid.

The helicopter was black and yellow, shaped like a bullet with three huge blades, now hanging limply, and thick metal runners. The front was all glass and I could just make out some of the controls with a few lights winking inside the cockpit. I had never seen a helicopter before, except in pictures, and looking at it now, the real thing, I found it impossible to believe that anything so heavy and so cumbersome could actually rise off the ground and fly. And to have it sitting in the middle of our village! All those years spent hiding and now it had landed as if it had known where we were all the time.

There was a woman standing beside it. Was she the woman I had heard on the phone? She was wearing a black leather coat that reached all the way to her calves, with black leather boots below. It certainly wasn't a uniform. It must have been the way she liked to dress. She had long ginger hair that fell in untidy curls and a thin, very pale face. Her eyes and lips gave nothing away. It was impossible to guess her age. She was quite near to me but she gave the impression of being far away, melting into the darkness that surrounded her. The darkness suited her.

Two men stood behind her, both wearing black police uniforms and helmets and visors that covered their faces. They were armed with machine guns.

"We know that the boy is somewhere in the village," she was saying. She wasn't the woman I had heard on the phone. Her voice was extraordinarily clear, reaching everyone in the square as if it was being secretly amplified. "He is the only one we have any interest in. Tell us where he is and we'll go away."

"I've got to tell them..." Jamie whispered to me.

"No." I gripped his arm. "You can't."

Everyone knew the woman was lying. They had heard the shots

in the forest. The village had been discovered, invaded and in that moment all its defences had gone.

I saw somebody push their way through the crowd and Miss Keyland appeared. She was wearing a shawl against the chill of the night and, as usual, her yellow wellington boots. She wasn't looking very pleased with herself. I think she was only just beginning to understand the consequences of what she had done.

"My name is Anne Keyland," she announced.

"Yes?" The helicopter woman sounded uninterested.

"I was the one who telephoned you." This caused a ripple, a mutter of disgust that spread through the crowd. The people who were nearest to her shrank away and suddenly Miss Keyland was on her own, separated from the rest of the village, watched from every side. I saw Sir Ian shake his head in disbelief. But she went on anyway. "You promised a reward for the boy. There are a lot of things we need here. The crops are beginning to die out. We all know that. The water levels are lower every year. We have no more medicine if anyone gets sick, no oil for the generator. These are all things you can give us." She had raised her voice and I guessed that she was speaking to us all now, trying to explain what she had done. "You promised me that no one would get hurt."

"I promised it if you co-operated."

"We are co-operating."

"Then where is the boy?"

"I don't know."

"If you don't know, you're no use to me." The woman's hand had disappeared into her pocket and drawn out a small gun. Without even hesitating, she shot Miss Keyland where she stood. There was a spray of blood, picked up by the lights. Miss Keyland crumpled in a little heap. Nobody moved.

"So who is going to tell me where I can find Jamie Tyler?" the woman demanded.

Once again I felt Jamie tense up beside me and knew that he couldn't stand any more of this, that he was going to make himself known. But before he could move, I heard a voice call out and recognized Rita, although I couldn't see her on the other side of the square, lost in the crowd. "Jamie's not here," she said. "He left before you came. He went through the wood, heading over to the east." Rita had built a lie into her response. She knew full well that Jamie and I had headed north. She had no idea, of course, that we were both back in the village.

"Is that true?" the woman asked.

"Yes."

She shrugged. "Then I've been wasting my time."

She raised a hand, almost like flicking away a summer wasp. It was a signal for all hell to break loose.

The two guards raised their machine guns and opened fire, the noise of the bullets deafening as it echoed off the buildings on every side. The circle of villagers, silent and resentful one moment, broke apart and suddenly everyone was screaming and stampeding into one another, forgetting everything in a desperate attempt to find a way out. At the same time, they found that the entire square was surrounded. The policemen from the forest had arrived even while the woman was talking and had taken up their positions, kettling us, with riot shields ... and worse. They had flame-throwers, machine guns, huge batons and gas canisters. They stood there, waiting to pick their targets off one by one.

As soon as the shooting began, Jamie and I took off, moving as fast as we could. I actually felt the breeze of bullets as they sprayed over my shoulders. One hit a man next to me – I think it was Mr Christopher, the baker – and he fell down with a little sob and didn't get up. Everyone was going crazy. We were penned in, trapped on all sides. The electric light, which had seemed such a miracle a while ago, made us into sitting targets with nowhere to hide.

Then the policemen moved forward. I saw three people, a mother and two children, shot dead right in front of me. On the other side of the square there was another whoosh of flame and a scream. Machine guns were clattering everywhere. Windows smashed. People running left and right were thrown off their feet, sent spinning to the ground.

"Holly!"

Jamie had shouted and I skidded to a stop with a policeman standing in front of me. He had come from nowhere. He was aiming a gun right at me and I saw my own face, like a death mask, reflected in his riot shield. I could have been killed right then. God knows how many people might have died in the square. The police had obviously been ordered to leave nobody alive. But then, further away, there was an explosion and all the lights went out.

Somebody had blown up the generator. I didn't know it then – but that was what had happened and the sudden fall of darkness, as fast as a guillotine blade, gave us the chance to escape. I was blind but Jamie dragged me with him, circling round the man who had been about to shoot me, breaking through the police line. We couldn't stop, not even to catch our breath. All the policemen were carrying powerful torches – we had seen them in the wood. It took them just a few seconds to find them and turn them on. Then, once again, the square was illuminated and the killing resumed.

Jamie and I had made it into the doorway of one of the houses just off the square ... Sir Ian's place, as it happened. The house was called Postman's Knock. We stood there, our chests heaving, listening to the shots, watching the bodies fall.

"Let's go inside!" I gasped. The door to the house was closed but it was sure to be unlocked. "We can hide."

"No. They'll search. They'll find us."

"Then what?"

"Back into the wood. It must be safer there now."

"Why?"

"Because they're all here, in the village."

It made some sort of sense. At least the forest would give us cover. A man staggered past us, screaming, clutching at his eyes. He had been sprayed with something horrible. He ran into a bush and toppled forward. The man was Simon Reade. Did I need any more reminding that it was time to go? Making sure that Jamie was with me, I launched myself away from Sir Ian's house and would have continued back past the garage for a third time, had I not found myself being seized by a hand around my throat. Suddenly there was a man with his face pressed against mine, whispering fiercely in my ear.

"Stay still. If you want to live, you'll come with me."

SEVEN

It was the Traveller. I was dazed; everything was happening so quickly and I'd only ever seen him occasionally. Even so, I knew him at once. He was holding me so tight, he was hurting me. There was a strange gleam in his eyes.

Jamie tore at his arm, trying to force him to release me. "Get off her!" he shouted. There was so much noise all around – screams and gunfire – that it hardly mattered if he was heard.

"Listen to me. Listen to me ... both of you! You have to get out of here and there is only one way. You have to trust me. There are only minutes left. There..."

He pointed up with one finger. What did he mean? And then I heard it, the thudding of more helicopters approaching, the same sound that I had heard in the forest only louder, more insistent. In the very far distance I saw the lights. There were lots of them. They would be here very soon.

"They will destroy the whole village," the Traveller said. "They'll leave nothing standing, nobody alive."

"Why?"

"Because, unfortunately, they believe what Rita told them. They think Jamie has gone."

"But why kill everyone?" I asked.

"Because that's what they do." The Traveller loosened his grip on my arms. "They kill for the sake of it. They kill because they enjoy it."

"Who are you talking about?"

"Hasn't Jamie told you? The Old Ones."

The Old Ones. He knew about them too.

We were still partly concealed in the doorway of Postman's Knock, protected by the ivy that grew up on either side. Standing there, I saw someone run past, trying to make it down the main road. There was a burst of machine-gun fire and the figure – I couldn't tell if it was a man or a woman – stopped, threw their arms in the air and collapsed.

Jamie stepped forward. "You said you know a way out of here," he rasped. "Where?"

"Will you do exactly what I tell you, even if it means abandoning your friends?" Jamie hesitated. "I'm not going to get myself killed," the Traveller snapped. "I need to know I can rely on you."

"All right. Yes. Whatever you say."

"Good. Then follow me. Stay close." He was talking to Jamie, not to me. "You stay here, Holly. Find somewhere to hide."

It took me a second or two before I understood what he was implying. My mouth dropped open. He was leaving me behind! Never mind that I'd been the one who had discovered Jamie in the first place and that tonight it had been me who'd raised the alarm. I was out. Dead meat like the rest of them.

But Jamie wasn't having any of it. "I'm not leaving without her," he said.

"What did you just promise me?" the Traveller snarled. "We can't take her with us. There's no room."

"I don't know who you are." Jamie was speaking through gritted teeth. "And I don't know where you're going. If I come with you, I'll do as you say. But I'm not coming alone. And that's not negotiable."

Another mushroom of flame. It was close by and for a moment all three of us glowed red. We had no time to argue and the

Traveller knew it. He nodded, angrily. "All right. But that's the last demand you make. From now on you do as I say."

I barely heard his words. They were drowned out by an explosion, louder and more powerful than any that had gone before. The ground trembled. The very air fizzed and a huge ball of scarlet flame rose into the night sky. The nearest helicopter had fired a missile. I didn't know if it had aimed deliberately or not but it had hit the church ... poor old St Botolph's, which had stood there for centuries and which had never done anyone any harm – unless you count having a magic door that had opened to allow death into our village. I saw the top of the tower crumble. Huge pieces of stone rained down, most of them in flames. The graveyard seemed to have caught fire.

And still people were running mindlessly, even though there were fewer of them now, less than half as many as there had been. They were trying to keep out of the glow of the fire, aware that it turned the immediate area into a death trap. But there was nowhere to go. The police were everywhere, waiting for them in the same way that George and I had often waited for a rabbit to come out of its hole. I no longer recognized any of the villagers. They had become leaping shadows, running hopelessly, being cut down by the silent men behind the visors and riot shields.

We were among them. Following the Traveller, we made our way down the main road. We didn't run. Moving slowly was the secret. Panic would kill us – we had to make certain we weren't seen. A single line of fire streaked across the sky and there was another shuddering explosion, somewhere near the garage. We were heading towards the river, the opposite direction from the one I would have taken because it led away from the wood. But after what he had said, I didn't dare argue with the Traveller. I found myself focusing on the red cloth that he was wearing around his neck. It made him easier to pick out and it stopped me seeing the horror that was taking place everywhere else.

More missiles fell. The ground shook. I was waiting for the single blast that would find our little group and blow us all to pieces. Dust and debris swept into my eyes, almost blinding me, and there was an endless, high-pitched screaming in my ears. A man was hurled, somersaulting through the air in front of me, and landing just ahead. I couldn't avoid him. It was the vicar, Reverend Johnstone. He knelt there as if at prayer, then lay down as though he was tired and wanted to go to sleep. I wondered if he knew that his church had been destroyed. I wanted to stay and help him but the Traveller had already gone past and I had no choice but to follow.

We reached the crossroads and the Queen's Head. The pub was still standing, although this was where the first explosion had come from, the one that had taken out the generator. It was quieter down here ... at least, there were fewer people and most of the killing was still taking place around the square. I wasn't sure I had any hearing any more. I looked back and saw that the whole village had become a firestorm. The muzzles of the machine guns were flashing white. We drew to a halt. Jamie looked stunned. Perhaps he was blaming himself for all this. It would have been even worse for him, if he thought that this was his fault.

"We can't rest," the Traveller said. His lips moved and I read the words without properly hearing them. "We have to keep going."

We continued down the hill. I was becoming more uneasy all the time. What was there here for us? A stagnant river and a houseboat that couldn't move because, long ago, we had eaten the horse that pulled it.

Another blast. More screams – but distant now and less often. There were fewer people to kill. Thankfully, we seemed to have been forgotten. And it was pitch-dark down here.

"What happened to the lights?" I asked.

"I blew up the generator," the Traveller said. "Now let's move..."

I saw the river ahead of us, a black ribbon that picked up some of the reflections from the fire. The water had no current. It was oily and dead. I smelled it too. For years now the river had had a thick, unpleasant odour, which in its own way warned you to stop and go back the way you had come. As we reached the quay, I tried to convince myself that we were on our own, that nobody had followed us. But I didn't believe it. It was as if the night were alive and watching us. It wasn't going to be as easy as this. They weren't simply going to let us slip away.

"Where now?" Jamie asked.

There wasn't much of a choice. If we went straight ahead, we'd fall in the water and drown ... if we weren't poisoned first. There were a couple of buildings – an old warehouse and the harbour master's office, which had been converted into someone's home. We could follow the towpath to the left or to the right. Either way, it ran out after a time, disappearing into nettles and mud, which of course had been allowed to happen quite deliberately.

"This way," the Traveller pointed to the right.

"Wait a minute," I said. My hearing had returned.

"What?"

"There's someone here..."

The Traveller stopped and looked around him. It was almost black down here, everything just vague shadows and shapes. His hand had dropped to his waist and I saw that he was carrying a weapon, a machete or some sort of sword. I knew that it wasn't me that he was worried about. He was staying close to Jamie, watching out for him.

"You're wrong," he said.

"I heard someone."

And that was when the policeman appeared out of the

darkness. I saw his hand rise to his shoulder and a second later, he had flicked on a torch which was strapped there, leaving him free to cradle the machine gun which was aimed at us. The powerful beam leapt out, dazzling us. The policeman had lost his helmet and visor but I still couldn't make out much of his face. He was in total command. There was nothing the three of us could do. He could cut us down where we stood.

"Stay where you are!" he grunted. A voice crackled somewhere inside his helmet and he spoke into a microphone that curved round in front of his lips. "I have them..."

"Where are you?" It was the woman from the helicopter.

"At the church," Jamie said. It took me a moment to understand that it was he who had spoken. He was staring at the policeman. There was something strange about him that I had never seen before, although somehow, I knew what was happening. Jamie had powers. He had already told me that. Now he was using them.

"They're at the church," the policeman said.

He knew that he had lied. It hadn't been what he wanted to say. He was struggling to break free of the spell or whatever it was that gripped him. His hand tightened on his weapon and I was certain he was going to shoot us right there. But then I heard a soft footfall, coming across the quay. Someone was rushing out of the darkness behind him and as the policeman became aware of the danger and turned, he was struck down from behind. The policeman fell. George was standing over him, holding the cricket bat he had just used to knock the man out. I had no idea how he had got there or if he had been waiting for us all along.

"You have to go, Holly," he said.

"You're coming with us, George."

"No. I can't."

He looked down and I saw the dark stain on his shirt. He had been shot or he had been cut or maybe he'd been hit by shrapnel from one of the missiles. I had no idea how he'd managed to make his way down here and I was amazed he'd found the strength to save us in the way he just had. At the same time, I knew he didn't have a lot of time left.

"George…" I began and choked on his name. Tears were pouring down my cheeks and I was wondering how all this could have happened. Only a few days ago, I'd been picking apples and he'd been making bread.

Then I heard the sound I dreaded most, the stamp of leather on concrete, and I knew that although Jamie had tried to trick them, there were more policemen on the way, running down the main road towards the quay. George slumped to his knees. He couldn't stand up any more. At the same time, he swept the dead policeman's machine gun into his hands and pressed it against his chest. I understood what he was going to do.

"Go on, Holly," he said. "Get out of here."

"George…" I couldn't believe I was saying goodbye to him.

The Traveller wasn't waiting any longer. He grabbed my shoulders and dragged me in the direction he'd wanted to take. Jamie came with us. He looked sick, in shock. George stayed where he was and I didn't look round.

I felt a slight rise in the ground. I knew that we were following the towpath along the edge of the river. We ran for about five minutes – and there it was in front of us, a black bulk that had to be the *Lady Jane*, the Traveller's home, stuck in the mud, where it had been for the last seven years. I allowed myself to be bundled on board. I felt the wooden deck beneath my feet and collapsed onto it. Behind us, on the quay, I heard machine-gun fire and knew that it was George, protecting me to the very end.

I didn't know what would happen next. I thought that we would hide here until it was all over. Perhaps the Traveller thought that the police would never look for us here. But then I heard the most extraordinary sound: a metallic cough followed by a rumble somewhere below. The entire boat began to vibrate and I realized that although the *Lady Jane* had been pulled by a horse when it arrived, that had just been a trick, a diversion, and that it still had a working engine. The Traveller even had fuel.

He and Jamie released the ropes. George was still firing short, uneven bursts, keeping everyone back, stopping them seeing where we had gone. The Traveller was standing next to me. He leant out and pushed us away from the bank. Jamie climbed in and crouched beside me. A last stammer from the machine gun, then a single shot and a sudden cry. The Traveller went over to the tiller.

The engine made little sound, a dull throbbing, as we slipped into the night. I looked back one last time and saw nothing close by, but in the distance a red glow spread across the landscape as the village burned.

ENDGAME – THE CONFERENCE

EIGHT

The car slowed down and stopped at the traffic lights and at once nine or ten children ran forward. They were the usual crowd – bare-footed, dressed in rags or half-naked, starving, with empty, saucer eyes, their hands cupped in the universal symbol for food. They almost seemed to be vying for who could look the most pathetic. *We're starving*, they pleaded, their shirts hanging open to reveal the skin stretched over their ribcage. *Give us something to eat. Give us money*. Their hairless heads swivelled on their scrawny necks, trying to catch the driver's eye. *Give us anything.*

The driver ignored them, staring straight ahead through his sunglasses, waiting for the lights to change. Outside, the temperature was well into the thirties and the streets stank of filth and decay, with raw sewage trickling down the gutter, actually moving faster than the traffic.

There were shops on both sides but most of them had been abandoned, plate-glass windows displaying grey interiors and shelves that had been emptied long ago. Any buying or selling was being done on the pavements. There were food stalls: foul concoctions, brains and entrails, bubbling away beneath a layer of scum in battered metal pots. Old men and women sat cross-legged in front of tiny piles of fruit and vegetables which they had brought in from the fields that spilt over into the suburbs, hoping to sell them to get money for what? For more fruit and vegetables to sell another day? One half-crazed woman crouched over a pyramid of dried milk in tins, a decade past its sell-by date. Another had a collection of batteries, as if anyone would have a use for them even if they could have afforded them. And, of course, there were beggars; blind, broken and babbling. A man with stumps instead of arms, another with no eyes, a third seeming to disappear into the roadside with nothing beneath his waist. A woman cradled a baby that was probably dead. A few stray dogs lay curled up in the shadows. The animals who hadn't already starved to death would feed on the ones who had.

As always, the noise was deafening, the traffic so snarled up that it was difficult to tell in which direction it was even supposed to travel. There were one or two expensive limousines carrying important people to important places, but most of the vehicles belonged on the scrap heap or had perhaps been rescued from it. There were crumpled, ancient cars with cracked windows and plastic seats, only kept in service with odd, spare parts and prayer. Buses stood rumbling, jammed with people pressed against each other without air for hours on end, slowly baking to death in the heat. And everywhere there were bicycles, rickshaws, scooters and tuk-tuks, motorized death traps that zigzagged through the traffic with their lawnmower engines buzzing like angry wasps.

The driver tapped his thumbs against the steering wheel, waiting for the lights to change. One of the children, a boy of about six or seven, rapped on the glass and pointed at his mouth, and the driver was briefly tempted to take out the gun which he always carried and shoot him right between those pathetic, staring eyes. The street-sellers would look up for an instant before going back to their work. And the blood would spread in the flyblown puddles that filled the cracks and the potholes in the road. One less mouth to feed! For a moment, he was seriously tempted. But to shoot the boy, he would have to roll down the window, and that would mean letting in the heat and the noise just for a few seconds. It wouldn't be worth it. His passenger wouldn't be pleased.

The lights changed but the car didn't move. There was an obstruction just ahead. An ox had been pulling a cart filled with old fridges and freezers – scrap metal – turning left across the carriageway. But the weight had been too much for the wretched animal, which had collapsed, blocking all three lanes. Its owner was standing over it, beating it again and again with a wooden stick. But the ox couldn't get up. It tried to raise itself onto its spindly legs, then collapsed again. Two policemen in black-and-white uniforms ran forward. They could have helped. They could have redirected the traffic or forced some of the children to help move the load. Instead, they began to shout, lashing out with their truncheons. Soon everyone was shouting at everyone. Horns blared. The ox lay still, staring out with saliva dribbling from its mouth.

"What is it, Channon?" the passenger asked.

"I'm sorry, sir. There seems to have been an incident..."

"It doesn't matter. We've got plenty of time."

The inside of the car was air-conditioned, the air filtered twice before it entered. The seats were leather, the windows tinted, the floor thickly carpeted. The passenger was reading a newspaper and there were several bottles of water in the compartment next to him. Even without the bulletproof glass, the thick military-grade armour built into the side panels, and the doors as heavy as those on a commercial airliner, he would have felt secure and suitably removed from the world outside. He was the chief executive officer of the Nightrise Corporation, the single most powerful business organization on the planet. He was protected.

Nightrise had come a long way in the last ten years. It was still active in the fields of telecommunications, energy and weapons development ... but it had added so many strings to its bow that there was barely any area in which it wasn't the market leader. It now controlled sixty-five per cent of the world's food. Its pharmaceutical wing owned the cures to virtually all the world's diseases. No newspapers or television station ever criticized Nightrise, because Nightrise had bought them all. The fact was that if you wanted to eat, stay healthy, and live with any degree of comfort, you needed Nightrise – although as Nightrise was quick to point out, it never needed you.

The chief executive officer was called Jonas Mortlake and he had been working for the company all his life. His mother, Susan, had headed the Los Angeles office of the corporation and had been highly regarded until she had died with a bullet in her head. Jonas had been working for the London office when he heard the news but he hadn't asked for time off to go to the funeral. He was far too busy and he had been brought up with one simple rule: business always comes first. He had never really liked his mother very much anyway. He only ever saw her a couple of times a year and he was slightly jealous of her success.

Jonas was still a young man ... which was just as well because old age, like any weakness, disgusted him. His curly blond hair had been cut short, in a style that was almost military, and he had the physique of a soldier ... the result of a careful diet and a personal trainer working with him every day at his private gym. Jonas was proud of his body, with every muscle perfectly developed, and he never covered it with anything less than a one-thousand-dollar suit. Even his nails were manicured, his eyebrows plucked, his teeth artificially whitened. Appearances are important. That was one of the things he had learned in business school. And business, of course, was his life.

Even so, he was not particularly handsome. Hours spent in front of the computer screen had damaged his eyesight and he now wore wire-framed spectacles that sat awkwardly on his face. He had never had plastic surgery but somehow looked as if he had.

There was a slightly sweaty, artificial sheen to his skin and everything was stretched a little too tight, making it hard for him to show any emotion. He spoke with a public-school accent and there was perhaps a part of him that had never left school. His lips were always twisted in a half-smile. He was very pleased with himself and couldn't disguise it. But then, he had managed to work his way to the highest level of Nightrise. He was even more senior than his mother had been at the time of her death. So why shouldn't he be pleased with himself? He was at the top of his game.

Jonas Mortlake was not married and had no children of his own. The idea of being close to another human being slightly repulsed him and he particularly disliked women, with their soft, flabby flesh, their emotions, their weakness, their constant demands. He glanced at the business newspaper lying open on his lap, at the tiny print and the endless columns of figures. That was where real pleasure was to be found.

He was excited.

As much as he mistrusted emotion, he couldn't deny it. He was on his way to a conference and he'd been looking forward to it for weeks. "ENDGAME" it had simply announced on the invitation, which, of course, was actually a command. He was aware that, elsewhere in the traffic, a hundred more limousines were carrying hundreds more men and women to the same event. They had all been summoned to meet the chairman of Nightrise, to hear him speak. But Jonas was different. He had already been told what was going to be said, and afterwards, when the chairman had made his surprise announcement, he was going to have a meeting, one-to-one, in which his own destiny would be spelled out.

They had managed to move the ox, which was now lying at the edge of the road, its eyes wide, its stomach heaving up and down. One of the policemen blew a whistle, frantically gesticulating, and somehow the traffic managed to untie itself and move forward.

Glancing up from his newspaper, Mortlake saw an open-air market spread out beneath a concrete flyover: more food frying, and water carriers – some only seven or eight years old – bent double under the plastic tanks which they carried on their backs and which would cripple them before they were nine. Women dressed in shorts, low-cut T-shirts, sandals and cheap jewellery with nothing to sell but themselves rested against the concrete pillars. At night, the area would be lit by coloured bulbs and open braziers and perhaps they would look a little less hideous and grotesque.

The car turned a corner and suddenly the river was ahead of them, the water as tangled up with old boats as the roads were with cars. The sun was even worse here. Out in the open, reflecting off the water, it made everything hard and brittle. With the smoke rising from the dozens of miniature bonfires that had been lit along the quayside, it was as if the ground itself was catching fire. There was no electricity or running water in this part of the city. The people sat, slumped in defeat.

At last they reached their destination. The building, with its famous curved front and multiple flags, stood in the plaza that had been named after it.

The United Nations. New York.

Two guards armed with machine guns stood and saluted as the barrier was raised and Jonas Mortlake was welcomed in.

NINE

There were one thousand eight hundred seats in the General Assembly and nearly every one of them was taken. Jonas Mortlake had been given a place in the second row and saw it as a sign of favour. The closer you were to the front, the more important you were considered to be. As he walked to his place, he was aware of the multicoloured crowd – many had chosen to wear their national costume – all sitting with their attention focused on the stage. There were Arabs in white robes and headdresses, Africans in brilliant woven shirts, Chinese and Japanese in silk, Indians in saris. It was important to show which countries they represented … which countries they had destroyed … and it was a reminder that delegates had come from every continent. Normally, at the end of the conference there would be a party and everyone wanted to look their best.

Jonas smiled to himself. There was indeed going to be a party in a short while, but it wasn't the one that everyone was expecting and he was glad he hadn't received an invitation. Just a few rows behind him, he noticed a man he had known at the London office. What was his name? The man nodded at him and Jonas nodded back. At the same time, he thought to himself, You're not going to be nodding in a few hours from now. He couldn't wait to see the look on their faces.

The hall had barely changed since the time it had been built, with vast, golden walls sloping inwards and an arched ceiling high above. There was a stage with a podium and behind it a circular disc that had once carried a map of the world bracketed by two olive branches, which stood, of course, for peace. But this had been replaced with a different symbol:

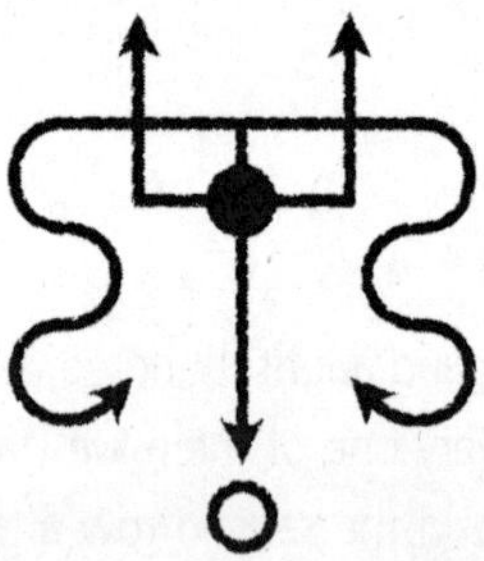

The sign of the Old Ones.

Jonas sat down, taking his place beside a silver-haired man whom he had also met before. He was a Russian, a man who had sucked so much money out of his country's oil and gas that it was said that you couldn't turn a light on in Kiev without his permission. He had lavished that money on himself with homes all over the world, a fleet of yachts and a premier league football team who played privately for him. Behind him, two women were whispering excitedly. Jonas didn't recognize them but the smell of their perfume was overpowering. It made him feel queasy. Ushers stood at the end of every row, showing the last arrivals to their seats. Everyone had arrived in good time. To have entered the room even a few seconds after the eleven-thirty start time would have meant immediate sacking … or worse.

And at half past eleven exactly, the conference began. There was no announcement. The lights didn't dim. The chairman of Nightrise simply walked onto the stage and everyone got to their feet, bursting into applause that wouldn't stop until he had reached the central podium.

It took a long time since the chairman was very old and moved like a tortoise, which in so many ways he resembled. He was completely bald and his head, at the end of an unusually long neck, bobbed forward as he made his way across, as if it was emerging from a shell. His eyes were red and watery. His skin was discoloured, covered in liver spots and so wrinkled that, from a distance, it could have been mistaken for scales. His black suit did not disguise how thin and fragile his body had become with age. There couldn't have been more than fifteen steps from the wings to the centre of the stage but he took each one of them as if it might be his last.

And finally he arrived. The applause rose in pitch, the audience congratulating him on having completed the journey. The chairman reached out a hand to steady himself and stood there, smiling, enjoying his reception. At last he raised the same hand, showing spindly fingers and grey, uneven nails. It was a signal for silence. The audience immediately obeyed, sitting back down in their chairs.

"My friends," he began. He had a croaky voice and an accent that could have been Australian or American. Nobody knew where he had been born or where he lived. Like many of them, he probably spent most of his time on the move. "First, let me welcome you all to New York. I know some of you have come a long way and you're all busy people. I take it as a personal compliment that you should have interrupted your schedules to be with me here today. At the same time, we couldn't have achieved what we've achieved without you. You are the inner circle. It's right that you should be here because this is the day you receive your rewards."

The chairman was speaking without a microphone but somehow his voice carried to the very back of the assembly hall. And although half the people in the room couldn't speak English, every one of them understood exactly what he said. How was it possible? Nobody wanted to ask that question. The truth was that the answer frightened them too much.

And what did it matter anyway? The last word – reward, *Belohnung*, *recompensa*, ανταμοιβή – echoed in their ears and once again they burst into applause. This was what they had all been waiting for. It was what this was all about.

Jonas Mortlake clapped too, but more slowly, his delicate white hands rubbing against each other. He wondered why the chairman was going through this performance. Perhaps he was simply doing it to amuse himself. These people ... the senators and statesmen, bankers and businessmen, millionaires, billionaires, power-brokers and king-makers ... what fools they all were! They were lapping it up. The women behind him were clapping so ferociously that their breasts were heaving, their earrings jangling. The man next to him was like an over-excited child.

"I want to talk to you about the Old Ones," the chairman continued, once the room had calmed down. "Who are they? Where did they come from? What do they want? I'm afraid there are no easy answers to these questions. I guess you could say that they've been around for ever. They're almost like a force. There are plenty of people who would claim that they're simply pure evil – but then I would have to ask you, what exactly is evil? I mean, they've looked after us well enough, I'm sure you'd agree. Three-quarters of the world is starving. We have food. Millions of people have no water. We drink champagne. Women and children are dying in wars while we pay ourselves huge bonuses and get richer and more comfortable. At the end of the day, I'd say that 'evil' is simply a point of view.

"The important thing for us to remember is that the Old Ones first came into this world about ten thousand years ago ... a long time before the Bible was written. And they had a Bible of their own. In the beginning was the word and the word was ... kill, damage, maim, destroy! Why? Because it was their nature. It was what they enjoyed. And they were helped by people just like us. It was always important to them that they should remain invisible. They never wanted to be seen as the enemy because that would just make everyone unite against them. The way they saw it, the greatest enemy of mankind was man himself, and people shouldn't be given the idea that they needed any help to make themselves extinct.

"The world was an amazing place ten thousand years ago, ladies and gentlemen. There was a civilization so extraordinary that it makes everything we have today look about as impressive as a Mumbai slum. There was art and poetry and cities full of beautiful buildings. People lived at peace with each other. Well, that quickly changed after the Old Ones arrived. They destroyed it so completely that there wasn't a single trace of it left for future generations to find. Maybe there are a few memories. People talk about the age of Atlantis. There are Bible stories like Noah's ark … or Sodom and Gomorrah. But basically it's all gone. Wiped clean.

"If the Old Ones had had their way, they would have continued until the planet had been sucked dry, until there wasn't so much as a single bacterium left. That was their aim. But at the very last minute, when there were only a few thousand people left alive, there was a rebellion against them and it was led by the very last people you'd have expected. Not adults but children! Yes … I can see the surprise on your faces and I don't blame you. There were four boys and a girl. They brought all the survivors together and fought against the Old Ones."

The chairman paused, as if he couldn't quite believe what he was about to say.

"And they won!"

He reached for a glass of water and sipped. The assembly sat in silence, watching as the liquid made slow, painful progress down his throat.

"As you can imagine, these were not normal children," the chairman continued. "I wouldn't go so far as to call them super-heroes, but they did have powers of a sort. One of them was a healer. One of them controlled the weather. Two of them – they were twin brothers – could read each other's minds and they were able to control other people's minds too ... a neat trick. We're not even sure what the last one was able to do. He could move things and smash them – just with the power of thought. And more. He was their leader and he was the most powerful of them all.

"Alone, the children were not a serious threat. They were strong, yes, but not strong enough. As long as they were separated, in different parts of the world, they posed no real danger. But if all five came together, if they formed a circle, then their abilities would be magnified. The Power of Five. That was what the Old Ones had to prevent at all costs. And in the end, they failed.

"There was a great battle which the children won, effectively by cheating. Yes. That's exactly what they did. They played a dirty trick and suddenly they were all there together and at that moment something astonishing happened. A great hole was torn open in the fabric of the universe and the Old Ones, with all their armies, followers and servants, were sucked through it – banished to another dimension.

"At the same time, a gate was built – a barrier to keep them out. It was given a name ... Raven's Gate, and for the next ten thousand years it stood there in what finally became the county of Yorkshire, in England. And the world, which had come so close to extinction, was given a second chance. It grew and it developed, and finally it became the world that every one of us here today inherited."

The speech showed no sign of coming to an end and already people were fidgeting in their seats, wondering what all this had to do with them. For his part, Jonas was beginning to get a headache. He just wanted this to be over – because then his own rise to ultimate power would begin.

The chairman coughed, swallowed some more water, and continued.

"Almost from the very moment that Raven's Gate was constructed, there were people who were determined to see it open again. Many of them were dismissed as witches and wizards but in fact they were believers, the disciples of the Old Ones. They were, ladies and gentlemen, people like us. They saw exactly what sort of rewards they would receive if they could bring the Old Ones back. Huge wealth. Power. Total dominance over their fellow humans. More luxury and comfort than it is possible to imagine.

"And finally, ten years ago, they succeeded. Raven's Gate stayed firm but it turned out that there was a second gate in the Nazca Desert, controlled by a combination of the stars and a great man, Diego Salamanda, was able to unlock it. At last the Old Ones were able to return … with results that you have all seen for yourselves.

"As I said in my opening remarks, the last ten years have been very good to us. Is there anyone here who wants to complain? Of course not. But there is a problem. It is what you might call a thorn in our flesh – and it brings me to the point of this conference. It brings me to the endgame.

"Somehow, the same five children – the four boys and the girl – have reappeared. Their names are different this time but it is almost as if they have been born again on the other side of time. And once again they are hoping to lead a rebellion against the Old Ones. Only this time, we are not going to let it happen. This time, they are not going to win."

The chairman had nearly finished. The effort of talking so much had exhausted him. His skin was sagging and there were strings of grey saliva between his lips. There was so much water in his eyes that he almost seemed to be crying.

"Very soon there will be another battle, a re-run of the one that took place ten thousand years ago. The King of the Old Ones is waiting for it. He has invited it. He has built himself a fortress at the very end of the world – in a place called Oblivion, in

Antarctica – and it is acting like a beacon, drawing all the forces of rebellion towards it. This is where the five children will go, bringing all their ragbag followers with them. And when they finally reach the frozen wastes of Oblivion, what do you think they will find waiting for them? A second victory? No. This time we will be ready. An army will have been assembled ... and all the resistance that is left on the planet will be wiped out in one fell swoop.

"Now, some of you may be thinking – I can almost hear you asking – why do you need to know all this? What has it got to do with me? You're all business people, aren't you. Politicians, consultants, celebrities, pleasure-seekers! You wear fine clothes and work in comfortable offices. You would never dirty your own hands ... not even to make yourselves a cup of coffee. So why all this talk of war and battles? Well, this is what it boils down to. In return for the many riches and rewards that have been bestowed upon you, the Old Ones are now asking for a display of loyalty on your part. They want you to join the army. When the last, great struggle comes, you are going to be on the front line."

There was a murmuring in the room. People were glancing at each other as if they weren't quite sure of what they had just heard. There had to be some sort of mistake, hadn't there? Many of them thought the chairman must be joking. Only Jonas Mortlake knew the truth and he was smiling to himself. This was what he had been waiting for.

"You have been chosen to become foot soldiers in the army of the Old Ones," the chairman exclaimed. "There are a thousand of you here, enough for twenty battalions. Most of you will die. That is tragic but unavoidable. The rest of you will have the satisfaction of knowing that you have repaid the debt you owe to the Old Ones, even at the cost of great pain and suffering to yourselves." He spread his hands, drawing them all in. "You've all been recruited and you will begin your new lives immediately.

There are buses waiting outside to take you to training camps, where you will be given clothes and equipment. You are also going to be adjusted to turn you into superb fighting machines..."

"Wait a minute!"

A man in the front row had got to his feet, raising his hand like a policeman stopping the traffic. Such a thing had never happened before. Nobody would have dreamt of interrupting the chairman while he was speaking. But the man was one of the most influential people in the room, with a business empire that stretched from Shanghai to New York. His name was Sir David Lang ... he had been knighted even though he wasn't a British citizen. He had made his fortune in airlines, hotels, expensive boutiques, film production and telecommunications. He was in his fifties, a small, neat man with silver hair and a slightly effeminate face.

"What are you talking about?" he demanded. "What's going on here? Are you seriously inviting me to join some sort of army?"

"I'm not inviting you, Sir David. The decision has already been made."

"You're crazy!" Lang looked around him, trying to draw the audience onto his side. "If you want people to fight for you, go out onto the street. There are millions of them out there. Pay them a dollar and you can do anything you want with them."

"We are not interested in the people on the street. We want you."

"Well, you can forget it. I'm not available."

The chairman seemed genuinely surprised. "Can I take it that is your final word on the subject, Sir David?"

"You most certainly can."

"Then I'm afraid we've come to a parting of the ways."

The chairman hadn't given a signal but a second later there was a gunshot, the sound echoing in the vast space. The sniper must have been hidden somewhere high up in the ceiling. Lang twisted round, his blood splattering over the women who had been whispering together before the conference began. The two of them reeled away, their eyes wide, screaming. Lang collapsed. Jonas Mortlake sat quite still. He had known that the businessman was dead from the moment he had opened his mouth.

And it was as if this first death was rippling outwards, like some fearsome disease. Everywhere, people were getting to their feet, shouting and crying, falling over each other as they tried to fight their way out. At the same time, doors burst open on every side and there was a commotion of whistles being blown, of shouting and barking. Security guards had appeared – the same guards who minutes before had been helping the business people to find their seats. Now their eyes were gleaming with undisguised pleasure as they marched back in, many of them with vicious dogs – Rottweilers and pit bull terriers – straining on leashes. The guards carried truncheons, whips and canisters of mace. There was no way out. The terrified audience was surrounded.

"Stay right where you are!" the chairman commanded. His voice had found new strength. It was louder than ever. "You must learn discipline. You're in the army now. Try to behave with dignity."

There was no dignity. People were sobbing, screaming, tearing at each other, trying to hide. A man in his sixties – red-faced and overweight – let out a bellow like a bull and charged towards the nearest exit. He hadn't taken more than a few steps before the guards rounded on him, clubbing him down with their truncheons and then continuing, pounding him long after he had lost consciousness. Several people had followed him but, seeing what had happened, they fell back, their hands raised in surrender, whimpering. There was a second gunshot. In the very centre of the room, a man stood clutching his stomach. His name was Haywood and he had been the head of a petrol company that had managed to pollute more than one hundred kilometres of the Australian coastline. Now blood, like oil, was leaking through his fingers. He fell to his knees, tumbling over the seat in front of him, and lay still. There was more screaming and confusion. The chairman watched, impassive, from the stage.

"Ladies and gentlemen, please!" he exclaimed. "Let's be civilized about this.

It took an hour to clear the hall. The delegates had become a seething mass, fighting against itself. They wanted to get out, to escape. At the same time, they were terrified of leaving, knowing what was waiting for them. Gradually, the guards beat them down, setting the dogs onto them or using the mace to blind them. They were laughing, enjoying their work. There were men here who had arrived with their noses high in the air. Women who had spent hundreds of dollars on their hair and nails and now found that they were worth nothing at all. They were jerked to their feet and sent spinning through the doors.

There was a fleet of yellow buses waiting outside. Once they had been used to ferry New York children to school but now they had been adapted – the windows barred, the seats removed. The men and women were jammed into them so tightly that they couldn't move, could barely breathe. Even at the end, they tried to find a way out, tearing off their own watches and jewellery to offer as bribes to the guards. The guards snatched the precious objects, then pushed them inside anyway.

At last it was over.

Jonas Mortlake was still in his seat, his hands resting on his knees. There were about twenty bodies around the hall. A few of them had been shot and some of them had been crushed in the stampede. But most of them had suffered heart attacks and were sitting there, facing forward with huge eyes and open mouths. The chairman had never left the stage. He was leaning against the podium, framed by the symbol of the Old Ones. The two of them were finally alone.

"Let's go to my private office," he said. "I don't know about you, but I'm dying for a drink."

TEN

The chairman's office had a panoramic view over the river that seemed to stretch on for ever to the north and to the south. Jonas Mortlake stood in front of the floor-to-ceiling, triple-glazed windows, looking at the women washing great bundles of clothes in the murky water, the children splashing around in the shallows, the old men turning scraps of meat on bonfires that had been built along the shoreline and that added clouds of grey smoke to the already polluted air. Dozens of ships were lashed together in the mudbanks, slanting at odd angles, the metal ones rusting, the wooden ones rotting. There were still a few ferries afloat, making the journey between Manhattan and Long Island City, but no one in their right mind went over there. The overcrowding was so bad on the island that some buildings had two or three families crammed into each room. The crime levels were off the scale. It was said that you couldn't walk the length of 21st Street without having your throat cut and that afterwards you would lie there until you rotted. The police never went into the area. There was no rubbish collection. The whole place was left to get on with itself.

Perhaps it was the air-conditioning but Jonas felt a cold shudder rise up between his shoulder blades. He was so glad he was up here, not down there. From as early as he could remember, he had always believed that he had been chosen. It didn't matter that he was alone, that his mother was always away on the other side of the world. All through his life he'd had the best food to eat, the finest clothes to wear. He had been educated, taken to theatre and opera, encouraged to read. If he became sick, doctors would look after him. He could not imagine scrabbling in the mud like the people he was looking at now. People? It wasn't even the word for them. They were little more than animals.

"A glass of white wine?"

The chairman had slipped into the office behind him and stood there with a bottle in one hand.

"Thank you, sir."

"I'm afraid it's not quite chilled. Even here in the United Nations, the power is not completely reliable. It goes on and off. Please, take a seat..."

The chairman seemed younger than he had on the stage, as if he had put the effort of his long speech behind him and could now relax. He moved carefully into the room and poured two glasses, then took his place behind the desk. Jonas took a glass and sat on a leather sofa. It occurred to him that he knew nothing at all about the chairman – where he lived, whether he had a family, or even his name.

"Your very good health, sir," he said.

"No, Jonas. I'm afraid you're drinking to something that doesn't exist. I'm old and my body is full of cancer. Fortunately, I have drugs to contain it but the truth is that I may not have more than a year left. Maybe we should drink to the Old Ones. And to the new world that they're helping to create."

"Of course." Jonas sipped his wine. It was excellent. He wondered how many hundreds of dollars the bottle would have cost.

"So what did you make of the conference?" the chairman asked. His face gave nothing away. There were so many folds, so many lines that it was barely more than a leather mask.

"I thought it was amusing," Jonas replied.

"The other delegates may not have agreed."

"I'm sure they didn't." Jonas paused for a moment, swirling the wine in his glass. "What did you mean by 'adjusted' – if you don't mind my asking?"

"Adjusted?"

"You said that some of them would be adjusted in the training camps."

"Oh yes." The chairman sounded uninterested. "They'll have their hands or their arms cut off and replaced with saws and blades. It's very hard for a soldier to lose his weapon when he *is* the weapon. Some of them will be disfigured in other ways. Their faces will be altered to make them uglier. You take someone's lips away, they never stop snarling. They'll all be branded – name, rank and serial number. It makes them feel they belong. And it terrifies the opposition."

There was a pause. The two men sipped their wine.

"Does it ever bother you, Jonas?" the chairman asked. "When the Old Ones have finished with you, they'll probably kill you too."

Jonas shrugged. "That won't happen while I'm still useful to them."

"And do you think you still are?" He paused. "Useful?"

"I'm sure I wouldn't be here if I wasn't, sir." Jonas leant forward. "I'll do anything to prove myself. You only have to ask."

"That's good." The chairman set his glass down. His eyes became hard. It was time for business. "You'll be leaving today for Italy. We have two prisoners for you to deal with. They were captured a couple of weeks ago in the Abbey of San Galgano, just outside the city of Lucca."

"Two of the Five?"

"Exactly. There was something I didn't explain back in the conference hall, but you need to understand it as it'll make sense of your mission. In fact, it's very important."

"Please go ahead, sir."

"Well, it concerns the Five. I said there were five children at the battle ten thousand years ago and five children now – and, as I explained, they're the same five children. But what I should have added was that, somehow, they have the ability to exist in two different times, simultaneously. More than that, they can replace themselves. Take the girl, for example. If you killed her today, she would be replaced immediately by the girl from ten thousand years ago."

"So you'd need to kill her a second time."

"Exactly. But you'd have to find her first and that might not be so easy. You see what I'm getting at, Jonas? If we want to control them, we have to keep them alive. We can lock them up. We can hurt them. Bu it's better for us if they don't die."

"Is that how they won ... the last time?"

"Yes." The chairman nodded. "There were five armies but they were hopelessly outnumbered. All the forces of the Old Ones – the shape-changers, the fly-soldiers, the monsters and the mutants – were lined up against them. And then, one of the Five, the boy called Sapling, was ambushed and killed at a place called Scathack Hill.

"The Old Ones thought they were safe. What they didn't realize was that killing Sapling allowed his modern self to travel back in time and replace him. The American boy, Jamie Tyler, went back without anyone noticing and joined with the four others to make five. That was the trick. The Old Ones didn't see what had happened until it was too late. The circle was formed, the gate opened, and the rest you know."

Jonas drank a little more of his wine. He wondered where this was all leading. The chairman had announced that he was dying. Well, good riddance to him. But was it possible that he was being groomed to take over Nightrise? His face gave nothing away but the thought of it thrilled him.

"Returning to modern times," the chairman continued, "the Five came together again very briefly in Hong Kong. It's extraordinary to think that they were actually in the same room, in a temple in Kowloon. If they had been able to stay together, if they had formed another circle, who knows what might have happened! But the city was being hit by a typhoon. It was falling down all around them. They had to get out fast so they all piled into a magic door, which had been specially built for them inside the temple and which could transport them to safety on the other side of the world.

"There are twenty-five of these doors and they've used some of them before. But this time they forgot the one simple rule. They had to know where they were going. Otherwise, they would be sent anywhere. And that's exactly what happened. They went in together through one door but they came out of different ones. Jamie Tyler, for example, turned up in a village in England and we very nearly captured him. We're still looking for him now. In a way, you've got to laugh. All that effort just to come together and they've found themselves scattered all over the globe.

"And there's something else. The door was blown to pieces even as they went through it. The typhoon destroyed the entire temple ... and this caused a gash in the fabric of time. Although the journey only felt like a few seconds for them, it actually took them ten years to arrive at the other end.

"I'm afraid they've come back to a world very different from the one they left. Their position is hopeless. They're alone, scared, weak and divided..."

"And we have taken two of them prisoner."

"Yes, Jonas. We knew the exact location of seventeen of the twenty-five doors and we have been watching them for ten long years, waiting for the children to appear."

"So which two are they?"

The chairman waited before answering and Jonas knew that he was toying with him, enjoying the moment. "One is a Peruvian boy. His parents died in a mud-slide in his village and he ended up scavenging and begging in the streets of Lima. His name is Pedro."

"And the other?"

"Scott Tyler."

The words were out and Jonas felt a warm glow of satisfaction. Scott and Jamie Tyler had been responsible for the death of his mother in California, ten years ago. One or the other of them – maybe it was both – had turned the hand of an assassin and sent a bullet straight into her head. Jonas had been seventeen at the time. Of course he didn't care about his mother – but that wasn't the point. This boy, Scott, had been responsible for her death and that made it personal. It would give Jonas great pleasure to meet up with him. Suddenly the wine tasted sweet.

"What do you want me to do?" he asked.

"Pedro is of very little interest to us. He's weak and he's loyal and it's unlikely that we'll be able to do very much with him. Scott is a different matter. Your mother already spent a certain amount of time with him and almost managed to persuade him of our point of view. She was using drugs and various brainwashing techniques." The chairman produced a memory stick and handed it to Jonas. "This is her report and there are video files too, which will give you a general idea of what went on. Obviously the process wasn't completely successful as Scott and his brother were reunited and your mother is dead.

"But it's still our belief that Scott is the weak link. He may be one of the Five but he's not really *one* of them, if you know what I mean. He's an outsider. He's not popular. From what we know, when the others went travelling to the UK and then to Hong Kong, he got left behind. They didn't want him. We can play on that. We can do anything, actually, but we want him on our side."

"And then?" Jonas turned the memory stick in his fingers. It was strange that he might be seeing his mother again soon in the video files.

"We can use him to get Matthew Freeman," the chairman replied. "That's what this is all about. It's like I said when we were in the conference room. Matthew Freeman did the impossible and hurt the King of the Old Ones in the Nazca Desert. For that he has to pay. There is an infinity of pain coming his way, Jonas, and it's your job to arrange it. You finish your mother's work and you make Scott one of ours. Scott draws Matt into a trap. And you get your reward."

"You mean … I end up getting adjusted too?"

The chairman smiled. His skin barely moved but it was there in his eyes. "It could come to that, Jonas. Let's face it. We're heading towards the end of the world as we know it. How many hundreds of thousands of people do you think have taken their last breath while you and I have been having this conversation in this nice office with this pleasant glass of wine? That's how it always was, even before the Old Ones arrived. You can't think too much about these things because there's nothing you can do – so why bother? If I were you, I'd take the same attitude to your future. Do as you're told and don't worry too much about what's going to happen. Because one thing is sure, if you fail in this, you'll be adjusted before you have time to blink!"

"I won't fail, sir."

"I know that. It's why you've been chosen." The chairman finished his drink. "There's a plane waiting to take you to Italy. Let me know when Scott is ready and I'll tell you what happens next."

"Thank you, sir. Thank you for this opportunity."

"You deserve it, Jonas. Enjoy it."

* * *

A few hours later, in the air above New York, Jonas Mortlake saw his mother again. Her face filled the computer screen which rested on the table in front of him.

He had always thought there was something deeply unattractive about her. She looked more like a man than a woman with her hair cut so short – and with those thin shoulders and long neck. As always, she was dressed in black, a trouser suit that didn't flatter her at all. She'd never worn make-up or very much jewellery. Her face was so washed out that had this been a black-and-white film, it wouldn't have made any difference.

It was the boy who was with her who fascinated Jonas. He was lying on a bed being fed by some sort of saline drip connected to his arm. He was wearing dark trousers and a black shirt that had been torn open to expose his chest. His feet were bare. He looked dazed as whatever drug was being pumped into him took effect. This was Scott Tyler ten years ago … although, of course, he would be exactly the same now after his little jump in time. He was a very handsome boy, Jonas thought, with that long, dark hair, sculptured features, Native American eyes. Fifteen years old but he had already packed so much into that young life. Jonas had read about his so-called uncle, a man called Don White who wasn't actually related to him at all. He had exploited the boy's ability and put him on the stage in Reno, Nevada. Scott had never had much education. He hadn't really had much of a life.

"It's always the good people who get pushed around," Susan Mortlake was saying on the screen. How long had it been since he had heard her voice? "The little people. Do you want to be a little person, Scott, or do you want to be with me? Because, you see, in the world that's coming, I'm going to be in charge, and you're going to have to start asking yourself: Which end of the whip do you want to be?"

The camera moved closer and Jonas froze the image. Scott

seemed very close now. He reached out and ran a finger down the boy's chest. It felt good. He was going to enjoy this assignment. Whatever happened to him in the future, it would be worth it.

The plane soared over the clouds, carrying him east to Europe and towards the blood red sun.

BLOOD AND SAND

ELEVEN

Scarlett Adams hovered between three different worlds.

The first of them, she knew, was the real one – and she spent as little time there as she could. It was a world of pain, harsh light, the smell of antiseptic and the knowledge of plastic tubes, twisting down, carrying fluid into her arm. She was lying on her back, in bed, obviously in a hospital. Once she had seen a woman, dressed in white, leaning over her. A nurse. The woman had said something but the words were far away, indistinct, and anyway, they seemed to be in a foreign language. Sometimes she thought there was a man in the room with her, but whenever she turned to look at him he was no longer there. She knew that she was drifting in and out of sleep and what seemed like a few seconds to her might in fact be an hour. She had never felt more tired. Her arms and legs were completely useless. There was a foul taste in her mouth.

The pain wouldn't stop. It was in the side of her head, like a knife pushed in between her eye and ear. The pain was throbbing in time with her heartbeat, so for every pump, pump, pump there was a stab, stab, stab. From time to time she was aware of someone pressing something against her lips, but she couldn't drink. She wondered if she was going to die.

And if this was a hospital, where was it and what was going on outside? She heard machine-gun fire, random shots, the occasional crump of a mortar or grenade. Sometimes it was very close and the whole world – the bed, the room, the building – trembled and she smelt dust and felt it sting her eyes. She had to be in some sort of war zone. The explosions were more or less continuous and although she had no real idea when day ended and night began, she was certain they stretched across both.

She had herself been shot – but not here. That had happened in Hong Kong, in the Tai Shan Temple. She still saw the flash of the gun and felt the shocking impact of the bullet. How long ago had it been? Lying on her back with the pain and the darkness, she tried to piece it all together, as if making sense of the past might somehow explain how she came to be here now.

The Old Ones had taken over Hong Kong. They controlled the entire city and had lured her in, using her as bait in a trap that had been set for Matt ... Matthew Freeman, a boy she had never met, even though the two of them had lived less than a mile apart for much of their lives. There were five of them. Gatekeepers. Matt was their unofficial leader. It was all very complicated and it made her head hurt (as if it wasn't hurting enough already) just to think of it.

She focused on the last day. Hong Kong was in the grip of a typhoon that was destroying everything and would have killed them too if she hadn't held it back. That was her power. She could control the weather ... make it rain, make the sun shine. And it was she who had brought them all to the temple, through the eye of the storm. Who else was there? Jamie, of course, the American boy. And Matt.

But there were also two others ... outsiders who had been drawn into the adventure, even though they really had nothing to do with it. The first of these was a journalist from a small, local newspaper in the north of England. Scarlett had barely met him but Matt had told her a bit about him while they were locked up together. His name was Richard Cole and he had become Matt's closest friend.

The other man was Lohan, her own protector even if "friend" wasn't quite the word for him. Dark-eyed, darkly handsome, always in control, Lohan was a member of the White Lotus Society, one of the Chinese Triads dealing in drugs, prostitution and God knows what else. He had never shown very much warmth or affection towards Scarlett and yet he had risked his life for her and would do anything to protect her. He was the man in the room with her, of course. It couldn't be anyone else.

They had reached the temple, knowing that there was a door that could take them out of Hong Kong, anywhere they wanted. She had got them there. She had seen the door with its five-pointed star. It had been built specially for the Gatekeepers, to take them across the world in the blink of an eye. Everything was going to be all right. They had won.

But then, at the last moment, it had all changed. Suddenly the door had opened and Scott and Pedro had appeared. Scott was Jamie's twin brother. And Pedro ... if only he were here now. Matt had also told her how he had met Pedro when the two of them were in Peru. Pedro was a healer. He could touch her with one finger and all the pain would be gone and she would be turning cartwheels out of the room.

For a few brief seconds, the five of them had been together. That was all that mattered. All they had to do was form a circle and a gate would open up and swallow the Old Ones. Wasn't that how it was meant to work? But before it could happen, someone had fired a shot. One of the guards must have been alive, hiding in a corner of the temple. Why had he chosen her? She had felt the explosion of pain in her head and had thought that this must be what it was like to die. And even as she fell, she knew her power had switched itself off and the typhoon would fall on the temple and demolish it. That was her last memory. She wasn't sorry she had been killed. She was just sad that she had let the others down.

But she wasn't dead. She had woken up here. One of them must have carried her. Maybe the others were waiting for her outside in the corridor: Matt, Pedro, Jamie and Scott. If only she could believe that, then the pain wouldn't be so bad and she would feel less alone.

That was world number one.

The real world. The here and now.

But sometimes she would slip back into the life she had left behind when she flew to Hong Kong and she would see herself almost as if she were watching herself in a film. There she was ... a confident, carefree girl moving across the screen in the uniform of a smart, south London private school (mauve dress, yellow jersey, ridiculous straw hat). On her way home, surrounded by her friends. She had to remind herself that this was her, how she had been, and not some stranger she would never see again.

She had lived in a comfortable house in Dulwich with a front garden and a gate and dustbins that were emptied once a week. Everything was ordered. School Monday to Friday and, annoyingly, Saturday mornings. Even weekends had their own routine, meeting up with Aidan, who was, she supposed, her first boyfriend, not that either of them would have ever used that word. They would hang out in the park, go shopping, see films, go to parties (home by eleven o'clock or else...). Looking back, she saw that she had been pinned down all her life like a butterfly in a glass case, but that was the way she wanted it. Didn't everybody?

Of course there had been upsets. She remembered the day her parents had told her she was adopted – which was hardly a great surprise as she was nothing like them with her Indonesian looks, her long, very black hair and green eyes. But the telling of it, the explaining made it real and somehow took her away from them. It was official now. *You don't belong to us*. What if they got fed up with her and sent her away again? They didn't owe her anything.

What would happen if her real parents turned up and demanded her back? She had been nine years old at the time and those had been the thoughts that went through her head.

And then, when she was fifteen, Paul and Vanessa Adams had got divorced. They had kept everything very civilized. There had been no plate-throwing or heavy-handed lawyers. But once again Scarlett had felt threatened. Everything she had taken for granted was being dismantled around her and there was nothing she could do. Her mother was moving to another country. Her father wanted her to go with him to Hong Kong. As her family life disintegrated, Scarlett had been struck by how little control she had over her own future – and it made her angry and afraid. Sitting on her own in her room, she had actually cried. How pathetic those tears seemed now.

Lying in bed with a bullet wound in her head, Scarlett felt she had plenty to cry about. One thing was certain. Her old life – Aidan, Dulwich, all the rest of it – was gone for good. She would never be able to return. At the same time, none of it mattered any more. She might die. She might never see Matt again. The Old Ones might have won.

She was determined it wasn't going to happen. Somehow she was going to get out of this hospital bed and back onto her feet. It wasn't over yet. She was going to fight back.

"Scarlett? Scarlett – can you hear me? I'm right here with you. You're going to be OK."

Someone was holding her hand. It was Lohan. She was sure of it. He had followed her through the door and across the world and he was with her now, as he had been when she was escaping from the Old Ones in Hong Kong. She tried to speak but her mouth was too dry, and anyway, she was exhausted. She needed to sleep.

Because sleep took her to the dreamworld – the third world –

that she knew so well and that she had been visiting for as long as she could remember. It was here, in this empty landscape that she had first met Matt, Pedro, Scott and Jamie, although she hadn't then known their names. The dreamworld seemed to have been constructed specially for them. It allowed them to communicate with each other. Although Pedro spoke only Spanish, he and Matt had been able to have conversations there, and when they woke up they remembered everything they'd said. If Matt was still alive, Scarlett was certain she would find him here. He was probably looking for her even now.

Scarlett slept and went back into the dreamworld. As always, there was no colour. The land was grey, the sea black, the sky a mixture of the two. What had happened here? she wondered. Had it always been like this? Surely dreams should be able to offer something more. She put aside her disappointment and called out for the others, her voice sounding as empty and lifeless as everything else.

And then, ahead of her, something moved. A man had appeared as if from nowhere, standing with his back to her. She saw that he was wearing a white shirt with a waistcoat but no jacket. Scarlett was completely shocked. She knew that the dreamworld could send strange messages. Jamie had met a cowboy figure who had seemed hostile but who had in fact warned him of an attempted assassination. Matt had been threatened by a giant swan.

Was this man here for her?

"Excuse me..." she said.

Slowly the man turned. Scarlett blinked. She was looking at a perfectly round face with a small, neat moustache. The man was wearing very black glasses, shaped like coins, that completely hid his eyes. He smiled at her, revealing more gold teeth than real ones.

"Five," he said.

The Five. She was one of them. He had recognized her.

Scarlett woke up and knew at once that something had happened. Doctors often talk about a tunnel of pain and she realized that, at last, she had come out the other side. There was a rush of light and a sensation of leaving the worst behind her. She saw the ceiling then, moving her head, the wall opposite. There was a picture in a frame: a young, very confident-looking man in Arab dress. He was standing in the wind with his fist raised above him. Next to the picture was an open door, leading to a corridor. Early morning light was slanting down, hitting the corner of her bed. She was desperately thirsty. She could feel the bandage tightly woven around her head but that was good. Before, she hadn't even been aware it was there.

"Scarlett...?"

Lohan was still with her. He was moving towards her bed, leaning over her. But as he came into focus, she saw that it wasn't Lohan at all. Somehow they had all got switched in the escape from the temple. The man had a lean, intelligent face, a slightly crooked nose and dirty blond hair, cut short and tangled. Scarlett recognized the journalist, Richard Cole.

"Can you hear me?" he asked.

She nodded.

"I'll get the doctor. Is there anything you want?"

"A drink."

"Here..." He picked up a glass, held it to her lips.

Scarlett swallowed. She felt the water go down.

"I was so worried about you," Richard said. "But you're looking much better now. You're going to be fine."

There were so many questions. The first one was the most obvious. "Where am I?"

Richard gritted his teeth. He sighed. "You're going to wish you hadn't asked."

TWELVE

The last minutes in the Tai Shan Temple would stay with Richard for the rest of his life.

Everything had happened so quickly. The race across the city with Matt and Scarlett as the typhoon relentlessly destroyed everything around them. The temple itself, with dead bodies littering the ground, killed by the Triad soldiers who had been sent ahead to prepare the way for them. The sudden appearance of Scott and Pedro, carried thousands of miles from Peru in the blink of an eye. Then the gunshot. For a dreadful moment, Richard thought that Matt had been hit, but then he had seen Scarlett fall right in front of him and he had scooped her into his arms, knowing that the wound was bad, seeing the blood spread across his shirt.

And with Scarlett unconscious, the entire temple had given itself to the storm. The walls had been ripped apart like damp paper and he knew that if they waited more than a few seconds, the magical door that was their only way out would disappear. Matt had given the order and of course they had all obeyed. Richard remembered the fourteen-year-old boy he had first met in the Yorkshire town of Greater Malling. Then, Matt had been almost helpless, a delinquent in trouble with the police, and fostered by a woman who delighted in taunting him. It was only after Matt had discovered his power that he had begun to change, taking his place as the leader of the Gatekeepers. He had stopped being afraid.

They had plunged through the door just seconds apart, and even then Richard had wondered how it was going to work. The doors had been constructed for the Gatekeepers but each of them was allowed to take one person with them – one passenger. Who would decide where they were going? Weren't they meant to have agreed on it before they left?

Through the door. If Richard had expected anything magical about the experience – a tunnel of bright lights and perhaps a whoosh of acceleration – he would have been disappointed. The other side was pitch-black. He was briefly aware of Jamie next to him, or maybe it was his brother, Scott, and then he was on his own with Scarlett still unconscious in his arms. He peered back through the darkness, but there was nothing. He wasn't quite sure what to do, but at the same time he was very aware of the situation he was in. No matter where he ended up, his first job was to get Scarlett to a hospital. She could die in his arms.

He had arrived in some sort of corridor and it was getting lighter ahead: a strange, orange light like nothing he had ever seen before. It was throwing shadows that swirled around the walls. At the same time, he heard a howling like a thousand wolves. The further he went, the brighter the light became and the louder the noise. At last he stepped out ...

... into a sandstorm.

He was almost knocked backwards. But for the weight of Scarlett, he would have been thrown off his feet. He could see nothing. The sand pounded him, blinding him. He could feel it stinging his arms and cheeks and he had to press his lips together to stop it entering his mouth, bowing his head into his shoulder so that he could breathe. His hands had been wet with Scarlett's blood and the sand clung to them, instantly forming a coating over his skin. He drew her tighter towards him, trying to protect her from the worst of it. He could have been anywhere. One thing was certain. This wasn't England. Where the hell was he?

Somebody shouted. The voice came from nowhere and meant nothing. Richard stood where he was as first one car engine then two more started up, moving in on him from different directions. It was only when they were very close that they became visible, looming out of the billowing sand as if from another dimension. They were open-top jeeps, dark green, military, driven by men partly in uniform but with their heads wrapped in scarves and dark glasses. They pulled up in an arrow formation, the lead jeep pointing at Richard. And suddenly there were soldiers everywhere, moving forward with automatic rifles, covering the two of them from every side.

Richard couldn't take it all in. His thoughts were still fixed on Scarlett, who seemed to be getting lighter in his arms, as if her life was slipping away from her. It didn't matter why these soldiers had come or what they wanted. Had they actually been waiting here? That was what it looked like. But it wasn't important now.

"I need help!" Richard shouted and the sand eagerly swept into his mouth, almost choking him. The howl of the storm whipped the words away. "A hospital!" he shouted again. "A doctor!"

One of the soldiers, the commanding officer maybe, reached him. He was wearing a green tunic and trousers, a tattered red-and-white bandanna and black wraparound glasses. He was a big man, almost six and a half feet tall, with wrestler's shoulders. He was unarmed. He shouted something and reached out, taking hold of Scarlett, pulling her away. Richard resisted, refusing to let go, then felt something huge and heavy thump into his back. As his knees buckled, he was aware that another of the soldiers had crept up on him from behind and clubbed him with the butt of his rifle. Richard fell. Scarlett was snatched away.

There was nothing he could do to stop them. He felt ill, ashamed of himself. But there were dozens of them and he was alone. He knew now that his instinct was right. Whoever they were, these people *had* been waiting for them ... which meant that they knew who Scarlett was. They were taking her into captivity ... and what of him? If they knew about her, they would know that he was of no use to them. As Richard lay there, cocooned in sand, he waited for the bullet that would be his end.

But at least he was wrong about that. They wanted him too. Richard felt two soldiers grab hold of him under his arms, dragging him towards one of the jeeps. Scarlett had disappeared, separated from him by the storm. He could barely see anything. His eyes were already cloaked with sand. He heard a door click open and he was thrown forward, landing on the soft leather of a car seat. Somebody was shouting again, the words falling over each other, and he guessed that he was hearing Arabic and that he must be in some desert in the Middle East. It was certainly hot enough. His clothes were clinging to him and he could feel the sweat trickling down his skin. But if this was a desert, what was the building he had left behind him?

All twenty-five doors were located in sacred places, although, in truth, the places were sacred for all the wrong reasons. It was the doors that mattered. They had been there first. The buildings – churches, temples, mosques, whatever – had sprung up around them, constructed by local people who had always remembered that the doors were special, even if they had forgotten exactly why.

He heard car doors slamming. The soldiers had got what they had come for and were now preparing to carry them away. The engines started up again. Richard felt the jeep begin to vibrate beneath him.

But before they could move, there was a sudden explosion of gunfire, bullets fired from unseen guns, slamming through the wall of sand. Richard looked up just as the windscreen of the jeep shattered, broken glass showering down onto his shoulders and head.

The soldier who had been about to drive him away jerked in his seat. Blood sprayed out of the side of his head and he slumped against the steering wheel, setting off the horn which began to blare continuously. Another bullet thwacked into the passenger door and Richard ducked down, afraid of being hit in the confusion.

All around him, people were shouting, panicking. The gunfire intensified. Richard glimpsed one of the soldiers get hit. He spun round, throwing away his own rifle as if in surrender, then allowed himself to be sucked into a whirlpool of sand. Whoever had been waiting for them on the other side of the door had themselves come under attack. Scarlett! He couldn't just stay hiding here. He had to find her.

Richard scrabbled for the door handle, opened it and tumbled out of the jeep, keeping low to avoid the bullets. The soldier who had just been shot was lying close to him and his bandanna had come free. Richard grabbed hold of it and tied it around his own face, covering his nose and mouth. The dead man was very young, dark-skinned, clean-shaven. Perhaps the sandstorm was beginning to subside, because Richard could make out the shapes of the other jeeps, parked a few metres away. He saw another soldier standing in front of him, firing at nothing. Then he was hit by a bullet and thrown off his feet. He didn't move again.

Richard ran forward and reached the nearest jeep. He had been lucky. Scarlett was there and she was on her own. For a moment, Richard stood there, uncertain what to do. She looked so fragile, stretched out on the back seat, her skin very pale and her eyes closed. She was barely breathing. Someone had covered her with a blanket but she had stirred in her sleep and it had slipped to one side. He didn't dare lift her up. Moving her again might kill her and how could he carry her through the sand and the gunfire – the one almost as lethal as the other? He glanced at the dashboard and saw keys dangling from the ignition. The driver must have left them there, joining the others in the fight. Now Richard knew what he had to do. He had no idea what was happening, who was fighting whom. He just had to get them out of there.

He threw himself into the front and turned the key. The engine coughed into life. He could see nothing out of the windscreen. His elbow had accidentally banged one of the controls and the windscreen wipers were scraping uselessly against the glass, pushing waves of sand left and right. He rammed the jeep into first gear, afraid that one of the soldiers would return at any moment. The wheels spun in the sand but then the vehicle leapt forward. They were away!

He was still driving blind, although the sand was getting thinner – he was sure of it. There seemed to be some sort of structure away to his left ... not a building but a statue or a memorial of some sort. It looked like a huge, crouching cat. His own jeep, the one he had just left, was in front of him. Richard swung the wheel and swerved round it. He was picking up speed. Out of the corner of his eye, he saw two of the soldiers running towards him, shouting, but he was away before they could get anywhere near.

Now just one man stood in front of him. From his size and from the colour of his headscarf, Richard knew he must be the commanding officer, the man who had snatched Scarlett in the first place. The jeep was doing about thirty kilometres an hour. Richard pressed his foot down on the accelerator, waiting for the man to dive out of the way. But he just stood there, huge and menacing, a concrete pillar in the driving sand. He was holding a gun but didn't seem to want to use it. Was he mad? Did he want to be killed? Richard didn't care. He wasn't going to let anyone stop him.

And then, at the last minute, as the man's figure filled the windscreen, something extraordinary happened. It was more horrible than anything Richard had ever seen.

It was impossible to see it clearly – what with the sand, the movement of the jeep, the chaos of the moment. The man's head seemed to split open. His shoulders peeled back. It was as if he had been hit by a mortar and blown apart. But there was no mortar. The man had done it deliberately, and even as Richard sped towards him, a snake's head and neck reared up from the ruin of what had been his neck. Huge tentacles slithered out, replacing his arms, and suddenly the man was only human from the waist down. Above, he was a monster, squirming in the sand, the snake mouth spitting, the eyes blazing, the tentacles writhing as if in pain.

Richard knew he couldn't avoid it. But nor could he stop. So he did the one thing that was left for him to do and stamped on the accelerator, driving straight into the man-thing. There was a dreadful thud as the front of the jeep hit it and Richard felt the shock travel up his arms. The creature let out a hideous screech and disappeared from sight. The jeep lost control, spun in a circle, nearly turning over on one side, then stopped suddenly. The engine stalled.

The creature hadn't been killed. As Richard looked round, it stumbled to its feet, the snake neck twisting from side to side, its tongue flickering in and out. Richard turned the key. The engine turned over but the jeep refused to start. The creature took a step towards him. Richard froze. Every instinct made him want to get out and run. But he couldn't leave Scarlett on her own. He tried the key again. The engine was dead. The creature came another step closer.

Then two more men appeared, stepping out of the sandstorm, dressed in pale grey and yellow. Desert camouflage. They were carrying machine guns, waist-high, strapped over their shoulders. They opened fire at the same moment, sending a blaze of bullets like two white-hot knife blades in front of them. The creature howled and twisted as it was cut into pieces by the continuous fire but the two men didn't stop, keeping their fingers pressed on the triggers until their cartridges were empty and what was left of the creature fell and lay still.

The men ran over to the jeep. One of them pulled open the door, briefly examined Scarlett then turned to Richard.

"*Vous êtes sortis de la pyramide?*" he asked.

"What?" Richard was too dazed to even realize that the man was speaking French, let alone translate.

"You came through the door – with the girl?" The man spoke English with a thick French accent.

"Yes."

"Then you must come with us. Now. Quickly. We are here to help you."

The other man was already lifting Scarlett out of the back. Richard slid out himself. There was less gunfire now and the sand-storm was almost at an end. Looking back the way he had come, he saw three constructions which he recognized instantly – which had appeared in tens of thousands of postcards and which would have been known to anyone in the world.

The pyramids of Giza. And in front of them, the statue he had partly glimpsed. The Sphinx.

Now he knew. He and Scarlett had escaped from Hong Kong. And the door had brought them to Egypt.

THIRTEEN

They drove Richard at speed through the city. He had never been to Cairo but he had seen enough pictures to be able to identify it – not just the pyramids but the great expanse of the Nile with its palm trees and slender feluccas, the mosques and minarets, the colourful markets filled with spices and tourist souvenirs. He was wrong. Cairo was unrecognizable. It was a city at war with itself and it had clearly been for some time. They sped through streets covered with rubble, buildings blown apart. Burnt-out cars and trucks lined the way. There was barely a single wall that wasn't pockmarked with bullets or shattered by mortar shells, and many of the pieces that were still standing were daubed in graffiti, political slogans in Arabic scrawled in dripping red paint.

As far as Richard could see, the shops were empty, the offices abandoned, the entire infrastructure destroyed. And still the shooting continued, in the far distance, sounding disconnected and almost harmless until they drove around the next corner, when it became ugly, loud and horribly close. A military plane flew overhead. There was a brief pause and then the heavy blast of a bomb finding its target. The ground shook and smoke rose into the air, still heavy with sand. There was smoke everywhere, trickling up in separate columns that finally joined together to form a thick pall in the sky. Nobody was moving in the streets, but when Richard examined the broken pavements and the wreckage of the buildings, he saw that there were dead bodies everywhere, lying where they had fallen and left to rot in the sun. He could smell them. Whoever had started this war in Cairo, whoever was fighting for control of the city, they clearly hadn't noticed that there was almost nothing left.

Their convoy consisted of two jeeps – one carrying Richard, the other Scarlett – a covered truck and two outriders on ancient, dusty motorbikes. Richard knew that he would never be able to find his way out of here without a guide. Even if he could read the street signs, which were in Arabic, most of them had been twisted out of shape or smashed and all the streets were so damaged that they looked the same. Turn left past the wreckage, continue through the wreckage, turn right at the wreckage. Already his mind was racing, taking in the impossibility of what he was seeing. When he had travelled to Hong Kong, less than a week ago, there had been no war in Egypt. Unrest – yes. There was always unrest in the Middle East. Libya had recently fallen, soon followed by Syria. Iran was making threatening noises to anyone who would listen. But there had been no war in Egypt. How could this violence have begun and spread so rapidly? What had happened?

He would worry about that later. Right now his thoughts were with Scarlett. She was in the vehicle ahead of him and he wondered if she was still alive. Would there be any hospitals still standing in all this wreckage that had the facilities to treat her? And what of Matt? Richard felt a wrench of helplessness, knowing that after all the two of them had been through together, they were suddenly apart. The door which had brought him from Hong Kong to Giza could have taken Matt anywhere. The two of them could be – and probably were – on opposite sides of the world.

The lead jeep swerved around a corner, through a shattered archway and continued down a narrow alley that had shuttered windows on both sides and dozens of washing lines criss-crossing each other with sheets and ragged clothes hanging down. It was as if they had entered a secret passage. The way ahead was blocked. A bus had been abandoned in the street, but as they approached, it was somehow drawn aside to reveal a gateway behind. Richard saw armed soldiers, dressed in the same desert camouflage, waiting in a courtyard beyond and he knew that they had arrived.

The compound was a rectangle of dust and concrete, surrounded by a breeze-block wall that was still intact and covered with faded posters and graffiti. Three anonymous buildings faced the main entrance, all of them three storeys high with barred windows, crumbling plaster and no sign of any decoration at all. As the vehicles pulled in, Richard saw goalposts with the tattered remains of a net and a wire hoop for basketball. This had once been a school. Or a prison. Behind them, more soldiers were sliding a heavy steel door across the entrance. There were wooden observation posts at each corner, manned by guards with guns and radio transmitters, doing their best to stay out of sight.

The jeeps came to a halt. As Richard got out, he saw Scarlett being lifted by two men and carried into the building furthest away. He tried to follow her but suddenly the Frenchman who had spoken to him at the pyramids was at his side.

"There is nothing you can do for her, Mr Cole. We have medical facilities here and she will be well cared for. We have been waiting a long time for you to arrive. You must come with me."

Mr Cole.

We have been waiting a long time...

The Frenchman knew his name. They had been waiting at the pyramids for the two of them to appear. None of it made any sense.

Richard allowed himself to be escorted towards the main building, the one that stood between the other two. But before he was allowed to go in, a guard appeared and barked at him in Arabic. The guard was young, no more than nineteen. War had quickly turned him into an adult.

"He wishes to search you before you can enter," the Frenchman explained. "Your backpack ... you are not permitted to carry weapons."

It was only now that Richard remembered the backpack that he had been wearing in Hong Kong and that was still strapped to his shoulders. It contained two precious objects. One was a diary, written in the sixteenth century by a Spanish monk, Joseph of Cordoba. It contained the only known history of the Old Ones and, Richard hoped, it might also hold a clue to how they could be defeated. The other object was indeed a weapon. It was a gold knife set with semi-precious stones that had been given to him by the Incas when he was in Peru. The knife was also known as a *tumi* and had once been used for sacrifices.

Richard had no choice. He handed the backpack over and watched as the young soldier, bearded with blank eyes, rummaged through it.

The soldier turned over his clothes. He found the book, took it out and glanced through it, then returned it without even looking at it. He unzipped the pockets and examined the insides. Then, with a cursory nod, he handed the backpack back to Richard. Once again, Richard found himself marvelling at what he knew had been nothing less than a display of Inca magic. The *tumi* had been in full sight of the soldier. He must have even pushed it aside as his hands burrowed into the pack. But he hadn't noticed it was there. This was what the *amauta*, the Inca wise man, had told him. The knife was practically invisible. That was its power. Richard had even been able to carry it through airport security when he had flown into London. But the old man had added something else.

"Do not thank me. One day you will curse me for giving it to you."

Richard often thought about that and wondered what he'd meant.

At least having the knife meant that if these people were enemies and this turned out to be some sort of trap, he would be armed. Richard reflected on that as he followed the Frenchman inside. He found himself being led down a short corridor and into an empty classroom with a blackboard at one end, a few scattered desks and chairs and a view over the courtyard. Now that they were out of the sandstorm, the Frenchman had removed his face covering to reveal long grey hair, sunken cheeks and eyes that were full of trouble. He was about fifty and seemed somehow suited to the room. Perhaps he had been a teacher or lecturer once.

"Are you hungry?" he asked. "I can arrange to have some food and water brought up."

"I'm fine," Richard said. He had forgotten how long it had been since his last meal but he couldn't sit down and eat until he had heard about Scarlett. "Where is Scarlett?" he asked.

"There are doctors here. We have a full working hospital in the block next door. You are very lucky. There is a bullet lodged in her head and without them she would not have a chance."

"What is this place? And you used my name. How do you know who I am?"

"I am sure you have a great many questions, Mr Cole. So, I must admit, do I. Perhaps it would help if you let me speak first. I will begin, if I may, with an observation. You have forgotten me but you and I have met before. It was in London, in a place called Farringdon."

"The Nexus...?"

Richard certainly hadn't forgotten the organization that had been helping them almost from the moment that he and Matt had met. The Nexus was made up of very important and influential people – police, politicians, churchmen, wealthy businessmen and women – who knew about the Old Ones and the threat they posed to the world and had come together to lead the fight against them. At the same time, they were smart enough to realize that if they went public, talking about demons and black magic, they would be ridiculed. The newspapers would tear them apart. And so they met in secret. They had used their huge collective wealth to set up a resistance movement that had branches all over the world. Richard had visited them in one such location, in central London. He remembered Susan Ashwood, the blind medium. And Mr Fabian, who had nearly got them killed in Peru. And then there was Mr Lee, the Chinese businessman who had helped them reach Hong Kong.

But this man was a stranger to him.

Unless…

Richard examined him more closely. Now that he thought about it, there had been a Frenchman in the room in Farringdon. He had seen him twice; once after the petrol tanker had destroyed Matt's school and the two of them had been sent to Peru, then again when they had returned on their way to Hong Kong. But the person he had met had been much younger than the man who was examining him curiously now. He'd had shorter, darker hair. He had been wearing a suit.

"My name is Albert Rémy," the Frenchman said. "You might as well know that now. But before you say anything else, let me ask you this. You remember me?"

"Yes…" Richard was hesitant.

"When did you and I last meet?"

"I was in Farringdon about ten days ago."

"Ten days…" Rémy smiled sadly. "It is as I suspected. A trick has been played on you, my friend. Or perhaps it has been played on both of us. For you, it has been ten days. But for me, it is more than ten years since we were last together."

"Ten years?"

"You were there with the American boy, Jamie. And also with Matthieu. We sent you to Macau, which we believed was the only safe way to enter Hong Kong." Rémy held up a hand. "Do not try to argue with me. It will drive you mad. Ever since the Old Ones came into the world, so many things have happened that do not seem possible, that we cannot understand. I will tell you how it is from my point of view and then you can say what you wish.

"I remember very clearly that last meeting with you. You had heard that Scarlett, the fifth Gatekeeper, was in Hong Kong and although we were certain it was a trap, we had to send you there. After that, we heard nothing more from you. There was a typhoon of great power that destroyed much of the city. Tens of thousands of people were killed and we wondered if you were among them. We had no way of knowing and could only do what we had always sworn to do. We waited for you. We have been waiting for ten long years."

"Why are you here in Egypt?" Richard asked. "Why not London?"

"London no longer exists, my friend. At least, not in the way you knew it." Richard looked shocked and Rémy continued. "I warned you not to ask questions. Let me explain…

"We all knew that there was a doorway in Hong Kong that you could use to travel across the world. You yourself had told us so, as you had found it in the diary of the Spanish monk. There were twenty-four other doors, some of which you had identified. We knew of St Meredith's in London, the cave at Lake Tahoe, the Abbey of San Galgano in Italy and the Temple of Coricancha in Cuzco, Peru. You also named other locations in Australia, South America and here in Egypt. It was clear to us that if you were ever to appear again, it would be through one of the doorways. It was therefore decided that agents of the Nexus would take responsibility for each one of the doorways that we knew and be there, should you ever arrive. I was sent to the Great Pyramid."

"But you weren't the only ones who knew about them," Richard muttered.

"Of course not. Have you forgotten that before you received the diary, it was in the hands of the industrialist Diego Salamanda? Before it reached you, he would certainly have studied it, and everything that is known to us is also known to the Old Ones. Not all the gates were identified in the diary. What this means is that some of them are safe. But the majority of them were surrounded, watched every minute of the day and night for ten years. The Old Ones were also waiting for the five children – Matt, Pedro, Scott, Jamie and Scarlett – to reappear. The moment that happened, they would be taken prisoner … as very nearly happened to you today."

"Except that you were there."

"You begin to see. Yes. The watchers were themselves being watched. I have spent thousands of hours waiting for you, Richard. It has been a long vigil and often I have thought to myself that it was a hopeless one. You have no idea how glad I am to see you now."

"So what's happening in Cairo? How come there's a war going on? Who were the soldiers at the pyramids? And there was a shape-changer with them…!"

"Ah yes. The shape-changer. It is very rare to see one, although we know they help the government forces. The Old Ones do not like to show themselves. They prefer to work behind the scenes.

"Much has occurred in ten years, my friend, and none of it has been good. In fact, when I look at what has happened to the world, I wonder if the Old Ones have not used their powers, playing with the fabric of time. Look at what they have done to you! You are gone for ten days but ten years have passed. Well, so it is for the world. It seems sometimes as if we flicker from crisis to crisis, that a year becomes a week, a week no more than a minute. How else can so many bad things happen in so short a space of time? The volcano that erupted in Japan. The tsunami that hit the coast of Australia. The plague in China. The earthquake in the west coast of America. The total failure of the crops and the famine that followed. Famine in the United States? Would you ever have believed it?"

"What about London?"

"Not all the catastrophes have been the work of nature, Richard. After the banking system collapsed, there were riots all over Europe. Much of my own city, Paris, was set ablaze. For London, it was a terrorist bomb. A nuclear bomb. Nine of them, in fact, each one destroying a major city in the United Kingdom on the same day."

Richard felt sick. So few words adding up to so much death. He simply couldn't take in the enormity of what the Frenchman was saying. What he was being told was insane. He had been away for ten days, not ten years, and it was as if he was hearing the history of ten centuries.

The Old Ones had made it happen. That was why they were here.

"I will not tire you with the rest of it – not all at once," Rémy said. "You only need to know the situation here. A military government has taken over Egypt. The same has happened in many places in the Middle East. The Supreme Council of the Armed Forces here is led by a man called Field Marshall Karim el-Akkad and he is utterly ruthless. He owes his power purely to the fact that he is supported by the Old Ones and he does everything that he is told. Citizens here are routinely kidnapped, tortured and killed. Everyone lives in fear.

"There is, however, a resistance movement. It has been partly funded by the Nexus. We have been supplying them with food, arms and ammunition, much of it flown into Dubai and then carried here, a thousand kilometres across the desert. In return, they have been helping us watch over the pyramid. Government forces were waiting for you when you emerged this morning. The rebels then attacked them and brought you here."

"Here...?"

"A rebel hospital and training centre. It is one of many. I will not say you are safe here because nowhere in the Middle East is safe. But they are operating on Scarlett even now and if it is at all possible for her to be saved, they will save her."

Richard was feeling exhausted. His mouth was dry. "I think I would like to have something to drink after all," he said.

"I will arrange it. We have a room here for you. We will get you fresh clothes and perhaps you need to have a sleep."

"And you'll tell me about Scarlett?"

"As soon as there is news, of course."

Albert Rémy stood up and went to the door. "You have no idea how happy I am to see you returned," he said.

Richard nodded. "Yeah," he muttered. "It's great to be back."

Field Marshall Karim el-Akkad sat behind his desk on the second floor of the Abdeen Palace, a huge building in the eastern part of the city. Once it had been the headquarters of the President of Egypt and it was only right that he should have taken it over. Everything about the room was out of proportion. The white marble floor seemed to stretch for ever. The windows looking out over Qasr el-Nil Street were triple-height. The potted plants were the size of small trees. Even the desk dwarfed the man who occupied it.

Akkad was exactly sixty years old. He was an ordinary-looking man, quite short and almost completely bald with just a few wisps of grey hair around his ears. His skin was dark, his eyes very brown. It would be easy to imagine him as a dentist or perhaps an accountant. There was a sort of willingness to please about him, a sense that he would apologize even as he was sentencing you to death. As if to make up for his physical appearance, he was wearing an elaborate military uniform. The jacket, trousers and shirt were all the same pale green. He had a dark tie and heavy epaulettes, both on his shoulders and on his collar. The only colour in the room came from the rows of medals displayed across his chest. There were so many of them that the effect was almost comical, as if the weight of them might actually make him topple over to one side.

Today's sandstorm had finally died down and outside, everything was quiet. Although much of Cairo was in ruins, Qasr el-Nil Street was still intact and a ring of steel had been thrown around the palace to protect it from rebel forces. Akkad was studying a report of a helicopter attack that had taken place the day before on Maadi, a wealthy suburb to the south which was believed to house a rebel stronghold. A nerve gas had been used and according to the report many thousands of people had died. The number was immaterial. If there had been rebels operating there, they were there no longer. Sometimes, to kill a wasp it was necessary to take out the entire nest.

There was a knock on the door and, without waiting for an answer, two men appeared, both dressed in crisply ironed uniforms. In perfect unison, they marched in, almost as if they were one creature, joined at the hip. They saluted and stood to attention. Akkad did not look up from his document, even though he had finished reading it. He was making a point, allowing the silence to add to the tension in the room. He knew what the men were going to tell him. He had heard about it long before they arrived. For their part, Colonel Bassir and Major Farouk stayed still, trying not to show how nervous they were. Both had taken part in the operation at the Great Pyramid that morning. They had come to report their failure and they knew perfectly well that, as far as Akkad was concerned, failure was never an option.

"So the girl escaped, I understand?" Akkad said at last, not looking up. He spoke in Arabic. He paused briefly, then allowed his eyes to travel from the page to the two men.

"Yes, sir," Bassir replied. He had been the commanding officer. He was thirty-two years old, married with two children, and right now he wondered if he would ever see them again. He had already decided on his strategy. He was going to blame Farouk. He had given the right orders. It was his junior who had failed to carry them out.

"How did it happen?"

"Rebel forces were waiting at the pyramid, sir. It seems incredible that they should have been there. How could they have known that the girl or any one of the Gatekeepers would appear? I had of course ordered Major Farouk to search the area, to make sure that it was secure. I am sorry to have to report that he failed in his duties."

Farouk knew what Bassir was doing. The two of them had served together for more than six years and were close friends. Their families met sometimes after evening prayer. And now Bassir was cold-bloodedly knifing him in the back. It was perfectly reasonable. Had their positions been reversed, he would have done exactly the same.

"Did you follow the girl into the city?" Akkad asked, in a tone of voice that suggested he already knew the answer and that anyway, he didn't really care.

"We were unable to, sir. Too many of our men had been killed. Even the shape-changer was cut in half. Most of our vehicles were disabled. Everything happened very quickly, and of course there was also the sandstorm..."

Akkad gazed at his commanding officer for the first time and suddenly there was a chill in his eyes which was anything but ordinary. There were stories that Akkad had been a ruthless fighter in the old Egyptian army. It had been his personal responsibility to interrogate political prisoners. Not a single one of them had lived to describe the experience. "Were you aware of how important it was to secure this girl?" he demanded.

"Yes, sir. Of course."

"Then how do you account for this failure?"

"I obeyed your instructions to the letter. I gave the commands. The men were slow and ill-disciplined."

"Major Farouk was responsible for their training?"

"Yes, sir."

The accusation hung in the air. Akkad turned to Farouk and now spoke to him. "Do you have anything to add?"

"No, sir." Farouk stood his ground and waited. He knew that there was no point in arguing or trying to raise a defence. The Field Marshall would have made up his mind before either of the two men had come into the room. Even so, the silence seemed to drag on for an eternity before he announced his decision.

"Colonel Bassir," he said. "I want you to assemble an execution squad in the parade ground. You will choose four of our most accurate riflemen … we cannot afford any more errors. Full ceremonial uniform."

"Yes, sir."

"And you can bring together a couple of regiments to witness the event. Shall we say one hour from now?"

"Yes, sir." Bassir hesitated. There was one detail missing. "Who is to be executed, sir?"

"You are, Colonel Bassir." Both men stared and Akkad went on quickly. "It is most unfortunate but this has been a serious blunder and you were the commanding officer. We have to make an example. That is all."

Bassir stood there, stunned. He tried to look at Farouk for help. But the other man turned away. Briefly, he thought of bringing out his own gun. It was there, hanging at his belt. No. That would be madness. In a way, Akkad had been generous to him. At least his death would be swift.

"Thank you, sir." Bassir saluted stiffly and left the room.

"I want you to organize search parties, Major Farouk," the field marshall continued as soon as the door had closed. "Speak to every informant. The girl must be in the city somewhere. Someone must know where she is."

"Yes, sir."

"And do make sure you find her soon. If there is any further failure in this matter, I will hold you personally responsible."

Farouk could barely speak. He spun on his heels and walked as quickly as he could out of the room.

Akkad continued working until twelve o'clock, when it was time for afternoon prayer. He didn't need to look at the clock. He knew instinctively by the length and the position of the shadows. He got up from behind his desk and dropped to his knees. But he did not face east. He faced south.

Field Marshall Karim el-Akkad had once been a good Muslim. But the old religions were almost forgotten. Along with Christianity, Catholicism and Judaism they simply seemed ... irrelevant. Akkad now prayed three times a day to his new master, to Chaos, the King of the Old Ones. And the best thing was that, unlike the old religions, his master answered back.

As Akkad muttered prayers of loyalty and devotion, the lights seemed to go out in the room. The shadows lengthened and dragged him in. The sunlight disappeared from behind the windows. Suddenly it had become very cold. Outside, there was the roll of a drum and a sudden blast of gunfire. And, almost at the same time, he heard the voice whispering in the room and he was aware that there was someone – or something – standing very close behind him.

"Find the girl," it said. "I need her. I must have her. Find the girl and bring her to me. Find her now."

FOURTEEN

"They've started fighting again," Richard said, listening to the gunfire coming from the west of the city.

He had developed a sense of distance and direction so that he could more or less tell where a battle was taking place just by glancing at a map. He had not yet been allowed to leave the compound – it was considered too dangerous – and anyway, there would have been no point with the sandstorms blowing almost continuously, twenty-three hours out of twenty-four, turning every street into a dead end. He was puzzled about the storms. He'd never thought of Cairo as a particularly windy place and wondered if there had been a catastrophic shift in the weather patterns, perhaps a result of global warming. Was that another curse that the Old Ones had brought down on the planet? The strange thing was that nobody in the compound ever mentioned it. Like the war itself, the storms had been going on so long that they had come to be expected as a normal part of life.

"Maybe it's Samir and his men," Scarlett said.

"What time did he go out?"

"About six this morning..."

By now, they knew half a dozen of the commanders in this outpost of the rebel army. They were all young, in their twenties, and – unless they were on a special exercise – they dressed in ordinary street clothes, with a single red ribbon pinned to their top pocket.

Red was the colour of the revolution. In ancient Egypt, it had been the colour of victory. The rebels all spoke a little English, although less than they might have done. With no television, there were no English-language programmes or films to learn from. There was no Internet either. For Scarlett, that was worse than almost anything, leaving her cut off and alone. But as Rémy had explained, it had simply disappeared one night a long time ago. Nobody could remember exactly when it happened, but then, Richard reflected, nobody had ever been quite sure when it had been invented either. It had just gone and that was that.

Two weeks had passed – but it was hard to keep track of time when every day was the same. And there was always the possibility that the Old Ones were still playing with them, that they might be jumping forward months or even years without even noticing it. Scarlett had been moved out of the hospital block and had a small room next to Richard, down in the basement, out of the way. They each had a bed, a basin and the use of a shower with only a trickle of cold water – although Rémy had told them to be grateful. There were now many cities within Egypt – and indeed many countries – with no water at all. At night, they looked out of small, barred windows that were half sunken below ground level so that their only view was of the boots of the guards on patrol as they walked past. The doors were unlocked. They were allowed to walk together around the compound. Otherwise, they might as well have been in jail.

At least Scarlett was well on the road to recovery. No matter what his own situation, Richard couldn't hide his relief. She had lost weight, which, with the meagre rations in the compound, she wasn't going to put back on, and the shock of what she had been through was still etched on her face. The surgeon had cut her hair short and there was an unpleasant scar from the operation, which wouldn't disappear until the hair grew back. Glancing at herself in the mirror, Scarlett had grimaced. "God, what a mess!" She was quickly recovering her sense of humour along with her strength and her determination to fight back. She was glad to be alive.

Richard had liked her from the start. He was still sorry that he had been separated from Matt and worried about him all the time – but the two of them had quickly bonded. How could they fail to, thrown together like this? Scarlett was thin and small and, with her cropped hair, had the look of a child beggar on the streets of Bangkok. But Richard never forgot that she was one of the Five and that she had immense power if she chose to use it. He had seen it for himself in Hong Kong. For her part, Scarlett was relieved to have Richard with her and, as much as he denied it, insisted that he had saved her life by bringing her here. She liked him because he was scruffy and disorganized and pretended to be completely helpless, drawn into an adventure which he didn't understand. At the same time, she saw his hidden strengths. He had been a good friend to Matt and would do anything for him, indeed for any of them. He would be with them until the end.

Richard had only recently told her what had happened to the world – her world, the one they had both known. He needed to be sure that she was strong enough to absorb it. He had briefly considered keeping it from her but had known at once that he couldn't. After all, it was the reason she was here. And so he had told her everything that Albert Rémy had told him.

She hadn't been shocked. It was all too much to grasp and – isolated, left on their own inside the compound with no newspaper or television images to make it all real – it had just added up to so many words. What proof did they have that it was even true? Rémy was as cut off as they were and had little information beyond what was happening in Cairo, and much of that was hard to prove. And yet neither of them had any doubt at all that the world was in chaos. That was the reason the Old Ones had broken through the gate at Nazca. From the moment they had returned, they had been swift and ruthless going about their work.

"I dreamt about London," Scarlett said.

The two of them were sitting in the classroom where Richard had been brought when he first arrived. The buildings had indeed once been a school and were now divided between living accommodation, the hospital, storerooms and military command. This was a neutral area. Richard and Scarlett knew they would be left on their own.

Richard waited for her to continue.

"I can't bear thinking about it, the idea that it's not there any more." She paused. "Do you really think there's nothing left?"

"I don't know," Richard said. "To be honest with you, Scar, I'm like you. I don't want to think about it."

Scarlett touched the side of her head. Her old nickname had become horribly appropriate. "Why would anyone want to do that? Blow up a city?"

"Terrorists don't really need a reason. It's always just hatred and fanaticism ... the complete opposite of reason."

"You know the terrible thing," Scarlett's eyes were far away. "I saw it in my dream. Everything in ruins ... all those people dead. But I didn't feel anything. It was as if I'd never lived there. And the only thing that makes me sad now is thinking about my school friends, and Aidan in particular. I don't suppose I'll ever see them again and I'll never even know if they lived or died."

"We have to work out what we're going to do," Richard said. "If we sit around here much longer, we're both going to go mad."

Scarlett saw that Richard was gently nudging her out of her mood. And he was right. Now that she had recovered, she was already bored, sitting in the compound with almost nothing to do. Rémy had found her a few dusty paperbacks in English, although they were barely worth reading, and there was an old chessboard that she and Richard had played on, using pebbles for the missing pieces. But they had been here too long already. It was time to move on.

"We have to get back to the Great Pyramid," Scarlett said. "That's our way out of here. I only have to think where I want to go and we'll be there."

"That won't be so easy," Richard said. "They know you're here now. Our friend Monsieur Rémy says they're looking for you everywhere. After what happened, they're going to have every soldier and shape-changer in Cairo around the pyramids. You'd never get through."

"We could go in disguise."

"As a camel?"

"I was thinking more of a burka."

"I don't think it would suit me."

The door opened and Albert Rémy came in. The Frenchman was always pleased to see them and regarded Scarlett's arrival as something of a miracle, but this morning he was particularly happy.

"I have wonderful news," he said. "Tarik is here – in the compound. Of course, nobody knew that he was coming until a few minutes ago. But I have seen him and he wishes to speak to you."

Tarik.

Both Richard and Scarlett had heard a great deal about him. He was the man in the photograph that Scarlett had seen from her bed, the leader of the rebellion. All the commanders revered him. Every night they told stories about operations that he had led, street battles that he had won. He had been fighting the forces of Field Marshall Karim el-Akkad for as long as anyone could remember, and many of the words painted on the walls around Cairo had been taken from speeches that he had made. Tarik was a warrior name in Arabic and that was why he had chosen it for himself. He was the ultimate warrior and urban guerrilla. He had dedicated his life to liberating the city and many people said he was the only hope they had left.

Rémy escorted them out of the building, across the courtyard and into the military wing of the compound. As always, there were guards at every door but Richard was aware that they were more disciplined and better dressed than usual. He could feel the tension in the air. He and Scarlett were shown into a room at the back, dominated by a round table covered with papers and files. There were maps on every wall, most of them showing Cairo and the surrounding area. An old fridge hummed in one corner. Electricity flickered on and off throughout the day but it was obviously working now. The room smelled of sweat and cigarette smoke. It had a shabby carpet, whitewashed walls and a scattering of classroom chairs.

The man who was waiting for them was young and good-looking. That was Scarlett's first impression. His clothes were semi-military; a combat jacket, jeans, army boots. Around his neck there was a cotton scarf which he would pull over his face when he was out in the sandstorms. He had black hair cut short, brown eyes and a face that seemed to be made up of straight lines: the chin, the cheekbones, even his eyebrows. He was about thirty years old. The picture that Scarlett had seen had been taken perhaps five years before. There was something about him that inspired confidence even before he spoke. Perhaps it was his eyes, which shone with passion and self-belief. There were two men with him – older, weather-beaten and bearded – saying nothing. Tarik dominated the room.

"You are Scarlett Adams," he said. His voice was soft, his English perfect.

"Yes."

"And Richard Cole. Mr Rémy has told me all about you. I am very glad you are here. I will confess that there were times when

I wondered if the stories about you were even true, but my men saw for themselves that you came out of the Great Pyramid. We have seen the shape-changers. We must accept that the world is no longer as it once was and that we are fighting an enemy who comes out of our worst nightmares and who makes us re-adjust our beliefs." He gestured at the table. "Please, will you sit down? I have asked for some tea to be brought. It is important that we talk."

Richard and Scarlett did as they were asked and a moment later a soldier came in, carrying a kettle of steaming green tea which he served in small glasses. The moment briefly reminded Scarlett of another time when she had been served the same drink. Then, she had been a prisoner of Father Gregory in the Monastery of the Cry for Mercy. Of course, this was different. Tarik was a freedom fighter. He was here to help them. But even as she accepted the hot glass, the memory nudged her and she had to repress a shiver down her spine.

"You speak very good English," Richard said.

"My grandmother was English. I learned it as child." Tarik seemed to dismiss the subject and turned instead to Scarlett. "A people's army physician removed a bullet from inside your brain," he said. His eyes were fixed on her, examining her minutely. "Without his help it is certain you would have died. You should be grateful."

"I am very grateful," Scarlett said.

"And yet many people are dying here every day. They are not as fortunate as you. Egypt was promised democracy but Field Marshall el-Akkad stole it from us. Anyone who dared to speak against him was imprisoned or killed, and in the end this war was all that was left to us."

"I'll do anything to help you." Scarlett wasn't sure why she said that, but it seemed the right thing to say.

Tarik nodded slowly. "Will you? Will you?"

"The only way to defeat the Old Ones is to get the Five together again," Richard said. "We need to send Scarlett back through the Great Pyramid and search for the others."

Tarik turned back to Richard. Now his eyes were hooded, thoughtful. "That may not be possible. Our enemies know the power of the doorway and they have been keeping it under close guard. Scarlett slipped through their fingers once. They will not allow her to do it a second time."

"Could she fly out of here? We've seen planes..."

"The only planes belong to the military and the airfields are well protected." He spoke briefly to Rémy in Arabic and Rémy answered in the same language. Richard realized that it was almost impossible to tell what Tarik was thinking, no matter what language he was speaking. He gave the impression of always being five or six steps ahead. Once again Tarik examined Scarlett. "Are you as powerful as they say you are?" he asked.

Scarlett hesitated. "I don't know," she said. There was a silence and she realized that they were waiting for her to go on. "I can control the weather."

"In Hong Kong, I understand, there was a typhoon."

"Yes. But I didn't create it. Maybe I helped hold it back..." Her voice trailed away.

"To hold a typhoon, to stop it in its path, that must have been worth seeing. You are just a girl. You are ... how old? Fifteen? And yet we heard of this typhoon that killed so many people and caused so much destruction all those years ago. You did not create it. But maybe you could now?"

Scarlett glanced at Richard. Both of them felt uneasy, unsure where this was going.

"To control the weather..." Tarik continued in his soft voice, his hands cradling his glass of tea. "The heat of the sun, the force of the wind, lightning and thunder, perhaps the very air itself! If you could do it in just one street, Qasr el-Nil Street, for example..."

"The presidential palace," Rémy muttered.

Tarik looked up suddenly and Richard saw a faint gleam in his eyes. "You say you want to help us, Scarlett. Could you do that for us? Could you kill Field Marshall el-Akkad by perhaps suffocating him or burning him or drowning him?"

"Wait a minute..." Richard cut in.

But Scarlett was already ahead of him. "I've never done anything like that before. I mean, I've never killed anyone."

"People died in Hong Kong."

"That wasn't my fault. I've already told you. I didn't start the typhoon and I wouldn't have done it, even if it had helped us escape. I'm sorry, Mr Tarik. Of course I want to help you. But not that way."

Tarik nodded and although his face still gave nothing away, a sense of sadness had crept into the room. "You think perhaps that I am a monster for even suggesting it," he said. "To ask a girl to kill a man is not easy. It is not pleasant. But the man himself is a monster. What he has done to this country is monstrous." Tarik fell silent, then seemed to come to a decision. "Please, come with me."

He got up and went out of the room. Albert Rémy looked briefly at the two of them, as if warning them to be careful, and they all followed. Tarik's two officers, neither of whom had spoken a word and who had given no indication that they even understood what was going on, came last. Tarik walked out into the compound, soldiers springing to attention and saluting as they saw him coming. There could be no doubting the effect he had on the men around him. Every one of them was delighted just to stand for a moment in his shadow. He continued into the hospital building, where Scarlett had been treated, and she wondered if he was going to reintroduce her to the surgeon who had saved her life. But instead he led her along a corridor on the ground floor and into a room at the very end, and she found herself in a long ward with sixty beds, stretching out in two lines, facing each other from wall to wall. The beds had been arranged with military precision. Each one had a small wardrobe and a side table. A nurse and a doctor were moving slowly along, checking the occupants, handing out pills.

It took Scarlett a moment to realize that every single patient in the room was a child.

Some of them were as young as nine or ten. They had all been injured in different ways, many of them swathed in bandages, some of them asleep, some staring rigidly at the ceiling as if they were afraid to move. What upset Scarlett perhaps more than anything was that there was nothing in the room to comfort them: no pictures, no toys, no teddy bears. It was as if being wounded had somehow turned them into miniature adults. And not a single one of them was complaining. The silence was almost unnerving.

The doctor and the nurse had stopped, seeing them come in. Both of them bowed as Tarik approached. For his part, the rebel leader walked from bed to bed, speaking softly to one child, rearranging a sheet for a second, offering a glass of water to a third. The children smiled when they saw him or felt him nearby. For a brief moment, Scarlett saw them forget their pain. Tarik made sure he connected with every one of them. He spoke briefly to the doctor. Then, with Richard and Scarlett still following him, he left the ward through a door on the other side.

They were glad to be back in the open air, even with the heat and the sand whipping around them. Richard was already wondering what point Tarik had been trying to make. He soon found out.

"Those children were taken from the street," he explained. "They had nothing to do with this war. Did you see their injuries, Scarlett? El-Akkad launched an attack on their neighbourhood, looking for insurgents, and they were caught in the crossfire. If we had not brought them here and looked after them, they would have been left to die. What sort of man, do you think, can behave like this? What sort of man wages war against his own people?

I will tell you. He is vicious. He is ruthless. And nobody in Egypt will be able to live without fear until he is dead."

"What are you asking? Scarlett said.

"You know what I am asking. You have this power – or so you claim." He couldn't keep the scorn out of his voice. "Use it! Help us! You can rain down fire from Heaven on this man and end his tyranny once and for all."

Richard stepped forward. "You're asking her to commit murder," he said.

"This is not murder. This is war."

"She's fifteen years old!"

"The youngest child in that ward is eight and a half."

"I'm sorry, Mr Tarik." Scarlett had never sounded so helpless. "I know why you're asking me to do this. I understand. But I don't think I could do it, even if I wanted to. I was only able to control the storm in Hong Kong because Matt and Jamie were there. That's how it works. We have to be together. We'll only be strong enough to take on the Old Ones when all five of us meet … which is why they've always wanted to keep us apart. And right now I'm on my own. I've never been more on my own and I don't think I could do it. I really don't.

"But I'll be honest with you. Even if I could, I wouldn't. I don't want to make you angry and I am grateful for what you've done for me. But no matter how bad this man is, I don't think it's my job to kill him. I'm not sure I'd be able to live with myself if I did. That's just how it is."

Scarlett faltered and came to a halt. Richard looked at her with genuine admiration. She was standing there, inside the compound, surrounded by heavily armed and grimly determined men. And she had defied them. But he wondered what was going to happen next. If Tarik couldn't use her as he had hoped, would he continue to protect her?

But the rebel leader had already come to his own conclusion. He lowered his head briefly, admitting defeat. "I understand how you feel," he said. "And there is no need for us to discuss it any further. Perhaps I was wrong to ask you but we cannot ignore any avenue in this great struggle. We must consider now what is to be done with you, Scarlett. One thing is for sure. You must leave Cairo as soon as possible. El-Akkad does not share your scruples and will do anything to find you. We are all in danger while you are here."

He snapped out a few words in Arabic to one of his officers, who nodded and left. Richard and Scarlett were standing together. Albert Rémy was looking at them gloomily from the side.

"I have a lot of work to do and we may not meet each other again," Tarik said. "We will see what can be done and I will inform you as soon as I have a plan."

And that was it. Tarik took one last look at her, then walked away. As he went, one of the soldiers raised a fist in a sign of defiance and suddenly, all around the compound, everyone was doing the same. At the same time, they called out his name, chanting it over and over again as he sprang into a waiting jeep and was driven towards the exit. At the last moment, he raised his own hand in acknowledgement. Then the metal gate was slid aside, the jeep disappeared into a cloud of sand and he was gone.

Rémy said nothing and Scarlett had no doubt that, whatever Tarik might have said, he was disappointed by the stand she had taken. Richard put an arm around her shoulders.

"You were right," he said, quietly.

"I wonder…"

Scarlett had seen the way Tarik had looked at her before he went. He was a hero to these people. He was fighting for their freedom. And he was on her side. But even so it had been clear that he was angry with her and she wondered what might be the result.

FIFTEEN

Two days later, with the sand clouds glowing orange as the sun tried to break through, the rebel second-in-command came to see them. They knew that his name was Samir but he had told them nothing else about himself. Maybe there was nothing else. He was utterly loyal to Tarik. For him, the war was everything.

Richard and Scarlett had hardly spoken to anyone since their encounter with Tarik and they had both come to the conclusion that even if all the details of their discussion hadn't been made public, everyone knew that there had been some sort of disagreement and that Scarlett had refused to co-operate. They were still given food and water. A doctor had come up to take one last look at Scarlett's wound. But generally the men avoided them, drifting away whenever they approached.

Only Albert Rémy stayed close and he didn't seem too concerned about what had happened.

"Of course he was disappointed but Tarik is a remarkable man," he told them. "He's devoted his whole life to his people and he would do anything – demand anything – to further their cause. It's hard for him to accept that the war we are fighting, the war against the Old Ones, is even bigger than the battle here in Egypt. I'm sure he'll see sense. We have to find the others … that's what matters. Matt and Pedro, Scott and Jamie. When the Five are together, everything will change."

But there was no sign of the other four. Whenever she could, Scarlett searched for them in the dreamworld, only to find herself utterly alone in the arid landscape. Just once she glimpsed someone and hurried towards them, but even as she drew close, she realized it was the man in the shirt and waistcoat who had made his first appearance when she was in hospital. Once again he turned his head and she saw his dark glasses and gold teeth and heard him mutter the same word: "Five!" She was glad to wake up.

During the day, she and Richard could spend a whole hour in silence, staring out at the endless sand as if just wishing it could make Matt and the others appear. The sand blew. Distant gunfire rattled through the streets. From time to time a jeep would come racing in and a broken, bloody body would be unloaded onto a stretcher and rushed into the hospital. But whatever was going on around them, they weren't part of it.

And then there was the question of Scarlett's power. Would she really have been able to do what Tarik demanded? Richard had to ask her – and did, while they were having lunch together.

"I don't know, Richard," Scarlett replied. Lunch was flatbread, some cheese and a dip made from chickpeas and garlic. "I think I do still have some sort of power. Do you remember this morning – about eleven o'clock?"

"The storm stopped for a few minutes. I could actually see some blue in the sky."

"That was me. At least, I think it was. I was just experimenting really. I wanted to see what would happen so I sort of willed the sand to stop blowing. And it did for a bit. I was only able to keep it up for about five minutes though…"

"Well, I'd keep practising if I were you. If we're going to bust out of here, we're going to need all the help we can get."

That had been the day before. And now, here was Samir; a thin, serious man who had been a student at Cairo University when the war began and, with his wispy beard and wire-framed glasses, still looked like one. He had been wounded in some of the earlier fighting. Scarlett had once seen him with his shirt open. The front of his chest was a mass of scar tissue. But he never complained. He was devoted to Tarik. He, more than any of them, had been shocked that Scarlett had refused to do what she had been asked.

He didn't greet them. He made no attempt to be friendly or polite. He simply marched in with two soldiers alongside him and Albert Rémy following behind. "You are leaving Cairo tomorrow morning," he said.

"Where are they going?" Rémy asked. It seemed to Richard that the Frenchman had aged since they had arrived. He looked tired and there were more creases in his face.

"To Dubai."

That made a certain amount of sense. The rebel army received its supplies from Dubai, as Rémy had already explained. It was still an independent country with a government in control and a working airport, although little had been heard from there for a while now. But at the same time, there was nothing for them there. It was a long journey to nowhere.

"What's the point of sending us there?" Richard asked. "The door is here, in Egypt, at the pyramids. That's our way out."

"It has already been explained to you, Mr Cole. An assault on the pyramids is not feasible. They are too well guarded."

"Then how are you going to get us to Dubai? Are we taking the bus?"

"You do not need to know that. Transport has been arranged. All you need to know is that you will be leaving here at first light. Six o'clock. Tonight you will return to your rooms early and you are not permitted to go out. Tarik will be coming here tomorrow morning and he will travel with you on the first leg of your journey." He turned to Rémy. "You will also go, Mr Rémy. You are no longer required here and you have no reason to stay."

"Of course. My place is with Scarlett."

"So what happens when we get there?" Richard asked. He wasn't sure why, but there was something he didn't like about this and he was unable to keep the suspicion out of his voice.

"That is not our business. You wish to find your friends. You can start from there. Six o'clock tomorrow. Be ready." Samir and the other two men wheeled round and left.

Scarlett didn't look much happier than Richard, but Rémy was delighted by the news. "I told you that Tarik would come through!" he exclaimed. "You have no idea how much it will have cost him – the time and the resources – to arrange this for us."

"And what's in it for him?" Richard asked.

"You don't understand the man," Rémy replied. "He's doing the right thing because that's what he always does."

"What about Dubai?" Scarlett asked. "Is it the same as here?"

"I haven't been there for three years but there is no fighting in Dubai," Rémy said. "We'll find other members of the Nexus waiting for us. It's better than being here."

"But there's no doorway in Dubai. Not like the Great Pyramid."

"There are planes. There are cars. There is fuel and there is food. Please, don't worry, Scarlett. I promise you this is for the best."

But much later, when the darkness had drawn in, Richard and Scarlett were still concerned. They were sitting in Richard's room, and although they were supposed to be asleep, they both knew there was little chance of them closing their eyes before the morning.

"I think we should just slip out," Scarlett said. "If we can make it back to the Great Pyramid, maybe we can take them by surprise. We can just run through the door and be gone before anyone notices us."

"I think it's too dangerous," Richard replied. "Field Marshall

Whatever-his-name-is knows about the door. It's all he knows. He will have made sure that we can't get anywhere close." He stopped. "Of course!" he went on. "That's what's been bothering me…"

"What?

"Why do we have to slip out? Why is it that suddenly they're treating us like prisoners? Why did Samir tell us we weren't allowed out tonight?" Richard went over to the window and craned his head so that he could see along the side of the building to the front door. A moment later, he turned back. "They've put a soldier outside," he said.

"They're protecting us."

"I wish you were right. But I think they're guarding us. There's something happening inside this compound that they don't want us to know about." Richard paced back and forth and Scarlett could see he was turning things over in his head. He came to a decision. "I want to take a look around," he said.

"Is that a good idea?" Scarlett asked. "I thought we were already in enough trouble."

"They're getting rid of us tomorrow so I don't see that it can hurt. Are you going to come?"

"Of course."

The two of them were still dressed. They opened the door and looked down the corridor, which was lit by a single bulb, burning low. There was nobody in sight. Together, they crept forward, passing the room where Rémy was quartered, and up to the door that led out into the compound. They saw at once that there was no way out. Samir – or maybe Tarik – was taking no chances. A guard had been posted there, standing in the doorway with his back to them.

Richard and Scarlett backed away again.

"We need a diversion," Richard whispered. He thought for a moment. "Look, I can do this on my own," he continued. "Do you mind? I'll say you're ill. Everyone worries about you and nobody really cares about me. While they're looking after you, maybe I can have a quick sneak around."

"Where are you going? What are you looking for?"

"I don't know, Scarlett. Actually, I want to start in that ward we were shown. The one with all the children."

"Why?

"I've just got a feeling. I don't think Tarik was telling us the whole truth."

Scarlett nodded, her face pale in the darkness. "Just be careful, Richard. I don't know what I'd do if anything happened to you."

"You'd be fine. You're the one with the power."

"Just make sure you come back in one piece."

The two of them separated. Richard waited until she had disappeared from sight, then hurried over to the guard, doing his best to look alarmed. The guard heard him approach and spun round, his hand automatically reaching for the gun that he carried. He was clearly unhappy to see Richard. This wasn't meant to be happening.

"It's Scarlett," Richard said. "She's not well. She's really ill. She needs help." He didn't know if the man understood English and as he spoke he rubbed his stomach and pulled a face as if he was being sick.

The guard hesitated. He didn't want to leave his place but saw that he had no option. "Wait here," he said, and ran off in the direction of the hospital block.

Richard followed him. It was almost pitch-black inside the compound and, as always, the swirling sand was adding to the cover of darkness. Of course there were guards at the gate and in the observation posts, but they had their backs to him, for if there was going to be an attack, it would come from outside and that was the direction they were facing. He saw the guard disappear into the building, waited a few seconds, then went in himself. The guard had gone upstairs. Richard heard his feet tramping on the concrete. He was alone in the wide corridor that he had followed just two days before. As in the accommodation block, a few light bulbs, barely glowing, lit the way ahead. He knew he had little time before Samir and the others were alerted, but still gambled on the fact that they would be so worried about Scarlett that they would forget about him. He hurried forward.

Once again he went through the doors and into the ward where the injured children lay in their two straight lines. Richard had been afraid that there would be a nurse or a doctor in attendance, but they were alone. Walking more slowly now, he moved between the beds. All the children seemed to be asleep but one or two of them were whimpering, unable to escape their pain. Richard hated being here. He felt nothing but pity for them. But there was something he had to know.

The cupboards. Each one of them was identical, with exactly the same space between them. That was what had puzzled him about the place. It all just seemed too uniform. And there had been something else. They were all boys. He hadn't registered it at the time but he saw it now and it made no sense at all. If, as Tarik had said, these had been innocent children caught up in the fighting, surely there would have been some girls among them. And where were their parents? Where were their relatives and friends? How could you have a children's ward without at least a few visitors?

He stopped between two beds and tiptoed between them. He opened the cupboard. And there it was, exactly as he had expected. A set of miniature desert khakis hung on a peg with the military red ribbon attached to the pocket. A rifle had been propped against the corner. He tried a second cupboard and found exactly the same thing, except that this time the weapon was a pistol.

These weren't innocent bystanders. They were child soldiers, part of Tarik's army. He had been using them to fight the government forces. Richard wasn't sure what shocked him more. The fact that Tarik had lied to them, using these terribly injured children to make Scarlett come round to his way of thinking. Or the fact that he had been prepared to use children in the first place. There were boys here as young as eight. What had been the point in sending them into battle? They would have been cut down where they stood.

Somewhere in the building, he heard raised voices and the stamp of feet as Samir and the others hurried over to examine Scarlett. Richard planned to fall in behind them. He would reappear and hopefully nobody would notice that he had ever been away.

But as he stepped outside, he noticed brighter lights at the other side of the compound. This was where the vehicles were stored overnight, a garage that was built into the corner but was actually open on two sides. Richard heard the slam of metal against metal, the bonnet of a car being closed. The main lights were turned off. Then three men walked out, two of them carrying torches. Richard recognized the one in the middle. It was Tarik.

They hadn't seen him. The three of them walked across the compound and went into the military wing. There was a part of Richard that didn't want to know what they had been up to. After all, he had been told that they were planning a journey at six o'clock the next morning. What could be more natural, or more sensible, than to make sure the vehicles were well maintained?

Except that they hadn't even turned over the engines.

And Samir had told them that Tarik was coming the next day. Why would the leader of the rebellion be involving himself with the maintenance of the jeeps?

Richard glanced at the accommodation block and tried to imagine Scarlett playing her part, writhing on the bed, surrounded by soldiers and doctors. How long did he have? It didn't matter. He had to know. Staying close to the walls, he edged round the compound then ran across, making as little noise as possible. Nobody saw him enter the garage. Everything here was silent.

There were two jeeps parked next to each other, the same vehicles that had brought them here on the day they had arrived. The keys were still in the ignition. The jeeps were almost identical – apart from the number plates and the fact that one had a bead necklace dangling from the steering wheel and a photograph of Tarik taped to the dashboard. In addition, there were three motorbikes, a dusty Land Rover and two other cars so beaten about that Richard doubted they would even start. He didn't dare turn on the main lights but fortunately there was a slight glow in the sky, perhaps the moon on the other side of the sand, that provided just enough light for him to see.

He examined the first of the jeeps, still with no idea of what he might find. There was nothing in the front or the back, just torn seats and the residue of sand. He opened the bonnet and glanced at the engine, then closed it softly. He still didn't know what he was expecting to find but he had heard the bonnet close so there must have been something about the engine that had interested Tarik and his men. He did the same for the second jeep, even though he was certain that he was wasting his time. What was he even looking for? He was being ridiculous.

He opened the bonnet and peered inside.

No.

It wasn't possible. He didn't believe what he was looking at.

Richard knew that he had to make the most difficult decision of his life. He lowered the bonnet again but very, very slowly. For a moment he stood there, his hands resting against the metal. He looked through the window at the bead necklace dangling from the steering wheel. He thought about the photograph stuck to the dashboard. Yes. It could be done. But was it the right thing to do?

He made up his mind. There was no other way. He moved away from the jeep, searching for a screwdriver.

Thirty minutes later, Richard returned to the building where he and Scarlett were staying. He arrived just as Samir was leaving and the second-in-command looked at him suspiciously.

"What have you been doing outside?" he demanded.

"I've just been waiting here," Richard said, innocently.

"I told you that you were not to leave your room."

"I had to leave the room because Scarlett was ill. How is she?"

Samir scowled. "There is nothing wrong with her. She complains of stomach pains but the doctor has examined her and he can find nothing wrong."

"Well, you can't be too careful," Richard muttered. "All this foreign food..."

Samir wasn't amused. "You must go inside now." The guard who had been there from the start had reappeared and Samir addressed a few words to him in Arabic. "It is late now," he said to Richard. "We will see you tomorrow."

"Six o'clock," Richard said. "I have to say, I'll be glad to get out of here."

Samir didn't reply. He walked off into the night.

Scarlett was waiting for Richard when he arrived back. "Did you find anything?" she asked. "I made a great fuss. I had a whole load of them down here. I was groaning and rolling my eyes and they made me drink some foul medicine and then I pretended I was better. I didn't know how long you'd be."

"I'm afraid it was a waste of time," Richard said.

"So you were wrong."

"It looks like it. Maybe we had better get a bit of sleep..."

He couldn't tell her what he had found. Nor could he tell her what he had done. Richard had decided he just had to go along with it and hope that it all worked out the way he wanted.

He just prayed that he hadn't made a terrible mistake.

SIXTEEN

It was still dark at six o'clock. If the sun was up, it didn't yet have the strength to break through the clouds. The wind had risen and the sand was more vicious than ever, chasing along the ground, whipping into any exposed flesh, blinding anyone who dared look the wrong way.

Richard and Scarlett were wearing the clothes they'd had on when they first arrived – washed and even ironed for them the night before. Richard had his backpack strapped to his shoulders. Albert Rémy had appeared in a crumpled safari suit, the sort of thing an archaeologist might have worn forty years ago, carrying a travel case tied with leather straps. He had been living here in Cairo for a very long time and Richard wondered what was so valuable that he needed to carry it with him. Maybe the bag was filled with sand, a souvenir of his time in the desert. The Frenchman seemed both nervous and excited. This was the day he had been waiting for. After ten long years he had finally found Scarlett and he was taking her with him to continue the fight.

Richard watched as both jeeps were reversed out of the garage and left with their engines ticking over. At the same time, Tarik came marching across the compound with Samir and three more rebel soldiers, all of them armed. He was more cheerful than he had been when they last saw him. He was holding what looked like a mobile phone in his right hand but as he approached, he slid it into his pocket.

"Good morning!" he exclaimed. "I heard you were ill last night, Scarlett. I hope you're feeling better."

"I think it was just nerves," Scarlett said.

"You have every right to be nervous. You are about to begin a long journey – two thousand kilometres. It will take you a week but the road is a straight one. It will mainly pass through Saudi Arabia, which is quiet now. The war there has been lost. There were very few survivors." Perhaps the words were meant to be pointed but Tarik seemed genuine enough. He took off his glasses and wiped them on his sleeve. "Are you all ready?"

"Just one question," Richard said. He gestured at the jeep. "Are we driving all the way to Dubai in one of those?"

"Oh no." Tarik smiled. "I have arranged something much more comfortable. I will explain everything on the way. We have a meeting point about one hour's drive from here."

"And who are we meeting?"

"The man who will take you to Dubai. I will drive with you, Scarlett and Mr Rémy. Samir and the others will follow in the second vehicle. I would advise you to keep your heads down and well away from the window. It's too early in the morning for a sniper and the sand will provide us with cover. But you never know..."

The eight of them split up and moved towards the two jeeps. Richard paused. This was the moment of truth. The jeep with the beads and the photograph was on the left. This was the second vehicle that he had examined the night before. Quite deliberately, he made for the other jeep. But Samir stopped him.

"You go in this one," he said. "It's more comfortable."

"That's very considerate of you," Richard said.

Tarik climbed into the driver's seat with the bead necklace hanging from the steering wheel and almost touching his lap. Richard sat next to him in the front. Scarlett and Rémy went behind. As soon as everyone was ready, one of the guards gave a signal from the watchtower and two men ran forward and slid open the metal gate. Tarik crunched the jeep into gear and for the first time in more than two weeks, Richard found himself being driven out of the compound. There was a sinking feeling in his stomach and he knew that he was full of anxiety about what lay ahead. He still couldn't be sure that he had done the right thing. In the next hour, everything could go horribly wrong. Even so, he wasn't sorry to leave the compound behind.

They drove slowly through the Cairo streets, the two vehicles staying close together, constantly on the lookout for government forces on foot or travelling in convoys of their own. The sand was howling around every corner and it was hard to distinguish between the walls that rose up and down in front of them and the ones that stood there permanently. In fact there was so much sand being thrown against the window that Richard was surprised Tarik could see the way ahead – but perhaps he knew these streets by instinct as much as anything else. As they rumbled forward, Richard remembered the journey coming here. It had struck him then that there wasn't very much left of this city that was actually worth fighting for. He thought the same now. Cairo had long since abandoned any sense of life or vitality. There was nobody in sight. It was as if the desert had decided to come in and bury it in a gigantic grave.

However, as they left the metropolis behind them, the storm began to die down and Richard was able to see more details: half-buildings with shattered windows and hanging doors, endless piles of rubble, a flyover that had been blown in half and jutted in the air like some grotesque concrete sculpture. They were more exposed now, following a six-lane motorway that must once have been jammed with traffic. If any of Akkad's planes happened to fly overhead, they would be easy targets and, knowing this, the drivers accelerated, keen to be out of the city. They passed an open space contained behind what must have been a mile of barbed-wire fence. Scarlett tapped Richard on the shoulder and pointed. A plane, a Boeing 747, lay on its side with a buckled wing and a crumpled fuselage, half-buried in sand.

"Cairo airport," Tarik said, the first words he had spoken since they had left.

"No flights to Dubai?" Richard asked.

"No flights anywhere."

They drove another thirty minutes and all the time the weather improved until it was almost like a normal day, the sun hot in the sky and the sand lying still for once. Richard wondered if this was actually something to be grateful for. It made them more visible. But at the same time, at least it meant they could see where they were going, and if they were about to set off on the long journey to Dubai, they would need a clear road. Now they were travelling down a wide avenue, empty of other cars apart from the ones burnt out and abandoned along the side.

"I am taking you to meet the man who will drive you to Dubai," Tarik said, speaking loudly so that Scarlett and Rémy in the back could hear too. "He is waiting for you with a Land Cruiser. It has a ninety-litre tank filled with diesel and he is carrying another hundred litres, which should be more than enough. The car is equipped with a compass and maps, water and basic rations. If you get lost in the desert, you will die. So I would advise you not to leave the road."

"Who is this driver?" Richard asked.

"His name is Ali. He has done the journey many times. You have no need to worry. You will be safe with him." Tarik brought the jeep to a halt. The other jeep drew up beside him. He pulled on the handbrake. "This is where we get out," he said.

They had come to the crest of a slight hill, with nothing around them apart from a few stunted palm trees. Taking out a pistol which he held beside him, Tarik ran forward. He was keeping low – it was almost a habit – and threw himself down on the very edge of the hill so that he could look down without being seen. The others did the same. Ahead of them, the desert stretched out to the horizon with a single road, a surprisingly modern strip of pale-yellow concrete, forming a straight line all the way. The hill itself sloped down for about two hundred metres to a rubble-strewn area that contained a small, white building with arched windows and a domed roof. Scarlett wasn't sure if it was a store house or some sort of miniature church. But that wasn't what caught her eye. Just as Tarik had promised, there was a fairly new Land Cruiser parked next to it, with supplies and spare tanks of fuel strapped high on the roof. A single man stood waiting, wearing traditional Arab dress.

Samir had brought binoculars with him and scanned the area. "He is alone," he said – in English, not Arabic. Richard noted the change. Normally, when the two men spoke together, they used their own language but Samir was obviously trying to make them feel more secure.

"So what happens now?" Richard asked.

"Now, you begin your journey. You can drive the jeep down and leave it there. We will collect it later."

"You're not coming with us?"

Tarik shook his head. "It is not in the agreement. The driver will meet with you and only you. If he sees more than three of you approaching, he will be gone long before you reach him." Tarik saw the doubt in Richard's face. "If you lived in my world, you would understand. Everyone is very careful. If they are not careful, they are dead. It is better for you to have us watching and to know that, in the unlikely event that you have been betrayed, we are here to help."

Richard nodded. "All right. Anything you say."

"Then leave us now. We will not waste time with goodbyes.

We have lost too many friends in the last years to wish to hear that word. I will only say to you – good luck. I hope you will find what you are looking for in Dubai."

Richard, Scarlett and Rémy walked back towards the jeep that had brought them this far. The other jeep was next to it but the driver was still standing at the front, as if warning them to keep away. That was when Richard knew for certain that he was right. There could be no more doubt.

"Listen to me," Richard said, speaking in a low voice. "This is a trap. I don't know how many men there are waiting for us in that building down there, but they're not going to let us get anywhere near Dubai."

"You are wrong," Rémy began.

"Don't tell me I'm wrong," Richard snapped. "And please don't give me any more lectures about your wonderful Mr Tarik. Because frankly I've had enough of it." He stopped at the door and rounded on the Frenchman. "Just out of interest, did you know that those children in the hospital beds were soldiers?"

"What are you talking about?"

"You know perfectly well what I'm talking about. Stop playing games with me. Did you know or didn't you?"

Rémy said nothing. He looked ashamed.

"Yes." Richard nodded slowly. "That's what I thought. You knew all along – but you let Tarik have his way because, like everyone else, you'd do anything to support him. He's a hero, isn't he! The saviour of Cairo." He jerked the door open. "Well, if you ask me, he's as bad as Field Marshall Karim el-Akkad. I can't say I know either of them personally, but I'm not sure I'd find it easy to choose between them.

"Richard..." Scarlett sounded shocked.

The three of them climbed into the jeep.

"There's something else you might like to know," Richard

continued. "It might not make this journey very pleasant, but right now we could be sitting on about ten kilograms of plastic explosive."

"What are you...?" Rémy's voice was a whisper. Next to him, Scarlett had gone very pale.

"Here's how it works." Richard started the car, then pushed it into gear and they jolted forward. There was a track leading down the side of the slope. It would take them a couple of minutes to reach the man who was waiting for them at the bottom. "Tarik wanted Scarlett to kill Akkad. As far as he's concerned, killing the Field Marshall is like Christmas all over again – if they have Christmas out here. She refused because, surprise, she isn't a cold-blooded assassin. So Tarik came up with his Plan B. What is the one thing in this whole, wretched country that would bring Akkad out of cover? What could Tarik offer him that would make him risk his own neck?"

"Me..." Scarlett answered the question with a single word.

"Exactly." Richard glanced at the black-and-white photograph of the resistance leader, taped in front of him. Tarik looked so young, so honest. Maybe he had been like that once. When he'd set out, he'd wanted to save the world. "Tarik didn't need Scarlett any more," he went on. "So he decided he would use her. He would turn her into a suicide bomber – and you and me with her, Mr Rémy. I'll bet you any money you like that the man waiting beside that very tempting Land Cruiser is Field Marshall Karim el-Akkad himself. That's the agreement he'll have made. He can have us but he has to turn up and show his face first. And as soon as we get close enough, Tarik is going to press a button and blow us all to smithereens ... you, me, Scarlett and Akkad too. Right now, we're delivering the payload."

"Why are you doing this?" Rémy asked. His voice was hoarse.

They were already halfway down the hill. They could see the

man much more clearly now. He was middle-aged, paunchy, almost bald with a little grey hair. He was watching them intently.

"For two reasons," Richard replied. "First of all, if there really is fuel in that car, I want it. Anywhere's got to be better than Cairo, and maybe if we get to Dubai, we'll be able to find a way out of this whole damned continent. And secondly, because the bomb is no longer in this car."

"Where...?"

"I found it last night, when Scarlett was pretending to be ill. I lifted up the bonnet and there it was."

"And you dismantled it?"

"Of course not. I couldn't actually move the bomb. There were too many wires and I was afraid I'd only manage to blow myself sky-high. But I did the next best thing. I swapped over a photograph and a bead necklace that were in the other car. I even found a screwdriver and changed the number plates. Otherwise, the two vehicles were identical and right now, the one with the bomb is up there on the hill. So when Tarik presses the transmitter – and I'm pretty sure he's the one holding it – everyone's going to have quite a surprise. And that's going to be the moment we start moving. Are you with me, Scar?

"I'm with you," Scarlett said. She was ready for this. Everything that Richard had said had made her determined that they wouldn't be beaten, that they would turn this situation to their advantage.

Next to her, Albert Rémy brought out a pistol. He checked that it was loaded.

Richard was surprised. "You always carry that?"

"Of course." Rémy loaded a bullet into the chamber. "But I do not believe that Tarik would do this, Richard. He is a good man."

"Maybe he was a good man once. But you fight any war long enough and in the end it's going to be hard to remember who you are. He's had too much blood. And maybe too much sand. I'd say he's become everything he set out to defeat."

They pulled in. Richard switched the engine off. "I really hope this is going to work out," he muttered to Scarlett.

"Now I know why Matt thought so much of you."

"Did he?" Richard smiled. "He never told me that."

They got out.

And stood face-to-face with Field Marshall Karim el-Akkad.

Although Richard and Scarlett had never seen him before, they knew it had to be him. After a lifetime in uniform, the Arab dress looked almost ridiculous on him. He had the face and the eyes of a soldier and he was examining them with undisguised pleasure.

"Scarlett Adams," he said, and even hearing the way he pronounced her name, Scarlett knew that he had little knowledge of English. "I am glad to see you," he continued, framing his words carefully, as if each one had been plucked out of a dictionary.

"I take it your name isn't Ali," Richard said.

"It is not."

Akkad raised a limp, carefully manicured hand. It was a signal. Two armed men appeared, tumbling out of the front of the building. They were dressed in the same dark-green uniforms that Richard and Scarlett had see when they first arrived. A third uncurled himself from his hiding place on the roof, aiming down with a machine gun.

"It is over for you," Akkad said. He had also produced a gun, which he aimed at Richard. "The Englishman dies here and now. He should have died before. The girl will come with me."

"And what do you get out of this?" Richard asked.

"My reward will be great…!"

He got no further.

The explosion was huge and deafening. It came from behind them, from the top of the hill they had just left. The force of it almost threw them off their feet and it was enough to blast the man on the roof onto one knee. A whole torrent of sand and smoke, scooped up from the desert floor, fell on them. They were blinded. But even at that moment, in all the chaos, Richard knew Tarik had paid the full price for his treachery.

Perhaps he and his men had survived the blast but Richard doubted it. Even if there had been time for it, he would have felt no pity for them. They had tried to turn Scarlett and him into unknowing suicide bombers, but they were the ones who had died. How he must have relished his moment of triumph as his finger pressed the button. He had detonated the bomb, thinking it was in their jeep, the vehicle that he had persuaded them to drive down the hill. He had thought that it would kill his greatest enemy, Field Marshall Karim el-Akkad, even if it killed the three of them too.

Richard had the advantage. He had known what was about to happen and so he was the first to react, throwing himself at the Field Marshall, fighting for control of the gun. And Rémy hadn't hesitated either. However strong his belief in Tarik, it had surely been shattered now. He had seen at once the danger they were in, and even as the blast echoed in his ears he fired three times. The man on the roof cried out and fell backwards. The other two tried to return fire but although one of them let off a couple of rounds, they were too slow and Rémy shot them both.

"Richard!" Scarlett stared in horror. The trap was bigger and more elaborate than any of them could have expected. All around them, men were appearing. They were all in desert camouflage and must have been lying flat until the moment of the explosion, but now they were rising out of the sand as if from the grave, fifteen or twenty of them, forming a circle about fifty metres away. Fortunately, they hadn't dared get any closer. They couldn't risk being seen. But they were already moving quickly, covering the distance between them.

Not all of them were men. Scarlett saw a creature with the head and pincers of a scorpion, another dragging broken wings, half-man, half-eagle. These were the mutations that the Old Ones had created to serve them, the shape-changers. The bird-thing screeched in anger and ran forward. The circle closed in.

There was nothing Richard could do. He was still struggling with Akkad, the man's face close to his, his eyes bulging. Richard could even smell the garlic on his breath. Akkad had his finger on the trigger. He was trying to bring the gun round. There was a gunshot, close and muffled. Richard stared. But it wasn't he who had been shot. Akkad tried to say something, then fell to his knees. Richard saw the light in his eyes go out. He released him and turned away.

The attackers were less than forty metres from them, moving in from all sides, lumbering across the sand. Scarlett couldn't wait any longer. She knew what she had to do.

Summoning up every ounce of her strength, she released her power, just as she had done in Hong Kong. She felt it at once, flowing through her like a breeze through her fingertips. The effect was astonishing. It was as if an invisible comet had smashed into the desert. A blast of wind came pounding down, causing the sand to explode outwards. The soldiers were thrown down, cart-wheeling then crashing into the ground. Even the shape-changers were forced back. The sky darkened. The wind howled.

"Into the car!" Richard couldn't make himself heard but he didn't need to. There was nothing else to do. They were in the eye of the storm that howled all around them, even if the immediate circle in which they stood was calm. Richard grabbed Scarlett and led her into the Land Cruiser. Rémy came with them, his face contorted with pain, one hand clutched across his chest. Scarlett saw that he had been hit by a stray bullet and that the wound was bad.

The three of them piled in, Richard in the driving seat, Scarlett next to him, Rémy sprawled out in the back. They couldn't see anything. The sand had formed a tornado around them – but it was a barrier through which no living thing could hope to come. For a brief moment, Richard wondered if Akkad had also tried to trick them. Suppose there was no fuel in the car? It might not even work. But when he turned the key, the engine started at once. Perhaps the Field Marshall had been concerned that they would send an agent ahead of them to examine it. So he had decided to take no chances and had provided them with exactly what they had demanded.

"Are you OK?" Richard shouted.

Scarlett nodded. She was controlling the weather. All her attention was focused on maintaining the spinning wall of sand.

In the back, Rémy groaned and slumped against the side.

Richard shoved the car into gear and they set off. They could see no more than a few metres ahead of them but the storm slipped back to let them pass. Gradually they picked up speed. They didn't see any of the soldiers or the shape-changers. None of them had got close.

The Land Cruiser slid and shuddered across the desert, leaving Cairo behind.

THE TREE

SEVENTEEN

Scott Tyler had come to the conclusion that he really didn't like Pedro very much.

They had been together in this stinking cell for ... how long now? Scott had already lost track of the time but it must have been more than three weeks, maybe as much as a month. However long it had been, Pedro never complained. He ate the disgusting food that they gave him and didn't ask for more, even though the portions were tiny and they were both starving. He never seemed to be bored. When they were allowed to exercise – just one hour a day – he walked around the empty yard under the black sky as if it were Central Park. They also had one daily visit to a shower and toilet complex, the cubicles arranged around a manhole set in a concrete floor. The water was cold and they had only a few minutes to wash. But he didn't seem to mind. It was like he was in another world.

Pedro never spoke very much either. That wasn't his fault. He had lived all his life in Peru and had only recently learnt English, mainly from his conversations in the dreamworld with Matt. But Scott got the impression that it was more down to the fact that he didn't *want* to talk. After all, the two of them had spoken together at the start, when they had both been captured. But as the days had gone by, Pedro had retreated into himself. And he had done it deliberately. Scott was sure of it.

He examined the other boy now. Pedro was stretched out on his bunk with his hands folded behind his head (neither of them had been given a pillow), gazing at the ceiling as if he could read something interesting there. Not that he knew how to read anyway. Pedro was much smaller than Scott and although they were almost exactly the same age, he looked five years younger, with the smooth skin and innocent brown eyes of a ten-year-old. His black hair had been cut short with a fringe that went in a straight line from ear to ear. It was the sort of haircut you'd get in a primary school. Even before they'd been put on starvation rations, Pedro had been incredibly thin. Stick Insect. That was the name Scott had given him and he'd even used it from time to time.

"So tell me what you think, Stick Insect...?"

It amused Scott that Pedro didn't know what it meant. He probably thought it was a term of friendship.

Scott still found it hard to believe that they had been thrown together after Hong Kong, as if by an unlucky toss of the dice. Why couldn't it have been Scarlett or even Matt? Why not his own brother? He wouldn't have minded if he'd ended up on his own. Anything would have been better than this.

He knew, of course, what had happened in those last few seconds in the temple. They had all rushed through the door without thinking, without knowing where they were going. So instead of taking them somewhere safe, it had scattered them like seed in the wind. That was down to Matt. Matt had given them the order to get out of there before the storm killed them all, and maybe he'd been right about that but he hadn't thought it through. Just a few seconds ... that was all it would have taken. He could have directed them back to Cuzco or to London or to anywhere they could all be together. But he'd been scared and he'd just run. Perhaps he wasn't quite the leader he thought he was.

And, for that matter, going to Hong Kong had almost certainly been a mistake in the first place. Chasing after Scarlett had meant walking into the most obvious of traps, something Scott had pointed out from the start ... not that anyone had listened. And Matt had even gone so far as to separate him and Jamie. How could he have done that?

Now that he thought about it, Scott disliked Matt even more than he disliked Pedro.

Scott and Matt had never got on, not from the moment that he and Jamie had arrived in Cuzco, Peru, at the end of a long journey that had nearly killed them both. Scott had already been captured once. He had been held prisoner and tortured by a woman, Susan Mortlake. (Scott couldn't think of her without seeing her ... the long, thin neck, the glasses, the piggy eyes.) She had wanted him to use his powers to help her kill a United States senator, using his powers, and in the end he had agreed. Anything to stop the pain. Was that so wrong?

At the same time, Jamie had been busy. He had broken out of a juvenile detention centre in Nevada, travelled in time, fought in the first battle against the Old Ones and ended up on the winning side. All their lives, Scott had looked after Jamie, acting as the older brother, even though they were actually twins. But from the moment Matt had come onto the radar, he had somehow been demoted. Jamie was the hero. Scott was the loser, someone you couldn't trust. The worst moment had come when Matt had decided to take Jamie with him to London, leaving Scott behind.

No. Even worse than that ... Jamie had agreed without putting up any sort of argument. After everything they had been through together, Jamie had simply turned round and betrayed him.

All these jumbled thoughts ran through Scott's mind as he lay there in the cell, cold and filthy in clothes he hadn't changed in weeks, remembering how he had got here and wondering what would happen next.

He and Pedro had come through the door from Hong Kong. He could see it still, the walls crashing down, the wind howling in. They had emerged into the cloister of some sort of church, which looked old and run-down. The sky was a dirty grey and smelled of ashes. Had there been a gigantic fire nearby? How he wished now that they had gone back the way they had come, but five seconds of curiosity had been the undoing of them. He had been about to say something to Pedro. *Maybe this isn't a good idea. Maybe we should try and find the others.* But the words never left his mouth. Suddenly there were men running towards them from all sides, figures in black uniforms with weapons in their hands and more weapons dangling from their belts. He heard shouting. Then something hit him on the side of the face and the world turned upside down as he crashed to the ground. He tried to get up but a foot slammed into the small of his back. His hands were seized and tied behind him.

There was nothing he could do as he was lifted up and carried into the building. He had been right to think it was a church – weren't all the doors hidden in religious places of one sort or another? He saw stained-glass windows and, on one wall, a statue of the Virgin Mary in a blue robe, although somebody had defaced it, chiselling out her eyes. The whole place seemed to be empty. All he could hear was the sound of his captors as they dragged him further in, up a staircase, along a corridor past a wooden screen. Nobody had said anything to him yet. Everything seemed to be happening incredibly quickly.

He heard a bolt being drawn. The door opened. Then he was propelled into a small room that might have been an office or a cell, with a stone floor, a tiny barred window, a mattress and a plastic bucket. He thought that Pedro would be thrown in with him but it turned out he was going to be left on his own. One of the guards knelt down and Scott felt a sharp blade cut through the plastic ties that bound his wrists. His hands came free. One of the men was right next to him – bald, unshaven, dark-eyed. Scott turned and spat in his face. The man stared at him and for a brief moment there was dark fury in his eyes. But he must have been given strict orders not to harm his captive. He simply straightened up and walked out.

Scott spent the next three days there. The window had no view. There was a wall directly opposite and he could only tell the time of day by the light reflecting on the brickwork. Nobody spoke to him. Nobody let him out of the room. The bald man brought him bread and water and occasionally a bowl of thin soup. He took out the bucket and emptied it. But he ignored the questions that Scott threw at him. "Where am I?" "Where's Pedro?" "What do you want with me?" Scott tried to provoke him, swearing at him, using every foul word he knew. It was a waste of time. The man showed no reaction at all.

Scott remained angry. He needed his anger to keep going. Because if he thought rationally about his situation, his complete helplessness, he knew he would get scared. So he blamed Pedro. He blamed Matt. He even blamed Jamie. Refused proper exercise, he paced the cell, slamming the heel of his hand into the stone walls until the skin broke and he bled. Eight paces from wall to wall. Eight paces back again. He was a caged animal, tracing out his territory. If he had stayed there much longer, he might have gone mad.

But after three days they came for him again. He was curled up on the mattress asleep when he felt hands grabbing at him, and before he could react there was a bag over his head and his wrists were locked together behind him once more. He couldn't see. He could barely breathe. He was scooped up and dragged out and he realized that there was absolutely nothing he could do. He might just as well have been dead. He found himself shouting, his whole body writhing. But the men didn't care. He thought he heard one of them laugh and kicked out even harder.

They took him upstairs. Scott was able to measure his progress by his heels hitting the steps. They must have passed through a doorway because he felt air against his hands and – even with the thick cloth pressing against his face – smelled the burning. He heard the whine of a helicopter. The wind from the rotors beat at him as he was bundled inside it – not onto a seat but onto the floor. His shoulders brushed against someone else.

"Pedro!" he called out.

"Scott!" He heard the single word shouted out from close by and felt a surge of relief. He had been glad to have Pedro with him then. He had to admit it. But that had been a long time ago. And as the hours had become days and the days had become weeks, Scott had found that he had changed. Maybe it was the anger that was changing him. He was getting used to being on his own. In a strange way, it was making him stronger.

This new prison had to be in some sort of castle, judging from the look of it, with thick walls, tiny windows and battlements. In the day it was cold and at night much worse, but even so they only had one blanket each and they shivered for hours before sleep came. The exercise yard was at the end of a short, white-washed corridor with just one door on the way leading into the toilet and shower complex. Apart from the men who took them there and back, they hadn't met anyone. Scott had decided that the guards were probably Italian. He had seen acrobats from Rome once, when he was performing in the theatre in Nevada, and they had much the same look. None of them ever spoke, though. If either of the boys hesitated, or refused to come out of the cell, they struck out with short, heavy batons, which didn't break their bones but left plum-coloured bruises that didn't go away for days.

Scott had preferred the church, or whatever it was, because

(he half-smiled at the thought) at least he'd had a room to himself. He was fed up with being with Pedro, day and night … not that there was a lot of difference between the two. There was no window. No TV. Nothing to read. Nothing much to talk about. Scott had given up thinking about the others. He didn't even know if they were still alive. The last he had seen of Scarlett, she had been shot in the head.

That bullet would have killed Jamie if it hadn't been for me.

Nobody had thanked him. They had just sent him on his way, bundling him through the door and into a cell with Pedro. And that was where he was now. Just the two of them. Stuck here.

Scott closed his eyes and tried to lose himself in darkness and anger and silence.

Pedro didn't understand the American boy.

He knew what Scott had been through. Before he had arrived in Peru, he had been held captive by people working for the Old Ones and they had used drugs, sleep deprivation, electric shocks and physical beatings to bend his mind and break him. Pedro had a special power. He was a healer. But that meant understanding and even feeling the pain of anyone who came to him, and with Scott it was almost unbearable. Pedro had known many bad things in his life. He had met people who were like brutes. In Lima there had been criminals and there had been policemen and often it had been hard to decide which of the two was worse. But he still found it incredible that anyone had set out to hurt Scott the way that they had done.

Matt had left the two of them together in the hope that Pedro could heal him – and Pedro had tried. Without saying anything, he had stayed close to Scott because that was the way it worked. It was like being a magnet and somehow drawing out the pain.

But Pedro had soon realized that this time it wasn't going to work. It was almost as if Scott didn't want to get better. The two of them had seen each other every day in Vilcabamba, the secret city of the Incas, but there had never been any friendship between them. Scott almost seemed to blame Pedro for what had happened to him and it was while they were in Vilcabamba that he had started calling Pedro a name – Stick Insect – and although Pedro hadn't understood exactly what he meant, he knew that it was something stupid and hurtful. *Insecto*. Insect. It was the same word in Spanish and English. The insult didn't bother him. But it worried him that Scott should be so hostile. Weren't they meant to be the Five? Didn't that mean looking out for each other?

The two of them had only been together for about a week, but by the end of that time Pedro knew for certain that there was nothing he could do. Something inside Scott had been broken and nothing in the world was going to put it back together again. Secretly, he wondered if Matt had made the right decision separating the two brothers. Pedro had seen how close they were. Maybe Jamie would have been able to help. He, like nobody else, knew what was going on inside his brother's head.

And then Scott had suddenly announced that he was going to leave the safety of Peru and travel to Hong Kong. Pedro hadn't argued. In fact he was glad. It seemed to him that it was a good sign that Scott wanted to help Jamie. Perhaps he was getting better after all.

The two of them had gone to Cuzco, the old Inca city, and then crossed the world to Hong Kong, only to arrive in the middle of an incredible storm with chaos and destruction all around them. Pedro had just had time to see Matt again. Jamie was there – and Richard, the English journalist. He had also glimpsed Scarlett, the girl that they had all wanted to rescue.

The five of them had been together in the temple and for a brief moment Pedro had thought it was all over, that they would have the strength to do whatever it was they were meant to do and that after that they could all go home. But then someone had fired a shot. The girl had been hit. The temple had fallen apart and they had all been forced to escape through the door that had brought Scott and Pedro there just moments before.

But it hadn't taken them back to Cuzco.

Scott had been the first through and Pedro was sure that Matt and Jamie were immediately behind. Then there had been a moment of darkness, barely more than the blink of an eye, and he had realized that although Scott was still in front, there was now nobody else with them. They were alone in a corridor with a rectangle of light, a courtyard, ahead of them. From Cuzco to Hong Kong and now to wherever this was ... it seemed that they were going to have no escape from each other.

Scott looked back and saw what had happened. "Pedro?" There was anger in his voice. "Where are the others?"

"They haven't come."

"Jamie was there. I saw him. I stopped him being shot. He must have come with us. He was right there!"

"There's no one."

"Where are we?" Scott might as well have been asking himself the question. Pedro had no idea.

"We should go back," Pedro said.

"No." Scott looked ahead. "Let's see where we are."

And that was the mistake they made. Pedro thought about it now as he had thought of it often. They could have turned round and walked two or three steps back through the door. How different things would be if they had returned to Hong Kong – or to anywhere else in the world! Instead, they had crept forward into a grey-lit courtyard, with weeds sprouting in what might once have been a garden and a cracked stone fountain, broken and still. He just had time to see that they were in the cloister of an old church but one that had been long abandoned by the priests.

Scott had been about to say something – maybe to call out a warning – but then a group of men had rushed out of nowhere, dressed in black uniforms and carrying batons and canisters of CS gas, which Pedro recognized instantly from his years on the streets of Lima. They had no chance. He saw one of the men swing his baton and knock Scott to the ground and leapt forward to help him. Somebody grabbed him and he lashed out with his feet and his arms, even trying to bite whoever was holding him. Then he heard a soft hiss and felt something damp on his skin. A second later his whole face exploded in agony, tears streaming down his cheeks. There was a fire in his eyes and down the back of his throat. When he tried to breathe in, he sucked the fire down to his lungs. Blind and helpless, he felt his arms being forced behind his back and guessed that exactly the same was being done to Scott.

Pedro knew very little more until the pain had ebbed away and he found himself on his own in a cell somewhere inside the building. He called out for Scott but got no reply. His hands had been freed and he wiped them against his eyes, working patiently until his sight had been fully restored. He had already guessed that these men had been waiting for them. The attack had been well planned and executed without any hesitation. But how could that be possible when even he and Scott hadn't known they were going to arrive?

Three days had passed. And then, while he was sleeping, they had come for him, tied him up, put a bag over his head and brought him here.

Pedro had been glad to see Scott at first but that feeling had long since faded. He was worried. He had no connection with the other boy. There wasn't even a hint of friendship. They barely spoke to each other any more. Maybe Scott was afraid – but Pedro knew that there was something else going on. It was worse than that. Scott had allowed them to get into his head. Maybe it was a result of everything he had been through. But he was changing. Gradually, day by day, he was becoming one of them.

Pedro slept. It was his one escape. And when he was asleep, he found himself in the dreamworld where he had first met Matt. It was the same as it had always been – a desert empty of colour and life, where the clouds never moved and the landscape never changed. Despite the fact that everything was so dead, Pedro felt comfortable here. He was certain that in some way this strange world was on his side. He hoped he would find the others there, but no matter how far he travelled, he arrived nowhere and he was always on his own.

And then, one night, he saw something.

It was so extraordinary that at first he thought he was imagining it; a dream within a dream. It was a tree, growing quite by itself in the middle of a piece of barren land. There wasn't anything else for a mile around, not so much as a weed – in fact it was the first sign of life that Pedro had ever seen in this world. The tree had no colour. Like everything else, it was different shades of black and grey, like the images on the old television set that had once stood in the village square where he had been born. It was a palm tree with a thick, round trunk soaring towards the sky and, far above, a ball of jagged leaves that seemed to have been captured just as they exploded outwards. Pedro walked towards it in the knowledge that it hadn't been there moments before, that he hadn't seen it on the horizon. It had just appeared, in front of him, and it was impossibly large.

The tree worried him. He knew that the dreamworld sent warnings – the cowboy and the giant swan. The images never made sense until the last moment and by then it was too late. Was that what he was seeing now? Was the tree telling him something that he needed to know?

* * *

The door of the cell crashed open.

Two guards marched in. Instinctively, Pedro drew his legs up, preparing to defend himself. But the men hadn't come for him. They closed in on Scott and dragged him to his feet.

And Scott couldn't prevent himself. His eyes widened. His voice cracked.

"No!" he shouted. "Not me...!"

The men laughed. They were huge, muscular, dressed in black uniforms. Pedro scrambled to his feet and lunged forward but he had no chance against them. One of them kicked out and he was sent sprawling, crashing into the far wall of the cell.

It was all over in a few seconds. Scott felt his arm being seized. His sleeve was wrenched up and there was a stab of pain as a needle was inserted into his flesh. Then they dragged him out. The door slammed shut. The lock was turned. And once again Pedro was on his own.

EIGHTEEN

Scott didn't even try to fight back. The men were holding him too tightly and after so many weeks without exercise, with barely any food, he knew how weak he had become. He wondered vaguely if he was going to be killed. They were taking him upstairs. Would there be a courtyard with a stake and an execution squad, like in an old film? That was what this reminded him of, and the truth was that he didn't really care. He was fed up with this whole business. Let it be over one way or another.

They stopped in front of a doorway. He heard a key being turned. And then they were inside a brightly lit room that already smelled and felt familiar and awakened in him memories that he had struggled to leave behind.

The guards released him.

Scott stood there, swaying on his feet. As he took in his surroundings, he felt a shudder of terror so overwhelming that his head swam and tears began to trickle down his cheeks. He felt the strength drain out of his legs so that they barely supported him. He thought he was going to faint. He heard someone whimpering and realized it was him.

This was worse than execution. This was worse than anything he could have imagined. He knew this room.

The bed with the dangling straps for his wrists, his ankles and his chest. The plastic tubes snaking down. The white metal boxes that pumped chemicals in carefully measured doses. The dentist's light. The electric cables with the plastic suction caps that could be attached to any part of his body … his stomach, his neck, over his heart. Just seeing them brought back the pain that had once torn through him, separating him from any coherent thought. He was in America, in the prison called Silent Creek! He must be. This was the room where they had first brought him.

This was where he had been tortured.

"Hello, Scott."

He knew the voice and looked up with dread. And there she was, smiling at him, even though he knew she was dead. He had actually seen her shot, right in front of him, with a bullet in the head. Susan Mortlake. She had been the one in charge, choosing the items on the menu that had been so carefully designed to destroy him. She had listened to his screams, analysing them as if they were a particularly complicated piece of classical music. And then she had made her recommendations. A little higher, Mr Banes. Let's try the knife. Or another injection. Always smiling, always reasonable. And Scott realized that there was nothing he could give her that would satisfy her. She wasn't hurting him because she needed information. What she wanted was him.

He had seen her die but here she was, walking towards him, dressed in a silvery-grey jacket and dress that clung to her too tightly, almost restricting her movements. He saw her close-cropped hair, her glasses, her thin, slightly upturned nose, the pitiless slash that was her mouth. There was something else. A circular hole gaped in the very centre of her forehead. As she reached him, Scott toppled forward, retching, his hands sprawled out in front of him. He didn't care what he looked like. He wasn't going to pretend to be brave. The simple truth was that he couldn't take any more.

He felt a hand rest on his shoulders.

"Scott?" the voice asked, but now it was a different voice. "What is it? What's the matter?"

He looked up.

It must have been the drug they'd pumped into him because in an instant the room had changed. It wasn't a surgery any more. And it wasn't Susan Mortlake. It was a man in a suit, although in a strange way he looked a little like her. He also wore glasses, round ones, and there was something about the shape of his face, the very thin mouth that reminded him of her. The man had short, almost military-style fair hair, made up of tight curls. His skin was smooth and there was no hint of any beard or moustache. He looked both puzzled and concerned, as if he didn't understand why Scott should have collapsed in front of him.

And the machines had gone. So had the bed. Scott was in a much larger room than he had first thought – it was actually more of a chamber – with a vaulted ceiling and a chandelier with at least a hundred candles. Was there even electricity? The room could have been modern or it could have belonged to the Middle Ages. It was hard to be sure of anything. There was an oversized fireplace on one side, with a neat pile of logs blazing cheerfully. The floor was paved with flagstones but there was a thick antique rug spread out in front of the fire. Two sets of glass doors led out onto a balcony with a stone balustrade. Although it was the middle of the day, it was very dark. The sky seemed to be full of soot.

"Are you all right?" the man asked.

Scott was on the floor, on his knees. He looked around him, afraid that if he so much as blinked the room would change again.

"I don't want to hurt you," the man said. "In fact, I've brought you some lunch."

He gestured. Scott hadn't noticed it before but there was also a table in the room – or maybe it was part of the same trickery and it had just appeared. It had been laid for two with plates of cheese, fruit, cold meat, cakes and a jug of some dark red liquid, like wine. There were paintings on the wall – portraits of people who might have died centuries ago – and an old tapestry showing men with bows and arrows, chasing a deer. None of this had been there before. It was as if everything was assembling itself around him. Like a dream.

"Are you hungry?" the man asked. Scott had no appetite. Not right now. But he was also aware that he hadn't eaten properly for weeks. His stomach had never been more empty. The man reached down and helped him to his feet. "Here, let me give you a hand. You certainly seem to have been going through the wars!"

Scott was sitting at the table, although he couldn't remember walking there. The chair was shaped like a throne with arms that curved around him. The food was very simple but the smell of it was absolutely delicious. He looked down. Incredibly, he seemed to be wearing different clothes: black trousers and a black shirt. It was the same sort of outfit he'd been forced to wear when he was working in the theatre, only the fabric was more expensive; the softest cotton.

"Please – help yourself."

The man poured some of the red liquid and Scott drank greedily. It wasn't wine but it had the same intoxicating effect. It was cold and tasted sweet – some sort of berries.

"Where am I?" Scott asked.

"You're in Naples. In Italy. You were brought here by helicopter from the Abbey of San Galgano. That was where you came through the door. I'm sorry you've had such an uncomfortable time but it took a while for the news to reach America. I came as quickly as I could."

"What about Pedro?"

"What about him?" The man seemed genuinely surprised that Scott had asked. "Do you want me to invite him up?" he asked.

Of course Scott wanted Pedro here. He couldn't possibly leave him on his own in a freezing cell, eating the scraps that were thrown his way. He was about to say so but perhaps he hesitated for just a moment too long because the man cut in again.

"We don't really want the Stick Insect, do we?"

"No." The word fell heavily from Scott's lips. He felt guilty but something in the man's voice had persuaded him. There was plenty of food on the table. He would save something and give it to Pedro later.

"I thought not." The man smiled again. "Pedro is different from you, Scott. And I'm afraid to say that we don't have very much use for him. We won't kill him. I'm told there's not much point in killing you boys ... it just complicates things. But we'll probably keep him locked up until he's a very old man. Maybe you can visit him from time to time if it amuses you, but my guess is that you'll probably forget him. Anyway, do tuck in. You must be starving!"

The food was in front of him. Scott hesitated, still wondering if this was a trick and it would all disappear the moment he reached forward. He picked up a peach. It felt soft and warm in his hand. He glanced at the man, who nodded, and he bit into it, the juice running down his chin. It was delicious. He had never tasted anything like it. And once he had started, he found himself eating ravenously, not even using a knife and fork, tearing into it with his hands. The bread was fresh, the cheese soft, the ham and salami thinly sliced and salty. Somewhere in the back of his mind, Scott was aware of the spectacle he was presenting. He was behaving like an animal. But he didn't care. It was the first time he had eaten properly in a month.

And all the time the man spoke to him in a voice that was pleasant and utterly reasonable. Perhaps an hour passed. Perhaps it was just a few minutes. Later on, Scott would remember it all.

"We haven't got a great deal of time," the man began. "We

have to leave Naples in the next forty-eight hours and we have a long journey together ... for you a journey in many senses of the word. Right now, Scott, you have a choice. There's a decision you have to make. And it's this. Are you with me or aren't you? Or to put it another way, do you want to travel in first-class comfort with an in-flight movie system and a choice of computer games – or are you going to leave, naked, in a cage? Nobody's putting any pressure on you. Nobody's hurting you. It's entirely up to you.

"Do you want to be a hero, Scott? Is that what you want? I'm sure you used to read lots of books about heroes who wanted to save the world. They never really had any reason. They were just ordinary people like you. But they were the hero and somehow it always worked out all right for them in the end. Harry Potter. Batman. James Bond! You name them.

"But you and I know that real life was never quite like that. It wasn't as simple. You'd try to help people but they were never that grateful. And I'd say that if you looked at most people living in your street, they were basically just plain bad. Did anyone ever try to help you when you were being beaten around by your foster parents in Carson City? I don't think so. They were too busy getting on with their own lives to worry about you.

"The fact of the matter is that since the world began – you know it and I know it – the vast majority of people on this planet have only been interested in themselves. Who are the heroes who have always been on the front pages of the press? I'll tell you. Footballers in fast cars. Actors and singers with their drugs and fat salaries. Models preening themselves on the catwalks all over the world. People were never judged by what they did. They were judged by what they earned – and it didn't matter that the rest of the world was going hungry. They were the heroes. Everyone wanted to be like them!

"If you ask me, everything you were taught at school was a

complete waste of time. There was only one lesson in life that mattered and that was how to be rich. The designer labels you should buy. The cars you should drive. Did you ever walk down Fifth Avenue in New York, Scott? Or Rodeo Drive in Los Angeles? You'd have seen shops crammed with things you didn't need. You could buy a watch for fifty thousand dollars. Designer sunglasses for five hundred and ten thousand. You could even spend a thousand on a shirt! And did you want it? Of course you did! And let's not think about the ten-year-old boy who'd been shackled to the workbench in Calcutta being paid four pence a day to sew on the buttons.

"Of course, there were the nurses and the doctors, the charity workers, the priests. They're still out there, even now. But what difference did they make? For all the millions that have been poured into Africa, there have always been children starving while the charity workers drive around in their nice, shiny four-by-fours, looking for people to save. Do-gooders may have felt good about themselves but you know and I know that nothing ever changed. There just weren't enough of them. They were wasting their time.

"There were never any heroes. But there weren't any villains either. All the problems that you see in the world right now – global warming, pollution, poverty, over-population, war, famine ... all the rest of it – whose fault is it? Is it the wicked businessmen? I don't think so. Because they'd all go bankrupt if people didn't want to buy what they were selling. Is it the politicians? Come on! Who voted for them in the first place? I know what Matt would tell you. He'd say it was the Old Ones. The Church has been saying the same for the last two thousand years – not of course that anyone listens any more. It's just like the Devil in the Bible. You've got to blame someone, so blame him. And when the five of you get together, you'll banish them and that will be the end of it. Everyone will live happily ever after.

"But you know that's not true. If you think about it for half a second, you can see it's ridiculous. Man is to blame. Not devils. Not demons. There is no Voldemort. There is no Darth Vader. There's just selfish, greedy, uncaring, destructive man."

The meal was over. Scott had left the table and was sitting in an armchair, facing the fair-haired man. Once again, he couldn't remember getting there. He was very full. He was feeling satisfied and slightly drowsy. He knew who the man was now. His name was Jonas Mortlake and Susan Mortlake had been his mother. That was why he had recognized him. But how did he know it? When had he been told?

"So that's why I say to you that you have to decide. You have to choose which side you want to be on."

The man was still talking. It seemed he had never stopped.

"Now, at one level, that's simply a choice between being here in this room having lunch with me or back in the cell eating left-overs with the Stick Insect. It means having nice clothes and a warm bed and everything you could possibly want to make you happy, or having your brain mashed up by chemicals and electric shocks. I would have said that choice was a no-brainer, if you'll forgive the expression. I could call my men in and have them beat you right now. I could make you agree to anything and I'd actually quite enjoy doing that, Scott. I like that sort of thing.

"But what would that prove? Nothing! As I sit here now, I'm much more interested in persuading you to see things my way *without* hurting you. I want to reason with you because at the end of the day the victory will be all the sweeter. To take one of the Five and to turn him against the others. To recruit him. That's what I'm hoping to do with you, Scott. That's what the Old Ones want. It's why they sent me here."

It was already night-time. Hours had passed since Scott had been given the lunch. And he was no longer in the same room. He was in a small and comfortable bedroom. There was a single bed with a pillow and a blanket, a wardrobe, pictures on the walls. He looked down and saw that someone had put a stuffed toy in the middle of the bed, a monkey. He'd had a toy just like that when he was six years old, living in the orphanage in Carson City. Maybe it was the same one.

"I don't know what you want," Scott said. He was feeling very tired and he had eaten too much too quickly. He wanted to get into the bed.

"It's what *you* want that matters, Scott. You can go back to that cell if you like. We can take those clothes off you and you can spend another night shivering with the Stick Insect. Stale bread for breakfast. Maybe a beating before lunch. The two of you can stay together for another month or a year or even ten years. Or you can stay here. The only trouble is, I'm going to need some sign from you, some proof that you've actually been listening to what I've been saying."

"I have been listening."

"I know."

"But I don't have anything…"

"You're going to have to give me a sign."

"What sign?"

Jonas Mortlake seemed to consider for a moment but Scott knew that he was only pretending. He had already worked this out. It was what he had been leading up to all the time.

"I want you to hurt Pedro. I want you to prove to me that he's no longer your friend. You don't have to do it yourself. You just have to give the order. You could be giving a lot of orders quite soon. You might as well get used to it."

"Hurt him…? How?"

Jonas stood in the doorway, considering. "Well, let's not do anything too unpleasant. Not to begin with. Let's break one of his fingers! There you are. You tell me which finger we're going to choose. His left hand or his right hand."

"No… I can't do that."

"Are you quite sure about that, Scott? Think about what you want! Look at the bed. Nice, clean sheets. Tomorrow you and I can have breakfast together and we can be on the same side. Pedro doesn't mean anything to you. You don't even like him. And it's Matt we're interested in. We need to know that we can trust you."

"I can't…"

"Why not? Do you want to be the one wearing that shirt or the one sewing the buttons?"

Scott was so tired. He could barely keep his eyes open. He could feel the weight of the world on him and he'd had enough.

"His left hand," he said. "The little finger."

"Whatever you say, Scott."

Jonas Mortlake left the room. Two minutes later Scott was asleep.

NINETEEN

Pedro was slumped on the floor in the corner of his cell, cradling his injured hand in his lap. It was wrapped in a bandage that had already become grubby, but at least it was throbbing less now and he wondered if he had somehow managed to channel his own healing powers into himself.

It had been six days since Weasel and Ape had come in and hurt him. Those were the names he had given the two guards. One was older and slightly paunchy, his stomach pressing against his black uniform, with sagging cheeks and heavy eyes. It was he who had held Pedro down, crushing him in a bear-like grip, while the other – younger, skinnier with a fuzzy beard and moustache – had quickly and deliberately taken hold of his little finger and pulled it back, away from his hand, until the bone had snapped. From that moment on they had been *Mono* and *Comadreja*. Ape and Weasel in Spanish. It made them easier to hate, giving them names.

He had no idea why they had done it. Neither of them had ever spoken to him – not before or since. After they had finished and Pedro was lying there, sobbing with pain and shock, they had tossed him a bandage and simply walked out. For a while, he had been afraid that this was going to be the start of a long process, that they would come back every day and kill him literally one bone at a time. But they hadn't returned – except to bring him the scraps of food that were his meals and to take him out to the shower and toilet complex and for one hour's exercise in the yard. Another twenty-four hours had passed – but Pedro had given up trying to keep track of the time. It was as if the attack had never happened.

He hadn't heard from Scott. In many ways he was more worried about the other boy than he was about himself. He knew what Scott had been through in the past and doubted that he'd be able to take very much more. Pedro was aware that he hadn't been able to help very much and that there had been a lot of tension between them, but he still thought they were better off together. At least they'd been able to talk.

There was still no sign of the others in the dreamworld. Pedro found himself there every time he went to sleep and he hated being so alone. He had kept walking in the hope that he would come across someone or something, but so far all he had seen was the tree which was now a long way behind him, on the horizon, the leaves sprouting in every direction, dominating the sky. He was glad to be moving away from it. Although he had no idea what it meant, he could sense that it was dangerous, that it was warning him to stay clear.

Warning him to get away while he still could.

Pedro had come to that conclusion quite simply. If he stayed in this cell very much longer, he wouldn't have the strength to escape. He was used to being half-starved. He had been brought up in poverty, in the province of Canta near Lima. There had never been enough food to go around and, of course, what food there was, the men took first. But things had been even worse when he had moved to the city. Living on the streets, he had eaten only what he had been able to steal – or whatever scraps he had salvaged from the dustbins in the wealthier suburbs. It had never bothered him, eating the cold and congealed pieces of fat that had been scraped off some rich man's plate. He needed to live. That was how it was.

But this was different. He was like an animal in a cage, starved not just of food but of hope. With every day that passed, he found himself accepting his fate, his one hour's exercise, the endless hours on his own. Even when they had broken his finger, he had barely fought back. There was a time when he would have bitten and scratched and kicked and done anything to protect himself, but this time he had been too slow. That was what scared him. He was dying on his feet.

He had just one advantage over them. They thought nothing of him. They saw a small, malnourished boy who didn't even speak their language and who probably cried himself to sleep at night. A stick insect. What they didn't know, what they had no way of understanding was that he had survived for two years in Lima, one of the most dangerous cities in South America. He had lived in a shanty town, sharing a room with a dozen other boys who would have put a knife in him to steal a single dollar. There had been the police, rival gangs, criminals controlling their little patch of turf, rich men who would bundle you into their car if they could and do things to you that you didn't even want to think about. To live in Lima without money, you needed to be strong and Pedro was strong in ways his guards couldn't imagine.

Breaking out wasn't the problem. Pedro knew that he was in the basement – the dungeon – of some sort of castle and that it was in the middle of a city. He had heard the noise of people passing – not traffic, there weren't any cars, but the dull murmur of crowds, occasionally punctuated by shrill police whistles. There seemed to be a lot of police. He was near a kitchen. The more starved he was, the greater his sense of smell and he would have been able to name everything that had been cooked in the past week. This building was more than a prison. People lived here in the rooms upstairs. But the two guards – Ape and Weasel – came in from somewhere else. Pedro knew this because of the ash on their uniforms every morning. For some reason, the sky was full of ash and every morning there would be a fresh coating on their shoulders and sleeves.

He could trick Ape and Weasel and he could get out of the cell – but the problem was, what would he do next? He had no friends. He had no money. He was in a strange country that could be anywhere in the world. Almost certainly, he wouldn't even be able to speak the language. And he didn't know where to go. The best thing would be to find the door that had brought them to the Abbey and to use it to return to Peru. But he had no idea where it was. On his own, he would have no hope of finding it.

And then there was Scott. He couldn't leave him behind. Somehow he had to find the American boy and take him along too.

One thing at a time…

Pedro had been watching his guards carefully, examining them as he walked around the yard, and he had noticed something. While he was pacing out his endless, pointless circles, Ape just sat there, occasionally smoking a roll-up cigarette. But Weasel had a hobby. He was carving something out of a piece of wood. It might have been a little statuette or a chess piece but that didn't matter. What interested Pedro was the Swiss Army knife he was using. When the hour was up and they escorted him back to his cell, Weasel slipped it into his right-hand jacket pocket. The knife was everything Pedro needed. It was a key. It was a weapon.

And he knew how to get it.

The next time they took him out, he was ready. His finger was already feeling a lot better. For anyone else, it would have taken a month to heal – but Pedro was not anyone else. From a very early age he had learnt how to survive and now all his energies were channelled into exactly that. He took a shower, standing naked under the dribbling cold water, idly watching it swirl around and drain out of the manhole set in the floor. He dried himself with the dirty rag that they gave him as a towel. He got dressed again and followed the two men into the yard.

As usual, he spent sixty minutes walking between the blank walls and beneath the dirty, black sky. He wondered why it always smelled of burning. Perhaps part of the city had caught fire – but surely it couldn't still be smouldering more than a month later? Well, he would find out soon enough. Out of the corner of his eye, he saw Weasel whittling away, the little shavings of wood floating down onto his black leather boots. Neither of the men ever came close and Pedro suspected that one of the reasons was that after several weeks of wearing the same clothes he must smell bad. Today that had to change.

Ape looked at his watch; an expensive watch for a man who worked in a prison. Pedro wondered who had owned it before and what had happened to him.

"*Tempo!*" he announced. Always the same word, spat out with no emotion. *Tiempo* was the Spanish for "time" and this obviously meant the same.

Weasel put his carving in one pocket and his knife in another, and then went back into the prison complex. But this time Pedro didn't follow him over.

"I want more," he called out. He spoke to them in English, then repeated the sentence in his own language. "I'm not coming in."

Ape turned to look at him. Not angry. Not even surprised. Just bored. He walked over to Pedro, his feet heavy in the dust.

Pedro swore at him.

The man punched him once, hard, in the chest, his fist pounding in above Pedro's heart. Pedro jerked backwards, almost collapsing onto the ground.

"OK! OK! I'm sorry!" Winded, in pain, Pedro held up his hands in a gesture of surrender, at the same time stumbling towards the door. But when he reached it, he seemed to lose his balance and fell against Weasel, who smiled, grabbed hold of his collar and threw him inside.

Pedro had got what he wanted. Every street child in Lima knew how to pick a pocket. American tourists usually kept their wallets in the back pocket of their trousers. The English preferred the inside of their jacket, near their right arm. And if you were fast enough, there were always expensive watches – a Rolex or an Omega could get you two or three dollars in the local market (where it would be sold on for twenty times that amount). The only trouble was, you had to get close enough to make the steal ... and that was what Pedro had just done in the yard. It had cost him a little pain but it had given him the excuse to brush against Weasel and in barely more than a second he had whipped the knife out of the man's pocket and concealed it under his own shirt. Pedro was still bent over, pretending to be hurt. The knife was safely pressed against his flesh.

The two guards threw him into the cell and locked the door, taking the key with them. Pedro already knew there were no bars or bolts on the outside. He waited until he was sure they had gone, then took out his prize and examined it. The knife had three blades, a screwdriver, a bottle opener, a nail file, scissors and tweezers. It was perfect. A gift from the gods.

But he had to move quickly. For all he knew, Weasel would want to start whittling again the moment he turned the corner and once he discovered his knife was missing, it wouldn't take him long to work out where it had gone. Pedro unhooked one blade and took out the tweezers. There wasn't a lock in Lima that he wouldn't have been able to pick. Again it was part of his street education. There was always the stupid shopkeeper who didn't pay someone to stand by the exit or who allowed himself to be distracted by one boy while another crept into his storeroom. Pedro ignored the pain in his chest. He knelt in front of the lock, the blade in one hand, the tweezers in the other. The mechanism was old and heavy but it had been used so many times that it had worn smooth. It took Pedro just five seconds. The lock clicked. The door swung open.

He was presented with a simple choice: left or right. Ape and Weasel had turned left and he didn't want to run into them again. But at the same time he knew that turning right would only bring him back to the shower complex and the exercise yard with no obvious way out. There was no choice. All he could do was move as quickly and as quietly as possible and hope he wasn't seen.

He found himself following a narrow, arched corridor that reminded him partly of a hospital, partly of a wine cellar. The floor was stone, the walls rough, whitewashed plaster. There were no windows but electric lights burned at intervals, showing the way ahead. He passed several doors and gently tried each one of them. They were all locked. More cells? Somewhere there had to be a staircase leading up. He couldn't hear anything now but the smell of cooking was still strong and came from ahead of him. He was aware that his stomach was empty and he was salivating. It had been a long time since he had eaten anything decent and part of him was tempted to go in and see what he could steal. But where there was a kitchen there would be cooks and the moment anyone saw him they would raise the alarm. It was more important to get out while he still could. Food would come later.

He was still holding the knife, clutching it in the palm of his right, undamaged hand. If he came upon someone – it didn't matter who they were – he was ready to use it. The corridor reached a T-junction with a brick wall ahead and a second choice of left or right. This time, Pedro turned right – and instantly regretted it. He heard a footfall and saw Weasel, the younger of the two guards, turn a corner and walk towards him. The guard hadn't yet seen him. He was in a hurry, his head bent low, one hand rummaging in his pocket. Pedro realized that he had just discovered that he was missing his knife and had returned in the hope of finding it. He was sweeping the floor with his eyes, imagining it must have dropped out of his pocket.

Pedro ran forward. Weasel saw him at the last moment when it was far too late. His eyes widened in surprise – and then in pain as Pedro kicked out with all his strength, smashing his foot into the man's groin. Again, they had underestimated him. Pedro was small but he was strong. He was wearing the boots he'd had on when he was seized, and had aimed the kick where it would hurt the most. Weasel screamed but the sound came out as a breathless grunt. He toppled forward. At the same moment, Pedro kicked him a second time, the underside of his foot slamming into the man's chin, then launched himself forward, leaning over him as he hit the floor, the knife poised to strike down. There was no need for it. Weasel was unconscious, blood trickling from the corner of his mouth. He might even have been dead. Pedro didn't care either way. This was the man who had cold-bloodedly broken one of his fingers. He deserved everything he got.

It was still bad news. If Weasel was here, Ape would be nearby and it wouldn't take long for the body to be discovered. Pedro backed away, taking the corridor that led in the opposite direction, even though it meant passing the kitchen. Sure enough, he came almost at once to an open door that led onto a wide space filled with ovens, fridges and silver work surfaces with dozens of pots and pans hanging from hooks. The kitchen was spotlessly clean. A huge cauldron, filled with some sort of soup, stood on a gas flame. That was what Pedro had smelled. It was as much as he could do to stop himself running over to it and scooping the contents out with his bare hands.

But he wasn't alone. A single figure stood close by, cleaning the floor.

The two of them saw each other at the same moment. Pedro stopped in his tracks. The servant, if that was what he was, was a boy of about his own age with long, light brown hair and a pale, emaciated face. He was so malnourished that his arms were almost as thin as the handle of the mop he was holding and his eyes and cheeks were sunken, his neck like porcelain. His clothes were clean. No germs would be allowed into the kitchen. He wore a white T-shirt, which hung loosely off him, and thin, grey trousers cut short above the ankle. His feet were bare. As the boy turned, Pedro saw that one side of his face was swollen and bruised. Somebody had hit him – and recently.

Pedro had already raised the knife and might have sprung forward and attacked the boy without a second thought before he could raise the alarm. For his part, the boy had already opened his mouth, about to call out. But then both of them stopped. Instinctively they understood that they were actually on the same side. Pedro had been kept in a cell. But the kitchen boy was just as much a prisoner … in his case sentenced to hard labour. Did he live inside this building or did he turn up every day? It made no difference. Hours of hard work and casual brutality were etched into his eyes.

They stood gazing at each other and then a bell broke the silence, jangling along the corridors, followed almost immediately by the sound of raised voices, stamping feet, doors slamming open. Either Weasel had been found or someone had glanced into Pedro's cell and realized it was empty. Pedro stood where he was, rooted to the spot. The noises seemed to be echoing all around him. He didn't know which way to go. Nowhere was safe.

The boy knew what was happening. "*Pa di qui, rapido*..." he whispered. He was speaking in Italian. He had to be. The words were almost identical to Spanish. At the same time he had hurried over to an oven and opened the door. Whatever the language, his meaning was clear. He wanted Pedro to climb inside.

Pedro stared at the flame-blackened interior. He would just be able to fit. He was small and the oven was industrial-sized, the sort of thing that might be used to cook a meal for fifty men. But the thought of it filled him with terror. It would be a tight squeeze and once he was inside, he would be completely helpless, unable to breathe. And what if someone turned it on? The boy could be offering him a particularly horrible death.

But there were voices coming down the corridor and they were getting nearer. He had no time to make a rational decision. If he was caught, he would be beaten and thrown back in the cell. He would never get a second chance. He was already moving. Climbing into the oven meant contorting himself and he had an image in his mind of a joint of meat. The boy helped to push him in. The oven was greasy and still warm. It had been used perhaps the night before. Pedro felt a rush of panic as the boy swung the door shut but he didn't close it completely, allowing just a centimetre for light and air. Pedro couldn't move. His shoulders, his neck, his arms and his hips were all jammed against the metal plates, his head folded into his stomach. Oven-ready. He couldn't escape the thought.

The boy turned away just as someone arrived in the kitchen. Pedro couldn't see them. He was facing the wrong way and could only see out of the oven by bending his head down and looking under his arm – but he was too low down and at the wrong angle. He heard a man's voice and somehow knew it was Ape. The words were indistinct but it was obvious he was asking if the boy had seen him. The boy replied in the negative, his voice high-pitched and innocent. The man said something else. The boy answered again. Then silence.

The man left. The boy went on mopping the kitchen. The alarm bell was still ringing and for Pedro the sound seemed to hammer against the sides of the oven. He wondered why the boy wasn't letting him out but understood when a second man came in and addressed a few words to him. This time Pedro caught a flash of white trousers and a white apron and guessed that this was the chef. The man uttered something angrily and walked towards the oven. Pedro tensed himself. The knife was still in his hand and if he uncoiled himself quickly he might still have time to use it. But the man didn't look in the oven. He simply slammed the door and Pedro had to fight against a sense of panic as he found himself trapped in a dark, airless, tiny tomb.

Closing his eyes, forcing himself to breathe slowly, Pedro mentally counted away the seconds. He had reached a hundred and five before the door opened again and the boy was there, his eyes wide, tugging at Pedro's leg. Pedro crawled out. He was covered in sweat and grease. His left hand was throbbing painfully. The alarm bells hadn't stopped but as far as he could tell there were no guards anywhere close. They must have decided that he was no longer in this immediate area and moved the search to the upper floors of the building.

The boy hurried over to the door and peered outside. He looked terrified and Pedro knew that he was risking his life to help someone he had never met before. Why? Perhaps it was because they were about the same age. Both victims. He wondered what would happen next. With the alarm raised and everyone looking for him, he would never find his way out. Somewhere inside him, Pedro resolved not to be taken alive. He had the knife. He would use it one last time rather than fall into their hands again.

The boy gestured frantically and the two of them slipped out of the kitchen and back the way Pedro had come. They passed the cell where he had been held and went into the shower and toilet complex. Pedro took one look at the open urinals, the toilets without doors and the shower cubicles. The place stank as always. He wondered why he had been brought here. There were no windows, no other way out.

At least, that was what he thought. But the boy was kneeling, pointing to something in the ground, and Pedro remembered the metal square he had seen so often, the cover of a manhole. There were a couple of rings to lift it out and the boy was already tugging at one end. Pedro hurried over and took the other with his good hand. The manhole cover weighed a ton, and years of damp and filth had glued it in place. It wouldn't budge. Pedro took his knife and ran a blade around the side, scraping through the mud. They tried again, pulling with all their strength, and this time the cover jerked free and, with straining muscles, they were able to slide it onto the floor.

Pedro looked in, then reeled back as the stench of raw sewage hit him full in the face. He could see a chute leading into darkness and a ladder built into the wall. About five or six metres down, the last rungs disappeared into a pool of filthy, brown liquid. He knew what he was being asked to do. But he couldn't. He would die down here.

"*Devi andare. In Fretta!*" the boy urged him and pressed something into his hand. It was a small torch. He must have stolen it from the kitchen while Pedro was in the oven. "*Sarò dall'atro lato...*" Pedro had no idea what the words meant but the boy mimed with his hands. He would be waiting when Pedro emerged from the building. And his eyes added something else. There was no other way. They had no choice.

"Thank you," Pedro said. At the very least, the boy would be punished when they found the torch was missing. And if they suspected that he had helped Pedro escape, he would be killed. He was about to climb down when something made him stop and turn round. "Pedro," he said, tapping his chest.

"Giovanni."

Somehow it helped having a name. It made the boy feel more like a friend and not someone guiding him into a horrible trap.

He eased himself over the edge and began to climb down. The closer he got to the sewage, the more overpowering the smell became. He had barely eaten anything in the past few days but still he felt his stomach churn and the contents begin to rise. And sure enough, a second later he had to twist his head to one side and throw up, the foul liquid splattering down into the equally foul pool below. It was almost as if Giovanni had been waiting for just this moment. Above his head, Pedro heard the metal cover grind against the stone floor and then there was a thud as it slid into place, and when he looked up he saw nothing. He was in a tomb. He was buried alive.

A huge part of him was tempted to climb the ladder and push the hatch open again. But he doubted that he would have the strength on his own, and anyway, there must have been a reason for Giovanni to send him down here. The boy had already shown he could be trusted in the kitchen. The trick with the oven had worked. Pedro gripped the knife between his teeth and the torch in one hand. He couldn't begin to imagine losing either of them. Still clutching the metal rungs as best he could, he continued down.

His foot entered the cold, thick liquid. He felt it rise over his ankle. The rungs continued down. How far was he expected to go? Another step and the sewage reached his calves, two more and it was over his knees. He had no choice but to continue. The closer it got to his nose and mouth, the sicker he felt. He was retching with every breath but he had nothing left to throw up. The acid from his stomach was burning the back of his throat. The smell was hideous, overpowering. Pieces of filth bobbed against him and he felt the liquid stir as he climbed down into it. It was between his legs now, in his groin. Above his waist. How many more rungs? Was he expected to swim? But even as he lowered his stomach into the hellish river, his foot touched something solid, concrete, and he realized that at least he would be able to stand and that if he kept his arms up, his chest and hands would form some sort of barrier beneath his face.

He flicked on the torch. A tiny, feeble beam revealed a passageway running in a straight line from the central shaft he had just descended. It also showed the surface of the brown river and the things that floated there and Pedro was forced to close his eyes, to turn his head away. At the same time, he turned the torch off. He could already see that the batteries were weak and he would need them later. He waited until his stomach had stopped heaving. Then gritting his teeth, trying not to let any of the fumes enter his mouth, he set off.

The walls of the tunnel were close together and he pressed against them, the soft slime nudging against his shoulders. The lower part of his body pushed through the liquid and he could feel it separating in front of him, then forming again behind. He was completely blind but every ten seconds he flicked on the torch to make sure that the way ahead was clear. He was terrified that the river would become deeper, that he would take one step and plunge beneath the surface. If he swallowed as much as one mouthful he would die. Half of him wanted to hurry, urging him forward. But his better sense told him to take it slowly. He couldn't stumble or fall. He had to take it one step at a time.

He came to an opening. His shoulders had lost contact with the wall. He turned on the torch and saw that he had come to a junction shaped like a letter Y and that he now had a choice of two directions. Why hadn't Giovanni warned him? Both the passages were identical, with black, glistening brickwork and curving ceilings a few metres above his head. For no reason at all, he went to the right and thought for a time that he had made the right choice. The further he went, the shallower it became. Soon he was only ankle-deep. But when he turned the torch on again, sacrificing his precious batteries, he groaned. There was a solid wall in front of him. He heard a noise above him, the clank of a chain and the sound of running water. Before he could move away, he was showered with filth. It clung to his hair and trickled over his shoulders. It was more disgusting than anything he could have imagined.

Angry, close to tears, he turned back the way he had come, once again lowering himself in the depths of the river. Everything was pitch-black. He didn't dare use the torch. But then he heard another sound and felt something knock into him. He cried out. The torch came on just as a rat the size of a small cat swam past, its claws beating at the surface, its nose and beady eyes straining for air, dragging behind it a long and greasy tail.

Pedro had almost had enough. He could see himself dying here. His hand was hurting more than ever and he felt physically empty. Even his cell would have been better than this. He reached the junction where he had made the wrong turn and followed the other passage. This time the river got deeper, not more shallow. He could feel the weight of it pressing against his chest, trying to force him back. He wanted to turn round. With each step it was getting worse, the level rising. But at the same time, there was a difference. Daylight was bleeding in from somewhere ahead. He could see it reflected on the walls. It was captured in the beads of liquid that dripped down by him. The corridor twisted and he hurried round, only to come to a shuddering halt.

The boy, Giovanni, had tricked him. There was an exit straight ahead, a glimpse of the darkening world beyond. The sun was setting but he could still make out a stretch of sand and shingle with the sea beyond. But the way was barred. Metal wires ran across the mouth of the tunnel – too close together to climb through, too thick to cut. Gritting his teeth, the worst swear words he knew echoing in his mind, Pedro staggered forward. His hands found the wire grille and he clung onto it with his fingers, rocking it back and forth, trying to pull it free. It wouldn't move. He could see the sea! There it was, just metres away from him, with the untreated sewage twisting its way across the beach. Yet he couldn't go on. He hadn't seen any other passages but he had to turn back and find another way.

He was about to do just that when he heard a voice.

"Pedro! Pedro!"

It was Giovanni. The Italian boy had made his way out of the building and now he dropped down and crouched on the other side. His face was filled with horror and disgust. He surely couldn't see very much of Pedro but the smell would be shocking enough.

"*Devi andare sotto!*"

Almost the same words as before, only this time Giovanni was pointing down at the surface, frantically jabbing with his finger.

Pedro understood. It was the last thing he wanted to hear. But once again he had to put his entire trust in this stranger. He took a great gulp of air. Then he dived down.

The filth rose over his face, over his head. He could feel it pressing against his eyes. It was utterly and completely revolting. It was worse than death. He used his hands against the wire mesh to guide himself downwards. It seemed to be a long way and he wondered for how much longer he would be able to hold his breath. He had lost the torch. That didn't matter. He wouldn't need it any more. The knife too. Oh God – this was horrible. But then his fingers found the bottom of the metal barrier and he realized there was a little space underneath. An adult would never have been able to pass through. It would have been too narrow for most children. But he was half-starved. He could do it.

He went feet first. He felt the metal rim rubbing against his thighs as he pulled himself under the grille. Now he was terrified of getting stuck. To be so close and yet to be pinned down here, to be forced to open his mouth and let the sewage flow into him. He couldn't bear it. In his haste, he tried to rise up too soon and the metal struck his throat, almost making him cry out. It hit him a second time, just above his nose – but then he was free, on the other side. There was almost nothing left in his lungs. He had to breathe. He pushed himself up, not exactly swimming ... more like burrowing with all his strength. His hands came free. The cool evening air hit him. He had reached the surface! For a moment he splashed around helplessly, then somehow he made it to the side and pulled himself onto the sand, sewage still streaming out of his hair, down his face, over his eyes and lips. He hardly dared breathe, afraid that he would swallow some of it. He was covered in filth and it could still kill him.

"Ti aiuterò!"

Giovanni had grabbed hold of him, smearing himself too, and the two of them staggered down the beach, arm in arm, as if they were drunk or had been fighting together for the past couple of hours. They were making for the sea but heading away from the outlet. The further they went, the cleaner the water would be. Pedro felt it lapping at his ankles and gratefully threw himself forward, allowing it to wash over him. Giovanni did the same. The water was black and polluted but after what Pedro had been through it felt and tasted delicious. He washed himself all over, particularly his hair and his face. For a long time he didn't move.

When he finally sat up, the sun had almost set. He could just make out the sprawl of a city, a port, a tangle of ships. In the middle of it there was a castle, a huge block with four massive towers and a scattering of tiny windows. This must have been where he had been held. It was from here that he had just escaped.

But there was something else that drew his attention. It was far behind the city and over to one side and yet still it dominated the landscape, soaring into the sky. At first Pedro thought it was a mountain, but then he saw the smoke pouring out of the top and realized that this was why the sky was always black and everything smelled as if it had burned.

Giovanni had followed his eyes. "Vesuvius," he said simply. "*Il volcano.*"

The smoke wouldn't stop coming.

It was forming itself into the shape of a tree.

TWENTY

Dripping wet and shivering, but no longer smelling quite as bad as he had a few minutes before, Pedro followed Giovanni through the darkening passages of the city, which he now knew to be Naples, Italy. It reminded him of Lima in some ways – particularly the cobbled streets and the palm trees, which somehow didn't seem to belong together. A lot of the buildings were old and very grand but they stood just around the corner from modern flats and offices that were uglier and more run-down. From the harbour where they had begun, they followed a complicated network of interlocking roads and alleys, which led them ever deeper into the metropolis. And all the time Pedro felt the bulk of the castle where he had been kept prisoner looming over him, and wondered if they were still looking for him inside or if the search had been widened into the city itself. Either way, he was glad to put as much space between himself and it as he could.

Naples was crowded. In fact, that wasn't the word for it. Pedro soon saw that there was an impossible number of people out in the open – thousands and thousands of them filling the pavements, crouching in the doorways, queuing for food, for shelter, for work, for a bed for the night or simply because they had nothing else to do. There were whole families clustered together: wizened grandmothers in black, children in rags, blank-faced mothers carrying babies. Many of the people were carrying huge bundles which surely contained everything they owned. Others had their possessions piled up on carts or wheelbarrows. And they were wearing so many clothes that they didn't even look human; they were just round masses of cloth – old jackets and shabby coats – shuffling forward, barely able to move.

And everywhere there were policemen. They wore the same black uniforms as the guards in the castle and patrolled together in pairs, with pistols and batons hanging from their belts. At first, Pedro thought they were looking for him and crouched down, afraid to go on. But Giovanni urged him forward. The policemen were here to control the crowds, stopping people at random to question them and examine their identity papers. Even so, the two boys kept their heads down, moving as quickly as they could without drawing attention to themselves. They were friends on their way home. What did it matter that they were soaked through and filthy? Maybe they had been fighting together by the sea. What could be more innocent than that?

There were no cars at all. That puzzled Pedro. How could you have a modern city without cars, buses or taxis? And, for that matter, there were tramlines but where were the trams? A few people overtook them on bicycles, weaving their way through the crowds, but otherwise everyone was on foot. And although there was electricity – he could see the wires criss-crossing above his head and white light shining out of some of the windows higher up – the streets and most of the buildings were dark. Nobody seemed to be enjoying themselves. Most of the shops were closed. There were no restaurants or cafés. No music – live or recorded – played anywhere. It was as if all the most miserable people had come to live in one place and had become even more miserable once they'd arrived.

He felt Giovanni take hold of his arm and the two of them left the avenue they had been following and continued down a series of narrower streets between buildings that were so close together that they almost seemed to touch. They passed a food shop with an open door and a long line of people stretching down the pavement. Next to it was a pawnbroker with an old bearded man sitting behind a desk, examining a gold ring with an eyeglass. They turned a corner, continued under an archway and finally followed a flight of steps into a private square formed by four crumbling apartment blocks, eight storeys high, with identical windows, shutters and cast-iron balconies. Clothes hung everywhere, limp and stripped of their colour by the fading light. The same uncanny silence that had characterized the city seemed to have followed them here. Pedro would have expected to hear a television playing or at least a radio – but there was nothing. The two of them made for a doorway and entered a dank, old-fashioned hallway with a flight of concrete stairs leading upwards. There were yet more families huddled together here. As Pedro brushed past, he felt their heads turn towards them and saw the whites of their eyes peering at him out of the gloom.

There was a lift but it wasn't working. They climbed six floors, passing twenty or thirty more people, stacked one above the other on different steps. They followed a corridor with light sockets dangling down on wires but no bulbs. Pedro could smell cooking … plain boiled rice or pasta. He heard a baby crying, a woman shouting at someone. In the distance, perhaps half a mile away, there was a single gunshot, then, a few seconds later, someone screaming. Giovanni stopped in front of a door and knocked – a special code, Pedro noticed – which he rapped out with his knuckles. There was a pause and then the door opened. The two of them went in.

They were in a flat that had just three interconnecting rooms, with high ceilings, bare wooden floors and windows looking out over the courtyard. It might once have been grand. Pedro observed some of the details; the finely carved shutters, the marble fireplace. But there were empty squares where pictures had once hung. The curtains had gone. There was barely any furniture.

A whole family lived here, several generations all sitting round a table together, lit by the oil lamp that was the only source of light. Most of them were adults but there were also children … two girls aged about four and six. They had all looked round as Giovanni had come in. They were obviously surprised and disturbed to see Pedro.

The door had been opened by a thin, serious-looking man with long grey hair and a beard. He was wearing a thick cardigan, a scarf and a flat cap. He slammed the door quickly, then grabbed hold of Giovanni and began to speak to him in fast, barely audible Italian. Pedro stood waiting, dripping on the wooden floor, aware that the rest of the family was still watching him. The man was angry, frustrated, but Giovanni held his ground, explaining what he had done. Eventually the man turned to Pedro.

"You speak Spanish?" he asked. He was speaking fluent Spanish himself.

"Yes." Pedro nodded.

"Are you from Spain?"

"No. Peru."

The man was astonished by this. "I also speak your language," he said. "A long time ago I used to be a professor of languages here at the university. That was before they closed it down. It is now used for housing. My name is Francesco Amati. You need to dry yourself."

He snapped at one of the women, who hurried into the next room, returning with a blanket which she draped over Pedro's shoulders. Pedro folded it around himself. Meanwhile, Giovanni had stripped off his own shirt and was drying himself energetically with a tea towel.

"I expect you are hungry," Francesco said. "Giovanni tells me that you have been a prisoner for a long time. You can join us. Please, sit down."

It seemed that Giovanni had won the argument and now that the man had acknowledged it, the whole family was prepared to accept him. They shuffled aside to make space for Pedro at the table and he found himself being served warm soup and bread, which he wolfed down immediately. The soup was thin and the bread hard but after a month of prison rations, they tasted delicious.

"We will tell you about ourselves," Francesco said. "But first there are some things I must know about you. Your name is Pedro. Is that right? Why are you here in Naples?"

"I didn't mean to come here," Pedro said between mouthfuls. He wasn't sure how much to tell these people. It wasn't just a question of whether he could trust them or not. It was simply that he wasn't sure how much of his story they would believe. "I was taken prisoner in a church, or maybe a monastery, about thirty minutes away. They brought me here in a helicopter."

"Why?"

"Because they think I can hurt them."

Giovanni said something in Italian and the older man muttered a few words in reply. "*Can* you hurt them?" he asked.

"If I can find my friends. There are five of us..."

A much older man on the other side of the table leant forward and spoke rapidly, in a low voice. Pedro heard the word "*cinque*" repeated several times. The Italian for five. He looked at the other people around the table: two women, two younger men, the children. They all looked similar and he guessed they were part of the same family but that wasn't what united them. They were all survivors. There was nothing left for them in the outside world. Everything, for them, boiled down to these three rooms.

The old man finished talking. Francesco turned back to Pedro. "I am Giovanni's uncle," he said. "His father was my brother but he is dead. This man –" he glanced at the man he had just been speaking to –"is my father. That is my wife, her sister and the two girls are her children. We are lucky because we still have this place to live in. My older brother, Angelo, works in the harbour, where he has a boat. He used to be a fisherman, but of course there are no longer any fish. And Giovanni is a kitchen boy at the Castel Nuovo, which is where they were keeping you. They treat him badly but he is able to bring home food and they also pay him, and it is only thanks to him that we can live.

"At first I was angry that he brought you here. The police will be looking for you now. If they find you here, it will be the end of us all. But Giovanni tells me that he heard them talking about you. He said that they were afraid of you, that you were their enemy – and that is why he brought you to this place."

"Why are there so many people in this city?" Pedro asked. "What are they all doing in the streets...?"

"They are refugees." Francesco muttered to his wife and she rose from the table, returning with the pot that held the soup. She ladled out another bowl for Pedro. The children looked at the food longingly and Pedro felt a twang of guilt, knowing that they were being refused. "Naples is overrun by refugees," Francesco went on. "They have come from the south of Italy, to avoid the floods, and from the far north because of the food shortages. There is fighting all over Eastern Europe and so they have escaped from Romania, Slovenia, Croatia – bringing everything they have with them in the hope of starting a new life. Some of them have come from as far away as Africa and India. Every night, hundreds of them die on the streets of this city and when the winter comes it will be even worse. There are huge camps out in Aversa and Arienzo – tens of thousands of people – but the authorities do not really want to help them. They would prefer them to die. Some say the camps are there to help them on their way." He paused. "You don't know any of this?"

Pedro shook his head. "No. I don't understand. What you're saying ... the world isn't like that!"

"What are you talking about? What do you mean?"

"I'm talking about the world that I knew. I saw the newspapers. I saw television. There was nothing about any fighting..."

"There are no newspapers and how can there be TV when we have no electricity?" Francesco examined Pedro carefully. "What you are saying is mad and I do not know if we should trust you. But Giovanni says that they are afraid of you and that is enough. We must help you. And my father, who once studied theology in the University of Rome, becomes interested when you talk about the five of you."

"*Cinque!*" The old man repeated the word again, vigorously nodding his head.

"But whoever you are and whatever reason you are here, you cannot stay in Naples. That is the first consideration before all else. I have to think about the safety of my family. You may believe it would be impossible to find you in a city with so many poor people who have no addresses and no identities. You even look Italian. But you have no idea what you are about to unleash. If you are who my father thinks you are, the police will tear down whole buildings and drag away everyone inside them to find you. And any one of the people who saw you tonight will be glad to sell you for the price of a meal. So far they have been slow because they did not expect you to find a way out of the Castel Nuovo. Unlike Giovanni, they did not know about the old sewer system. But soon it will begin and by then you must be gone."

The old man spoke again and Francesco raised a hand, silencing him.

"It is too dangerous for you to travel by land. There are checkpoints everywhere. But we can talk to Angelo. He has the boat. He can take you up the coast to Rome and there are friends there who will shelter you. All that matters is that you leave here as soon as you can."

Pedro tried to take all this in. The trouble was that it was all happening too quickly; first the prison, then the escape, Giovanni, the nightmare of the sewer, the city and now this family, sitting in the half-light of an empty flat, telling him what he had to do. Nothing added up. Naples was a big European city, a place where people went to art galleries and smart restaurants. He had seen pictures of it in magazines. But this Naples seemed to be nothing more than a giant camp for refugees – and all these things that the man was talking about ... flooding and wars. Whatever Francesco was telling him, Pedro had watched television when he was in Nazca with Matt and Richard. They had read the news and surfed the Internet. There had never been anything about any of this. Why were the schools closed? And how could a boy as young as Giovanni end up working in a kitchen? In Lima that might be possible, but not here. Was this man lying to him? He surely didn't have any reason to and he genuinely seemed to want to help. But nothing he had said had any connection with the world that Pedro knew.

Only one thing was certain. He couldn't leave. Not on his own.

"I have to see Scott," he said.

Giovanni had understood nothing of the conversation but the mention of the name caused him to look round sharply.

"Scott?" Francesco asked.

"He was a prisoner with me. He's my friend. I can't go anywhere without him. I certainly can't leave him with them."

"Is he in the castle?"

"Yes. He was in my cell but then they took him away. I have to go back for him..."

Pedro hadn't touched his second bowl of soup, which had gone cold in front of him. He was still hungry but he slid it towards the two girls, who glanced briefly at Francesco for permission. He nodded and they began to eat greedily, attacking the bowl with their spoons.

"You broke out of the Castel Nuovo by a miracle and only because you happened to meet my nephew. He brought you across the city to one of the few places where you would be safe. And you want to go back?" Francesco laughed briefly. "You're out of your mind."

Giovanni leant forward and began to ask his uncle questions. Francesco answered him briefly. Pedro heard the name Scott mentioned and Giovanni scowled. They talked for what seemed like a long time until finally the older man turned back to him. "This friend of yours is the same age as you? A dark-haired boy? An American?"

"Yes."

Giovanni began again but Francesco held up a hand, warning him to be silent. "You cannot see him," he said. "You are mistaken about him. He is not a prisoner in the castle. He is a guest. He sleeps in a fine room with sheets and everything he could want. In the day he walks out in the streets of Naples and although he is accompanied by guards, they are there only to protect him. He can go where he likes."

"No. You're wrong." Pedro shook his head. "That's not possible. That's not Scott."

"I am not wrong." Francesco was deadly serious. He rested his fists on the table and spoke softly, as if he didn't want the rest of his family to hear. "Listen to me, Pedro," he said. "Giovanni works in the kitchen but sometimes he has to serve food in the dining hall. That was what he was telling me just now. He was there two nights ago. They had a banquet, a whole load of important people eating the best food and drinking fine wine. There was a man from America there, some sort of big shot. But he wasn't at the head of the table. Do you know who was? It was Scott Tyler. Is that right? He was wearing black trousers and a black shirt. And they all raised their glasses to toast his health. That was when Giovanni heard his name."

"No." Pedro refused to believe it.

"Giovanni, whose father was a doctor and who should be at school, works fifteen hours a day in that place. He sweeps and he cleans and does everything he is told and they beat him for the slightest reason. You see his face? Maybe he'll show you his back and you can see the whip marks. Two nights ago, he bowed in front of your friend, as he had been told to do, and took the dirty plate from him. And when he thought nobody was looking, he scraped the food that was left into his own mouth. But Scott saw him. Scott smiled. It amused him. He thought it was funny."

"I have to see him," Pedro said. "You don't understand. They did things to him. They hurt him. But Scott isn't like that. He isn't what you think."

"So you're just going to walk back in and ask to meet him?"

Giovanni was glaring at him. And Pedro understood why he was angry. The Italian boy had risked everything to help him escape and had brought him back to his own family because he believed in him, and because he thought that in some way Pedro could help fight back against the people who ruled over the city. But Pedro was repaying him by calling him a liar. Everything he had done was being thrown back in his face.

Could he be wrong about Scott?

Could his friend have joined the other side?

Pedro sighed. He turned to Francesco. "I have to see Scott because there is nothing any of us can do without him," he explained. It had been a long time since he had spoken his own language at such length. "Obviously I can't go back into the castle but if he is free, as you say, perhaps he can come to me. I don't want to put any of you in any danger but I cannot leave here without seeing him. He is one of the Five. You seem to know what that means. We can't do anything without him." He thought for a moment, then glanced at Giovanni. "Is there any way that Giovanni could pass him a message? Maybe there is somewhere in the city, or outside it, where the two of us could meet. Somewhere safe. I'd have to make sure that he was on his own, but whatever you may think, I know he wouldn't hand me over to them. All I need is to talk to him for a few minutes. After that, I'll go anywhere you want."

Pedro had to wait while Francesco translated all this for Giovanni. The older man, Francesco's father, cut in a few times and one of the women joined in too. It was clear that nobody around the table was happy with what Pedro had proposed. Finally Giovanni spoke. Once again, Pedro was impressed by how confident he was. Nobody interrupted until he had finished.

"Giovanni thinks he can do what you ask. Tomorrow they change all the sheets and it's his job to carry them down to the laundry room. That means he will go into Scott's bedroom. Do you understand that? To change the sheets for him, like a servant." Francesco paused. "And you realize that if they find out that Giovanni is helping you, they will kill him. He has been in the Castel Nuovo for two years and he has seen many other servants die. One of them was found stealing food. He was taken out and shot."

But you can't just kill people like that, Pedro thought.

Instead he said, "I promise you. You can trust Scott. He's playing a game. It's not what it seems."

Francesco translated again. Giovanni nodded. Pedro was relieved. It had been agreed.

"We will have to think of somewhere safe for the meeting,"

Francesco said. "The police are certain to be looking for you and that will make it doubly dangerous. I still wonder why we are doing this, why we are endangering ourselves for you."

And suddenly the old man spoke. "He is one of the Five," he said. The words were in Spanish. "Gio found him and brought him to us. He is our one hope."

Francesco nodded but his face was grave. "Maybe you're right, father," he said. "So let us hope he does not let us down."

TWENTY-ONE

They met in the afternoon, in the very heart of the city.

Francesco Amati had considered many possibilities for the meeting point – churches, shopping arcades, gardens, the Catacombs of San Gennaro, one of the jetties stretching out from the harbour front – but he had come to the conclusion that none of them was safe. The simple fact was that if Scott chose to betray Pedro, then there was nothing that any of them would be able to do. As soon as the place had been agreed, he could have five hundred men in the streets around any part of the city. The government still had helicopters and jeeps, even if the people didn't. With a single command he could make sure Pedro was captured and that would be that.

The police were already busy. There had been house-to-house searches in Vomero, Santa Lucia – the southern area close to the sea – and in a dozen other areas of Naples. Hundreds of arrests had been made. At the same time, notices had gone up everywhere offering a reward of ten thousand lira, an unimaginable sum of money, to anyone who came forward with information leading to the arrest of a fifteen-year-old Peruvian boy, thin with black hair, on his own somewhere in the streets. For the last six hours, Pedro's description had been blasted out on police loudspeakers all over the city and with it had come a stark message. Anyone found guilty of helping him would be shot – and their entire family with them.

Even travelling to the meeting place would be dangerous, and in the end that had given Pedro an idea. The police would be expecting him to leave Naples. He certainly had no reason to stay there. Already there were road blocks on all the main motorways. If he was still in the city, he would surely be hiding in the darkest corner he could find. The last place they would expect him to be was in the middle of a wide open space with no protection whatsoever – so as crazy as it sounded, that had to be the best place to meet. Francesco had quickly seen the logic of it and had suggested the Piazza Dante, a public square high up on the Via Toledo, once one of the busiest streets in Naples. It would also be an easy place for Scott to find. The meeting was set for four o'clock, next to the statue of the famous poet Dante Alighieri, which stood at the very centre.

It was an unpleasantly warm and close afternoon without a breath of wind. There seemed to be more smoke in the sky than ever. Francesco had explained to Pedro that it was all down to Vesuvius, the volcano that stood ten kilometres to the east. There had been a minor earthquake followed by an eruption three months before. Nobody had been killed but the volcano had been spewing out smoke and ash ever since, poisoning the atmosphere and filling the people with dread of worse to come. And yet, strangely, the inhabitants of Naples had got used to it now. Perhaps it was because they had other things to worry about. There hadn't been a serious eruption for almost a hundred years and even without weather forecasters and meteorologists to give their assurances, everyone had decided that there wasn't going to be another one any time soon.

Pedro stood in front of the statue, which had once been white but which now, like everything else, had a thin coating of grey. There were tall, handsome buildings all around him and arcades which were once filled with outdoor cafés and flower stalls but now contained only a few clusters of people, slumped on the concrete, sleeping out the heat of the day. A huge gateway rose up on one side and above it there was a clock, which had stopped permanently at eleven o'clock. The eleventh hour. It was somehow appropriate.

And there was Scott, moving towards him across the paving stones, on his own, without a bodyguard. Even before he got close, Pedro could see that he had changed. He was healthier, stronger, more sure of himself – walking as if the square and the entire city belonged to him. His hair had been cut shorter and he was wearing new clothes – an expensive shirt, jeans and trainers. He saw Pedro and raised a hand in greeting, but there was little emotion on his face and he clearly wasn't in any hurry. Almost at once, Pedro got the impression that something had gone badly wrong. The boy approaching him was nothing like the Scott he had known. He wondered if he should turn and run.

It was too late. Scott was here. There was nobody with him, no armed soldiers or police closing in on the square. Pedro relaxed a little. At least it seemed that he had come on his own.

"Hello, Pedro," Scott said.

"Hello, Scott."

"I was really surprised to get your note. I didn't even know you could write. There's a kid called Giovanni ... I think that's his name. He cleans my room and works in the kitchen. Was he the one who helped you escape?"

"No. I don't know who you're talking about." Pedro hadn't intended to lie but even as the words left his mouth, he realized that he didn't trust Scott and wasn't going to give anything away. He was already wishing that he had never come to this meeting. It wasn't just that he had put himself in danger. If Scott really had guessed how Pedro had been helped to escape from the Castel Nuovo, the whole Amati family would be killed.

"I have to say, I was impressed. The whole place went completely crazy after they found you were gone. In the end they worked out you must have gone through the sewers. That must have been pretty gross ... having that crap all over you. But I've got to hand it to you – I didn't think you had it in you."

Pedro wasn't sure what to say. He knew that Scott wasn't really complimenting him. He was mocking him.

"Are you OK, Scott?" he asked.

Scott raised his hands, showing off his new clothes. "You can see for yourself. When they dragged me out of the cell, I was expecting the worst. But in fact they've been pretty good to me. I can't complain." He shrugged. "They're looking after me."

"And what have you offered them in return?"

"What makes you think I've offered them anything?" Pedro didn't answer so he went on. "That's the trouble with you. That's the trouble with all of you. From the very start, none of you have ever rated me. I was always the weak link, wasn't I. You think I'd turn you in right now for a steak sandwich and a can of Coke. Is that what you think, Pedro? Do you think I've become one of them?"

Pedro gestured. "You have everything. I have nothing."

"That's because of the choice you've made."

"And what choice have you made, Scott?"

"I've chosen to stop running around and stop being hurt. I never wanted any of this hero thing in the first place. You have no idea what sort of life I've had, Pedro, from the very start when I was found dumped in a seed box beside Lake Tahoe. Nobody ever wanted me. I was beaten up in the orphanage. My foster parents treated me like dirt. I spent two years in a crummy theatre in Reno doing tricks without even getting paid, and if I refused I got beaten up again. And why did this all happen to me? Because I was 'one of the Five'. I'd been chosen. Lucky me!

"Except I was never really one of you, was I. You were all over my little brother … best buddies … but I got left out of the loop. I know why Matt wanted you to be my nursemaid when he went off to London. He didn't trust me – just like you don't trust me now."

"I'm here," Pedro said.

"But you're looking over my shoulder. I can see you twitching, Stick Insect. You think the big bad policemen are on their way any minute. You can't believe that I'd simply come out here on my own and meet you face-to-face."

"Why did you?" Pedro asked.

"Because I wanted you to know how I felt. I wanted you to tell the others – if you ever get to see them again, which, frankly, I doubt. Or maybe you'll see them in the dreamworld. Do you ever go to the dreamworld, Pedro? I've been there quite a few times but there's nobody ever waiting for me. It seems they've decided to leave me on my own."

"I can't find them either."

"Then maybe they've dumped both of us." Scott stopped, suddenly tired. "We were never going to win this fight," he said. "And it's all over anyway. Have you worked it out yet? When we went through that door in Hong Kong, we somehow jumped ten years into the future. Half the world has gone. Look at this place! Naples was once a pretty cool city. It was where all the rich people went. Now it's just a big refugee camp and soon it won't even be that. When Vesuvius blows a second time, it'll be wiped out … which brings me to the point of this little meeting."

Scott glanced at his watch. It was new, a great slab of precision engineering on a silver strap. It would have cost him two thousand dollars if he'd had to pay for it. But that was the deal he had made. He would never have to pay for anything again.

"I have to get back," he said. "But if you want, you can tag along. I can talk to my friends. Right now they want to do a lot of bad things to you but I think I can persuade them to take you with us. I can't promise they'll let you travel first class but at least they won't kill you."

Pedro shook his head. "I can't come with you."

"What's the alternative?"

"I don't know."

"Then why are you here?"

"I hoped you would come with me."

Scott laughed briefly. "Back into the sewers? No way."

"We can get out of Naples. We can find another door."

"You just don't get it, Pedro." Scott was scowling now. "I'm finished with you. I'm finished with Matt. I'm finished with the Five. I just don't want to know about it any more. I'm flying out of here with Jonas, in comfort, and the only reason I've come here is to give you the chance to come with me. And if you know what's good for you, you'll take it."

"Who is Jonas?"

"He's a friend. He looks after me."

"I thought I was your friend," Pedro said.

Scott shook his head. "You're wrong. You and I were thrown together but I never wanted that. I don't care if I never see you again."

Pedro gazed at Scott and knew that there was nothing more he could say. The meeting had been a waste of time and he had never felt more depressed. He had let Matt down. Far from healing him, he had allowed Scott to slip away. The boy who stood there, lording it over him in his new clothes, wasn't anyone he recognized. How had it happened so quickly? Pedro wondered briefly if Scott had been drugged or if he had been hurt again. He wanted to forgive the other boy. But looking into his eyes, he could see the truth. Scott had caved in. He had allowed the Old

Ones to reach inside him and this was the result.

Was there any way Pedro could still reach him? Did they have any connection left? He remembered the one person Scott had always been close to. "What about Jamie?" he said.

"What about him?"

"What do you want me to tell him?"

Scott shrugged. "Don't tell him anything."

"You know that without you, we can't win."

"We could never have won anyway. That's the whole point."

There was nothing more to say. Pedro turned round and would have walked away but Scott called out to him, stopping him. When Pedro turned back, the other boy was holding something out: a handful of money.

"I stole this for you," Scott said. "I don't know if it will help you or not, but you might as well have it."

"Thank you." There was no point in refusing it. Pedro reached out and took it and it was then that Scott noticed the filthy bandage that was still tied around his hand.

"What happened to your hand?" he asked.

"It was the guards. They broke one of my fingers."

"When?" For the first time, Scott's voice faltered and he seemed to have lost a little of his confidence.

"I don't know. It was the same day you left."

There was a brief silence. Then Scott spoke once more, the words pouring out rapidly. "Listen," he said. "This was always going to happen. The world was going to end and there was nothing any of us could have done to stop it. Me joining them or me staying with you, it would never have made any difference."

"Is that what you believe, Scott?" Pedro asked. His voice was tired.

"The Old Ones aren't evil. It's the world that's evil."

"And what are you?"

"I'm not anything. I just want to live."

And that was it. This time it was Scott who turned and walked off. Pedro watched him as he continued across the square, finally disappearing underneath the archway with its clock. He looked down. He was still holding the banknotes in his broken hand.

He shoved them in his pocket, then turned and walked the other way.

TWENTY-TWO

Jonas Mortlake was waiting for Scott in one of the great state rooms of the Castel Nuovo. It was a huge space that had been specially furnished for him with soft, comfortable furniture, thick rugs and a grand piano – although he couldn't play it. Masterpieces of classical and modern art hung on all four walls; works by Rembrandt, Leonardo da Vinci and Picasso, all of them taken from famous art galleries shortly before they had been looted or demolished. There was a fire blazing in the hearth and stretched out on the flagstones in front of it, the skin of a white tiger with its paws spread, its glass eyes staring and its teeth bared in one final roar before it became extinct.

Jonas was sipping coffee from a white porcelain cup when Scott arrived. He was dressed for the flight out of Naples, wearing a grey silk suit, white shirt and pink tie. Earlier that afternoon, while Scott was in the Piazza Dante, he had spent two hours in the gym next to his bedroom in the castle. But despite all the work he had done lifting weights, despite the press-ups, the rowing and the stretching, he hadn't managed to get rid of the anger he had been feeling ever since he had heard that Scott had gone. His muscles were still warm but the anger was burning cold inside.

"Where have you been?" he asked.

"Out." Scott took a biscuit from the table, broke it in half and ate it idly.

"I know that. But that's not why I asked you. I'd like to know where you've been."

"Why?"

Jonas considered the question. He knew that a week ago Scott wouldn't have dared to ask it – but then a week ago Scott had been a very different person. He decided to tread carefully. "I was worried about you," he said. "I've told you how dangerous it is out there. There are a lot of very desperate people. If they see anyone with money and possessions, they'll try anything."

"I can look after myself."

"I have no doubt." Jonas raised the cup to his lips and sipped. "Even so, you've left it rather late. We ought to be on our way to the airport. The plane is waiting."

"I'm ready to go. I don't need a passport, do I?"

"No."

"Well, I'm all packed." It was true. Jonas had provided him with enough new clothes to fill three suitcases. There were jeans, jerseys, shirts and jackets but also thermal underwear, padded jackets, hoods and gloves. It was going to be cold in Antarctica. That was where the two of them were heading, apparently. "You can get one of the servants to carry it down."

"I'll do that." Jonas took another sip. "So where did you go, as a matter of interest?" he asked, casually.

"I was in a place called the Piazza Dante."

"And what took you there?" Scott didn't answer. Jonas lowered the cup and leant forward. His eyes were hard behind the wire-frame glasses. "You saw Pedro."

It was an accusation, not a question. Scott shrugged. He couldn't see any point in denying it. "Yes."

"May I ask why?"

"He wanted to see me."

"You are aware that I am extremely annoyed about his escape.

You and I may have come to an understanding, but it's still going to make me look careless and stupid."

"You *were* careless and stupid, Jonas. That's the point."

Jonas frowned. The boy was going too far. He would have to devise some sort of punishment. Not here. They had no time. But perhaps while they were on the plane. It was a Boeing 747 and there were only the two of them flying. There would be plenty of room. "I would have very much liked to have had Pedro back in my hands," he said. "If you knew where he was, you could have warned me. At the very least, you could have told me who helped him escape. Presumably you know. How did he even contact you?"

"He sent me a message."

"I'm very disappointed in you, Scott—"

"You don't need Pedro," Scott cut in. "He's nothing to you. You've got what you want. You've got me." His voice was cold. At the same time, he seemed to be completely relaxed. Jonas felt a sense of unease. It was he who had made the boy like this but what exactly had he created? "Now if you want to go, let's go. But stop talking to me like I'm a child."

"I think you're forgetting yourself." Jonas had decided he'd had enough. It was time to reassert himself. "How dare you speak to me in this way!"

"I'll speak to you how I like." The hatred was pouring out of him. It was in his dark eyes, in his voice. The American boy was consumed by it. "I think you're the one who's forgetting, Jonas. You serve the Old Ones. We both serve the Old Ones. But there's a difference between us. You are a human being who has been indulged and been given a little power in return for his service. But I am one of the Five. I was there at the very beginning when the Old Ones were defeated and they've always been a little bit afraid of me. I have power – and the strange thing is that since I have accepted what I am, since I joined you, I've become stronger than ever. I can't tell you how I feel. It's extraordinary. But do you want to see my power, Jonas? Do you want a taste?"

"Let's just leave..." Jonas muttered.

But it was too late.

"I can see right into your mind," Scott went on. He had folded his arms across his chest and although he was a few inches shorter than Jonas, he seemed to tower over him, staring straight into his eyes. "I have read every dirty secret of your life. I know what you think when you get up and I know what you dream when you go to bed. But more than that, I can control you. I was always able to do that, to push people and make them do what I wanted. I killed my foster father when I was twelve years old. I made him climb up a ladder and hang himself. I could do the same to you now."

"That's enough, Scott."

"I don't think it is enough, Jonas. I think it's time you learnt who I am and what I can do. I know you like breaking fingers. That's what happened to Pedro. So why don't you find out what it feels like? Why don't you break one of your own?"

"What...?"

"You heard me."

"You're not serious."

"I am."

Scott stared and it was as if Jonas had been electrocuted. His whole body shook, his arms jerking as he fought to keep them still. "Scott..." he managed to whisper.

"I don't care what you do to me," Scott said. "But you leave my friends alone!"

"He wasn't your friend!" Jonas gasped out the sentence, his eyes bulging, his face contorted. His entire body was fighting against itself and as he stood there he looked as if he was about to topple over. Scott was still gazing at him, and without wanting to, Jonas took hold of the little finger of his left hand. All the muscles in his arms and shoulders were shuddering. "Please…" he whimpered. There were beads of sweat on his forehead. His whole face was twisted in anticipation of the pain to come and tears leaked out of the corners of his eyes. He was clutching the finger in his right hand, bending it away from the others. "Scott…" he tried one last time.

"Break it!"

Jonas couldn't stop himself. He had no control. He screamed as the finger broke and at once it was as if he had been released. He pitched forward, falling to his knees. His whole body was shaking. Huge tears rolled down his cheeks.

"Don't even think about punishing me," Scott said. "The Old Ones don't care about you but they have a great deal of interest in me. I am the master here, Jonas, not you. That's what you have to remember." He smiled. "So when does the plane leave?"

"What have you done to me? What have you done to me?"

"When does the plane leave?"

"The car's outside." Jonas hissed the words. He was cradling his injured hand, unable to believe what had just happened.

"Good. I'll get my things." Scott began to walk towards the door, then stopped. "By the way, there was only one person who could have given me the message to meet in the square and that was the little servant boy, Giovanni."

"Why are you telling me…?"

"Why shouldn't I?" Scott smiled. "We're both on the same side."

Giovanni was throwing a few possessions into a small suitcase: some clothes, letters and photographs. He had almost nothing to take with him but Pedro understood the significance of what he was doing. He wouldn't be coming back. Meanwhile, his uncle, Francesco Amati, was standing over him, watching both the boys anxiously.

"We have no time," he was saying. "The two of you should have already left."

The other members of the family – Giovanni's grandfather, various aunts and cousins – were clustered together in the room next door, gazing through the open door, frightened and perplexed. Pedro understood what they were going through and knew, with a heavy heart, that it was all his fault. They hadn't had much of a life here. Every day had been a struggle for them. But at least they had had each other. They had these rooms. They had been able to live together in relative safety. And then he had come into their lives and overnight everything had changed. Everything they had could soon be ripped away. Someone at the Castel Nuovo would work out that it was Giovanni who had passed the message to Scott. Putting two and two together, they would know that he must have helped Pedro escape. And then they would come and find him ... and not just him. His family would suffer too.

Giovanni had finished packing. He closed the case and Francesco immediately picked it up. "Angelo is waiting for you at the harbour," he said, speaking in his own language. Angelo was the name of the brother with the boat. "He will take you up the coast. And when you get to Rome he will help you find Carla Rivera. She worked at the University of Rome with your grandfather and she has always been a friend to this family. She lives with her son and her daughter, close to the Vatican. She will know what to do." He turned to Pedro and spoke in Spanish. "Giovanni will take care of you and you are less likely to be stopped, travelling together. You even look a little Italian. Remember, it is illegal to travel in Italy without an ID card. If you see any policemen or officials, you must try to avoid them. If you are stopped, do not try to run or they will shoot you."

"I'm sorry," Pedro said, miserably. He knew the two words were useless. They didn't begin to express what he felt.

How could he have known about Scott? The two of them had only been apart for a week, but in that time Scott had changed to the extent that he was almost unrecognizable. He was Jamie's brother. The two of them were twins. But something had happened that had ripped them apart and turned one of them into…

No. Pedro still wouldn't accept it. Scott had been hurt. He had been frightened. Any one of them might have chosen to do what he was doing now. Pedro simply refused to believe that Scott really had switched sides.

So why was he in such a hurry to leave now? Why did he believe that armed soldiers might already be on their way to the house?

Thinking of Scott reminded him of the money he had given him and he pulled it out of his pocket. "Here…" He offered it to Francesco. "You can have this."

"Where did you get it?" Francesco stared at the handful of banknotes.

"Scott gave it to me."

"I don't want it!" Francesco snapped out the words, then softened. "That's a lot of money, Pedro. Several months' salary."

"Then take it. Your family needs it."

Francesco stood for a moment, fighting with himself. Then he took the money, kept about half for himself and handed the rest back. "You and Gio will need money too," he said. "Did you hear the name I told him? Carla Rivera. She is the woman you must look for in Rome."

"Papa … they're here!"

The voice came from the room next door. It was Isabella, the younger of the two girls, who had been standing at the window all this time, her face pressed against the glass. Francesco rushed in and looked over her shoulder. Outside, it was already dark, although night had not yet fallen. The sun had been obliterated by the smoke pouring out of Mount Vesuvius, thicker and blacker than ever. But even so, he could make out the uniformed men crossing the courtyard, heading for his front door. There were about twenty of them, masked and helmeted, carrying automatic weapons. Their feet were stamping in unison on the concrete.

An old woman appeared from the side, a grandmother in a shawl and apron. She shouted at them in a high-pitched voice. What were they doing here? Why were they disturbing the neighbourhood? The soldiers ignored her. Somewhere, a baby cried. A dog began to bark.

"You have to get out of here, now!" Francesco cried.

"You have to come with us," Pedro said.

"No. We can hold them off. We can buy you time."

"But they'll kill you. They'll kill all of you."

Francesco seized Pedro between his hands. "There is no room on the boat," he hissed. "We're dead anyway. But we need you to live. You are one of the Five, Pedro. You are the only hope we have left."

"*Zio*..." It was the Italian for "uncle". Giovanni was in tears. He grabbed hold of Francesco and the two of them embraced.

Then the two boys were out of the door and hurrying down the corridor. Pedro heard the front door being smashed open and could imagine the leather boot that had done it. There was another burst of gunfire, shockingly loud, and although they were six floors up he caught the unmistakeable smell of cordite.

"This way!" Giovanni was leading him once again, just as he had done in the Castel Nuovo.

The two boys hurried down the corridor in the opposite direction to the main staircase. Pedro could hear the soldiers coming towards them, twenty pairs of feet stomping on the steps. They came to a window at the end and Giovanni threw it open. There was a fire escape leading down. Pedro climbed out.

"Not down. Up!" Giovanni was still speaking Italian but he stabbed with his finger and Pedro understood. There would almost certainly have been someone waiting for them at the bottom. There had to be another way.

They climbed two sets of metal steps to the roof and ran across a flat concrete wasteland covered in soot and piled high with broken pieces of metal and wood, mangled bicycles, smashed-up machines that hadn't worked for years. Ten years. The sight of them reminded Pedro what Scott had told him. They came to the edge of the roof and Pedro looked for a second ladder. There wasn't one. A gap of about five metres separated this building from the next and Pedro saw what Giovanni was intending to do.

The Italian boy threw his suitcase over. It seemed to hang in the air for a long time before it crashed down on the other side. Then he walked back, took a deep breath and began to run. Pedro saw him launch himself across the chasm. He made it easily, landing on both feet and rolling onto his side. Pedro was shorter than Giovanni and not as strong. But there was no point in staying here on his own. He took one glance down. He was eight storeys from the ground and he could imagine himself falling, smashing into the pavement below. There was a longer burst of gunfire from inside the building. Pedro felt the brickwork vibrating beneath his feet. Suddenly everyone was screaming, or so it seemed to him. He couldn't take any more. He ran and jumped. At that moment, he wouldn't have even minded if he had fallen to his death.

But he didn't fall. He hit the other rooftop, rolling over and taking the skin off his elbow and knees. Giovanni had already retrieved his suitcase and as Pedro got to his feet he propelled him towards a fire escape on the other side. The whole neighbourhood was in an uproar by now. People were pouring out of their homes, knowing that soldiers had come and that it would be safer to be far away. By the time Pedro and Giovanni reached ground level, the street was crowded. They had to push their way across, disappearing up an alleyway on the other side.

Behind them, there was the scream of a whistle. Whoever was in charge at the Castel Nuovo was taking no chances. There were about twenty men inside the building and easily a hundred more outside. The entire area was surrounded. While Pedro and Giovanni had been packing and arguing about money, the net had been closing in and, with a sick feeling in his stomach, Pedro knew that there was no possible way out.

Even so, they kept moving. It was early evening but there were still masses of people in the streets, taking up every inch of space. The crowds refused to get out of the way. They moved like syrup, reluctantly separating, then sliding back together again. Giovanni had his suitcase up against his chest, using it like a battering ram. Pedro glanced to one side and saw several men in black uniform, hacking and stabbing with their truncheons, beating a path towards them. Giovanni shouted and they took another turning. The wrong turning. There was a wall straight ahead of them, too high to climb, with no way around. They had come to a dead end.

And they had been seen! The soldiers knew where they were. Pedro came to a breathless halt, the sweat dripping off his forehead, running down beneath his arms. He wondered if Scott had sent the soldiers here and knew in his heart that there was no other way that they could have been found so quickly. Perhaps it still wasn't too late. Perhaps Pedro could appeal to him ... on his knees if he had to. A word from Scott and the family that had helped him would be spared. But Pedro knew it wouldn't happen.

He wished that he had never come to Italy. He should never have left Peru.

The first soldier appeared right in front of him. He had already unbuckled his revolver and now he raised it, aiming at Giovanni. One boy was to be captured, the other to be killed. He knew which was which.

Pedro closed his eyes.

The ground began to shake. It was so sudden, so violent that it was as if the whole world had been seized in a giant hand and thrown down like a tennis ball. All the lines broke up; the edges of the walls, the doors, the windows, the streets. At the same time there was an explosion like nothing Pedro had ever heard before. It was impossibly loud. And it wasn't stopping. It just went on and on, echoing through the city, tearing through the sky, hammering at the buildings as if determined to bring them down. The shaking was becoming more violent by the second. Pedro felt like his eyeballs were being pulled out of his skull. He was twisting and spinning, out of control. He could no longer feel the ground beneath his feet. Then, in an instant, the sky turned from black to red and Pedro finally understood.

Scott had warned him.

The volcano was erupting.

The soldier had gone. Maybe he had turned and run. Maybe he had fallen. But none of the men from the Castel Nuovo was going to have any interest in the boys. Not now. Pedro looked up and saw a blaze of brilliant red cutting across the sky like an enormous firework. There was a hideous rumbling and more explosions. Balls of flame appeared above the rooftops like falling comets, except that these were soaring upwards, fired into the darkness. At the far end of the alley – it was where they had come from just moments before – a five-storey building with flats and a shop underneath began to tear itself apart, one brick at a time. One after another the windows shattered. Then the whole thing collapsed sideways and came shuddering down, great chunks of wall and shards of glass smashing into the crowds of people who were still below. More flames sprang out of the ground. The whole sky was on fire. The noise was deafening. Thousands of people were screaming but Pedro couldn't hear them.

Where was Giovanni? Pedro staggered around in a circle and found him, his suitcase gone, his arms hanging limp by his side. For a second the two of them were close together and Giovanni shouted something, but Pedro couldn't understand him. It didn't matter. There was only one place they could go.

The harbour.

Vesuvius was already spitting poisonous gases, ash and pumice into the air. A column of smoke had risen up, fifteen kilometres high, the top of it branching out so that it resembled a massive palm tree. Pedro glanced at it and remembered it at once. It was the same tree that he had seen in the dreamworld, the same size and colour. A river of lava, burning at nine hundred degrees Celsius, was edging forward, flowing slowly but inexorably towards the city. Everything it touched disintegrated. Trees vanished as if they were matchsticks, flaming up as they were caught in the conflagration. The earthquake could be felt eight hundred kilometres away. The sky was on fire. And this was just the beginning. Worse was to come.

Pedro and Giovanni were right in the middle of it. Together they set off, staggering, running, fighting their way through the screaming crowds, trying to reach the sea.

The Boeing 747 had already taxied to the end of the runway when the eruption began. Scott was sitting with his seatbelt fastened, his face pressed against the window.

"You should look out, Jonas," he said. "It's quite a view."

"We should have left an hour ago," Jonas rasped.

"I'm glad we didn't. This is something I wouldn't want to miss."

The interior of the plane had been converted into a single room that ran almost half its length and it was absurdly luxurious. There were leather sofas, a dining-room table, an open-plan kitchen, a gym, a cinema screen, a bar and even an entertainment area with computer consoles and miniature football. Two doors led to full-sized bedrooms and there were also en suite bathrooms with sunken baths, showers and saunas. Scott had read about Russian billionaires who had planes like this, complete with gold taps and caviar in the fridge, but he had never dreamt he would fly in one. He had been excited from the moment he had climbed on board.

Jonas Mortlake was not in such a good mood. He was sitting in an armchair, his face pale, thinking how much pleasure it would give him to murder Scott. Of course, the chairman wouldn't allow it. These children had to be kept alive. But circumstances had changed. The world was ending anyway and, as the chairman had told him in New York, there was little chance that he would survive. Maybe, just maybe, he would disobey orders and take matters into his own hands.

Those hands were currently resting on the table in front of him. Jonas hadn't had time to get his little finger bandaged before they left for the airport, so he had wrapped it in a silk scarf. He had swallowed two paracetamol and was sipping a large whisky to deaden the pain. Scott hadn't referred to the incident again. It was as if he had forgotten it. But Jonas would never forget. One way or another, he would have his revenge.

There was another explosion outside and the whole plane shook, the metal joints straining against each other. All the windows were burning red. Scott, sitting opposite him next to a window, let out an exultant whoop, but Jonas scowled. Couldn't the boy see the danger they were in? They had to fly through this mess. If particles of soot or molten glass got sucked into the turbines, the plane would fall out of the sky. Why, why, why hadn't they left earlier? Jonas had been completely in control when he had left for Naples but now he felt he had lost everything.

The pilot had finished his on-board checks and dimmed the cabin lights. Not that there was any need to. It was just habit. Nor did he have to wait for permission to fly. This was the only plane leaving Naples Airport. After today, Naples Airport would no longer exist. Jonas heard the engines being revved and a moment later they were shooting down the runway, the whole fuselage trembling, the wheels bumping over the potholes. There was a moment when he wondered if they would get off the ground. The smoke and the flames seemed to be everywhere, closing in on them from all sides. Was it his imagination or had the temperature risen inside the cabin? They were being cooked alive! His breath caught in his throat and he reached out with his good hand and held onto the edge of his seat. Without knowing it, he had closed his eyes. He was squeezing the whisky glass so hard he was sure it would crack.

But then they were up. He felt the wheels retract and leant back in his chair as they slanted up into the sky. There were two more huge explosions. The plane was almost torn apart, thrown madly from side to side, the walls creaking. Some of the compartments had been thrown open. Books and DVDs tumbled to the ground.

"Did you see that?" Scott howled.

Jonas opened his eyes. Everything was black and red. Clouds of ash folded in on them like giant fists. The whole sky was blazing. Jonas moaned softly. He wanted to scream.

But they didn't crash. Ninety seconds later they had risen above the swirling smoke, the clouds spinning in circles ... the hideous eye of the storm. The worst of the eruption was already behind them. Looking ahead, he could see patches of sky that were almost clear. Jonas stared out of the window and imagined the city he had just left behind. He wondered how many people would die tonight. Ten thousand? A hundred thousand? Somehow it didn't matter when you got to numbers like that. You stopped thinking about them as human beings. With enough zeroes on the end, they just became ants.

The pilot turned the plane in a gentle arc. The cabin lights came back on again. The Boeing 747 began its journey south.

Black smoke, like oil, was oozing out of the crater, spreading outwards, swallowing up the light. Ash was pouring down, as thick as snow. It was as if the air was being sucked away, but what little remained stank of sulphur. And still the flames were spreading. The city was on fire. The sun had disappeared and the whole world had turned red.

Somehow Pedro and Giovanni had made it to the harbour, pushing their way through the crowds of people who had lost any semblance of sanity, screaming and running in every direction, fighting with each other, staggering blindly from street corner to street corner. Some had given up, falling to their knees on the pavements, praying for salvation while others stampeded over them. Children, separated from their parents, ran around in hopeless circles. Babies had been left, abandoned in prams.

Whole sections of the city had disappeared in flames and darkness. Vesuvius was shooting at it, like some monstrous fairground game, firing huge fireballs that plummeted down, one after another. The Castel Nuovo itself had been hit. One of the towers was wrecked and the rest of the building was on fire, flames spitting out of the windows. Further to the north, the Duomo, the main cathedral of Naples, which had stood over the city since the thirteenth century, had almost gone. More than a thousand people, believing even now that God would protect them from the volcano, had taken refuge inside moments before it had been hit by one of the blazing missiles. They were pouring out again, surrounded by smoke and broken stone.

The harbour was a nightmare of fire and smoke, of choking gases and water that was already being whipped into a frenzy. Most of the boats that could sail had already left, and had so many people crowded onto the decks that they could barely stay afloat. There were people fighting on the quays, flailing and screaming at each other, or standing there with hands outstretched, begging for a passage out. But the boat owners were forcing them back. They were on the decks, lashing out with boathooks and oars while the other crew members struggled with ropes and sails, trying to get out into open water before it was too late. As Pedro skidded to a halt, gasping for breath in the poisonous atmosphere, he felt another huge shockwave travel under his feet and had to cling to Giovanni for support. The two boys watched in disbelief as the entire quay, a giant slab of cement, suddenly tilted as if trying to set sail itself. If they had been any closer, they would have been killed. As it was, dozens of people were thrown into the foaming sea. They had no chance. There were ships all around them, rising up and crashing down. Many of them were crushed. The rest must have drowned.

Giovanni looked around him, his hair being whipped by the wind, his eyes filled with panic. "Angelo..." He shouted out a sentence but most of it was lost in the din.

Pedro wondered if they should have come here. At least half the city seemed to have had the same idea. A lot of the boats had already gone. For an insane moment he was reminded of a funfair he had once seen in Lima. He had only been about nine or ten years old and he had been fascinated by the dodgem cars, so many of them packed into such a tight space. The harbour looked the same ... only without the lights and music. It was a hellish scene of destruction as the huge vessels smashed into each other, the water black and frenzied below.

"There!" Giovanni pointed and shouted out.

Miraculously, his uncle's boat was still there, waiting for them. Perhaps it had been overlooked by the rest of the crowd because it was so small and looked so fragile; a seven-metre fishing boat with two sails and a single cabin. It was called *Medusa*, the name painted in gold letters on blue. There were three men on board. Two of them were desperately clinging to the ropes that kept them moored to the quay. The third, a dark, bearded man, soaked to the skin, was searching for them.

"Angelo!" Giovanni called.

The man didn't hear but saw them a moment later as they ran forward, following the edge of the quay. Suddenly there were fewer people around them. Pedro leapt over a jagged crack in the concrete. It hadn't been there seconds before. The entire harbour was breaking up, the pieces tumbling into the sea. The air was thicker than ever. Every breath was an effort. His throat and lungs felt scalded.

The boat was heaving around as if it were a living animal and Pedro wondered how it could possibly sail out of here. The wind was too strong, coming at them in short, vicious punches. The sails were writhing, trying to tear themselves free of the masts. But as he clambered aboard, allowing Angelo to haul him off the quay with Giovanni right behind him, he heard a metallic cough and a rattle and knew that incredibly, the *Medusa* still had a working engine and that somehow the men had saved enough fuel for this journey.

They were instantly away, a void opening up between them and the harbour's edge. Pedro lost his footing and sprawled on the deck. As he looked back, he saw a man and two women leap towards them, hoping to reach the last sailing boat to leave. But they were already too far away. All three of them fell into the black, churning water. Pedro didn't see any of them come back up.

There was a roar like the end of the world, like the universe splitting in two. A twisting column of flame blasted out of the top of Vesuvius, rising straight up into the sky. As the *Medusa* fought its way out of the harbour, blazing balls of lava rained down, hitting the water all around them, and suddenly they were surrounded by a dense forest of steam. Pedro saw a bigger sailing ship about twenty metres away. It was impossible to say how many people were on board. Every inch of the deck was crowded. But as he watched, it was hit by one of the lava balls, exploding instantly into flames and sinking even as it burned. Two other boats had been trying to get out of the way and crashed into each other, their masts and sails becoming hopelessly entangled. More people, tiny figures, fell into the water. It was all madness. Everything was being destroyed.

But the *Medusa* had broken free, racing through the jet-black water with the fire reflected in the surface all around them. The wind had become very hot. It was burning them. Pedro felt warm water lapping at his face, splashing over the side. The boat was pitching and tossing. He was spread-eagled on the deck, unable to move.

Somebody screamed something in Italian.

Pedro looked up and saw a wave travelling towards them. It was like nothing he had ever seen before. The wave was the size of a ten-storey building. It was massive, hideous, unstoppable. They were steering right for it. There was no way around it. Pedro reached out. He found a rope and wound it round and round his right arm. He closed his eyes.

The *Medusa* was still making for the wave. Angelo was gripping the wheel, his face locked in an expression of total horror. And then the wave was right in front of them and they were climbing,

climbing, trying to make it over the top. But thousands of gallons of water were crashing down on them, blotting everything out. Pedro felt himself being battered down. It was as if the weight of the world had fallen on him. He couldn't see. He couldn't breathe. He was scooped up and swept away.

After that … nothing.

MATT

TWENTY-THREE

"How much you want for him?"

Matthew Freeman stood with his head bowed and his hands tied in front of him, waiting to be sold. He had a cracked lip and there was a thin trail of blood trickling under his chin. A moment before, he had said something without being spoken to – and this was his punishment. He wasn't alone on the platform. There were four other children, three boys and a girl, with him. They were all younger. The girl couldn't have been more than seven or eight and she was wearing a black dress covered in sequins, as if this were some sort of high school beauty parade. One of the boys had been beaten and starved. He was standing there, swaying on his feet with an empty expression in his eyes, and Matt wondered if he would even make it to the end of the sale before he collapsed.

Matt was the centre of attention. Most of the buyers had been drawn to him at once – a well-built fifteen-year-old boy with broad shoulders, close-cropped hair and intense blue eyes. His clothes and the colour of his skin marked him out as a foreigner, and Americans in particular were highly prized at slave markets. He guessed that nobody would be able to tell where he really came from. These people only spoke English with an accent that made every word sound ugly. Their native language was Portuguese. Nor did they really care. For the last fifteen minutes he had been prodded and poked. His shirt had been ripped open to show off the muscles on his shoulders and chest. His eyes, ears and throat had all been examined, and one of the buyers had even checked if he had head lice. He was healthy. That was all that mattered. It meant he was worth more.

Of course Matt was a world apart from the other poor kids who were being sold alongside him. He had only arrived in Brazil five weeks ago, while they had grown up here, sold as soon as their parents had run out of food and then sold again two or three times, always at a lower price. He shuddered to think what they might have been used for. Manual labour, domestic service … or worse. It was probably better not to know.

And now it was his turn.

Matt wasn't allowed to look up. If he so much as lifted his head, he would feel the crack of a cane across his shoulders. But he couldn't resist raising his eyes to see who might be about to buy him. The speaker – the man who had asked the price – was short, fat, dark-skinned with a black moustache and little ratty eyes. A *cafuzo*. Half African, half Brazilian. He was dressed in jeans and a striped shirt that stretched across his belly, and one glance told Matt that he wasn't in the market for himself. He was an agent. That was bad news. If the man had been a farmer or a log-worker or even a bandit, that would have given Matt a clue as to where he might end up. But as the man was representing someone else, it could be anywhere.

"The price is two hundred dollars."

"The boy not worth half that."

"When was the last time you saw a boy in this condition?"

"Where you find him?"

"That's my business. You buy him, maybe he'll tell you. But you're not having him for less than two hundred."

"A hundred and twenty."

The slave market was taking place in a village that looked more like a prison or a military compound. A white church stood at one end, with an ornate roof and a bell tower surmounted by a cross. Otherwise, all the buildings were identical: long, white-washed and low with red-tiled roofs, laid out as neatly as houses on a Monopoly board. They were arranged around a wide square of grass cut so short that it was as if the ground had been sprayed green, and it was here that the platform had been built. There were about a dozen buyers. The villagers were keeping their distance. Matt had glimpsed a man dressed in what looked like dirty white pyjamas, carrying two buckets on a rod over his shoulders and another pushing a wheelbarrow. But they didn't want to know. The village was surrounded by jungle. Not the lush and mysterious rainforest that Matt had once seen on TV programmes but a flat, dark green shrub land that seemed to stretch on for ever.

"A hundred and fifty. That my last offer."

"A hundred and eighty."

"One seven five."

The two men shook hands.

Matt watched as a roll of American dollars was unwrapped and a number of notes peeled off. He knew that US currency was used almost everywhere, while the local money – the *real* – was almost worthless. To one side of him, the malnourished boy let out a moan and fainted. His owner swore and lashed out at him and the buyers laughed. The boy's price would have just been halved and it would have been barely in double figures to begin with.

For his part, Matt had a new owner. There was a rope around his neck and – just as if he were a dog – he saw it being passed from the seller to the buyer. Then he was jerked forward, off the platform and down onto the grass. Just for a moment he found himself right next to the man who had sold him.

Lohan, the Triad member who had protected Scarlett when she was in Hong Kong, the son of the criminal boss who called himself the Master of the Mountain, the man who had somehow got tangled up with Matt when they had escaped from the Tai Shan Temple, stood in front of him.

Lohan shrugged. "I'm sorry, Matt," he said. "But I've got to survive."

Matt swore at him.

The *cafuzo* jerked on the rope so that Matt's head snapped round and he was led away. Behind him, Lohan counted his money and the sale went on.

There was a truck with a driver waiting at the edge of the village. Matt's new owner used one end of the rope to lash him across the shoulders and he climbed into the back. There was another boy of about his own age already sitting there, chained to the floor with a shackle around his ankle. The boy was Brazilian, with curly hair and a pockmarked face, dressed in jeans and a T-shirt that advertised Skol beer. Matt wondered vaguely if it still existed. He squatted down as his ankle was also fastened to the floor. Nobody had spoken to him but that was quite normal. He was property – nothing more. He wanted to ask for water. The afternoon was hot, the air heavy and still, and he could feel the sweat trickling under his clothes. He would have given anything for a bath or a shower but there was no point in asking. If he was going to be made to work in a kitchen or wait at tables, they would dress him and make him presentable. If he had been bought for outside labour, they would keep him as he was. He would find out soon enough.

"What's your name?" he whispered to the other boy.

The boy spat but otherwise gave no answer.

The man climbed into the front of the truck and about a minute later they set off, rattling through the village, hooting frantically at anyone who got in the way. They drove for about an hour over rough, pitted roads that threw Matt around in the back and soon took all the skin off his ankle. He had no view. The man had drawn a tarpaulin across the back, and the front – with the driver's and passenger seat – was boarded off. When they turned corners, Matt and the Brazilian boy were thrown against each other or sent sprawling across the rough floor of the cabin. Matt's hands were still tied and there was nothing he could do but endure the long journey in silence. The worst of it was that he had no idea where he was going or what might be waiting for him when he got there. The other boy was silent and surly and didn't seem to care.

At last they slowed down and drew to a halt. Matt heard shouting. Then they rumbled forward a few more metres and stopped again. The engine was turned off. Several moments passed before the back of the tarpaulin was thrown open and green sunlight, the last rays of the day reflected by the surrounding forest, flooded in.

The first thing Matt saw was men with machine guns – not in military uniform but jeans and black shirts, some of them bearded, some with baseball caps. He was in a sort of encampment, which at first reminded him of a monastery as he was in a courtyard between two covered passageways, like cloisters, built of bricks with rooms beyond. A wooden stockade surrounded the place, and although they were in the middle of the jungle, there had to be electricity here as he saw arc lamps, CCTV cameras and a radio mast. The driver came round and unfastened his shackle, and as he climbed down from the truck Matt saw a large wooden house that had shutters and a veranda and – of all things – a children's play area with a slide and swings. Somebody rich lived here and they were well protected. Matt had already seen more than a dozen armed guards.

The *cafuzo*, the man who had bought him, appeared with a knife and roughly cut through the cords that had tied his hands. Matt rubbed his wrists together, teasing the circulation back. He noticed some of the men looking at him and he didn't like what he saw in their eyes. They knew something he didn't, and whatever it was, he wasn't going to enjoy it. He glanced to one side. One part of the compound had been given over to their work being done here. There were steel cylinders and plastic buckets piled high. Beyond, behind glass doors, men in white T-shirts leant over long tables, surrounded by laboratory equipment: glass cylinders, bunsen burners, different tubs of chemicals.

Drugs.

Matt knew at once where he was. The wooden house was the home of one of the many drug lords who were now, as they had always been, the wealthiest and most powerful men in Brazil – and this was where his supply line began. Whoever lived here had his own private army and his own scientists producing pure cocaine, which would spread all over South America and north to the United States. The only question was – how were he and the other boy supposed to fit into all this? Matt had a nasty feeling that they hadn't been brought here to help keep the compound clean.

The two of them stood by the truck, stretching their legs, avoiding the eyes of the men who were staring at them, weighing them up. The evening was already closing in. It was uncomfortably hot and airless. Matt heard the whine of a mosquito close to his ear and resisted the temptation to try and slap it. He was determined not to show that he was afraid, but there was no escaping the thoughts that whispered constantly in his mind. *You are alone. You are thousands of miles away from home. Nobody knows you are here. These people can kill you quickly or slowly and nobody will ever find out. Nobody will care. One hundred and seventy-five dollars – that is all you are worth.*

A man appeared from one of the laboratories – a doctor. At least, he was dressed like one, wearing a grubby white coat with a stethoscope around his neck. He was bald, with glasses and a shaving rash. He went over to the Brazilian boy first and examined his eyes, lifting the brows with his thumb, then pulling back his lips to look at his teeth. At first the boy resisted and the doctor slapped him on the side of the head and muttered something in Portuguese. After that he stood still as the doctor listened to his heart and lungs using the stethoscope. At least Matt was prepared when it was his turn. He tried not to show any expression, even though the doctor's breath stank of rum.

Both examinations had taken no more than a couple of minutes. At the end of them, the doctor stepped back, rubbing his hand against his chin. He was obviously trying to make up his mind. Then, abruptly, his hand shot forward, pointing at the curly-haired boy, and he turned and walked back the way he had come. At the same time, Matt's travelling companion went mad. He must have known something that Matt didn't because he ran forward, screaming, and would have made it all the way to the perimeter fence if two guards hadn't caught up with him and clubbed him down. Even then he writhed and kicked out, shouting and sobbing all the while. Two more guards caught hold of his feet. Then they dragged him across the central yard, his head trailing in the dust, and disappeared into one of the laboratories.

"*Rapidamente – porco!*"

With his eyes on the other boy, Matt didn't see the guard shouting at him and a moment later he felt his legs fold underneath him as he was struck down from behind. He collapsed into the dust

"*Le vantai!*"

Matt got to his feet as quickly as he could, knowing he would be hurt more if he hesitated. The guard – a small, bearded man who looked like a teacher with glasses and thinning hair – gestured in the direction of a building on the other side of the compound. As he went, Matt caught sight of a square, brick shed with an engine running inside. This was surely the main generator. He looked at it carefully, imprinting an image of it on his mind. He would need it later.

The guard took him to a room that might have once been a store cupboard but that was going to be used as a cell. There was a mattress on the floor but nothing else. However, as Matt was led in, the guard handed him a plastic bottle – a litre of water – filtered from the look of it. That told him two things. They wanted him alive and hydrated, in reasonable health. It wasn't good news. Matt already had a good idea what they were needed for ... he and the Brazilian boy. The appearance of the doctor and, now, the drinking water confirmed it.

He stretched out on the mattress as the door slammed shut. He heard the rattle of a chain being drawn on the other side. There was no window in the room and no light. Matt had to force himself to breathe slowly, not to panic in the intense dark. He had to remind himself that, in a way, he had chosen to be here. And he didn't intend to stay long. He lay back with his eyes closed.

Five weeks had passed since he and Lohan had found themselves in the Brazilian city of Belém. The door from Hong Kong had led them to a huge church – the Basílica de Nossa Senhora de Nazaré – although it had long been abandoned to the floods, the filthy Amazon water that had swallowed up much of the city, spreading through the streets and under doorways, lapping through the once magnificent nave. The church itself was fairly modern but there had always been a holy building in the same place. An image of the Virgin Mary was said to have appeared there three hundred years before. Nobody had ever taken much notice of the little door, with its five-pointed star, that was concealed behind the altar.

Belém was almost completely abandoned, the few thousand people who remained either killing each other or letting disease and starvation do it for them. Matt and Lohan had quickly realized that they had been away for many years and had come back to a world that was very different from the one they had left. Worse still, the door in the church no longer worked. They were stuck here.

Matt was shocked to find himself separated from Richard. It had seemed to him that they had been together for so long and had faced so much danger together that they would never be apart. At the same time, he blamed himself for what had happened and the thought of it was still bitter in his mind. He hadn't been thinking straight in those last moments at the Tai Shan Temple. If he had shouted out a single word, a destination, they would have all arrived there together. It could have been London, Cuzco, Lake Tahoe – anywhere. Instead, he had allowed them to pile in mindlessly and as a result they had ended up in different corners of the world.

And yet of all the travelling companions he could have chosen, he had considered Lohan the best equipped. Lohan had spent his entire life working inside one of Asia's most dangerous criminal organizations. He spoke five languages, including Portuguese. When the two of them had been attacked by a street gang on the outskirts of Belém, just a few days after they had arrived, Lohan had responded with a speed and ruthlessness that had astonished Matt, leaving one man dead and two more in need of intensive care. Lohan had also refused to allow Matt to blame himself for what had happened after the escape from the temple.

"You had to get us out of there," he said. "And you did. There was no time to sit down and look at a map, so why waste your energy going over it? It would have made no difference anyway. If we had all gone to one place, the Old Ones might have been waiting and we would have all been captured. Maybe it's better this way. At least no one knows where we are."

They had gone south together with only two aims: they had to avoid the Old Ones, and they had to survive. They had no money and were forced to steal food – again, Lohan was completely cold-blooded and efficient, and Matt soon saw that he would kill anyone who got in his way. Not that he was going to argue about it. There was no point, not with a man like this. As they had travelled, they had learnt that there was an airport still operating in Salvador and that it might be possible to buy a flight to another South American city or even to the United States. But Salvador was more than two thousand kilometres away. And a flight would cost thousands of dollars they didn't have.

The slave markets were the only fast way to make money in Brazil. When people became desperate, they sold their children. If they were really desperate, they sold themselves. After five weeks on the road, when they had run out of food and knew that they could go no further, Lohan had sold Matt. It was as simple as that. There had been no other way.

Matt drank the water. It was warm and tasted of chlorine, meaning that it had probably been purified just as he had expected. He wondered about the other boy and wished he could help him but knew there was nothing he could do until later in the night. Eventually he dozed off, not so much sleeping as floating on the very surface of sleep. He wanted to go back to the dream-world – but not tonight. He had enough to do already and it had been so long since he had seen Pedro, Scarlett, Jamie or Scott that he wasn't sure what he would say to them if they met. When he opened his eyes again, he guessed that three or four hours must have passed. It was enough. It was time to make his move.

There was a chain on the other side of the door. Matt hadn't seen it but he had heard the rattle as it was drawn through the bolts, somewhere above the handle. Still lying on the mattress, he visualised the bolts, the screws connecting them to the wood. He had the picture in his mind. He held it there, then sent out an instruction. How else could he describe it? A thought wave? A guided missile? He simply ordered the metal to break and a moment later he heard it do just that, cracking open as if someone had used a bolt cutter.

His power had increased ever since he had arrived in South America. As the days passed, he found that he could use his mind as effortlessly as he had once used his fists. He could move objects – even if they were several times heavier than himself. If he had wanted to, he could have stalled the vehicle that had brought him here, by simply telling the engine to tear itself apart. Maybe that would have been the easier way, but he had been interested to see where it would take him. And he was going to need the truck later on.

The door of the room swung open. Matt saw harsh electric light, leaking into the passageway from the arc lamps outside. He needed darkness. He thought about the generator building, imagined the mechanism inside, the turning cylinders, the wires. Once again, he pushed. The lights died instantly. The darkness was followed, seconds later, by the sound of shouting.

Matt stood up and finished his water. He felt good. He was in control.

It was time to go.

TWENTY-FOUR

There was no moon, no stars. The compound was utterly black. As Matt left the storage room where he had been kept, he heard voices – men shouting at each other in Portuguese – and saw the beams of torches leaping through the darkness. He took his time. Everyone would be concentrating on the generator and the loss of power. They wouldn't have any time for him and provided he made his way carefully, he would be able to slip out before anyone realized he had gone.

The stockade was open. There was no need for locked gates when you were in the jungle, far from anywhere. And the drug lord had enough protection to hold back an army. Matt could have walked out, there and then – but as much as it exasperated him, he couldn't do it. There had been the other boy in the truck with him. Matt hadn't even learnt his name but somehow he still felt responsible for him. Right now, Matt could have been in his place. It was just his bad luck that the doctor had chosen him first, as casually as if he had flipped a coin. He had to know what they were doing to the boy and, if possible, prevent it. If it wasn't already too late, they could escape together.

He had to cross the compound, to the arches on the other side. This was where he had seen the laboratories and it was to somewhere here that they had taken the boy. Matt didn't dare walk straight across. There were too many men coming from too many directions, converging on the generator. Instead, he continued around the very edge, keeping close to the covered passageways, then hurried across the front of the house, passing the swings and the slide. He heard someone from inside calling out, a man's voice, deep and gruff. Was it the drug lord, waking from his sleep, wondering what was going on? A guard ran past, only a few metres away, but didn't see him. In the distance Matt heard a dog barking and that made him stop and turn round anxiously. Dogs wouldn't be tricked by the darkness. They would find him by smell. If the drug lord kept guard dogs anywhere near the house, he might be in trouble after all.

He still hadn't been seen so he quickened his pace, following the arches opposite where he had been. About half a dozen torches had converged on the generator building, the beams criss-crossing in the darkness, and he caught glimpses of men with unshaven faces and crumpled clothes, peering in to see what had happened. Matt knew that they would be confronted by cogs and pistons that had inexplicably bent themselves out of shape, cables that had been torn in half – and unless they had a back-up system, the only light they were going to see out here would come from the rising sun.

But as he continued on his way, he saw that one room was illuminated. There was a soft yellow glow coming from behind the glass windows ... either candles or an oil lamp. Matt crept forward, his feet making no sound on the tiled walkway. He reached the window and looked in.

From the day that he had been arrested by the police and sent to be fostered in North Yorkshire, Matt had seen many horrors. The last minutes that he had spent at Raven's Gate, his first encounter with the King of the Old Ones, had been enough for a lifetime. But he knew that he would never forget what he saw on the other side of the window. He was almost sick. It was hard to believe that any human being could be so monstrous, so cruel.

The drug lord had been buying boys to act as drug mules, to carry drugs inside them from country to country, crossing borders without being suspected or stopped. Matt knew that drug mules had flown into London and other major cities years before his adventures had begun. But the drug lord had taken things one step further. The Brazilian boy was lying on an operating table with a doctor and two male nurses leaning over him, their gloved hands bright with blood. His operation had been interrupted by the sudden loss of light.

He had been cut open and his body used to provide a hiding place for many packets of white powder. The plastic bags were packed into the cavities beneath his ribs and around his stomach. Anything that wasn't vital had been removed to make room for more. Right now the boy was a glistening mess of blood and plastic, but Matt knew that he would be sewn up again and that he would live. He would make the journey to wherever the drugs were being sent and then he would be operated on again and the bags removed. How many times would he manage it before he died?

And he had been next. If the doctor had decided otherwise, it would be him lying there, unconscious and anaesthetized. Matt had to force back the fury he was feeling. If he released it, he would kill them all … the doctor, the assistants and the boy too. Perhaps he would be better off dead. But that wasn't for Matt to decide. All he knew was that there was nothing he could do. He would have to leave him behind.

"Quem são você?"

The words came rasping out of the darkness. Matt turned, angry with himself, and saw a guard looming over him, inches away. He had been so fixed on the horror on the other side of the glass, he hadn't heard him coming and now it was too late.

The man was about to raise the alarm and even with his powers, Matt doubted that he could get past the dogs, the drug lord, the men with machine guns. Why had he even concerned himself with a boy he had barely met? His job – his one responsibility – was to get out of here in one piece.

The man opened his mouth to call out, then stared at Matt, his eyes widening, reflecting the light from the operating theatre. He pitched forward, a knife jutting out of his back. It had been thrown in almost total darkness, twisting twice in the air before it had found its target.

Lohan ran forward on soundless feet. "Matt?" he whispered.

"Yes..."

"I thought I saw you round the other side. What are you doing here?"

"I was just checking up on someone."

Lohan followed Matt's eyes back through the glass and saw what was happening. He showed no emotion at all and Matt realized that he had smuggled drugs all over Asia and Europe in his time with the Triads. He had probably used children himself. He might even have cut them up if it suited his plans. Lohan was eight years older than Matt, a few inches taller, slim and strangely detached. It was only the thin scar that ran diagonally across his lips that stood out, a reminder of his criminal past. And that was what he was. A criminal. The man he had just killed meant nothing to him. There had almost certainly been dozens of others.

"These people are bastards." Lohan muttered the words matter-of-factly. "Do you want to do anything about it?"

"Yes. But we should leave."

"I agree. I have a jeep outside. I've seen to the rest of their vehicles. Let's go."

The two of them set off together, leaving the dead guard and the dull glow of the operating theatre behind them. Most of the guards were still grouped around the generator and nobody stopped them as they approached a cluster of vehicles parked near the main entrance. The clouds had parted, allowing a little moonlight to steal through. Matt was grateful for it. They would need it as they navigated their way back through the jungle. Lohan pointed at a jeep and Matt hurried forward, almost tripping over a pair of legs stretched out on the ground beside it. They belonged to another guard, who was lying there with a thin strip of cord around his neck. After spending so long with Richard, Matt still found it hard to get used to a companion who killed people with such ease.

They climbed into the jeep, quietly closing the doors behind them. Lohan started the engine and at once another guard appeared, blocking the way ahead of them, already swinging his machine gun around. Lohan stamped on the accelerator. The jeep leapt forward and the man dived out of the way. Somebody shouted. But then they were through the gate and off down the track. Matt remembered what Lohan had said. Somehow, without being seen, he had managed to disable all the other cars. They weren't going to be followed.

They drove slowly, the stunted trees and bushes sweeping past on both sides. Lohan pointed in the back. "I got you some bread, cheese and water," he said.

"Thank you." Matt reached behind him. He hadn't eaten for twenty hours and his stomach was growling.

"It was expensive. It's a shame we couldn't get more for you at the market. Your value is going down."

"Maybe we should sell you next time," Matt suggested.

It had been Lohan's idea. The two them were going to need money if they had any chance of travelling across Brazil and there was only one easy way to earn it. Lohan had so far sold Matt three times in three different villages, each time pocketing almost two hundred dollars. Then he had come after him and rescued him. The first two times it had been easy. Matt had been chosen for manual labour on farms with hardly any security. But this latest adventure had reminded them both that there were far more unpleasant things happening in Brazil, worse even than human slavery. They might have six hundred dollars in their pockets but the risks were getting too great.

"How did you get here?" Matt asked, chewing a piece of bread.

"I travelled with you. On the top of the truck."

So Lohan had travelled on the roof! Matt hadn't heard him climb or jump down. But he wasn't surprised. Lohan could walk into a crowded room in broad daylight without anyone noticing. It was just one of the skills he had been taught.

"How much fuel do we have?"

"The jeep's full and we've got another hundred litres in tanks. The good news is they carried you south when they took you to Fernandinho."

"Who's Fernandinho?"

"The drug lord who just bought you. They call him Fat Freddy – but not to his face. Anyway, the compound is one hundred and sixty kilometres south of Laua." Laua was the name of the village where the slave market had taken place. "So if you still want to go to Salvador, we're on our way."

"Can you think of a better plan?"

"No. But six hundred dollars isn't going to be enough if we want to get tickets on a plane."

They drove for two hours in silence, following a road that must have been a major thoroughfare at one stage: the concrete was still in good repair and there were even painted lines down the middle. Lohan had brought maps and a compass with them. That was typical of him. No matter where they were, he had the ability to find anything they needed, disappearing for half an hour and then returning with food, medicine, supplies … whatever. Matt was careful not to ask too many questions. He had never met anyone who could be so cold-blooded about their own survival.

At last they pulled to one side, driving behind a clump of bushes where the jeep would be concealed. Lohan wasn't worried that anyone had followed them from the compound but if other drivers happened to pass, he didn't want to be a target. There were any number of people who would cut their throats to steal their transport.

It was about half past three, the night heavy and close. Matt had just about got used to the mosquitoes, but the darkness – the way the jungle stretched out with no seeming end – still unnerved him. Lohan drank some water and helped himself to what was left of the food while Matt climbed into the back and tried to make himself comfortable on the seat. He had spent many nights like this and knew he could sleep with the window open and wake up covered in bites or he could close the window, turning the back into a hot, airless oven – in which case he would barely sleep at all. It wasn't much of a choice.

"Did you ever use children?" Matt said. It was what he had been thinking earlier. Suddenly he wanted to know.

"Children?"

"To carry drugs."

Matt hadn't asked Lohan about his life in Hong Kong before the two of them had met. The more he learnt about the Triad leader, the more difficult it might be to travel with him. But he knew he wasn't going to sleep while the image of the Brazilian boy remained in his head. He looked over the front seat and saw Lohan's eyes reflected in the driver's mirror. They were dark and cruel, and Matt knew that they had seen more violence and death than he could begin to imagine.

"Yes." Lohan answered the question as if it were obvious, as if it were nothing to be ashamed of.

"Why?"

"Sometimes it was easier. Especially in airports. When the customs officers see a little boy clutching a teddy bear, they probably won't want to look inside the bear."

"Or inside the boy."

"We had people who swallowed drugs and carried them for us inside their stomachs. But they were paid. It was their choice. What you saw today – that we would never do."

"But you still smuggled drugs." Matt hadn't meant to throw out the accusation and regretted it immediately. But Lohan didn't seem to mind.

"It was part of our business, yes." The voice – reasonable, considered – floated out of the darkness. "Does it bother you, Matt?"

"Drugs have killed a lot of people."

"Cars have killed more. So have cigarettes and alcohol."

"But they're all legal."

"Who decides what is legal or not legal? Politicians! And do you think that politicians are always right, that they always know what is best? People all over the world wanted drugs and it was part of my work to supply them. I think this was reasonable. Supply and demand. It is at the very heart of capitalism. Unfortunately, a politician in some room decided to interfere and because of this I found myself operating outside the law. I was a criminal. I am not ashamed of this. To be honest with you, I would rather be a criminal than a politician. Certainly, I have done less harm."

"Why are you helping me? Why did you help Scarlett?"

"I had no choice. My father saw very quickly that the Old Ones were our enemies. They killed thousands of people in Hong Kong, threatening first our livelihoods and later our lives. I have never thought of myself as evil, Matt. I am in my own way a businessman. But what you saw tonight in that compound, that was evil. And you and I must fight it together."

"I have to find the others," Matt said. "I need to know why the doors have stopped working."

"I thought you were looking for your friends while you were asleep."

"I am. There's no sign of them. Maybe it's because we're all in different time zones now. We're never asleep at the same time. But I've had another idea. There's someone else I know."

"In your dreamworld?"

"Yes."

Lohan nodded. His eyes were still fixed on Matt. "We are in the middle of Brazil with a few litres of fuel, six hundred dollars and limited supplies of food. The Old Ones will be looking for you already, I expect. So I suggest you stop asking me foolish questions and close your eyes and sleep. Go back to the dreamworld, Matt. Find what you are looking for. Right now we need all the help we can get."

TWENTY-FIVE

Matt hadn't wanted to go back to the library. The truth was that it frightened him. It was like walking into a cemetery in the certain knowledge that he would find his name on one of the graves.

What was it doing there anyway?

Matt had been visiting the dreamworld just about all his life. As far as he was concerned, it was a grim, empty place that had been created as much to keep him prisoner as to help him. It was a world without colour. The sea, the sky and the dust that made up much of the land were all different shades of grey. Nothing grew there. Even the wind had no life to it. To begin with, he had been trapped on an island surrounded by waves that crashed onto the beach, warning him to keep back. But he had seen the other Gatekeepers – Pedro, Scarlett, Scott and Jamie – on the shore and eventually he had reached them. The dreamworld had brought them together and seemed to want to help them with strange warnings, signs and symbols of what would take place.

It had come as a shock to stumble upon a building – and one so large that it was actually the size of a city. The library must have been there for thousands of years, growing all the time, so that there were parts of it that looked ancient – massive stone towers and battlements – and parts of it that were positively futuristic, with titanium-clad walls bending like waves, solar panels, and triple-height windows. Every country and culture in the world had been drawn into its design so that when Matt had looked at it for the first time, it was as if a hundred famous buildings had somehow got jumbled up together, with the onion domes of the Kremlin, the pure white minarets of the Taj Mahal, the pillars of the Parthenon, the metalwork of the Eiffel Tower and even the clock face of Big Ben. They were all tied together by arches, staircases, bridges and passageways, like the dream of a mad architect.

Not only was there a library – there was a librarian. Matt had met him; a man with vaguely Arab looks, long grey hair, a hooked nose and the sort of eyes that might contain all the knowledge in the universe but did their best to keep it hidden. Was he even a man at all? The trouble with the dreamworld was that it was hard to tell what was real and what was not and certainly the Librarian looked as if he had dressed up for the part, with his loose-fitting jacket – pastel shades of mauve, orange and green – his baggy trousers and sandals instead of shoes. He hadn't been unfriendly but he spoke in riddles. He seemed to know Matt from the past. He knew all the Gatekeepers. But how? He had refused to say.

Why didn't Matt want to go back? Almost every night, while he had been in Brazil, he had returned to the dreamworld but had spent his time there searching for the others, retracing his footsteps all the way to the sea and the island where they had first met. He had persuaded himself that he would find them there again and had felt a crushing sense of disappointment to see the black rock jagged and empty, lashed by sea spray, abandoned. Part of him knew that this was all his fault. He had led them through the door in Hong Kong and he had lost them – not just in one world but in two.

The library was his only hope. He would find all the answers to his questions there – after all, that was what libraries were for. Where were the others? Why were the doors no longer working? What did he have to do to win the struggle against the Old

Ones ... especially when everything seemed so hopeless and, with a whole decade on their side, it seemed they had already won? All he had to do was ask. The Librarian had been helpful enough. Surrounded by thousands – millions – of books, he seemed to know everything about the past and the future. But Matt was certain that the information would come at a price. He had already been offered the chance to read his own future and had turned it down. Had that been another mistake?

He had looked for the others and he couldn't find them. Maybe he had been doing nothing more than putting off the inevitable. At the end of the day, he knew there was no real choice. He couldn't afford to waste any more time.

And so he made the decision and turned round. Retracing his steps back to the library was surprisingly easy. They were etched out in the dust, footprints like the ones left by the astronauts on the moon, winding all the way back to the horizon. He had been walking for days, or even weeks, but of course it took him only a few minutes to get back ... that was exactly the sort of time-trick that the dreamworld liked to play. Ahead of him, the ground rose up slightly – a sand dune but one that was grey not yellow. He might have covered a hundred kilometres or more but his legs weren't even tired as he reached the top and stood there, willing himself to continue down the other side.

The library was spread out in front of him, sprawling across the landscape in every direction. It was still impossible to believe that it was actually a single building as there were so many sections – annexes, vestibules, covered walkways and bridges added over the centuries as each part of it became too small to house the collection of books that it contained. Every human life that had ever been lived had been given its own volume, meaning that there had to be billions of them just to cover the world of the present day. Add thousands of years of history, whole populations growing up and dying, and you arrived at a figure with too many zeros to make sense.

Matt's own life was somewhere among them. He had held it in his own hands but he had refused to open it and read. He still didn't want to. Was that really so unreasonable? Would anyone?

He climbed down the sand dune. After a while, he felt smooth marble under his feet and realized that this was the same path that he had taken before. The main entrance, a spectacular arched doorway with stone carvings of plants and animals, loomed over him. The front wall soared upwards, blotting out the sky. If it had been constructed to make him feel tiny and insignificant, then it was working. Keeping his head down, forcing himself on, Matt walked into the entrance hall, taking in the great pillars and a vaulted ceiling. And there was the Librarian waiting for him – as if he had never left. He wasn't surprised. He wasn't particularly pleased. He was just there.

"Hello, Matt," he said.

"Hello."

The Librarian had never told Matt his name. Indeed, Matt had the impression that he didn't have one.

"I thought you'd come back eventually. How can I help you?"

"You know what I want. Why ask?"

"You sound tired. Would you like some tea?"

The Librarian had been sitting behind a desk, studying a page of a manuscript with a magnifying glass. Matt almost smiled. Had somebody been vandalizing the books? And what would have happened to the unfortunate person who had had a page torn out of his life? The Librarian put down his things and, gesturing at Matt to follow him, walked through an archway partly concealed behind an ornamental screen. There was a smaller, more welcoming room on the other side. Staff quarters? Two low sofas had been set facing each other with a table on a thick rug between them. A copper teapot, two glasses and a small bowl of dates had already been laid out. Again, the set-up seemed vaguely Arabian to Matt. It reminded him of the inside of a Bedouin tent.

He sat down and waited while the Librarian poured two glasses of tea, the liquid pale green and steaming hot.

"Please, help yourself..."

Matt picked up his glass, holding it between the very tips of his fingers so as not to burn himself. In the dreamworld, nothing had any colour. There was never any temperature or taste. But the tea was different. Matt could smell the fresh, aromatic scent of peppermint. He sipped the tea. It was delicious.

"I'm afraid things haven't been going well for you," the Librarian said.

"We've lost," Matt said. The words fell heavily from his lips but even as he spoke them he knew that they were true. "The whole world has changed. We jumped forward ten years and it was as if every warning we were ever given had suddenly come true. Global warming. Floods. Famine. Wars. It's all happened at once."

"The Old Ones have been busy."

"What can we do to stop them? Can we do anything? When we arrived in Belém, half the city was under water and there were dead bodies floating in the streets. There are slave markets! People are so desperate, they're selling their own kids. And we've heard things are almost as bad in America. Whole countries have been wiped out. It's like the end of the world. Even if we managed to beat the Old Ones, there's hardly anything left."

"And yet this happened before," the Librarian reminded him. "The world came very close to the edge when the Old Ones visited it the first time. There were very few survivors left. But thanks to you – the five of you – mankind had a second chance."

"Yes. And they blew it again. Like they always do."

"There's still hope."

"I'm not so sure." Matt set his glass down. He had finished his tea and felt better for it. The Librarian leant forward and poured some more. "The five of us are scattered," he went on. "That was my fault. We were together in Hong Kong and that should have been the end of it, but then everything went wrong and now we're right back where we started. I don't know who made me the leader of the Five but they can't have known what they were doing. When I wake up, I'm going to find myself back in the middle of Brazil! What use is that? There are no phones any more. No TV. All the doors are locked. How am I ever going to reach the others?"

"I never remember you being so defeatist," the Librarian remarked.

"I've had enough of it," Matt said. He was thinking of the Brazilian boy. He suddenly saw the open wound in his stomach, the plastic bags sticky with blood. He hadn't been able to save him. He hadn't even learnt his name. "I never asked for any of this. Why does it have to be me?"

"You can give it up if you want to. That choice is still open to you."

The Librarian sounded calm and friendly. Yet Matt still felt the accusation in his voice. He knew that he was being judged, and right now, when it mattered most, he was failing. He forced himself to remember why he had come here. "Why are the doors locked?" he asked.

"I can tell you that," the Librarian replied. "It's actually very simple. The twenty-five doors that carry you and your friends across the world are all interconnected. This means you can go from anywhere to anywhere at any time. However, if you lock one of them, you lock all of them. And that's exactly what the King of the Old Ones has done. He's locked the twenty-fifth door."

"Where is it?"

"That's the problem. It's in Antarctica ... in a place called Oblivion. That is where Chaos has built his fortress and the door is somewhere inside. It's also where he is gathering his armies. There's absolutely no doubt that he wants another battle, a final confrontation with you to make up for the last time when you beat him. He also wants revenge for what you did to him in the Nazca Desert. You caused him pain and that is unthinkable ... unforgivable. And so he has put down this challenge. Finding you is not so easy. So he's waiting for you to come to him instead."

"In Antarctica!" The very thought of it made Matt's head spin. It was so far away, a totally hostile environment. How was he even supposed to get there? "If I found this door, could I unlock it?" he asked.

The Librarian shook his head. "Not really," he replied. "Well, you could. But it would kill you. There's an electric charge running through the lock ... except it isn't really electricity. You could say it's a sort of cosmic force, but the end result would be the same. Even if you managed to break it open, you would die. And to be honest with you, I'm not sure how you'd get into the ice fortress to begin with. The King of the Old Ones has all his forces around him. Shape-changers, fly-soldiers, fire-riders..."

"But there has to be a way! You just sit there as if all this doesn't mean anything to you. Why won't you tell me what I want to know? Why can't you help?" The Librarian said nothing. Matt took a grip of himself. Getting angry wasn't going to do any good. "Even if I get to this fortress, what am I supposed to do?" he went on. "You say he's got a whole army there. There are just five of us! And he's waiting for us. Everything is on his side..."

"I am not the one who creates the stories," the Librarian said. "I just look after them. And in this particular story, Matt, I'm not the hero. You are."

Matt nodded. He had known all along that it would come to

this. As far as he could see, there was no other way. "All right," he said. "The last time I was here, you showed me the book of my life. You said it contained everything I had ever done and everything I would do. You even said it would tell me how I die."

The Librarian nodded slowly.

"So all the answers I'm looking for must be in there – right? If I do beat the Old Ones, it will tell me *how* I beat them. And if I make any more mistakes, like I did in Hong Kong, they'll be in there too."

"Yes."

"When I was here before, you said I could read it. But I didn't want to. There were things in it I didn't want to know. There still are – but now I see I have no choice. So is the offer still on?"

"Of course you can read it, Matt. It's your life."

"Then I want to read it now. Let's go..."

The Librarian looked neither happy nor sad. It was as if he had been expecting the request and was here simply to oblige. He stood up and Matt followed him back into the entrance hall and over to a simple wooden door near the desk where the Librarian had been working. Matt knew that it could lead to any room in the library city. It worked the same way as the twenty-five doors in his own world and would take them wherever they needed to go. The Librarian went through first, with Matt close behind, and they came out in a wide, modern space that might have been built just a few years ago. Matt understood why. He had been born at the very end of the twentieth century and so the architecture – plate-glass windows, metal walkways and platforms – corresponded to that time. If he had wanted to read the life of Julius Caesar, he would probably have been taken to a Roman temple.

Matt had never seen so many books. They were stacked in mile-long rows that dwindled in the distance until they finally became a blur. The shelves started at floor level and rose all the way to the ceiling, with spiral staircases connecting them and narrow metal walkways and handrails stretching from one end to the other. Some strange artificial light filtered through the room. It couldn't have been coming in from outside – with the roofs and the spires of the other sections closing in, everything was dark – but there was no sign of any electric lamp. It was as if the room was somehow trapped in perpetual daylight. Matt climbed up after the Librarian, vaguely remembering his last visit. But with so many books, and all of them more or less identical, he wouldn't have known where to start.

The Librarian went six levels up, then turned left, trailing his finger along the spines. Finally, he stopped. "This is what you want," he said, picking out a thin grey volume. He handed it to Matt.

Matt weighed it in his hands. His first thought was how light it was, how little his life added up to. He thumbed to the back page and for a crazy moment he felt like he was back at school, being given a novel to read in English class. He had never found books easy and it had always been the first thing he had done … look to see how much he would have to struggle through.

His life lasted one hundred and fifty pages.

He knew that the book would tell him everything he wanted to know, everything he had ever done, everything he would be. He *was* the book – and he could feel his heart thumping. His mouth had gone dry. The very thought of opening it, of starting at the beginning, filled him with a sense of unease. But try as he might, he could think of no other option.

"Is there somewhere I can go?" he asked.

"There's a table downstairs," the Librarian said.

The table suited the room. It was large and industrial, with a single plastic chair waiting for him.

"I won't be far away," the Librarian said. "Just call as soon as you've finished and I'll be right back."

He walked away.

Matt placed the book on the table in front of him. The cover was completely plain, covered in grey fabric. There was no author listed, no title, no illustration. If he hadn't known better, he would have said it was a textbook; maybe a study of something that nobody was very interested in, the sort of book that's left at the back of the shelf and is never read. He tried to get his head around what was about to happen. The book would describe his life. Presumably, he would come to a chapter where he would find himself here, in the library, reading. And then the book would tell him what he did next.

He would know. So did that mean that he could do something different? Could he change his own future? Suppose the book told him he was shot by an arrow and killed leaving the library, then why couldn't he just stay where he was, or go out by another door? But then again, if he changed his future, the book would be wrong ... and that wasn't possible, was it? If it was in the book, it must have happened. Who had written the bloody thing anyway? Matt had asked the Librarian the last time he was here but the Librarian had refused to say.

It didn't matter. Matt wasn't here to change anything. He was here to find out what he was supposed to do. The answer was in front of him. He opened the book and began to read.

Six hours later, a lifetime later, he called the Librarian.

The man appeared almost at once. Matt was still sitting at the table. His whole body was rigid and there was no colour in his face. He looked ill. His hands, curled into fists, were stretched out in front of him. The book, closed and with the cover facing down, was on the table between them.

"You read it," the Librarian said.

"Yes. I read it." Matt looked up accusingly. "You knew what was in it."

"No."

"You never read it?"

"No."

"Why did you let me read it?" Matt asked. His voice was little more than a whisper.

"I'm afraid it's not my job to prevent you," the Librarian said. "I'm sorry. Is it very bad?"

"I know how I'm going to die!" Matt heard himself speak the words. It was as if they came from someone else. He thought about the last ten pages of what he had just read. The last ten pages. One hundred and forty to one hundred and fifty. There was going to be no page one hundred and fifty-one. Not for him. "I've read what I'm meant to do. I've read what happens. And it's horrible." He pointed at the book. His hand was trembling. "Nobody could be expected to go through that. I mean, nobody would do it if they knew how it was going to be."

The Librarian shrugged. "You want to save the world," he said. "I suppose that always comes at a price."

"It's too much. The price is too high. I won't do it. I can't."

There was a long silence. Matt sat there, in shock, his chest rising and falling. Eventually he wiped his face with the back of his hand and turned again to the Librarian. His eyes were pierced with anger. "Just because it's written this way, I don't have to do it," he said. "I still have a choice. I can walk away. I don't have to be part of this. Maybe there's another way."

The Librarian said nothing.

"I thought you were on my side. I should never have come here."

"Leave the book on the table," the Librarian said. "I'll return it later. Let's go back to the entrance hall. Maybe I can get you something else to drink."

"I don't want anything more from you."

"Whatever you say, Matt. I understand why you're angry but I would remind you that this was your idea. I had nothing to do with it."

They left together, taking the door back the way they had come. Matt didn't know how long he had been in the library. Normally it would have taken him several days to read a book.

Not this book.

He wondered how long he had been sleeping in the Brazilian jungle while he was here. And yet he wouldn't have been surprised to wake up and find that only minutes had passed. Different world, different times. None of it made any sense.

"I want to see the others," Matt said. "Do you know where they are?"

"The library has a bell," the Librarian said. "If you ring it, they'll hear it and they'll come."

"I know," Matt said. "I read it in the book."

They were back in the entrance hall. The Librarian was standing in front of him, his hands folded. As ever, he was unperturbed. "Is that what you'd like me to do?" he asked.

"It doesn't matter whether I'd like it or not. It's what happens. You leave me here. You climb up the tower and you ring the bell. The others arrive. We meet outside. And as for you and me, we never see each other again."

"Then I'll go."

"Yes. Go."

"Matt… I'm sorry."

"Just do it. Please."

The Librarian turned and walked back through the door they had taken, but of course it could now open somewhere completely different. Matt sat where he was, staring ahead of him, trying to block out the thoughts that were running through his head.

Pain. Humiliation. Death.

Eventually he heard the tolling of a bell. The same sound would be heard all over the dreamworld and the others would come. Jamie would be the first, then Scarlett and Pedro. And finally Scott. Matt knew all about Scott.

The bell rang out.

Matt waited.

When the bell fell silent and the Librarian came back through the door, Matt had already gone.

The five of them met at the top of the hill, where Matt had first seen the library.

Jamie was the first to arrive and, despite everything, Matt was glad to see him. Jamie was always positive, always upbeat, and the two of them had struck up a friendship when they had travelled to London. Matt sometimes thought that if the five Gatekeepers had a leader, it should have been Jamie, not him. After all, Jamie had been at Scathack Hill. He had taken part in the first battle long ago, when the Old Ones had been defeated. He had even helped to construct the first gate.

They embraced warmly.

"I thought I was never going to see you again," Jamie said. He looked past Matt at the vast construction. "What is this place?"

"It's a library."

"Scar told me about the library when I travelled back in time. And there's supposed to be some sort of woman who lives here too."

"I haven't seen her." Matt smiled, grateful for this moment. "Where are you, Jamie?" he asked. "In the real world?"

He knew the answer. He knew all the answers. But if he stopped talking, he thought he might break down. He had to hold it together for all their sakes.

"I'm back in England. I was in a village but it was attacked and now I'm on a canal boat heading for London. There's that church you told me about. St Meredith's. I reckoned if I could find the door, I could somehow get to join you."

"You know that London has been destroyed."

"London and pretty much the whole world, from what I can gather. Nothing is the same any more. Somehow I managed to lose ten years."

"We all lost ten years. If we'd just spent a few more seconds in Hong Kong..."

"It wasn't your fault, Matt. You had to get us out of there and you did. It's just bad luck we ended up all split apart..."

"Matt! Jamie!"

Scarlett had appeared, quickly climbing the hill towards them, with Pedro just behind her. She was dressed in exactly the same clothes she had been wearing when she had entered the Tai Shan Temple, but Matt could see that she had been hurt. She was thinner and she had a slightly pinched look in her eyes; the memory of recent pain. Pedro too was different. Although he did his best to smile, and he was evidently glad to see Matt again, he was hiding something and he couldn't disguise it. One of his hands was wrapped in a bandage.

His finger was broken. Matt knew about that too.

Matt went over to them.

Scarlett kissed him on the side of his cheek. At that moment she was close to him and looked deep into his eyes. She pulled away. "What is it, Matt?" she asked. "What's happened?"

"Nothing," Matt lied. He had already decided not to tell any of them about the book. "I'm really glad to see you."

"I've really missed you."

It helped to keep talking. Say anything. Ask questions.

"Where are you?"

"I'm in Egypt, on the way to Dubai. I'm with your friend,

Richard. He's going to be so relieved that I've seen you. He asks me about the dreamworld every morning. What do you want me to say to him?"

"Just tell him I'm glad he's OK. And say I'm glad he's got you to look after him."

"Actually, I think it's the other way round."

"Scott!" Jamie had seen his brother walking towards them and ran forward to greet him.

But even as Scott appeared at the bottom of the hill, Matt could see that he was lingering. He had probably thought twice before responding to the sound of the bell and had only come because he had to, because if he wasn't there, Pedro would tell them what had happened. He was still reluctant to join the group. Matt glanced at Pedro and saw him turn away, deliberately avoiding having to look Scott in the eye. Matt tried to force what he had read out of his thoughts. He wasn't the only one with problems. This adventure was going to hurt them all.

Pedro was his friend. Without him, Matt would never have survived Peru. He rested a hand briefly on his shoulder. "Hello, Pedro."

"I am happy to see you, Matteo."

"I'm glad to see you too." He went on quickly, keeping his voice low. "Don't worry about Scott. I know what's happened and it's going to be all right. Don't say anything to the others."

"But Scott—"

"I know. But everything's happening the way it's meant to. What matters is that we're together again. The Five. It's all going to work out."

They talked for a few more minutes. Scarlett was amazed to learn that Lohan was now with Matt. She quickly described the civil war in Egypt and the death of Tarik, killed by his own bomb. She still couldn't believe what Richard had done.

"He only did it because there was no other choice," Matt said. "That's the way he is. He says he doesn't want to be part of this but he'll do anything to protect you."

Then Jamie described his time in the village in England, his escape on the canal boat. "I guess I'm still there right now," he said. "With Holly and this guy – the Traveller. It'll take us about a week to get to London and we're just going to have to hope that St Meredith's is still there."

They were all so glad to see each other that they didn't notice that Scott hadn't bothered to tell anything of his story. He was almost silent, making sure he kept his distance from Pedro. They hadn't spoken a word to each other.

"I was going north," Pedro said. He was choosing his words carefully. Scott was listening and Pedro was concerned. He might repeat everything he heard here to Jonas Mortlake. He wondered why Matt had stopped him from warning the others. "There was a volcano eruption … in Naples. I still don't know what happened. I was on a boat and then I was here."

And that was what mattered most. They were finally together … even if these were only the dream versions of themselves. From now on, it would matter less that they were thousands of miles apart in the real world. All they had to do was fall asleep at the same time. They would meet each other again.

"We ought to get on with it," Matt said. "Lohan is going to wake me up at any moment and we have a long drive ahead of us through the jungle in Brazil. What's important is that the five of us know what we're doing and how this is going to work out. Let me tell you straight off that it's not going to be easy…"

Not easy. Not easy at all.

"You probably guessed that much already. The Old Ones have stolen ten years from us and somehow they've stretched those years and made them much longer. The whole world has changed. But we're still here – the Five – and we can still win. We were born for this time and we have to hold onto that, no matter what happens now or in the future. I always thought this sort of thing was meant to be fun … becoming a hero and saving the world. But it's not going to be fun. Remember that. Maybe not all of us are going to live. But we don't have any choice except to go on because that's how it has been written."

Written.

"We need to get to Antarctica, to a place called Oblivion. Chaos is there, surrounded by his armies, in a fortress built out of ice and stone. He's waiting for us and that's where we have to go."

"But why?" Scarlett said. "That doesn't make any sense, Matt. All we have to do is meet. Isn't that it? So we should go as far away from him as possible."

"It has to be Oblivion, Scarlett. There are things you don't know, things I can't tell you."

Alone among the Five, Pedro understood what he meant. Scott had left Naples with Jonas Mortlake and presumably he was now inside the fortress. That was why the other four had to travel there. It was the only place in the world where they could be together.

"And there are people there who need our help," Matt went on quickly, before Scarlett could argue. "Word is leaking out. Somehow people have found out that there's going to be a last battle and that it's going to be fought in Antarctica. They're already beginning to move south. They call themselves the World Army. But they don't have any real understanding of what they're up against. A lot of them are going to die for no reason – but without us, it'll be much, much worse. Trust me, Scarlett. You're needed."

"But I told you. I'm in the middle of the desert. In Egypt."

"There are still planes flying. You can persuade someone to take you."

"What about the doors?" Jamie asked. "If they're not working any more..."

"The doors will open again eventually. Somehow, you have to make it to St Meredith's in London. You can trust the man who calls himself the Traveller. He'll look after you. And, Pedro..." Matt turned to him and for a moment Pedro thought there was something strange in his eyes, something he didn't quite understand. "You're going to St Peter's in Rome," he continued. "There's a door there that will take you to Antarctica. Giovanni will help you."

"How do you know all this?" Pedro demanded. "How do you know about Giovanni?"

Matt shrugged and looked away. "I've been to the library," he said.

"And what's my part in this?" Scott asked. The others looked at him curiously. His voice was dull and hostile. He was sitting, cross-legged, on his own, slightly apart from the rest of the group. And he was dressed differently from them. He was wearing an expensive black shirt and jeans. His clothes were new.

"You and I can talk about that in a minute," Matt said. He got to his feet. "The five of us are together again and that's all that matters. We're still alive. And I will make you a promise. The price may be high but we are going to win."

He walked over to Scott. "Let's go..."

"We've got nothing to say," Scott muttered.

"That's not true."

"I've got nothing to say to you, Matt. I mean it."

"Give me five minutes, Scott. That's all I'm asking. After that, you never have to see me again."

"Five minutes?"

"What difference does it make? You're asleep anyway. When you wake up, we'll be miles apart."

"OK. Whatever you say." Scott rose lazily to his feet. He was still ignoring Pedro. But he was also ignoring Jamie and that was much worse.

Scarlett watched the two of them walk away. She turned to Pedro. "What's going on?" she asked. "You were with Scott in Italy. What happened?"

"Nothing happened," Pedro replied, miserably.

"No? So how come you look half-starved, you're in rags and you've got a broken finger, while Scott looks like he's just walked out of a fashion show?"

"Pedro...?" Jamie pleaded with him to say more.

"I can't tell you!" Pedro sprang to his feet and walked off in the opposite direction, kicking up grey dust. He quickly disappeared down the side of the hill.

Jamie and Scarlett were left alone. "The five of us together again?" Jamie muttered, echoing what Matt had just said. "It doesn't feel that way."

Matt and Scott were still together in the empty grey landscape. Matt was doing most of the talking, trying to make Scott understand something. Scott was shaking his head. Matt stopped him, then spoke quickly and urgently. He seemed to have regained his confidence.

He knows something we don't, Jamie thought.

Scott muttered something. He was trying to back away but Matt was staying close to him, refusing to let him leave.

Scarlett wished she could hear what they were saying. She didn't know if Matt had persuaded Scott to see his point of view and wondered if she could help. She thought of going over to them but then she saw a man walking towards her. He was still dressed in a white shirt but, from the front, she could see that there was a pattern of some sort on his waistcoat. He was an Arab. She saw that too. The two black discs covering his eyes glimmered in the fluorescent light.

"Five," he said.

Always the same word. Nothing else and no explanation... "Matt!" she called out.

But Matt was far away, still talking to Scott. At the same time, she heard the sound of an engine revving and somebody shouting at her. There was blood on her hands. She jolted forward as the car she was in hit a pothole.

She was in the desert, in the front of a Land Cruiser. Rémy, the Frenchman, was slumped in the back.

Egypt was behind them. Dubai was eighty kilometres ahead.

WHEEL OF FORTUNE

TWENTY-SIX

Albert Rémy was dead. The Frenchman, who had been part of the Nexus in London and who had waited ten years for them in Egypt, hadn't made it through the night. Richard wasn't surprised. For three days, Rémy had been in constant pain, every jolt and every bump on the deserted main road causing him to cry out, a bubble of blood appearing on his lips. A bullet had entered his chest just under his left arm and Richard suspected it had punctured his lung. His breathing had been horrible, a constant rattling that competed with the engine of the car, and both Richard and Scarlett had known the moment he had slipped away. That had happened during the fourth night but they had kept going, afraid to stop in the dark.

Then the sun rose, the road was empty with nothing but desert all around – as it had been almost always during the long, sweltering journey that had taken them out of Egypt across the Suez Canal bridge and through no fewer than three countries, including the full length of Saudi Arabia. Richard had driven the entire distance, his eyes glazed, his hands grimly clutching the steering wheel. For her part, Scarlett had talked to him almost incessantly, not because she had anything to say but because she knew she had to help keep him awake. There had been almost nothing to look at, nothing to separate one dreary mile from the next. Even the sight of a burnt-out bus or armoured vehicle became a landmark, something to break the monotony. As they continued south, they had passed a few scattered villages, electricity pylons, abandoned frontier posts with twisting barbed wire and ragged flags … but not a single sign of human life. The sand was still blowing and it might have disguised the truth. Perhaps people had heard them as they drove around Eilat in Israel or Aqaba in Jordan and had run to intercept them. If so, they had been too late. Richard had kept his foot down. The car hurtled on.

The sky was grey, the sand a dirty orange as they dragged Rémy out and laid him on the ground. Richard climbed onto the Land Cruiser and pulled a spade from the various supplies and pieces of equipment that were strapped to the roof. Scarlett realized that he was going to dig a grave and felt guilty because, if she'd had her way, she wouldn't have bothered. Rémy was dead. What difference would it make to him?

"Richard, let me do it," she said.

Richard shook his head. "No. I'm fine. In fact I need the exercise. I've lost count of how many hours I've been cooped up in that thing."

"We're only about an hour from Dubai."

"I know. If he'd waited just a little longer we might have got him to a hospital."

"If there are any hospitals…"

"Yeah. Take a look at this…" He handed something to her, a thick wallet made of pale brown leather.

"What is it?"

"It's Rémy's. It was in his pocket."

Scarlett opened the wallet. Inside, in one of the compartments, there was a wad of banknotes; American one-hundred-dollar bills, neatly pressed together. Scarlett flicked them with her thumb. "How much is there here?" she asked.

"There's fifty of them. Five thousand dollars." Richard took the spade in both hands. "I guess he was keeping them for a rainy day."

"Not much chance of that out here."

"It's funny though. There are no photographs. No pictures of his wife or kids. Nothing about him. Just a pile of cash. We'll never know anything about him."

"He tried to help us. That's enough." Scarlett closed the wallet. "The money may help us. Maybe it'll buy us a ticket out."

The sand was soft and it only took Richard about half an hour to cut a trench a metre deep. That was enough. He threw down the spade, then he and Scarlett went over and dragged Rémy in. As she took hold of the dead man's ankles, Scarlett had one of those moments where she seemed to be looking at herself and couldn't quite believe what she was seeing. What would Mrs Ridgewell say if she were here now? she wondered. Somehow she doubted that the head teacher at her old school in Dulwich would have any advice on how to bury dead Frenchmen in the Arabian desert.

Keep the feet together, Scarlett. And try not to get any more blood on your hands. You're covered enough already...

Had this really happened to her? How had her life come to this?

The body slumped into the grave. Before Richard could do any more work, Scarlett snatched up the spade and began to fill it in. Richard took out a canister of water and drank, his face covered in sweat and grime. At least they still had water. They had been careful, rationing themselves over the course of the journey. They couldn't be sure what the water situation would be in Dubai. Neither of them said the obvious, even if both of them secretly thought it. Rémy had drunk more than either of them in the last three days. And it had all been wasted.

Scarlett finished her work. "Do you want to say anything?" she asked.

"You mean – a prayer?" Richard handed her his canister. "I was never really the religious sort."

"Me neither. I used to hate chapel at school."

"Let's get's back in the car."

"Actually, I've got something to tell you, Richard." Scarlett had been waiting for the right moment. "I saw Matt last night."

"Matt?" Richard's face brightened. "He was in the dream-world?"

"He called us all together. We were all there. Matt, Pedro, Jamie, Scott..."

"That's great news. How is he?"

Scarlett hesitated. She knew how close Richard was to Matt and how much he'd worried about him – but she was determined not to lie. "I don't know, Richard. I got the feeling there was something he wasn't telling me. He was very serious. I thought he was upset about something."

"Where is he?"

"He's in Brazil. Lohan is with him."

Quickly, Scarlett told Richard everything that had happened outside the library. The sun was rising and although the colour of the sky hadn't changed, it was getting hotter. They needed to set off soon. Without the Land Cruiser's air-conditioning, they would both melt.

"We have to get to Antarctica," she said.

"Antarctica!" Richard shook his head. "That's a funny thing to be talking about in the middle of the desert! Right now we must be, what, ten thousand miles away?"

"Rémy said there were planes flying in and out of Dubai."

"That was a while ago. Things may have changed."

"We'd better find out. And at least we've got money now. We can pay."

"You're right." Richard nodded. "Maybe that's where it all ends ... this whole thing. On the ice."

"I really hope so," Scarlett said.

The two of them got back into the car and drove off. The unmarked grave dwindled into the distance behind them. Neither of them looked back.

Dubai took them by surprise. One moment they were driving through the unremitting emptiness of the desert, the next they were boxed in, with modern streets and buildings appearing all around them, as if the city had been lying in the sand and had leapt up to ambush them. Their first impression, particularly after Cairo, was one of extraordinary cleanliness. There was no war going on here and they had left the sandstorms behind. In fact the sky was a dazzling blue, the shops and offices gleaming – as if they had only just been built. The streets were wide and evenly spaced with what might once have been lawns stretching their entire length. All the grass had died but the earth that remained was neat and symmetrical. The city didn't seem to have grown. It could have been laid out deliberately, piece by piece.

And it was completely deserted.

Richard and Scarlett had driven down half a dozen empty avenues before they saw what should have been obvious from the start. There were cars parked everywhere, many of them very expensive ones... Ferraris, Jaguars, Rolls Royces. But there were no drivers and they were alone on the road. The traffic lights were still working uselessly, blinking from green to yellow to red, but nothing moved. There was nothing to move. Most of the shops had been stripped but they saw fridges, furniture, plasma screen TVs and even grand pianos on display. They were too heavy to carry so they had simply been left behind. As they continued forward, they passed fountains without water and palm trees which, against the odds, had managed to survive. The traffic lights changed and changed again. After a while, they learnt to ignore them.

All around them, huge hotels, shopping centres and skyscrapers seemed almost to mock them – or to mock each other. The buildings were extraordinary, the visions of architects with all the money in the world and the desire only to outdo each other. There were constructions that curved and rippled and shone silver or white. They were shaped like knives, like rockets, like the sail of a ship. And at their very centre, soaring above all of them, stood the Burj Dubai, which had briefly been the tallest building in the world and which appeared like a futuristic steel syringe, desperately trying to puncture the upper atmosphere. They were all empty. Scarlett wasn't sure quite why she could be so certain. But they had the same sort of lifelessness as a group of statues in a museum that has closed for the night. They faced each other, solid and unmoving. Dead. There wasn't a flicker of movement anywhere. And the very motion of the car as they rolled slowly forward seemed alien and unwanted.

"It's quiet," Richard said, as much to hear the sound of his voice as to say anything that mattered.

"There's no one here."

"But there hasn't been any fighting. There are no smashed windows. Look at these cars! They could have been parked overnight."

It was true. All the parked cars were clean and polished and looked as if they would start at the turn of a key. There was no litter blowing in the street, no rubbish waiting to be collected. It was as if the city had woken up one morning and the people simply hadn't been there.

"Richard ... what are we going to do?"

"We could find a five-star hotel."

"I don't think I want to stay here."

"Then let's see if there's a way out."

They drove past a Shell garage and Scarlett wondered if they would be able to refill the Land Cruiser. After they had buried Rémy, they had filled their tanks, using the last of their fuel. The pumps all looked in working order and clearly the electricity supply hadn't failed, at least in this part of the city. The forecourt was spotless. But if they were going to continue driving, where exactly could they go? Scarlett vaguely remembered old geography lessons. Dubai was on the northern coast of the United Arab Emirates. Oman was next door. Or there was always Iran just opposite, on the other side of the Persian Gulf. It was completely hopeless. They could drive for weeks or months and even assuming they could find more fuel on the way, they wouldn't necessarily arrive anywhere they wanted to be. Scarlett wondered about Mecca, another sixteen hundred kilometres to the west. They needed a door like the one that had brought them to Cairo. The doors were supposed to be in religious places. Surely they would find one there?

But Richard had other ideas.

He had been following a six-lane motorway towards a roundabout with a slightly more antique-looking monument, two giant pincers supporting a clock that had, perhaps ominously, stopped at one minute to midnight. They drove past it, curving around some very ordinary blocks of flats, and there was the airport ahead of them – a great swathe of empty concrete almost the size of a small city itself, with a few low-rise buildings and a single control tower, vague and indistinct on the other side of the heat haze. Scarlett's heart sank. She hadn't expected any signs of activity here, not after what she had seen so far. There would be no passengers, no airport workers, no ground crew. But Rémy had told them there were planes here and as far as she could see, there wasn't so much as a glider. If she and Richard were going to find their way out, then flying wasn't going to be an option.

"Don't worry. The airport's huge," Richard said, echoing her thoughts. "There might be a plane somewhere."

They drove through the main entrance, past a security barrier that was raised and a control post that was empty. Both of them felt as if they were entering another desert … this one made of concrete. There was no point even looking for a car park. It wasn't as if someone was going to leap out and give them a parking ticket. They left the car between a silver Aston Martin and a Rolls Royce – both of them could have been driven here direct from the sales room. They didn't have to worry about the Land Cruiser being stolen either. If there was a thief in the area, he would have a hundred much more luxurious cars to choose from.

They walked into the main terminal, glad to be out of the car. Ahead of them, on the other side of a gleaming marble floor, dozens of check-in desks stretched in long lines, waiting for passengers who would never arrive. Escalators stood, frozen. All the TV screens that might once have announced the departures were blank. The atmosphere inside was warm and clammy – it had been a long time since the air-conditioning had been turned on – and the palm trees had wilted and died in their pots. The terminal was huge. Scarlett was reminded first of a factory, then of a cathedral. Everything here – the floors, the windows, the desks, the stairs – was hard and brittle. It was a place with no comfort at all.

"Do you want to go on?" Scarlett asked. Her voice sounded very small.

"Why not? Maybe we can pick up a drink in Duty Free."

They passed through the departure gate (PASSENGERS ONLY) and through the security area with its silent conveyor belts, its metal detectors and X-ray screens. It was a reminder of how the world had once been, the endless fear and suspicion that went with people's determination to keep on travelling. Then there were the passport controls, modern cubicles at the end of a long stretch of marble. *You are now leaving Dubai and entering the no-man's-land of an international airport. You have hours of shopping and hanging around ahead. Thank you for coming.*

Only the Duty Free area was empty. All the shelves had been wiped clean. Richard and Scarlett found themselves in a long, subterranean arcade that ran the entire length of the terminal, with shops everywhere, a sports car parked at one end (WIN THIS CAR – US$25 A TICKET) and a bar decorated with a plastic palm tree. It was the same as the city. There had been people here, and then, quite suddenly, they had gone. It was as if they had bought everything that could be bought, right down to the last packet of cigarettes and the last king-sized tube of M&M's and then leapt on the first plane and gone home.

Richard and Scarlett kept going. Neither of them spoke. They didn't want to express their disappointment. There was nothing here for them. They weren't going to get so much as a drink.

They reached a window looking out onto the runway. Richard pointed. "Look!"

It was there after all, right in front of them. A plane. Perhaps the only plane in the whole airport. An Emirates airline Airbus, sitting on its own in the middle of the tarmac. A flight of steps had been wheeled against the cabin door and there was a man sitting there, dressed in dark blue trousers, a white shirt and sunglasses. The pilot. It had to be. He seemed to be waiting for them.

Richard grabbed hold of Scarlett and the two of them set off, looking for a way out.

TWENTY-SEVEN

Despite its name, getting out of the departure building was much harder than it had been getting in. Richard and Scarlett became increasingly frustrated as they followed winding corridors past door after door, each one of them locked with security codes known only to ground staff who had left long ago. Even though the electricity inside the terminal had either failed or been switched off, the magnetic locks hadn't released themselves and the doors refused to open. Huge windows gave them tantalizing views of the tarmac they were trying to reach. Richard would have been tempted to pick up a chair and smash the glass but the chairs were bolted down, and anyway, the glass was probably too thick.

Eventually they found what they were looking for. There was a boarding desk with a British Airways sign and, next to it, an open door with one of those long passageways that bent back on themselves and that used to lead directly onto an aircraft. This one jutted into open space. When Richard and Scarlett reached the end, they found themselves looking at a square of bright light with a drop to the ground that would break both their ankles if they weren't careful. But there was no other way. They clambered over the edge, taking their full weight with their hands and their arms outstretched, then dropped. Even so, it was a hard landing. And the tarmac was burning hot.

"You OK?"

"Yeah." Scarlett dusted herself down and looked around. The Airbus that they had spotted was now some distance away but the man was still there, smoking a cigarette.

They hurried towards him. There was no breeze at all but it was drier and more pleasant than it had been inside the terminal. Scarlett was very aware of the silence. It was the last thing she would have associated with an airport and she felt lost in her surroundings, with the ground, completely flat, stretching out in front of her and a mile of glass and steel blinking in the sun behind. The pilot of the Airbus – if that was what he was – saw them coming and dropped his cigarette. He reached into his pocket and even before he had drawn his hand out, Scarlett knew that it would be holding a gun and wished that they hadn't been quite so quick to make themselves visible. They could be anyone. So, for that matter, could he. He could shoot them both down before they even had time to tell him their names.

But it was too late to stop now. Richard had raised his hands, showing that he was unarmed. And with a fifteen-year-old girl beside him, he couldn't have looked like too much of a threat. The pilot lowered his gun but remained wary.

He was young, fair-haired with a thin face and crumpled cheeks. As they approached, he had taken off his sunglasses to reveal watchful blue eyes. He was athletic-looking, quite wiry. Scarlett thought he had the body of a surfer and could easily imagine him on the beach in brightly coloured shorts. But he kept himself out of the sun. His skin was pale and he had placed himself in the shadow of the plane. Despite the heat, he hadn't rolled up his sleeves.

"Who the hell are you?" he demanded, when Richard and Scarlett reached him. He gestured with the gun. "Don't come any closer – all right?"

"It's OK." Once again, Richard lifted his hands in a gesture of surrender. "We're friends."

"Everyone's friends," the pilot responded. He spoke with an Australian accent. "The question is – who are you friends of?"

"We've only just got here," Scarlett said. "We don't know what's going on."

"Got here? From where?"

"We were in Cairo."

The pilot whistled. "You came all that way? How did you get here?"

"We drove." Richard gestured back at the terminal. "We have a Land Cruiser. It's parked out there." He lowered his hands. "You're Australian," he said.

"That's right." The pilot hadn't lowered his gun. "And you sound English. What were you doing in Cairo? Are they still fighting?"

"Yes. They're still fighting. What we were doing there is a very long story. My name is Richard Cole. This is Scarlett Adams. You wouldn't have any water, would you? We've been driving all day and it took us a while to find our way out here."

The pilot examined them both carefully. He was clearly weighing them both up. Then he came to a decision and put the gun away. "OK. You can come on board if you like. But I'm warning you, if you try anything fancy, I'll shoot you right between the eyes without giving it a thought. The name's Martins, by the way. I'm from Sydney – or I would be if Sydney were still there."

"Are you the pilot?"

"No. The co-pilot."

They followed him up the steps and into the plane, and saw at once that the Airbus had been adapted. All the seats had been taken out apart from a few at the front, leaving a long, cigar-shaped space that was filled, floor to ceiling, with crates. Martins reached into one of them and took out two plastic bottles of water, which he passed to Richard and Scarlett. "Let's go upstairs," he said.

There was a spiral staircase leading up to what must have once been the business-class cabin. The upper area had also been adapted. It had been turned into a bedroom and a living room with two single beds, a couple of armchairs, and an area with a PlayStation and about a hundred games, scattered across the floor. There were also dozens of old food cartons, empty plastic bottles and overflowing ashtrays ... the last thing Scarlett would have expected to see on a plane. The air smelled of cigarette smoke. A half-empty bottle of whisky and a glass stood beside the bed and there was a pile of paperback books with cracked spines and dog-eared pages. The cockpit door was open and, looking through, Scarlett could see the two seats with the joysticks and the banks of controls. Richard nudged her and she knew that he was thinking exactly the same as her. There was every chance that this plane could fly.

Martins had thrown himself down on one of the beds, but had arranged himself so that the pocket with the gun faced up and could be reached easily. His eyes were still wary. Richard and Scarlett took the chairs, opened their bottles and drank. The water was warm and tasted stale.

"So where have you come from? Martins asked. "I mean, how did you get to Cairo? What were you doing there?"

"We were prisoners," Richard said. "There was a freedom fighter called Tarik."

"I know Tarik. I've flown supplies in for him. How is he?"

"As a matter of fact, he wasn't looking too good when we left."

"I'm sorry to hear it. So you're English. The girl looks Indonesian. What are you doing together? You meet on the road?"

This was always the difficult bit. Richard never knew how much to say. He'd never had to explain himself to Tarik because Rémy had been there and knew all about the Gatekeepers. Anyway, Tarik had seen shape-changers in Cairo and after that, any story about magical doorways, the Five and the war against the Old Ones would make some sort of sense. But this man might make nothing of it. In which case, it might simply be easier to lie.

"We've been travelling for a long time," Richard said. "We met in Hong Kong and we've sort of been thrown together since then. We want to get to Antarctica."

"Antarctica?" The co-pilot didn't sound as surprised as Richard might have expected. "It's funny you should mention that," he went on. "I've been hearing a lot of chatter about that on the radio."

"You have radio!" Scarlett said. Things were beginning to come together. The plane had power (the video games had hinted as much). And the world wasn't quite as empty as she had thought.

"Not national radio," the co-pilot replied. "But there are plenty of amateurs out there. Radio hams, they used to be called. I listen to them at night. Everyone who can has headed south. Whatever planes they could find ... boats ... they've gone overland to the tip of South Africa or South America. People say they've been having dreams about Antarctica. It's like some crazy religion."

"Could you fly this plane to Antarctica?" Richard asked.

The co-pilot shook his head. "Not on my own."

"So where's the pilot?"

"That's a long story. Do you have any idea what's happening here in Dubai?"

"I already told you," Richard said. "We only just got here."

"And came straight to the airport. Well, I guess I'd have done the same. As you've probably seen, there aren't many people around."

"Where is everyone?" Scarlett asked.

"They've all gone."

Martins reached out. He poured himself a glass of whisky and lit another Marlboro Lite. Scarlett noticed that he had hundreds of cigarettes, still in their duty-free cartons. Maybe he had looted them from Dubai Airport or from somewhere else on his travels. She suddenly saw that this plane was more than his way out. It was his home, his depot, his survival pod. He turned on his back and blew grey smoke in the air.

"Don't ask me to explain the history of the world," he said. "I never paid much attention to it when I was in school. All I ever wanted to do was fly. And when I got a job with Emirates, I was as happy as Larry." He smiled to himself. "Since I mention it, Larry is the name of my pilot. Larry Carter. He's a nice guy, except that he doesn't completely trust me. For example, he's never given me the codes that allow me to get into the on-board computers, which is one of the reasons why I'm sitting here instead of being on my way to somewhere a little more pleasant."

"What has happened in Dubai?" Richard asked.

"I was just getting to that, Richard. Would you like a Scotch?"

"No thanks." It had been a long time since Richard had drunk alcohol, and if it had been a cold beer he might have been tempted. But the idea of a whisky without ice in this confined space in the middle of the day slightly disgusted him.

"What happened to Dubai actually happened a very long time ago," the co-pilot explained. "It went bust. In the beginning there was oil, but that ran out soon enough. Well, it didn't matter because Dubai had set itself up as a playground for the super-rich, a sort of never-never land based on business, shopping and property. They built these islands that were shaped like palm trees, with multi-million-dollar houses that were bought by Hollywood actors and footballers. You saw the Burj Dubai in the centre of town? Well, you couldn't miss it, could you! That was what it was like here. Everything had to be the biggest, the tallest, the most expensive, the best. They say that at one stage, ten per cent of the world's cranes were operating here in Dubai. That's one hell of a lot of cranes. But they were all needed, to help build the miracle in the desert.

"Only the miracle wasn't as miraculous as everyone thought. Once the recession hit, the pop stars and the footballers stopped coming. Half the properties here were suddenly empty and the palm-tree islands never worked properly anyway because they fouled up the tide and suddenly people started noticing they were surrounded by sewage. Then the business dried up too. Nobody was doing any shopping. And here's the funny thing. It was actually illegal to go bankrupt in Dubai. You weren't allowed to do it. And finally, one day they woke up and found that Dubai itself was bankrupt.

"That was when everyone left. They drove out of here. They took planes. Some people even rode out on camels. They took everything they could carry with them – you may have noticed that most of the shops are pretty empty. But that still left enough for people like me. You want a nice Rolex watch for yourself, Richard, or maybe a diamond necklace for your young friend, I can show you where to find one. There's plenty of food and water too. This city's got everything! Except people."

"So where is the pilot?" Richard asked. "It looks to me as if you're stuck here without him."

"I am stuck here," Martins agreed. "I suppose I could put this hunk of metal up in the air. I have thought about it. But the fact is, I'm better off where I am … at least until the booze runs out. After that, we'll see." He reached for his glass. "Larry was an idiot but until he turns up, there's not very much I can do about it."

He threw back his whisky and swallowed, screwing up his eyes. It was hard to tell if the liquid gave him pleasure or pain.

"I say that everyone got out of here," he went on. "But actually, that isn't true. Dubai always had a royal family … you know, a sheikh. And the man in charge when everything went down the pan was Sheikh Rasheed Al Tamim. He has a palace overlooking Dubai Creek, although I don't suppose the views will have been quite so pretty since the water dried up."

He poured himself another whisky.

"He's still there. He's got a wife … and several kids. He's surrounded by ministers and advisers. Sheikh Rasheed is an important man. As well as being king, he's president of the United Arab Emirates and vice-president of the Supreme Council of the Union. He has an extensive military bodyguard. And then there are the diplomats, the civil servants, the advisers … everyone you'd expect to find in a busy court. And there's something that everybody knows but that nobody ever says. Here are the two things you need to know about Sheikh Rasheed. One – he's an evil bastard. And two – he's completely, utterly and certifiably mad.

"Maybe he always was. These people, locked up in their palaces with billions of dollars in their pockets and everything they could possibly want … it's probably all too easy to lose touch with reality. Or maybe it was the shock of waking up one morning and realizing that he was the absolute ruler of absolutely nothing! The city was empty. Everyone had gone and his beloved Dubai had about as much relevance as—" he searched vaguely for the comparison— "as a check-in desk in an airport with no planes.

"So here's what's happened, Richard. Sheikh Rasheed goes on ruling. He has important meetings in which he discusses new building projects that are never going to happen, traffic control schemes that are never going to be implemented, education policies that no longer matter and state banquets to which nobody is going to come. Last week he inspected his army. It's a shame you weren't here. He stood on a balcony and they marched the same one hundred soldiers round and round the building for three hours, making him think he was in control of thousands. Oh yeah – and they brought out the tank too. There is only one working tank. But he stood there, taking the salute, with the deputy prime minster on one side and all the other ministers around. I was there too. I saw him. And I'll never forget the idiot grin on his face."

"Why do the ministers stick with him?" Scarlett asked.

"Because he'll shoot them if they try to leave. They smile and they bow and they applaud when he says something witty – and they're all terrified of him. More to the point these people chose to stay behind and now they've got nowhere else to go. There are tons of supplies stockpiled in the royal palace. He controls the electricity supply and he's even got his own desalination plant for water. Provided they play ball and try not to say anything that will get them killed, they're probably more comfortable in Dubai than they would be anywhere else. So why rock the boat? Maybe some of them have even managed to persuade themselves that the streets are busy and the shops are full. That's one of the reasons they keep the traffic lights running. It's all part of the illusion. The point is, nobody steps out of line."

"What did Larry do?" Richard asked.

"Larry was stupid. He and I had been talking together. Things are OK here. Apart from anything else, there's still a certain amount of aviation fuel at the airport and we were doing plenty of jobs for Rasheed, running stuff up and down into Egypt. But at the same time, we were getting bored. It's not much fun being the only sandwich at the picnic when everyone else is a fruitcake. So we agreed we were going to do a runner. We'd heard there's a community doing OK in the Northern Territory in Australia, near Alice Springs, so we thought we'd fly out and join them. The trouble is, Larry got greedy. He decided to help himself to some of the sheikh's very considerable treasure. You might wonder who needs diamonds the size of ping-pong balls when the whole world is slipping down the gutter, but maybe Larry was thinking ahead.

"He sneaked into the palace one night while everyone was having dinner and broke into the royal vault – but of course he got himself caught in the act. You can imagine there was quite a song and dance about that. They weren't angry. They were delighted! You see, it gave them something real to do. They were able to set up a whole series of courts – the Court of First Instance, the Court of Appeal, the Court of Cassation – with defence lawyers and prosecution lawyers and witnesses and all the rest of it. Rasheed took the role of chief judge and he had himself kitted out with a wig and a red coat, even though it must have been a hundred degrees in the courtroom.

"Anyway, this lasted a couple of months and the upshot of it was – surprise, surprise – Larry was found guilty."

"What are they going to do with him?" Richard asked.

"They haven't decided yet. They may cut off his head. They may cut off his hands. Or they could just put him in front of a firing squad. It depends on Rasheed's mood and that can change in the blink of an eye. One thing you can bet on is that they'll make a big thing of it. Without TV, they've had to find other ways to amuse themselves." Martins lit another cigarette. "Whatever happens, he isn't going to be flying this Airbus any time soon."

"Can't he give you the codes?"

"I haven't been allowed to see him. And anyway, it isn't as easy as that. There's no air traffic control any more. There's no sat nav. If you want to fly one of these things, you more or less have to do it with maps and a compass. I'm not even sure I could find Alice Springs without him."

There was a long pause. The cabin was full of cigarette smoke but Martins didn't seem to notice.

In the end it was Scarlett who broke the silence. "Does Sheikh Rasheed speak English?" she asked.

"They all do. English is the language of international business so they like to speak it all the time."

"If we were able to persuade him to release your friend, would you fly us to Antarctica?"

The co-pilot shrugged. "You want me to be honest? I can't answer that. Larry's the one in charge."

"But if Larry agreed, you'd go along with it?"

Martins thought for a moment. "I don't really care where I go or what I do. It seems to me that the whole world has somehow got itself blown to infinity, and what difference does it make if I end up drinking myself unconscious in the outback or freezing my balls off on the ice?" He glanced at the tip of his cigarette. "Or dying of lung cancer here," he added. "But you're not going to persuade Sheikh Rasheed to let him go. He's been found guilty – and that's the end of it."

"We might be able to make him change his mind," Richard muttered. "Can you get us in to see him?"

Once again, Martins shook his head. "Sorry, mate. Right now I'm not Mr Popular at the palace. There's a faint suspicion that Larry and me were in it together. Pinch the diamonds and jump on the plane. All in all, it's better if I don't show my face."

"Could we go in ourselves? Is there a way we can get to meet him?

"Yeah. Actually, that's easy."

"How?"

"The sheikh used to gamble in London and he enjoyed it so much, he made it legal in Dubai. So they still have horse racing once a month, even though it's always the same horses going round the track and they're so lame now that it takes them half an hour to finish. And there's also the casino and the sheikh goes there almost every night."

"People still have money to gamble?" Scarlett was amazed.

"I know it's crazy. You'd think money wouldn't matter any more. You can walk into pretty much every shop and help yourself to a new car, a diamond necklace ... whatever. But you try buying a bottle of water! That's when you need hard cash and the sheikh just loves making his people squirm. People in Dubai are gambling for their lives, quite literally. Last week we actually had one man die playing a fruit machine. He put in his last coin and when the bells didn't come up, he just fell off his stool and he was dead. Dehydration.

"So, you want the sheikh to notice you, you go in there and win big or lose big and either way it'll happen. Just remember – if he scowls at you, be scared.

"And if he smiles at us?"

"Be scared too. You'll see how it is. The man's got all the charm of a rattlesnake. But if you can get Larry out of there, I for one will be grateful." Martins glanced at his watch. "The casino opens in an hour, at seven o'clock. Good luck if you're going in there. I'm telling you ... you're going to need it."

TWENTY-EIGHT

The casino was on Baniyas Road: a squat, low-rise construction, it was completely dwarfed by the various ultra-modern towers that surrounded it. Had Dubai been populated, if there had been any sign of life behind the thousands of windows, perhaps they might have seemed less threatening. As it was, Scarlett felt she was walking through an enormous cemetery. Everything was crowding in on her and it was all dead.

The casino could have arrived from another planet. It was covered in red and gold panels with two words – DUBAI CASINO – in glowing neon. But some of the letters had burned out so that it was the legend DUBAI SIN that flashed on and off as they approached.

There was a time when the casino would have looked out over the wide canal that flowed through the city, and Scarlett tried to imagine it with water taxis bobbing about, and sleek white yachts rocking gently at anchor. But the water had almost dried up, leaving two sloping banks of brown mud with a narrow trail of dark green slime where they met. A few boats remained but they had tipped over on their side. Any pretence of elegance or beauty that this place might have had, had long since gone.

Richard and Scarlett had both changed, picking fresh clothes from one of the many abandoned stores. Richard had expensive designer jeans, a new polo shirt and new trainers. Scarlett had picked out an ankle-length dress with a silk scarf. Martins had warned her to keep her head and arms covered. The two of them parked their car a short distance away and covered the last few hundred metres on foot. Richard left the keys in the car ... just in case they needed to make a fast getaway. He also concealed his backpack with the precious knife in the boot.

A doorman stood in front of the entrance – only the second person they had seen since they had arrived. Despite the sluggish heat of the evening, he was dressed in a long coat with over-sized gold buttons, epaulettes and a cap. As the two of them approached, he spoke to them in English.

"Good evening, sir. Welcome to the Dubai Casino."

It was their first taste of the madness that Martins had described. They had come out of nowhere, from an empty city. Despite their new clothes, they hadn't been able to wash. Richard hadn't shaved for days. They both looked – and smelled – less than their best. And yet the man in his smart uniform, already holding the door open for them, was behaving as if they were regular customers, as if they had just stepped out of a chauffer-driven Rolls Royce or perhaps strolled in from the Sheraton Hotel a short way up the road.

They walked past him and into a reception area that was all glass and marble. Scarlett felt the cold breeze of an air-conditioning unit as it found its way beneath the silk that covered her arms and brushed against her skin. There were more men here, all of them Arabs: a concierge dressed in black tie and dark glasses, and three or four others wearing traditional white robes and headdresses. They were chatting among themselves as if they were old friends who had chanced to meet, but even here, Scarlett sensed a certain falseness. They were nervous. They needed to win in order to eat and drink. This was no pleasant social occasion. They were all at the mercy of the sheikh, who would be watching over them as they played.

They turned and walked towards a pair of swing doors set

between two sculptures ... palm trees, heavy and golden. One of the doormen noticed Richard and nodded in welcome. There was a metal detector at the door and they all passed through it. To one side, a woman in a tight-fitting, sparkly dress was being patted down by a blank-faced security guard. A huge, bearded man in Arab dress walked past, cradling a tiny chihuahua dog with a heavy platinum collar. Richard and Scarlett glanced at each other. They didn't need to say anything. This place was weird.

But they needed the plane. And if they were going to fly, they needed its pilot. There was no other way. They walked through the metal detector and went in.

They were in a large, thickly carpeted room, with a ceiling illuminated by hundreds of tiny lights that had been set out at random, like stars. There were no windows, no exit signs – so that once they were in, they might imagine that there was no longer any way out. The air had a cold, antiseptic feel, like the inside of a fridge. About a hundred people had gathered here, a few of them in Arab dress but the majority in expensive Western suits – Armani, Prada, Paul Smith, Versace. Despite the low lighting, Scarlett had never seen more sunglasses. It was almost impossible to look at anyone without seeing reflections of herself. There were women too, whispering together, drinking brightly coloured cocktails. And everyone, the men and the women, were smothered in watches and jewellery, the different coloured stones glittering as they moved around the room.

In the middle of the casino, standing back to back, there were two lines of fruit machines. Huge mirrors on the walls reflected the blinking lights, the promises of pay-outs, the endlessly spinning reels. The players, perched on high stools, many of them smoking cigarettes, fed their silver coins into the slot, one after another, barely reacting whether they won or lost. Scarlett saw poker and blackjack being played, with croupiers, in white shirts and multicoloured waistcoats, dealing the cards out onto tables covered with green baize. There were two roulette wheels and a long table where a crowd had gathered to watch the throw of the dice. The atmosphere was hushed, expectant. But nobody really looked as if they were glad to be there.

And then two doors – wood-panelled with gold handles – crashed open and for a moment the games were forgotten as all eyes turned and Sheikh Rasheed Al Tamim made his entrance. It had to be him. He commanded the room before he had taken a step into it.

He was also wearing Western clothes; a silvery silk suit and a black shirt open at the collar to reveal the gold chain around his neck. There were gold rings on three of his fingers and a gold Rolex on his wrist. He himself was a thin, weedy man – and yet everything about him seemed designed to conceal it. He was wearing designer sunglasses, real gold, with large frames, and much of his face was covered with a black growth that wasn't quite thick enough to be a beard and a moustache. He was surrounded by bodyguards in shiny suits. There were three of them, with bald heads and watchful eyes. A single woman came behind. His wife? She also seemed unhappy to be here. She was wearing a sober black dress with a scarf over her head, tied under her chin. Her eyes were downcast.

The sheikh looked around the room as if this was the first time he had ever been here and was surprised to find that anyone else had come. "Hello, hello, hello!" he called out. His voice was high-pitched, almost girlish. Richard and Scarlett looked at each other. It was obvious at once that the sheikh had been drinking. He was swaying on his feet and his face was fixed with a stupid grin. "Are we all having a good time?"

Everyone in the room applauded. Waiters hurried forward carrying glasses of champagne. There was a sofa – red velvet cushions and a gold frame – set up on a raised platform and the sheikh went over to it, followed by his retinue. His bodyguards stood around him, warning the crowds to keep their distance. The woman who had come with him sat down at the very edge. The gamblers returned to their games.

"So what do we do now?" Scarlett whispered.

"I don't know." Richard watched as the sheikh twisted a cigarette between his lips and one of the bodyguards leant forward with a gold lighter. The guard said something and he burst into childish laughter. "I suppose we've got to get his attention."

"How do we do that?"

Scarlett looked around her – at the fruit machines, the dice table, finally at the roulette wheel. The ball had just finished spinning and the croupier was settling the bets ... more people had lost than won. As he swept the multicoloured chips off the baize surface, he looked up and Scarlett started. For a moment, he seemed to examine her. Then he turned away, waiting while the bets for the next game were placed in front of him.

Scarlett turned to Richard. "I know what to do."

"What...?" Richard began.

"Trust me!"

Before Richard could stop her she had marched forward to the roulette wheel, placing herself right in front of the sheikh, partly blocking his view. She spoke directly to the croupier and her voice was deliberately loud. "I want to play roulette," she announced. "Is there a limit on this table?"

"There is no limit," the croupier replied.

"So I can put on as much money as I want?"

"Yes, miss."

"That's very good." Scarlett produced the wallet that Richard had taken from Rémy. "In that case, I want to bet five thousand dollars."

The sheikh had been holding out his glass, waiting for it to be refilled, when this strange girl had made her appearance in front of him. He had also heard what she had just said. Slowly, he reached up and took off his sunglasses, examining her with small, lizard-like eyes. The croupier glanced in his direction, unsure whether to accept the bet.

"You! Young woman!" Sheikh Rasheed pointed at her. Scarlett turned. "How old are you?" the sheikh demanded.

"Fifteen."

"You're too young to gamble."

Scarlett looked him straight in the eye. Again, she spoke so that everyone could hear. "Are you afraid I'll win?"

Something flared briefly in those lizard eyes. The sheikh examined her more closely and she wondered what was going on in his mind. It was probably better not to know. There was a half-smile tugging at the corner of his mouth. "Have you got five thousand dollars?" he asked.

"Yes."

"And you don't mind losing?"

"Maybe I won't lose."

"Are you going to put it on red or black?"

That was the obvious bet. The odds were fifty-fifty. If Scarlett won, she would double her money. If she lost, it would all go.

"I want to put it on a single number."

"All of it? Five thousand dollars on a single number?" The sheikh's voice was more high-pitched than ever. He burst into laughter. "You really want to do that? Then go ahead! That's an awful lot of pocket money to lose but I'm not going to stop you." He snapped out a command in Arabic and the croupier produced a handful of black chips, which he handed to Scarlett. Scarlett took out the banknotes and handed them over. She was aware of Richard, watching in horror. The croupier folded the money and slid it through a slot next to the table.

The entire casino was watching her, knowing that what she was proposing was insane. She could have bet on red or black, high or low, odd or even. These were all known as outside bets – with the lowest risk but also the lowest return. There were thirty-five numbers on the wheel but there was also a green zero and a double zero that pushed the odds heavily in the casino's favour. Scarlett had a one-in-thirty-seven chance of winning. But if by some miracle the ball did land in whatever slot she chose, she would receive almost two hundred thousand dollars in return. The casino never made pay-outs like that.

"What number?" the croupier asked.

"Five," Scarlett said.

The croupier took her chips and slid them into place. At once, there was a rush to the side of the table. A great many of the other players in the room had decided to follow her example. It often happened that way in casinos. One person's courage would inspire the others. Perhaps she knew something they didn't. Perhaps she'd been studying the wheel. Number five was red, odd, low. More people crowded in, the chips piling up on those bets. Some of them even followed her, betting on the number itself. Five dollars, fifty dollars, even a hundred dollars. Soon there was a pile of plastic on the square and the croupier was looking very nervous indeed. If Scarlett's number came up, the entire casino could fall.

Richard Cole couldn't believe what he was seeing. It didn't matter to him very much if Scarlett lost the money. He had no use for it anyway. But she had set herself directly against the sheikh, and by betting with her, his own people had shown they were on her side. They really wanted to see him get a bloody nose.

"What is going on here? What is going on?" The sheikh hurried forward, pushing people out of the way until he reached the edge of the roulette table. "You do not understand what you are doing, you stupid girl. You do not understand the rules." He looked around him and saw the sullen faces of the crowd. For once, he was isolated, on his own. "All right!" he exclaimed. "Spin the wheel! In a minute I am going to be very rich!"

The croupier did as he was told. First he spun the wheel. Then he dropped the ball in, sending it flying in the opposite direction, so fast that it was no more than a blur.

Richard moved closer to Scarlett. "Are you going to win?" he whispered.

"I think so," Scarlett whispered back.

But was she? The ball was already slowing down. She could see it rolling over the numbers. Seven, twenty, thirty-two, seventeen ... and there it was. The number she had chosen. The ball was moving too fast. It couldn't possibly slow down enough to fall into place on the next revolution.

The crowd was getting uneasy. Those who had backed Scarlett, particularly with the larger bets, were already wishing they had been less hasty. It wasn't only the money that they might lose; they had also taken on Sheikh Rasheed and he wouldn't forget it. There were stories of torture chambers deep underneath the royal palace. It was well known that if you offended the sheikh on one day, you might well disappear before the next.

The ball was dipping in and out now. It hit one of the pockets and bounced out again with a rattle. Scarlett took a deep breath. The ball had almost fallen into number twenty-seven. It travelled on – past thirteen, one and double zero. Five was coming up again. As if suddenly losing its strength, the ball fell one last time. There was complete silence in the room.

The ball was being carried round and round. It was in slot number five.

The croupier was the first to react, looking down at the ball and then up at Scarlett as if she was somehow connected to it by a thread. And once again, Scarlett examined his face: the neat moustache, the round glasses, the gold teeth. She knew him, of course. She had seen him several times in the dreamworld and always he had said the same thing to her. "Five". Nothing to do with the Gatekeepers, everything to do with the game she would one day play. Scarlett had gambled this evening ... but only on her certainty that the dreamworld was there to help her. And she had been proved right.

Sheikh Rasheed grimaced. His face was a riot of emotions as he was torn between shock, disbelief, the knowledge of how much he had just lost and the need to reassert his authority.

"What is happening here?" he quavered. His eyeballs were almost bulging out of his head. "How could this be allowed to happen?" He stared down at the scattered piles of plastic chips crowding the number five. Then, without warning, he seized the croupier and punched him hard on the nose. The man was thrown onto the roulette wheel, sending chips flying. "The game is disallowed!" he announced. "The girl is under the age of sixteen. She should not have been permitted to play." He turned to address the rest of the crowd. "The casino is closed for the evening. You must all go home. The gambling is over!"

The gamblers didn't look happy but none of them were foolish enough to complain. The bodyguards were waiting for the first sign of dissent and would have cut them down before they could utter a word. Slowly, they began to move away. The croupier picked himself up. There was blood streaming from his nose. He began to collect the plastic chips.

Sheikh Rasheed came over to Scarlett. His mood seemed to have changed once again. He was smiling. "You are a very clever young lady!" he exclaimed waggling a finger at her. "I have not seen you here before. What is your name?"

"I'm Scarlett."

"Tell me how you did that. How did you know where the ball was going to fall?"

"I didn't," Scarlett said, tiredly. "I was just lucky."

"You came here to win money? To buy supplies?"

"Yes."

"There is no need for that. You will come to my palace for dinner. You and your friend will sit beside me as my guests of honour and we will talk. Come, Jaheda! Let us leave..."

The sheikh examined her one last time, then turned on his heel and left the room. Scarlett looked at Richard. They both knew that she hadn't received an invitation. It had been a command.

They watched as the sheikh disappeared through the doors that had brought him here. His wife – Jaheda – followed him, but at the last moment she turned and looked at Scarlett with an expression of intense hatred.

Then the doors closed and the two of them had gone.

TWENTY-NINE

There were thirty people invited to dinner at the palace that night. Like the casino crowd, they were all dressed in their finest clothes and displayed enough jewellery to fill a treasure chest. Many of them were smoking – cigars and cigarettes – sucking in smoke between mouthfuls of food. They sat on cushions around a low table, with Sheikh Rasheed at the very centre so that none of his guests would miss his jokes or his observations. Scarlett had been placed on his right. Richard was concerned to find himself separated from her, some distance away. And to make matters worse, the sheikh's wife, Jaheda, had been banished from her usual place and placed next to him.

The palace was a sprawling mass of white marble and gold fittings, where every door seemed to open onto a room larger than the one before. The building had been put together with one single aim: to prove that the owner was the richest and most important person in Dubai, surrounding him with pillars, arches, ornamental balconies, latticed windows, glittering chandeliers, fountains, pools and fish tanks. And yet at the same time it was a strangely ugly place. It reminded Scarlett of a department store, stuffed with expensive objects that nobody wanted to buy. On the way into dinner she had counted no fewer than seven portraits of Sheikh Rasheed. Even the elaborate mirrors seemed to have been positioned so that they would always reflect him.

The dining room led to a courtyard and a garden. There might not be enough water in the country to serve the people but there was certainly enough to keep the plants and trees blooming. The air was thick with the smell of flowers. A classical quartet wearing dark suits and bow ties, was sitting outside, playing pop songs and hits from American musicals. And inside, waiters – crowds of them – circulated with food piled high on silver plates. Each guest had half a dozen glasses. Red wine, white wine, champagne and spirits were being served non-stop. It was almost impossible to hear anything. The noise of people talking in English and Arabic, the clatter of plates and glasses, the music – all these had blended together into a general din, broken from time to time by a high-pitched squeal of laughter from the sheikh himself.

He was piling food into his mouth … but only after everything had been tasted by one of the three bodyguards who stood behind him, taking each dish from the waiters and then passing it on. Very little of the food was fresh but all of it was expensive. They had started with caviar, great mounds of it. Sheikh Rasheed had scooped the oily black eggs out of the tin with his fingers, laughing in delight as the juices trickled down the palm of his hand.

"Lick it! Lick it!" He had thrust his hand at the woman sitting opposite and she had done exactly that.

Scarlett was sickened. She was also hugely relieved that he hadn't asked her to do the same.

Then there were traditional meze, a selection of Arabic dishes that included stuffed vine leaves, red cabbage, falafel, cream cheese and pancakes. Scarlett had lost her appetite but she forced herself to eat. It had been more than twelve hours since her last meal and she couldn't say how long it would be until the next. She glanced at Richard, who was also eating without much enthusiasm.

Then Sheikh Rasheed leant over her. He had been drinking

heavily and he was already very drunk, his eyes rolling, his smile crooked. Despite the air-conditioning, he was sweating alcohol. Scarlett could see it on his skin. There were black caviar eggs on his lips and caught in his beard.

"So, Miss Scarlett," he asked. "Where have you come from?"

"I was in Cairo," Scarlett replied. It seemed the easiest and the safest answer.

"Cairo! I hear things are very difficult there. The people are at each other's throats. I will tell you the mistake they made. Not enough fear! The people of Dubai love me but they are afraid of me. Tomorrow you will see why."

"What's happening tomorrow?" Scarlett asked.

"There is a man, an Australian, who tried to steal from me. His name is Larry Carter." He spoke the two names slowly, with distaste. "And tomorrow, at midday, I am going to have him executed at the Meydan Grandstand. I am going to have him boiled alive. It is not something I have seen before. I think it will be quite a spectacle."

One of the bodyguards handed him a stuffed vine leaf. He had already bitten off one end. The sheikh pushed the rest of it into his mouth.

"Would you like to come?"

"I'm not very interested in executions," Scarlett said.

"You'll get used to them in time." The sheikh chewed and swallowed. He drank some champagne. "You are a very attractive girl, Scarlett." He leant towards her and took hold of her wrist. Scarlett had to fight not to show her horror and disgust. "I want you to stay with me."

"I'm afraid that won't be possible," Scarlett said. Everything about this man made her recoil. It was like sitting next to a slug. "Richard and I have to get back to Cairo."

"I don't think you understand me." Suddenly his eyes were very black, the madness all too obvious. "I do not want you to leave. There is something about you that fascinates me. You come here from nowhere. At the roulette table, you win a great fortune..."

"I didn't win anything," Scarlett reminded him. "You took it away."

"Only because you cheated. It seems to me that, somehow, you glimpsed into the future. I will be fascinated to know how you did that, Scarlett. I am looking forward to getting to know you better. I want you at my side." He tightened his grip. The idea had come to him all at once. "I want you to be my wife!"

"I thought you were married."

"Jaheda bores me."

"I'm only fifteen!"

"In Yemen, in Egypt, in many parts of the Gulf, girls get married as young as ten!"

Scarlett jerked her hand free. "It's very kind of you," she said and there was nothing but scorn in her voice. "But I'm not interested."

Rasheed's face darkened. He stared at her, his black eyes burning into her. Suddenly his lips were very close to her ear so that only she could hear. "This is my kingdom," he said. "Everything that I want, I take. Nobody argues with me. I have made my mind up about you, Scarlett, and if you try to leave here, I will have you locked up and your friend – the man who came with you – beheaded. Do you understand? You should not have come here if you were not prepared to stay. And I, only I, will be the one who will tell you when you can leave."

He picked up his glass and thrust it out, demanding to have it refilled. A waiter hurried forward but in his haste he spilled some of the champagne. The yellow liquid splashed down. Some of it splattered onto Rasheed's sleeve. His reaction was so instant, so fast, that Scarlett thought of a snake lashing out from behind a rock. The sheikh cried out. He brought the wine glass down and smashed it against the table, then sliced it through the air. The waiter cried out as the jagged edge missed him by inches. "You fool!" the sheikh screamed. "You idiot! You're fired. Get out of here!"

There was a sudden silence in the room, apart from the quartet outside who were halfway through "The Sound of Music". Scarlett sat there, rooted to the spot. Across the table, Richard was about to get up to go to her, but suddenly he felt a hand grab hold of him, pinning him down. It was Jaheda. "Do not give him an excuse to kill you," she said.

The sheikh seemed to realize what he had done. He suddenly laughed and clapped his hands. "Time for pudding!" he crowed. "And more champagne."

The guests cheered and applauded. The meal went on.

Richard looked more closely at Jaheda, wondering why she had changed her mind and suddenly decided to help him. The two of them had barely spoken throughout the meal and he remembered how angry she had appeared as they left the casino.

"What does he want with her?" Richard asked.

"What do you think he wants with her?" Jaheda was angry again. "If you care for her, why did you even bring her here?"

Richard's first instinct was to lie. He knew nothing about this woman. He didn't know if he could trust her. But at the same time, he wondered if she might be able to help them. She seemed to have an agenda of her own. "We came here to get the pilot," he said. "That's all we want. We need him to fly us out of here."

"That is not possible. He is in prison. He is being executed tomorrow."

"Can you talk to him?"

"To Rasheed?" She shook her head and when she spoke again, she didn't attempt to conceal the bitterness in her voice. "Not all the men in this country are like Rasheed," she said. "And even he was not always like this. He was cruel. He was always spoilt. But when he lost control of his world, that was when he turned into this ... child!"

"Why do you stay with him?"

"Because I want to. Because it is my duty. I am his wife!" Jaheda's eyes flickered towards Scarlett and at that moment Richard understood exactly what was in her mind. "I will not be replaced by a child," she said. "I knew that this girl would cause trouble for me the moment I saw her in the casino. And look at him now." The sheikh had his arm around Scarlett, trying to force her to eat a piece of Turkish delight. "He is besotted by her. It makes me sick!"

"Then help us leave," Richard said. "Do you know where Larry Carter is being held?"

"Of course I do."

"Then get him out. Bring him to us. There's a plane at the airport and we have a car just down the road."

"I cannot do as you say. Rasheed will kill me."

On the other side of the table, Rasheed threw the Turkish delight in the air and caught it in his mouth. He was doing tricks for Scarlett, trying to entertain her.

"I don't think he'll kill you," Richard said. "I think he's forgotten you."

Jaheda nodded slowly. "We will see..."

THIRTY

By midnight, Jaheda still hadn't come.

Richard and Scarlett had been given adjoining rooms in the palace. They were certainly comfortable enough. The beds were enormous, covered with Egyptian cotton sheets and silk duvets, buried underneath an avalanche of pillows. Anything that could be made of gold turned out to be just that – from the mirror frames to the light fittings to the bathroom taps. They had hot and cold water too. The baths were deep and surrounded by oils and shampoos. It was like staying in the most luxurious hotel in the world, apart from two small details: the windows were barred and the doors were locked.

They were both still awake. After everything that had happened during the course of the evening, sleep would have been impossible. Scarlett could still feel the clasp of the sheikh's fingers on her wrist. She saw his black eyes and the food caught in his beard. She remembered what he had said. The one thing she hadn't done was to tell Richard the threats that he had made. He would kill Richard to make her change her mind. Maybe that was why he had allowed them to stay near each other tonight, to remind her what her refusal would cost. But she had already decided that she wouldn't let it happen. She would marry Sheikh Rasheed if she had to – but she would deal with him in her own way before she allowed him to touch her again.

For his part, Richard was angry with himself.

It had been his idea to come to the palace. What had he been thinking of? Martins had warned them that the sheikh was unstable. Had there really been any chance that they could persuade him to hand over the pilot and let them fly out of here to Antarctica? Richard had allowed them to walk in here without any plan at all and now they were both prisoners. His position was bad enough but from what he had seen at the dinner table, Scarlett's was worse. He had brought her to this. It was his fault.

It seemed so long now since he had been a writer, working on a local newspaper in the north of England. The *Greater Malling Gazette* ... he could see it so clearly, the drab offices set behind the High Street, filled with cheap furniture and computers that were forever crashing. It had been his first job after leaving university. Not *The Times*, not the *Telegraph*, not even the *Yorkshire Post* but his next step towards a career that he had wanted since he was a boy. Richard had always been fascinated by the news, by the way people's lives all over the world could be changed and moulded by events over which they had no control. Why should a flood in Bangladesh mean anything to a housewife in Yorkshire? It was the journalist's job to make the connection, to make people care.

Not, of course, that he ever covered such stories in Greater Malling. Almost from the day he had arrived, he had been bored rigid, writing about marriages and funerals, charity events, local councillors and bright school kids. He had thought about leaving several times and had only stayed because there were no other jobs. He had a flat in York. He had occasional girlfriends. Life wasn't too bad and he was sure that if he stayed around long enough, something would turn up.

That something was a fourteen-year-old boy who had arrived in the office one afternoon, just after lunch, with a story so incredible that Richard had given up on him within five minutes of their meeting. Matthew Freeman claimed he had been kept prisoner in a local farm, Hive Hall, that he had stumbled upon a conspiracy that involved a disused nuclear power station, a circle of witches and God knows what else. It was all completely unbelievable. Richard had said so and Matt had stormed out of the office.

What was it that had made Richard decide to take a second look, to drive out to the old power station that night? He doubted now that he would ever know, but as things had turned out, he had met up with Matt again and at once he had been plunged into a different world. And it really had been like that … as if he had dived off a cliff, into a cold sea. His own life had been torn away from him. Everything he believed had been shattered. Yes, there were witches and demons and blood sacrifices. There were children with special powers and secret societies that existed to protect them. There were the Old Ones. He had been forced to accept all of it and had known from that moment on that there would be no escape.

From Yorkshire to London to Peru, back to London and then to Hong Kong – Richard had been swept along, trying to work out what his role in all this might be. The five Gatekeepers had been chosen for this adventure long before they had been born … but why him? He had consoled himself with the thought that he was there to help Matt. Certainly the two of them had become friends of a sort. But even that role had been taken from him when he had found himself in Cairo with Scarlett.

Since then, he had tried to give her the same support he had given Matt. He had barely left her side after she had been wounded. He had managed to save her from Tarik and had brought her here to Dubai. And now he had failed her. It was as simple as that. He should never have brought her here.

Richard went into Scarlett's room. "We're leaving," he announced.

"What?" Scarlett had been lying on the bed but now she sat up.

"We're getting out of the palace. It doesn't matter about Larry Carter." Richard went on quickly, before she could interrupt. "He probably wouldn't have taken us where we want to go anyway. We can get back in the car and drive to Oman or even down to Yemen. If there are planes here, there may be planes there. It doesn't make any difference. All we know is we can't stay here."

"But what about the door? It's locked."

By way of an answer, Richard leant down and seemed to take something out of his shoe. When he straightened up, he was holding the gun that had once belonged to the Frenchman, Rémy.

"Where did that come from?" Scarlett asked.

"I had it in my sock."

She stared, then remembered the entrance to the casino. "What about the metal detectors?" They had both passed through them.

"Yes. I was worried about that. But they weren't even plugged in. I knew when I saw a man go through, carrying a dog. It had a metal collar and it didn't set anything off. I guess the security was all part of the make-believe." He gripped the gun. "I wasn't going to come here empty-handed. And I can use this to get us out."

"Someone will hear if you shoot."

"I don't think so. There were no guards in the corridor as far as I could see, and most of the people here were so drunk when they left the dinner that they're probably fast asleep. But you can help me. Run the bath and put the shower on. That'll make a bit of noise. And as for the rest of it..."

He grabbed one of the pillows off the bed and wrapped the muzzle of the gun inside it, then pressed the whole thing against the lock of the door. Meanwhile, Scarlett had run into the bathroom and turned on all the taps. With so much metal and marble around, the sound of the water seemed amplified. Richard took a deep breath, then pulled the trigger.

Even with the pillow acting as a silencer, the explosion was enormous and must surely have been heard throughout the palace, if not in much of Dubai. Richard lowered the pillow – there was a scorched hole right through the middle – and tried the handle. The door swung inwards. He and Scarlett waited, hardly daring to breathe. But there was no sound of any alarms, no guards running. Someone must have heard the gunshot but it was always possible that they had no idea where it had come from. It could have been a drunken guest trying to make a point ... perhaps even the sheikh himself.

Richard wasn't going to wait any longer. "Let's go," he muttered. He and Scarlett slipped out.

After the sudden interruption, the palace had returned to that strange, absolute silence that only comes at night. The corridors were empty, illuminated by lamps shaped like candles, set at intervals along the walls. There weren't very many of them but the light was reflected by the white and pale grey marble, allowing them to see far ahead. Richard still had no idea how many people lived in the palace. It seemed to him that only half the dinner guests had actually left, meaning that around fifteen of them might still be under the sheikh's roof. Then there was the sheikh himself, his three bodyguards and at least a dozen servants. Add in guards, attendants, ministers and hangers-on and there could be a hundred people here ... certainly the palace was big enough to house them all.

"Which way?" Scarlett asked.

"Follow me." The truth was that Richard had little idea which way they were going. He had been careful to follow their progress from the dining room, along a maze of twisting corridors and passageways, up two flights of stairs ... but even if he could make his way back to the main door, he had little doubt that it would be locked and guarded. He still had the gun, but that wasn't going to help them if they were surrounded. He knew only that he had very little time to find a way out. Someone must have heard the gunshot. They might be investigating it even now.

They reached the end of the corridor, passed through an archway guarded by two onyx lions, one on each side, twisted round on themselves and finally came to the main staircase, a swirl of gold banisters and red carpet that would bring them down to the entrance hall and the doors to the street. They hurried down, but as they got to the hallway, Scarlett grabbed hold of Richard and pulled him back. She pointed. A CCTV camera was mounted high up on a crossbeam and, unlike the metal detector, it was definitely working, a red light blinking in the half-light. They were out of range, but one more step and they would have been seen.

"What now?" Scarlett whispered.

"A service entrance. There must be one..."

They found their way back to the dining room and went through the swing doors into the kitchen. Fortunately, there were no more cameras and if there were any guards on patrol, they didn't come across them. Together, they hurried past the stainless-steel surfaces, the fridges and the ovens. This was where all the food was prepared. It had to come in from somewhere.

It was on the other side, a set of double doors at the end of a short corridor. Without knowing quite why, Richard was certain that they had found the delivery entrance. He hurried towards it, realizing only when it was too late that he had made a mistake, that there was a second corridor that he hadn't noticed, with a man standing in the shadows. A guard stepped out, his rifle already loaded and at the ready. He stared at Richard and Scarlett in disbelief, then spoke to them in Arabic. Richard didn't move. He was still holding the gun and wondered if he could bring it up and fire it in time. The guard was aiming directly at him, less than five metres away. He would certainly shoot Richard down before he himself was hit – but at least that might give Scarlett a chance to get away. The exit door was so close! Richard cursed himself for not being more careful.

There was the tinkle of glass. The guard's eyes went white and he folded in on himself. It took Richard a moment to see that something had smashed into the back of his skull. Then Jaheda appeared behind him, holding the broken neck of a bottle of champagne.

The two of them looked at each other.

"You…" she said.

"Jaheda."

"I was coming to your room. I was coming to find you." Was it true? The woman's face, still partly concealed by the black silk scarf that hung around it, gave nothing away.

She was not alone.

There was a man standing behind her, dressed in the rags of what had once been blue trousers and a white shirt. He was barefoot. Richard knew at once that he was looking at the pilot, Larry Carter. He had been badly beaten. Richard saw the whip marks where the blood had dried across his shirt, and one side of his face was swollen. He had sand-coloured hair, matted and bedraggled. He looked as if he hadn't eaten properly for a week.

"Who the hell are you?" he demanded.

"I'm Richard Cole. This is Scarlett."

"What are you doing here?" He didn't sound at all pleased to see them. In fact he was sullen and hostile.

"As a matter of fact, we came to get you out."

"Did you? And why would you do that?"

"There is no time for a conversation," Jaheda interrupted. "You can do that when you are gone from here. I have the man you wanted. I have kept my side of the bargain and taken him from his cell. But now you must go. I want you far away."

She hurried towards the doors that Richard had first seen. Carter might have been released from his cell but his hands were still tied behind him and he stumbled forward, his arms and shoulders straining against the cords. Richard and Scarlett followed.

The doors led into a service area with a forklift truck resting against a wall and piles of empty crates all around. Richard had hoped he would see the street on the other side but they were still inside the palace compound, in a walled-in parking area with about fifty cars neatly positioned in two long rows. Even at a glance, it was clear that many of them had never been driven. They were brilliantly polished, the tyres free of any dust or dirt. Some were brand new, some vintage – from the twenties and thirties. Together they would have been worth hundreds of thousands of pounds.

"The sheikh likes cars," Jaheda said.

"Even though he has nowhere to go," Richard muttered.

The woman turned on him. "He collects cars. He does not need to drive them. You wouldn't understand."

She led them to yet another door with a push-bar. Surely this had to be the way out into the street! The door was locked and this time there was an electronic keypad, demanding a numeric code.

"The number is 5455," Jaheda said. "But opening the door at this time of the night will set off an alert throughout the palace and there is nothing I can do about that. Once you are outside, you will find yourselves on Baniyas Road. Do you have a car?"

"Yes."

"It will take them a few minutes to come after you. Go as quickly as you can. If Rasheed catches you, have no doubt, he will kill you slowly"

"Thank you," Richard said.

"Do not thank me," Jaheda snapped. But then she turned and looked at Scarlett and just for a moment there was a softness in her eyes. Perhaps she was remembering how she had been at that age. "I have done this only for myself."

She turned and went, hurrying back the way she had come. Richard, Scarlett and Larry Carter were left standing beside the door.

"I don't suppose either of you would have a knife on you?" the pilot asked.

Richard shook his head. "We'll cut you free later."

"So what happens now?"

"We go to the airport."

"The plane's still there?"

"That's right. You're going to fly us out."

"Oh yes? And where do you think you're heading?"

"To Antarctica."

"You've got to be kidding!"

Richard had never taken a dislike to anyone so immediately. He and Scarlett were saving this man's life. The sheikh would have executed him. But he wasn't remotely grateful. In fact, all he seemed to want to do was argue. "Let's not discuss it now," he said.

He keyed in the four numbers that Jaheda had given him.

The door opened and at the same moment alarm bells exploded throughout the palace. Richard, Scarlett and Carter burst out, running into the sluggish heat of the night. It took them a moment to orient themselves. There was the dried-out canal in front of them, the casino on their right…

"Where's the car?" the pilot shouted.

"This way!"

Richard led them down Baniyas Road. There were no lights anywhere in the city but they were lucky. There was a full moon and the sky was full of stars. Richard had left the Land Cruiser about a hundred metres away and they ran towards it, their footsteps echoing on the pavements, the pilot cursing as he had to fight for balance with his arms behind him. Back at the palace, lights were already starting to come on. Someone shouted. Could it be possible that they had been spotted? Richard was already wishing he had parked the car closer. He felt in his trouser pockets for the ignition key. It wasn't there! Just for a moment, his blood froze – then he remembered that he had decided it was better not to carry it with him and had left it in the glove compartment.

They reached the car. Richard threw open the door and scrambled in. Scarlett helped Larry Carter into the back, wasting precious seconds as he contorted himself and swore out loud, banging his head against the top of the doorframe. Then she climbed in next to Richard.

Richard found the key, jammed it into the ignition and turned it. The car started at once. They pulled out and began to drive. For the first time that evening, Scarlett thought she could relax. They had made it! The airport was less than twenty minutes away.

"There's something I think I should tell you." The voice was Larry Carter's and it was utterly cold, coming from the back seat. "I don't know what you two jokers think you're up to, but there's absolutely no way I'm flying you to Antarctica. I don't quite know why you want to go there. It wouldn't be my choice for a vacation. But just so there's no misunderstanding, I'm telling you now, it's out of the question."

Richard glanced at the driving mirror. "Suppose we dump you on the road," he muttered.

"Then you're not going anywhere. Zack needs me to fly that plane. Or didn't he tell you?"

Zack was Martins, the co-pilot. And Richard knew that Carter was telling the truth.

Scarlett twisted round. The pilot was sprawled out uncomfortably, sitting on his own hands and arms. But there was a thin, unpleasant smile on his face. At the end of the day, he held all the cards … and he knew it. "We have to go to Antarctica," she said.

"Why do you have to do that?"

"I can't explain it to you. And you wouldn't believe me if I did."

"Well, let me explain something to you. There's nothing there except freezing wind and maybe a few penguins. Nowhere to refuel. If I come down on the ice, I may not be able to take off again. I don't want to die out there."

"You won't die. There are people waiting for us."

"Really?" Carter didn't sound convinced. "Well, they're going to have to wait a little longer. I'm heading back to Australia. Maybe you can hitch another ride from there."

Scarlett opened her mouth to argue with him, but just then there was a flicker of light in the back window and she saw three cars pulling out onto the road far behind them. "Richard...!"

"I've seen them." Richard glanced again at the rear-view mirror. The cars were some distance but they were already catching up. He thought of the vehicles he had seen in the lock-up. They contained some of the most powerful engines ever built for the road. There was no doubt at all that whoever was following would catch up with them long before they got anywhere near the airport.

The pilot had seen them too. He was leaning forward, the lights of the dashboard reflecting green in his face. He looked scared. "Where's your gun?" he demanded. With a cry of desperation, he jerked at the ropes, trying to free himself.

"The gun won't help us," Richard said. He turned to Scarlett and there was a moment of understanding between them. "Can you?"

Scarlett thought briefly, then nodded. She took one last look behind her. The pursuing cars had already halved the distance between them. She had to do this quickly. She closed her eyes. Fifteen seconds passed. They were still speeding forward through the empty streets. Richard was gripping the wheel, concentrating on the road ahead.

"What are you doing?" the pilot shrieked. He was staring at

Scarlett. "You think falling asleep is going to help?"

"Listen to me, Mr Carter," Richard said, through gritted teeth. "We're going to get to the airport and you're going to get us into the air. And then you're going to take us to Antarctica because this girl is very special and if she says she has to be there, then that's what happens."

"Special...?"

"If you don't believe me, look behind you."

Larry Carter hesitated, then turned around in his seat and looked out of the rear window. He stared. Then he faced forward again. Then he looked back. His mouth fell open. He looked more frightened than ever.

"She did that...?" he whispered.

"That's right," Richard said. "She did that."

The way ahead was clear. They were driving through the empty city, the road a pale white, reflecting the moon. The skyscrapers were silhouetted like huge paper cut-outs all around. But behind them, the rain was pounding down. It was falling so heavily that everything was obliterated. The road had become a black river. The cars that had been following them had disappeared. Almost certainly they would have had to stop. Nothing would have been able to drive through the rainstorm.

The pilot looked ahead again. Dry. But as they drove forward, the rain closed in, separating them, protecting them.

Impossible.

"She did that?" he said again.

Scarlett was still deep in concentration. Richard nodded. "You know, if I were you, I'd think very hard about upsetting her."

Ten minutes later, they reached the airport. They parked in the same place and Richard retrieved his backpack, using the Inca knife to cut the pilot free. Together, they ran through departures, through security, back out onto the tarmac and round to the plane. Martins, the co-pilot, was sitting in a deckchair on the tarmac, smoking and drinking whisky, but scrambled to his feet when he saw them.

"Larry? I can't believe they found you ... got you out." He saw the look on the other man's face. "What's going on?"

"Just get into the cockpit, Zack. Behind the controls. We're getting out of here right now."

They climbed the steps into the plane. The co-pilot closed and sealed the door. Larry was already on his way to the upper deck. Richard and Scarlett followed him, choosing two seats in business class, where they had a view of the controls. As Martins strapped himself in, they saw Larry go through the start-up procedures, flipping open the battery switch cover, turning on the standby power, the electronic engine control, the navigation lights. Finally, he switched on the IRS – the Inertial Reference System – which would send all the necessary information to the flight computer.

"This is going to take ten minutes," he shouted at Richard.

"Can't you do it any faster?"

"No. And we can't do it in the air."

Scarlett peered out of the window. She couldn't see anything in the darkness and it was always possible that Rasheed's men were closing in on them from behind. Meanwhile, both Martins and Carter were pressing more switches. The computer screens had burst into life, displaying numbers and diagrams that would have been meaningless to anyone but them. The engines started. Scarlett could feel their energy, vibrating in the air. But they still didn't move. The seconds ticked away, agonizingly slow. Richard was standing with his hands resting on the pilot's seat, leaning forward. Everything seemed to be taking for ever. She wanted to scream.

And then, finally, Carter opened the throttle panel, set the flaps, released the parking brake and at last they jolted forward. Scarlett had never seen so much activity taking place in such a confined space. The two men had flown together long enough for each of them to know exactly what they were meant to do and at what time. The huge plane had begun to move, leaving the stairs slanting up into thin air. Richard knew that they must be using all their skill to guide the Airbus without a tow truck, without airport staff showing them the way. Nobody was speaking. They were all gazing out of the window, their eyes fixed on the navigation lights.

Slowly, the plane wheeled round.

They taxied to the runway and although all of them wanted to be in the air and on the way, they had to stop again. Final checks. There were no lights to help them take off. If it hadn't been for the moon, Richard knew it would have been impossible.

Carter turned to the co-pilot. "You ready?"

Martins nodded.

No need to wait for air traffic control. No need to look out for other planes. In the darkness of the cabin, the two men reached out and made the last adjustments. "OK. Let's go."

Scarlett heard the pitch of the engines rise. They began to roll forward, picking up speed. She had the seat nearest the window and suddenly she saw them, racing across the tarmac to cut them off. There was a Land Rover, a Jaguar and a Ferrari, a bizarre trio of vehicles. They must have entered the airport from the other side because they were ahead of them, at the far end of the runway.

"Richard!" Scarlett pointed.

Richard leant over her. "It's OK," he said. "They're not going to make it." But he didn't sound convinced.

The plane was hurtling forward, moving faster and faster. The lines on the runway had already become a blur. They could see the cars, directly in front of them. The drivers were committing suicide. If there was a collision, the drivers would be killed instantly. But the Airbus would crash too. Was that their aim, to bring them down, no matter what the cost?

They had reached take-off speed.

"Let's do it!" Carter shouted.

He pulled back on the controls, glancing at the primary flight display to check that the pink lines were centred and their climb rate was secure. Martins was already reaching for the switch to raise the landing gear. The cars were right in front of them. Richard actually saw the drivers crouching there, their faces white. They would be deafened by the noise of the engines. They were going to crash! They weren't high enough.

The plane rose. They were clear. There could only have been inches in it, but they were away.

Richard and Scarlett saw the ground disappear below them. They couldn't believe they had done it. Scarlett was exhausted. Beside her, Richard let out a huge sigh of relief.

In the cockpit, Martins said nothing until they had reached six thousand metres. Then he turned to the pilot. "You want me to set a course for Alice Springs?" he asked.

There was a long silence. Then…

"We're not going to Alice Springs."

"No?"

"No."

"So where are we going?"

Another pause.

"Antarctica."

Martins screwed up his face in puzzlement. "Are you serious, Larry? Why?"

The pilot took a while to answer. At last he spoke. "I don't know, mate. It just seems like a good idea."

The Emirates airline Airbus reached nine thousand metres over the desert. Then it changed course and began the long journey south.

LEGACY 600

THIRTY-ONE

They found another slave market soon enough. It seemed that every village and every town in Brazil had one, that there was no other way for the people to live. Men sold their wives and women sold their children ... the younger and fitter they were, the higher their price. The most desperate people of all simply sold themselves. As Matt and Lohan drove south, they passed several chain gangs, like something out of an old American film, dusty figures shuffling forward with their hands tied and chains connecting them from ankle to ankle.

It seemed as if months had passed since the two of them had found themselves in the submerged, rotting city of Belém and had come to terms with the fact that the world had changed utterly in the few seconds it had taken them to travel there from Hong Kong. Environmental catastrophe, political breakdown, the dark influence of the Old Ones ... they were aware of all these things but they hardly mattered when they were faced with the practical matter of how they were going to make it to the next day. They had no money, no food and no transport. It was only when they had stumbled on the Mercado de Ferro – the old iron market close to the quays – and discovered what it was now being used for that they had seen what they had to do. Matt hadn't argued. In the end he had been sold three times and although the process was humiliating and sometimes painful, it had brought them the money they needed to survive.

The third sale had been the worst. It had brought them to Fernandinho. The drug lord was probably looking for them even now, and many of the traders in the country would have been warned about a Chinese man with an American boy and the trick that they were playing. But they had to try again. From the moment Matt had woken up in the stolen jeep, he had taken command. They were no longer heading for Salvador and Matt had no interest in trying to get to the United States. He had been back to the dreamworld and he had a new destination.

"Antarctica!" Sitting in the grey light of the jungle, cramped and mosquito-bitten after a bad night's sleep, Lohan hadn't believed what he had just heard,

"The Old Ones are there," Matt said. "In a place called Oblivion. They're waiting for us to arrive."

"If they're waiting for you, then that's the last place you should go."

"No. They have Scott. That's how they know we'll come. Their armies are already there." Matt looked into the distance, at the sun struggling to force its way through the grey clouds. "We're not the only ones, Lohan. All over the world, people are heading south. There are still a few planes flying. They have ships..."

"How do they know about Oblivion?"

"I don't know. Maybe they've heard about it ... like a rumour, spreading from country to country. Maybe they've dreamt about it. But it's already begun. And I have to be there to help them..."

That had been three days ago. Since then, the jeep had run out of petrol and Matt and Lohan had been forced to continue on foot. They hadn't even come across another vehicle they could steal. Matt knew that Lohan would kill anyone who got in his way, simply taking what he needed without any thought. The two of them were unlikely partners and although he had never said as much, Matt found himself badly missing Richard Cole. Lohan might be better equipped for survival but his very ruthlessness made him cold and untrustworthy. When Matt had been taken prisoner in the drug compound, part of him had even wondered if Lohan would stick to their agreement and come to his rescue. He wouldn't have put it past the Triad leader to abandon him and make off with the money.

In fact, Lohan had considered doing exactly that.

Lohan was twenty-four years old and for much of his life he had been involved in organized crime. He had carried and sold drugs. He had sold weapons – to other criminals and to terrorists. He had been involved in gambling, blackmail and vice. In the course of his career, he had killed eleven men, finally rising to become Incense Master with the rank of 438 in the White Lotus Society in Hong Kong.

He was not ashamed of anything he had done. After all, he had never applied for the job. He had been born into it. His father had been the Master of the Mountain, the undisputed leader of the Triad, and Lohan had been groomed to take his place one day. Part of the lesson was to obey every instruction, to have no scruples, to be loyal only to the Triad and to himself.

It had come as a shock to him to find himself babysitting a fifteen-year-old English schoolgirl. Of course, he had always known about Scarlett Adams. She had been taken from the Pancaran Kasih Orphanage in Jakarta when she was a baby and sent secretly to England. For some reason, the White Lotus Society had sworn to protect her and they had been watching her ever since. Lohan had once asked his father why they should waste time and resources on a single girl, thousands of miles away. It was one of the few times the Master of the Mountain had ever turned his anger on his son.

"Ask no questions. Never question my commands. The life of

this girl matters more to me than your own. She is more important than any of us."

And then the Old Ones had come to Hong Kong and Lohan had understood. It was, at first, impossible to believe. It was as if the city had been invaded by aliens, creatures from outer space. They killed everyone who stood in their way – first hundreds, then thousands – and nobody noticed! The bodies were piling up in the harbour and nobody cared. The Old Ones infiltrated the government. They controlled the police. They turned the entire city into a giant trap – simply so that Scarlett Adams would fall into their hands.

Lohan had managed to grab Scarlett, even though she was surrounded by her enemies, and had tried to smuggle her out of the city on a cruise ship. The plan had only failed at the last moment when they had been betrayed – one of the few failures he had known in his life. The two of them had only met again at the Tai Shan Temple in the last few moments as Hong Kong had been destroyed.

And now this.

Despite everything, Lohan had been sorry to find himself separated from Scarlett. He had grown to like her. After all, she was an English schoolgirl, brought up in comfort in a quiet London suburb. She knew nothing about real life. She had never been in danger. And yet she had adapted remarkably quickly. There had been no hysterics, no tears. At the end of the day, she had actually saved them all, using powers that she had never known she had.

From one fifteen-year-old to another. It seemed to Lohan that Matt was very different from Scarlett. There was something detached about him, an inner strength and certainty that made him quite difficult to understand. When the two of them had found themselves together in Belém, with water lapping at the buildings and rotting corpses floating past in the gutter, he hadn't even seemed surprised. And although Lohan was a lot older than him, with all the experience that his life in the Triad had brought him, it was Matt who had taken command.

Matt was still the one making the decisions. They were going to Oblivion. It didn't matter that it would be almost impossible to get there and that anyway it was the worst place on the planet, even more dangerous than Brazil. He didn't care that the ice and the cold would kill them even if the Old Ones didn't. That was their destination.

And there was something else. Lohan was aware that Matt had changed since the business with Fernandinho. Maybe it was something he had seen or heard in the dreamworld. There was definitely something he wasn't saying.

Tired and footsore, they had reached a shabby, whitewashed village where a slave market was actually about to start and that was where they were now, watching from the edges. As far as Lohan could see, it was ideal. There were just a few children for sale, as well as some animals and a one-armed man who probably wouldn't raise as much as five dollars. But the very fact that it was quiet and out of the way was in its favour. If Fernadinho was looking for them, he would be unlikely to find them here.

Matt was leaning against a wall, looking weak and exhausted after the long walk. It occurred to Lohan that his value was probably going down with every day that passed, although the fact that he could pass as an American still added to his price. American slaves were highly prized. "I think we should go somewhere bigger," he said.

"Why? This is perfect!"

"We'll get a better price in a town."

"I can sell you here for a hundred dollars. Then I can pull you out and sell you again for two hundred dollars when we get to a town. We might as well get all the money we can."

"No, Lohan." Matt shook his head. "We're just wasting time here. Let's keep going."

Lohan was astonished that he could be ordered about in this way. Just six months ago, he would never have dreamt that such a thing could happen. But there was something in Matt's voice that told him there was no point arguing. They turned away from the slave market and set off again.

It took them three hours to arrive at a much busier town, a place called Jangada, which stood at a busy intersection, with houses and shops piled up on each other like a traffic accident. There was a football stadium with broken floodlights and mouldering grass and even as Lohan and Matt arrived, another, larger slave market was about to begin. Once again, Lohan was suspicious. Could it just be coincidence that had brought them here? Or had Matt somehow known that the market was taking place?

A large platform had been constructed in the stadium, with twenty men and a dozen boys aged from about eight to eighteen huddled together in shared misery. There were no women for sale. Jeeps and trucks were parked along the edge of what had once been the football pitch and there were groups of men – the buyers – already examining the merchandise. The whole place stank of animal dung and there were flies everywhere. It occurred to Lohan that even slavery might be preferable to life in this drab, forgotten place.

Matt and Lohan were standing out of sight at one of the entrances, with empty seating rising above them. Lohan had brought a rope with him from the abandoned jeep. He began to tie a noose.

"It may not be so easy to find me this time," Matt said. "But don't give up."

"Why should it be any more difficult than the last three times?" Lohan asked.

Matt didn't answer. Lohan lifted the rope over his head and pulled it tight around his neck. Matt flinched. He knew what was coming next and although he didn't like it, he knew it had to be done. "OK," he said. "I'm ready."

Lohan hit him across the face. Matt jerked backwards, making no sound. They both knew what they were doing. Matt had to look subdued, the servant with his owner. He bowed his head. His eyes were filled with tears of pain and there was a fresh bruise on his cheek. Now he looked just like the other boys.

Lohan led him across to the trader, a small, mean-looking man dressed in an old football shirt with the name FLAMENGO printed in red on his back. He was bald and carried a bullwhip, curled up at his side. As he saw them approaching, his eyes filled with suspicion and Lohan wondered if he had heard of them and knew the trick they were about to play.

"You're selling him?" the trader asked, speaking in Portuguese.

"That's right." Lohan spoke the language fluently. He had been taught it when he was at school in Macao.

"Where did you get him? He's clearly not your son. Is he American?"

"I bought him," Lohan spat. "Now I've got no further use for him. So I'm selling him. Do you have a problem with that?"

Matt knew that Lohan was being aggressive on purpose. He wouldn't want to spin out long stories or make the trader think he had something to hide. There was a long silence and Matt didn't dare look up. If he did, Lohan would have to hit him again. But then he felt the trader's hands on him, pulling up his shirt to examine his torso and chest, feeling the muscles in his arms, and knew that he had been accepted for sale. The trader prised open Matt's mouth and peered inside, looking for evidence of tooth rot or disease. Finally, he ran a hand through his hair, just as if he were a dog.

"All right," he said. "The kid's in good shape. He can join the others. But I warn you, prices are low today. They're all being sold in a job lot."

"Who is the buyer?"

"Over there..."

Lohan glanced at the platform and his heart sank. There was a group of them standing in front of it, dressed in khaki with guns dangling from their shoulders. These weren't farmers looking for cheap labour or rich men who liked having good-looking boys to clean their houses. They were soldiers and they had done this before, many times. He could tell from the way they stood there, working as a unit, relaxed with each other, uninterested in their surroundings. They were men without feelings and Lohan knew that such men were the most dangerous of all.

He glanced briefly at Matt, wondering if he should make an excuse and pull them both out before it was too late. Matt had seen the soldiers too. He shook his head very slightly. The message was clear. He wanted to go on.

Lohan handed the rope across and the trader led Matt up to the platform, where he stood with the other boys. The soldiers barely acknowledged him. They were buying everyone who was there and it didn't matter to them if he was fat, thin, strong or weak. A job lot. The trader negotiated briefly with one of the soldiers – a bearded man with a broken nose and crumpled cheeks. A deal was made. The two of them shook hands. The soldier reached into his pocket and took out a bundle of banknotes, which he began to count.

The trader took the money and walked back to Lohan. He handed over five crumpled ten-dollar bills.

"Fifty dollars?" Lohan was contemptuous. "You're not being serious. He's worth five times that."

"I warned you that prices were low today. If you're not happy, you can leave."

"OK." Lohan made a decision. He gave the money back. "You can forget it. I'll take him with me."

It was already too late.

Lohan's attention had been on the trader, on Matt and on the money. He hadn't noticed the other man who had crept up behind him and only became aware of him as something slammed into his back. He toppled forward onto his knees, already reaching for the gun that was concealed in his waistband. But his attacker was too fast. Before he could produce it, he was hit a second time, this time a leather boot crashing into the side of his head. If Lohan hadn't reacted instinctively and ridden the blow, it would have cost him a fractured skull. As it was, he was sent flying into the dirt and he could only lie there, dazed and furious, as the gun and everything else he owned was removed.

"*Olhe para mim, seu porco...*"

"Look at me, you pig." The voice was ugly, filled with contempt.

With the side of his head on fire and blood in his mouth, Lohan rolled over and looked up. The trader was standing over him with a second man. That was when Lohan realized just how much trouble he was in. Short, dark with black eyes and a moustache ... he recognized him at once. It was the *cafuzo* – half African, half Brazilian – who had bought Matt the last time he had been sold.

"Is this him?" the trader asked.

"This is him," the other man replied. Lohan saw him draw back his foot and tried to roll out of the way as he lashed out a second time. The foot caught him on the shoulder, sending a bolt of pain all the way down his arm.

Matt watched helplessly from the platform. There were too many soldiers here, too many guns. He was tied up. There was nothing he could do. A small crowd had gathered around Lohan. People weren't having a lot of fun in a place like Jangada and a man being beaten up was the closest thing to entertainment that they got. The *cafuzo* had Lohan's gun in his hand. There could be no doubt that he was going to use it to kill him.

The soldier with the beard and the broken nose stepped forward. "What's this all about?" he demanded.

"This man is a thief," the *cafuzo* explained. "He and the American boy – they have this thing together. He sells him, then he takes him back again. Fernandinho sent me to find them. He wants them both dead."

"You can't kill the boy," the soldier said. "He belongs to me now ... and where he's going, it's a living death anyway. It'll come to the same in the end. You can tell Fernandinho that. As for this other one..." He looked down at Lohan, who was lying there, his eyes sullen, furious with himself for allowing this to happen. Suddenly a thought came to him. "I'll take him too, if you like."

"You mean you'll pay for him..." the *cafuzo* said.

"I'll take him for nothing. You've got his money. How much did he have on him?"

The *cafuzo* had ended up with a bundle of notes which he had taken from Lohan's pocket. He counted them quickly. "Six hundred."

"That's plenty." The soldier laughed humourlessly. "You can pay back Fernandinho what he's owed and split the rest between you. It looks like the Chinese guy's got plenty of work in him so I'll take care of him. I get an extra pair of hands for nothing. I'd say that works out all round."

There was a brief pause. But what the soldier had said made sense, and anyway, he had his men close by and if there was going to be an argument or even a fight, the trader would have got the worse of it. He knew that. He glanced at the *cafuzo,* who must have thought the same thing. He nodded. The agreement had been made.

After that, things happened very quickly. Lohan was pulled to his feet. His hands were tied behind his back and he was propelled forward, joining the others on the platform. All at once he was standing next to Matt. Even at that moment, it occurred to him that Matt didn't seem particularly surprised by what had just happened. Certainly, he wasn't concerned, even though they were now both prisoners with no one to come after them wherever they were taken. At the same time, the trader completed his negotiations with the soldiers and suddenly it was over. There were thirty-four people on the platform, but they were no longer human beings. They were possessions.

"*Vamos lá!*"

One of the soldiers shouted the order and the pack of them began to move off. The other men used the butts of their rifles to lash out at anyone who was slow or who tried to break away. The local townspeople watched with blank faces. Lohan knew what they were thinking. It might have amused them to see the slaves being bought, but in their hearts they knew that one day their food and their money would run out and they would end up just the same. The captives were herded down the main street past shops that were empty or closed and houses with the windows boarded over. Everything was dirty and run-down. Finally, they came to an old bus station. There were still one or two buses left behind, missing their windows, their wheels and their seating ... nothing more than rusty, burnt-out cans.

There was a helicopter parked there, waiting for them. Matt and Lohan had seen nothing in the air since they had found themselves in Brazil so the sight of it was both surprising and alarming. Clearly, they had a long journey ahead of them. The helicopter was a four-bladed Super Puma painted in the colours of the national air force, sitting on its own in the rubble, hardly in better condition than the buses. It had been constructed to hold just eighteen passengers but almost twice that number were going to be crammed inside.

"OK. Começar dentro!"

Once again the order was barked out in Portuguese, but the sight of the helicopter had been too much for one of the prisoners, an older man with wide eyes and a thin, pockmarked face. As the soldiers pushed the others in, he panicked and broke free, running across the bus station, weaving from side to side with his hands still tied behind his back. One of the soldiers lifted his rifle, aimed and fired. The man's legs tied themselves in knots and he went down. Lohan watched the body hit the ground. Well, there was fifty dollars wasted, he thought. But on the other hand, the soldiers probably didn't care too much. After all, they had got him for nothing.

Nobody did anything that would get themselves noticed after that, climbing into the helicopter and taking their places on their feet in the metal cabin. The seats had been taken out, but even so they were jammed in so tight that there was barely room to breathe. Lohan and Matt had become separated. They couldn't have been far apart from each other but it was impossible to be sure. Their faces were pressed against the necks and shoulders of people they didn't know. They could taste sweat on their lips.

The soldiers slammed the door shut. Only two of them were making the journey. One was the pilot. The others would presumably follow another time. The engines started up. The blades began to turn, picking up speed until the noise became deafening. The cabin began to vibrate. Some of the boys were sobbing.

The helicopter left the ground. It hovered, turned, rose into the sky, then soared, carrying its human cargo into the unknown.

THIRTY-TWO

At last the helicopter landed.

They had been flying for about two hours but it had been impossible to tell which direction they were taking, whether they were heading inland or out to sea. Nobody could see anything unless they were pressed up against the cabin window, and even then the clouds had covered everything for much of the time. The helicopter might be droning forward but time seemed to have stood still for the unfortunate passengers who were there, breathing in the damp air, suspended in darkness and misery with the noise of the engines all around. At last they felt the pressure change as the helicopter began its descent. There was a sudden bump. The door was opened. And there it was ... the most secure prison in the world, in the middle of the rainforest, surrounded by it, thick and impassable on all sides. If anyone was going to leave here, it would certainly not be on foot ... not without a compass, drinking water, a machete, food and medicine.

A miniature airport had been hacked out of the middle of the jungle and this was where the helicopter had come to rest. It was sitting in a wide compound, penned in by a tall wire fence which had been built fairly recently, although it was already covered in rust. A tarmac road followed the fence on the inside and there were more slaves, part of an earlier intake, hard at work, unloading heavy boxes from a truck. A single armed soldier watched over them.

A runway stretched into the distance, stopping at the edge of the rainforest, which stood there like an impenetrable barrier. The soldiers had constructed an ugly, uneven control tower using a patchwork of wooden panels ripped out of crates and squares of beaten tin. It was surrounded by covered wagons and a jeep and a second helicopter. Battered drums of aviation fuel were stacked to one side, partly covered by tarpaulin.

Lohan realized that Matt was standing next to him. He looked at the boy almost reproachfully, wanting to blame him for the situation in which they found themselves but at the same time knowing that it would do no good. But Matt's eyes were fixed on something behind him. Slowly, Lohan turned.

And there it was, the one sign of hope in this nightmare, the one small chance that there might be a way out. It was parked on the rubble, waiting to take off. Lohan knew it at once ... a Legacy 600, made in Brazil, old and dusty with fading paint but surely still capable of flight. Already, Lohan was doing the sums. A Legacy had a range of six thousand kilometres. They couldn't be more than four thousand kilometres from the tip of South America. The plane could take them to Antarctica.

"Can you fly?" Matt asked.

Lohan nodded slowly. "Yes."

How could Matt have known? There had been a time when the Triad had been given the task of smuggling illegal immigrants from Asia into Australia – for a price. Lohan's father had always insisted that his sons should involve themselves in every area of his business and so he had ordered Lohan to study for his pilot's licence. He was unfamiliar with the controls of the Legacy but he had flown a Hawker 4000, which was similar. Not that it mattered anyway. There wasn't a plane in the world that Lohan wouldn't have attempted to fly if he had thought it would get him out of here.

More armed soldiers had come to meet them, all of them dressed in the same khaki uniforms, although they carried a range of different guns. Lohan could see that this was not a military installation. The men were too slovenly and ill-disciplined, many of them unshaven, smoking, with long, dirty hair. Mercenaries? A private army? They stood and watched over the new arrivals as they formed themselves into a line. It was extremely warm and damp in the jungle. It wasn't actually raining but the moisture hung constantly in the air. Matt and Lohan had only been here for a few minutes but their clothes were already damp and uncomfortable. Mosquitoes whined in their ears. Doubtless there would be snakes in the undergrowth. Disease and sickness were all around them.

"Did you know it would be here?" Lohan asked.

Matt looked up. "What?" he asked.

"The plane."

"I hoped it would be."

Lohan shook his head. "You knew it was here," he said. "This is your plan. You want me to fly us to Antarctica."

Before he could answer, one of the soldiers struck out with the butt of his rifle, driving it into Matt's chest. "*Nenhuma fala!*" "No talking." Again the instruction was in Portuguese. A Brazilian boy, aged eleven or twelve, had been standing next to Matt and for him this casual act of violence was the final straw. He burst into tears. There was nothing Lohan could do for him. His hands were still tied behind his back, and anyway, any further talking would only invite the same punishment. But looking at the boy, he thought to himself, if the pain of others means so much to you, you will be dead in a week. For his part, Matt reeled back, straightened up, but said nothing. The soldier moved on.

The prisoners stood with the helicopter behind them for about ten minutes. Finally, the man with the beard and the broken nose who had been at the market stepped forward to address them. He had travelled in the front, with the pilot. He was holding a half-empty bottle of rum.

"Welcome to Serra Morte," he began. "This is where you will live and where you will die. If you work hard, you will not be badly treated. You will be given water – one litre a day – food and a place to sleep. If you do not work, if you try to escape, if you are disobedient, you will be punished. There is only one punishment at Serra Morte and it is death. But do not think that it will be painless, a quick release from your labours. We have a game here. We like to see how long we can make a person suffer before they die. The record is one hundred and six days. Remember that.

"You will begin work immediately. We work here for fifteen hours a day, every day. There are no holidays. If you become too sick to work, you will be taken into the jungle and left there for the snakes and the alligators. After work you will be taken to the place where you will sleep. But sleep has to be earned. There are rules that you must learn but it is very simple. You are slaves. You have no rights. Nobody cares about you. You will do as you are told and you will work and that is all. Now – follow me."

They set off, shuffling through the gates, along the track and into the rainforest. Matt was still next to Lohan, his face grim and yet submissive. At the same time, the fire seemed to have gone out of him and that worried Lohan almost more than the terrible situation in which they found themselves. Neither of them spoke, afraid of another beating and saving their energy for the long walk through the heat. Within seconds they were smothered in the thick, tangled vegetation of the rainforest, and when Lohan glanced back, the little airport had already disappeared. The path was well trodden. A great many people must have come this way as they were led into captivity. Some sort of creature, a monkey maybe, moved in the branches overhead, but looking up, there was no sign of it. Nothing could be seen, not even the sky. It was as if they were walking through a dark green tunnel.

And then the rainforest opened out and they found ourselves at the edge of a clearing. The helicopter had dropped them on high ground, on a plateau, and suddenly a whole panorama opened up in front of them. It was a sight that none of them would ever forget.

There was a vast, monstrous hole in the ground. It was as if an entire mountain had been scooped out and this was the empty space that had been left. In fact that was exactly what had happened. The hole was man-made. The earth had been cut into, layer after layer, with long ridges and platforms that continued down for five hundred metres. To get from one level to another there were ladders – hundreds and hundreds of them – cut from the branches of trees and roped together so that they looked horribly fragile and unsafe.

And there were people still digging. It was impossible to say how many of them there might be. The ones in the distance were tiny, the ones close by packed together in dense crowds. They were climbing the ladders – swarming up them – carrying wooden buckets filled with earth. Most of them were half-naked. Some of them wore only a loin cloth wrapped around their groin. And they were filthy, so caked in mud and sweat that they barely looked human at all, smothered in brown and grey, their hair matted, their eyes staring out hopelessly.

They were taking soil from the bottom to the top, a back-breaking journey up one ladder after another, with long lines of people in front and behind. Up to the top with a full bucket and then immediately down again with an empty one. Fall and you would die. You could break your neck. You could suffocate in the soft earth. You could be trampled underfoot by the others. Nobody was speaking. These people were worse even than slaves. They had been turned into caged animals: mindless, helpless, existing only in exhaustion and pain.

And Matt and Lohan had been chosen to join them.

"This is the Serra Morte mine," the bearded man exclaimed. The new prisoners were huddled on the edge of the plateau, looking down at the chasm, knowing that we were going to be sucked into it, that they would become part of it and it would never let them go. "It is the largest gold mine in Brazil," he went on. "Your lives mean nothing any more. All that matters is the soil that you bring to the surface, the flakes of gold that it contains.

"From now on you will work together and you will live together. Your team name is 1179 *Verde*. Remember that." "*Verde*" was the Portuguese for green. "Your own names do not matter any more. If a guard asks you who you are or what team you belong to, you must answer '1179 *Verde*'. If you are unable to tell him, you will be punished. Now, before I take you down, are there any questions?"

Nobody spoke. Then one of the boys who had been on the platform with Matt put his hand in the air. He was thin, dark-haired with a sullen face, aged about eighteen.

"Yes?"

"When can I get some water?" he asked. "I'm thirsty."

The bearded man walked over to him and stopped in front of him. Everyone knew that something bad was going to happen – and they were right. He held out a hand and one of the other soldiers tossed him a plastic bottle of water.

"You want water?" he said. "You can have water."

He weighed the bottle in his hand for a moment then suddenly swung it with all his strength, crashing it into the side of the boy's head. Water exploded all over him as the plastic broke. The boy crumpled. It must have been like being hit by a club.

"Learn from this," the man said, addressing all of them. "You do not ask for water. You do not ask for food. You do not ask for rest. You take it when you are given it and you are grateful. Now let's get to work."

Nobody else had any questions. Several guards moved forward, carrying knives, and although some of the slaves writhed or whimpered, it soon became clear that their task was only to cut the bonds and set their hands free. Someone helped the boy to his feet and the whole group was about to make its way down when suddenly something moved through the sky above them, causing them to stop and look up. It was the Legacy 600. It had made no sound on the other side of the forest but suddenly it was roaring right above them as it cleared the treetops.

Lohan watched as it arced over the pit and veered away into the distance, then he turned back to Matt and his eyes were filled with anger.

"Was that your ticket out of here?" he snarled. "Well, it looks as if it's taken off without us. So what do we do now?"

Somebody pushed them forward. By the time they reached the edge of the pit, the plane had already gone.

THIRTY-THREE

Matt and Lohan spent the next week working in the gold mine of Serra Morte and by the end of that time they knew that if they didn't escape soon they would die. Their strength was being sucked out of them ... by the long hours, the gruelling labour, the lack of food and the constant presence of disease. And this was how it was for the thousands of people around them. It was as if they had been fed into some kind of hellish machine. Individually, they no longer mattered. They were being processed. Eventually they would die, just as others had died in front of them. And there were hundreds more arriving every day to fill the spaces that they would leave when they themselves had gone.

The mornings began with a klaxon, sounding out across the empty pit, echoing in the darkness before the sun began to rise. It might have been five o'clock. It might have been six. Nobody had watches or clocks so what difference did it make? The slaves slept in a town that had been constructed about half a kilometre from the pit, a dark and festering sprawl of huts made from wood, plastic, corrugated iron and canvas, or a mixture of all four. Lanes ran between the huts, giving the impression of a community, but in fact the town was lifeless, with nowhere to go, nothing to do. There was no electricity, no running water, no sanitation. Hundreds of people were forced to share the same latrine, a foul trench dug in the jungle where they would queue in line, waiting to relieve themselves. There was no privacy. The stench was stomach churning and the air was thick with black, buzzing flies.

Each building contained twenty or thirty people lying side by side on camp beds, so close that their shoulders touched. Old sheets and blankets hung uselessly over doorways in a vain attempt to keep the mosquitoes out, but all they did was keep the warm, sweat-filled air locked in. Evening meals were distributed in metal buckets and shared out, the men and women crowding round and filling their own tin cups. The food was always the same: a stew of beans with a few scraps of meat from an animal it was probably better not to identify. After they had eaten, they slept, knocked out by the fifteen hours' non-stop work that were just behind them but which they knew waited for them again the next day. Mosquitoes droned endlessly throughout the night. There was no respite.

Every morning began with a body count. There was a work detail – they were known as "*os coveiros*", the gravediggers, and it was their job to drag out the dead and carry them on wagons to a clearing in the jungle. In fact, there were no graves. The bodies would be dumped here, and once a week, when the pile had grown high enough, they would be doused in petrol and set alight. No night ever passed without someone dying. Sometimes it would be from malaria or exhaustion. More often, it was the snakes. Matt would sometimes hear the scream as someone was bitten. It would be followed by raised voices and panic as the other men and women in the same hut tried to find the creature by candlelight before they were bitten themselves.

The work was always the same.

Every morning, in the pale glow of the dawn, the workers picked up a wooden bucket and a wooden spade and climbed down the ladders, all the way to the bottom. Even this could be dangerous. The ladders were slimy with dirt and sweat, and it was all too easy to slip. On their very first day, Matt and Lohan saw a man fall to his death. Perhaps he broke his neck. Perhaps he suffocated in the mud. Either way he didn't get up again and the other workers simply curved around him, trying to pretend he wasn't there. Matt and Lohan did the same. They had quickly learnt not to draw attention to themselves, not to do anything that would separate them from the crowd. They had only one plan. They had to live long enough to be there when the Legacy 600 returned.

They dug, they filled their buckets, they climbed. It was dark at the bottom of the pit. The sky seemed miles away and the guards, standing on the edge or patrolling with their Alsatian dogs, were tiny. It was as much as Matt and Lohan could do to stay close to each other. Talking was forbidden, not that they would have had the strength to exchange anything except swear words. Climbing up was much harder because of the extra weight. The edge of the rope cut into their shoulders, the heavy buckets rubbed the skin off their backs. By the end of the day they were in a daze, pulling themselves up, rung after rung, with the next person's feet in front of them, someone's hands scrabbling at their ankles. One ladder then another and another. Matt didn't dare look up to see how far he had to go. If he knew, he might give up.

They dumped the mud that they had collected at the top and there were more workers ready to wash it, to sieve through it, searching for the flakes of gold that were the reason the mine existed. Torrents of muddy brown water flooded back down the hill. There seemed to be very little gold.

They were given water three times a day – when they woke up, at noon and before they slept – but it was never enough. The water was warm and thick with chemicals that were supposed to prevent them from getting sick but both Matt and Lohan suffered from nausea and stomach cramps, and all around them people were collapsing and lying in spasms on the ground.

Before the week was over, the two of them were almost unrecognizable. The sun had burned them, even though it never seemed to shine. Matt's neck and shoulders were raw and red. His shirt had been stolen from him while he was asleep and he was naked to the waist, although he was so filthy it was impossible to tell where his flesh ended and his trousers began. Lohan kept himself contained in a bubble of hatred, which he directed against the guards, against the *cafuzo* who had sold him and even against Matt.

The strange thing was that there were only a couple of hundred soldiers in the entire area, even though they were responsible for thousands of slaves. At first, Lohan had thought that he might be able to persuade people to join him in a general uprising. Surely it would be possible to break free if they all acted together. But he had soon realized it wasn't going to happen. A great many of the slaves had chosen to be here. They had sold themselves into slavery and at that moment it was as if something inside them had died. As for the rest, they knew they were going to be worked to death. But they no longer cared.

Just once, at night, Lohan and Matt talked about escaping. They were lying next to each other, whispering as quietly as they could in English. If anyone overheard them, they would almost certainly inform the guards in return for a little extra food.

"I can get us guns," Lohan said. "All I need is for one of the guards to come close enough..."

"And what then?" Matt sounded defeated.

"We can make a break for the helicopter. Or if that doesn't work, we could head off on foot, through the jungle."

"We'd never make it, Lohan. We're miles from anywhere. And they've got dogs. They'd come after us."

"Then what do you suggest, Matt? Do you want to die here?"

"We wait for the right moment."

"There are no right moments. There is only death."

And then Matt became ill.

It was what Lohan had been dreading more than anything, even though part of him still blamed Matt for bringing them here. It was on the eighth morning when the two of them woke up that Lohan saw that the worst had happened. Matt had a fever. His whole body was bathed in sweat and his eyes were glazed. Desperately, Lohan turned him over, forcing a little water between his lips. The other prisoners in the hut stole out as quickly as they could, not wanting to catch whatever the American boy had. It might be malaria. The mosquitoes had been more than usually aggressive. It might be dysentery. It might be something worse.

"Get up, Matt. I can help you..." Lohan tried to pull Matt to his feet but he soon saw that it was useless. Matt's whole body seemed to be broken, his arms and his legs lacking any strength. His breath was rasping in his throat. Outside, he heard one of the guards calling out a warning. Latecomers were beaten. Sometimes, as an example to the others, they were tied up and left without water or food, roasting in the heat. Lohan had no choice. "I will come back later," he said. "Try to rest. Try to get well..."

Lohan knew that the hut would be inspected as soon as he had gone. They would find Matt and they would make a decision. There was no medicine at Serra Morte and no doctors to administer it. If the soldiers thought there was any chance that Matt would get better, they would leave him lying there. If they decided he was finished, they would drag him out and throw him onto the pile of bodies waiting to be burned ... they wouldn't even check he was dead before they lit the match.

It was the longest day Lohan had known since he had been brought to this terrible place. All he could do was concentrate on his work, trying to force Matt out of his mind. Already he was making his plans. If Matt died, he would escape on his own. It didn't matter if he was killed in the attempt. He was dying anyway. He couldn't take any more.

He was the first back into the hut that evening. Matt was still there, looking not much better than he had been when Lohan had left.

"Pedro…? he asked, as Lohan leant over him, pressing another water bottle to his lips.

"He's not here," Lohan said, wishing that he was. Matt had told him that the Peruvian boy had the power to heal. It was exactly what was needed right now. "I'm Lohan. How are you feeling?"

"Weak."

"Well, at least you got a day off work." Lohan tried to make a joke of it, to conceal how worried he had been. "Do you want to eat? Can I get you anything?"

"The plane…"

"It's not here, Matt. It left more than a week ago and it hasn't come back." Lohan tried to keep the anger out of his voice. The other slaves were trooping into the room, collapsing on their beds. Some of them were already asleep. "I don't know what you saw in that dream of yours," he went on. "But it was a mistake coming here."

"The plane…"

"Didn't you hear me?"

Lohan was gripping Matt by his shoulders, almost as if he wanted to shake some sense into him. But then he heard it. Matt wasn't talking about the plane they had seen when they had arrived. There was another plane, approaching even as they spoke. Lohan looked up. There was a low humming in the air. It was still some distance away but it was getting closer all the time. The hum became a roar. The other prisoners looked up. It was right overhead. Lohan wanted to run out of the hut but he knew there was no point. He wouldn't see anything in the darkness and there was a risk he might get shot. But he listened as the plane landed and knew that it had touched down on the runway that he had seen eight days before.

He turned back to Matt. Despite everything, the boy seemed to be a little more peaceful, as if he had somehow managed to prove a point. Lohan smoothed the bundle of rags that he had been using as a pillow beneath his head. "It's OK," he whispered. "We're going to get out of here. We'll try tonight."

"No." Matt was also whispering but his voice was strong. "Not tonight. Tomorrow morning. Need to be strong..."

"It'll be easier when it's dark."

But Matt's eyes had closed and Lohan saw that he had fallen asleep. For a long time he crouched there, looking at the unconscious figure. He seemed to be struggling, trying to come to some sort of decision. Finally he nodded, as if he had won a battle with himself.

He stretched out on the bed next to Matt and a few minutes later he too was asleep.

THIRTY-FOUR

Lohan woke up early. His body might have been exhausted but his mind was in turmoil and he opened his eyes long before the sun began to rise, the hut shrouded in darkness. He lay there for a long time, listening to the sounds around him. A few people were snoring, some whimpering in the grip of bad dreams. The mosquitoes were whining as usual. Outside, a dog barked a couple of times then yelped as it was kicked. The best thing was that as far as he could see, Matt was sleeping soundly. Perhaps it would help him. He might even find someone in that dreamworld of his to look after him. Somehow, Lohan knew that the next day was going to be their last at Serra Morte – no matter how it actually turned out.

It was strange but he still had no idea who actually owned or organized the gold mine. Who, in fact, was getting the gold? It could have been the Brazilian government – but then Brazil didn't really have a government any more. Maybe it was the military or the drug lords. And what did they do with the gold when they got it? Presumably it was refined, melted down and traded in the international banks. Lying there as the light began to creep in, Lohan tried to imagine the men in suits weighing the bars in their hands, not thinking of the pain and misery that had produced it. He himself had bought bracelets and necklaces in the many gold markets in Hong Kong. He and his father had often traded in gold bars ... it was more secure and less easy to trace than paper money. Had some of the gold produced here ever passed through his hands? If so, he was being punished for it now.

Outside, the klaxon sounded and there were the same, tired movements in the hut, the occupants rolling off their camp beds and readying themselves for the day's work. Matt opened his eyes. Lohan examined him anxiously.

"Lohan..."

"How are you feeling?"

"I'm better. I'm OK." Matt lifted himself onto one elbow. "I'm coming with you today."

He was far from OK. Lohan could see that the fever hadn't left him and he was so weak that he was swaying on his feet. But somehow the two of them made it outside, drank their water and ate their bean stew, crouching in the damp morning air.

"Matt..." Lohan began.

"I know," Matt replied. "We have to make our move today."

"When?"

"I'll tell you."

Lohan nodded, amazed that he was taking orders from a fifteen-year-old boy – and one who was barely able to stand.

The guards shouted their orders and team 1179 *Verde* moved off. By now, Lohan recognized most of the faces of the prisoners who had been brought with him from the town of Jangada – but he knew none of their names and nothing of their histories. That was the way it worked at Serra Morte. Nobody trusted anybody and there was no point in making friends when you were all certain to die. Lohan snatched up a spade and a wooden pail for himself. He did the same for Matt, noticing with a sense of gloom that Matt was barely able to carry the weight.

Together they trudged the half a kilometre back to the pit, neither of them speaking, then stood there as the first workers began to climb down. Lohan glanced at Matt. They couldn't go down the ladders. If there was going to be any chance of escape, it had to start here, while they were still at ground level.

"Move!" One of the guards had seen them hesitating. He was like all the others, anonymous in his khaki uniform with a machine gun cradled in his arms and a dog following him on a leash.

Matt turned to Lohan. "Take him out," he said. For a moment Lohan thought he'd misheard. What was Matt saying? "Take him out..." He repeated the words.

"He has a dog," Lohan muttered.

"I'll take care of the dog."

The rest of their team had already entered the pit, making their way down the ladders. Lohan looked around. There were no other guards nearby. Next to him, Matt closed his eyes and at that exact moment the dog whimpered and sat down. It had simply forgotten that it was meant to be ferocious. The guard looked down, puzzled, and that was enough for Lohan. He took two steps forward and struck out, the side of his hand driving into the man's throat. All the anger of the last eight days was in the blow and the guard wasn't just knocked out. He was killed instantly. Lohan didn't care. He and Matt had committed themselves. The punishment for an attack on any guard was death. There could be no going back.

Some of the other workers had seen the exchange and were already backing away in terror, not wanting to share the blame. Matt and Lohan were standing on the very edge of the mine. The guard lay on the ground. The dog was sitting there, ignoring them. Matt took a deep breath and seemed to focus on something in the mid-distance. Lohan knew that Matt, like all five Gatekeepers, had powers that went beyond anything that was human and waited to see them in evidence now. Nothing happened. For a brief moment he thought that Matt was too weak, that his illness had neutralized him ... in which case they were both dead. But then there was a tiny movement. One of the ladders inside the pit had come free and fallen away from the wall. It was followed by a second and then a third. As Lohan stared, the ladders began to tear themselves apart, the thick wood snapping, the pieces tumbling down. Nobody had been hurt. Matt had only chosen empty ladders. But the way down was rapidly becoming unreachable and all work searching for the gold flakes would come to a rapid halt.

Snap, snap, snap... The breaking wood reminded Lohan of Chinese firecrackers. There were soldiers everywhere, running to the edge of the mine and staring down. But Matt had only just started. He swung his head round and suddenly an entire stretch of the mine exploded, the huge mud walls folding in on themselves and plunging down. If anyone had been below, they would have been killed, crushed under the weight, but it was still early morning and the lower levels were empty. Lohan watched in disbelief. How many hundreds of tonnes of earth had the slaves at Serra Morte carried to the surface? In seconds, tonnes more of it had been returned. An entire cliff face had collapsed. A huge section of the mine had once again been filled in. And Matt was responsible. He had done it with a single movement of his head.

There was a brief silence, then confused shouting as the guards reacted to what had just happened. Now Lohan understood what Matt was doing. Nobody knew what had caused the collapse but right now nothing else mattered. He had just created an incredible diversion.

"Let's go," Matt whispered.

The effort had taken away what remained of his strength. Lohan could see that he was shaking, soaked in sweat. He put his arm around him and dragged him away. The other workers saw them move but not a single one of them tried to join them. That was what life in Serra Morte had done to them. They had reached the point where many of them would have been unable to tie their own shoelaces without being given the order. Their spirits had been broken. They were no longer really human.

With Lohan supporting Matt, the two of them hurried towards the path that would take them back to the landing strip. Matt was stumbling and if it hadn't been for Lohan's arm around his waist, he would have fallen. For his part, Lohan was hoping that nobody would see them, that all the soldiers would be concentrating on the devastation they had left behind – but, of course, it didn't happen that way. Almost at once they were seen. Somebody shouted out a warning. It was followed by a single gunshot.

They didn't stop. They couldn't stop. They had attacked a guard and giving themselves up was no longer an option. The edge of the rainforest and possible safety were about twenty metres in front of them. Matt was forcing himself forward, leaning against Lohan. There was another shot and Lohan cursed himself for not taking the gun from the man he had killed. Even if they made it to the landing strip, the plane would be guarded and he couldn't just walk up to it unarmed. And a second, grimmer thought crossed his mind. If he was captured, he would have been glad to have had a gun in his hand. He could have turned it on himself.

There was the shriek of a whistle, a burst of sustained gunfire. Lohan was still holding Matt, almost lifting him off the ground. Matt had no shirt and Lohan could feel the heat and the dampness of the boy's skin. Matt's legs were hardly working at all. Bullets were whipping around them and it occurred to Lohan that Matt must still be using his power. Otherwise, surely one of them would have been hit. The rainforest loomed in front of them. There were more shots and the leaves of the nearest trees were shredded. But then they were inside, letting the darkness and thick green light swallow them up. The commotion behind them was abruptly cut off. It was as if they had plunged into another dimension.

Within seconds, they were lost. The track that had first brought them to the work place was some distance away and there was no way they could reach it. The forest itself was too dense, too unwieldy. It alone would decide which direction they took. Lohan knew that they had to lose themselves in the interior, to get as far away from their pursuers as possible. They could worry about the airstrip later. Almost blindly, the two of them followed whatever paths they could find, twisting round the trunks of huge trees, climbing over the tangled roots that covered the ground, pushing through creepers that hung down like solid walls. There was no sound now except for their own tortured breathing. Matt stumbled and collapsed, his legs giving way beneath him. With a curse, Lohan swept him up in his arms, carrying him like a child. Matt's eyes had closed. He didn't seem to be conscious.

Lohan looked back, resting against a tree. At least it seemed that nobody was following them. Perhaps the soldiers had decided that the mine was more important than two escaping prisoners who would probably end up dying in the rainforest anyway. He realized that he had no idea where he was, that he had lost any sense of direction. Matt was heavy in his arms. He wouldn't be able to continue for more than five or ten minutes and he had no food or water. A movement caught his eye and he weaved sideways as a huge spider with a red and furry back scuttled down the trunk of the tree. If he hadn't moved, it would have bitten him. And what then? A fast, painful death for him. Matt left on his own. The rainforest would cover them over and neither of them would ever be found again.

He continued forward as far as he could, then set Matt down on his own feet. "Can you stand?" he asked.

Matt opened his eyes and nodded.

"We have to find the landing strip. And when we get there, I'm going to need your help. Do you understand me? You have to open the gates ... like you did at the mine. And get rid of the guards."

Matt nodded a second time. "I can do that." His voice was little more than a whisper. "Don't leave me, Lohan."

"I won't do that."

How had he known? Even as they had stumbled through the rainforest, Lohan had thought about dropping Matt and continuing on his own. Why not? It was how he had always been trained. His first responsibility was to look after himself and Matt was slowing him down. He had only kept faith with Matt because he needed his powers – but if Matt lost consciousness a second time, Lohan had already made up his mind. The two of them weren't friends. They had been thrown together by chance. At the end of the day, it was each to his own.

They pressed forward, Matt somehow managing to keep going. Lohan was certain that the airstrip was somewhere over to the left but the vegetation kept forcing him to go in the opposite direction and he knew it would only waste his strength to push his way through. He wished more than anything that he could have equipped himself with a machete. A bird hooted overhead. During all the time they had worked at the pit, they had never seen a bird in flight but the rainforest was full of them. Something moved in the undergrowth and Lohan remembered the spider. He thought of the snakes, of the screams he had heard in the night. They were still going the wrong way. The rainforest was playing tricks on them, leading them ever further into its embrace. The path behind had gone. It was as if the trees and the vegetation had closed in on them, deliberately preventing them from finding their way back.

And then came the sound they had both dreaded most. Somebody shouted. The soldiers hadn't seen them yet but they were close. How many of them were there? It was impossible to say in the green nightmare in which they found themselves, but one thing was certain. The soldiers would know the rainforest better than they did. They might have dogs with them. It wouldn't take them long to track the two prisoners down.

Matt was stumbling again, his legs tying themselves in knots, and Lohan put an arm around him, not just propping him up but urging him forward, forcing him to keep up the pace. Once again he thought of abandoning him. At least the vegetation was screening them from their pursuers, deadening any noise they made. They needed somewhere to hide ... a tree to climb or a burrow to crawl into. But they couldn't go on much further, not together. He would have a better chance on his own.

He pushed a veil of leaves aside and stopped.

It was impossible.

He couldn't believe what was in front of him.

The rainforest simply ended, like a chapter in a book. In front, the landscape was blank. As far as he could see, and he could see for miles, the ground was empty and flat with just a few stumps of old trees sticking out of the dirt. It was as if a gigantic wind had somehow swept the rainforest away, leaving nothing behind, but even as Lohan stared at this lifeless, empty desert, he knew the truth. This had been done on purpose. Men had come here. They had cut down the rainforest for cattle ranches and farms. Slash-and-burn agriculture. They had grown bananas, maize and soyabean until the soil had refused to yield any more and then they had left.

They say that the rainforests are the lungs of the world. But there was nothing breathing here. The Serra Morte mine had cleared away a few hectares of rainforest. But this destruction continued all the way to the horizon and it would be hundreds of years before it was repaired. Lohan gazed with a certain wonderment. Who needed the Old Ones to destroy the planet when mankind was doing such a good job of it already?

"Lá são!"

The shout came from behind then and it was close enough for Lohan to hear the actual words. They couldn't go back.

"Matt..."

"Keep going!"

Matt could have been answering Lohan. He could have been talking to himself. Without a moment's hesitation, they continued forward, crossing the empty space, horribly exposed in the open, with nowhere to go, nothing to guide them. Lohan had never been anywhere so completely dead. There were no birds in the sky. Even the insects seemed to have abandoned the few roots and creepers that still covered the ground. There were just two of them, Matt and him, jogging forward, arm in arm, waiting for the two bullets that would bring them down.

They came to a track, defined only by the vehicles that had left their tyre prints. It might quite possibly have led to the airstrip – but they couldn't follow it now. As Lohan glanced back, two things happened. The first of the soldiers emerged from the rainforest, saw them and shouted to the others. And, at the same time, a jeep suddenly appeared, bursting out of the undergrowth and racing towards them, with two men in the front and two in the back. All of them were armed.

It was over. Lohan stood where he was, his face covered in sweat, his chest heaving. He was ready for death. In truth, he had never expected to live long, although he couldn't have imagined that this was how he would finish his days, shot like a dog in the middle of Brazil. He turned to Matt. Could the boy have one final trick up his sleeve? But Matt didn't even seem to be aware of the danger he was in. The jeep was getting closer. It would reach them in seconds. More soldiers were stepping out of the rainforest, appearing as if by magic, forming a long line.

But then, at the last second, Matt stepped forward. He seemed to have briefly shaken off his illness. As Lohan watched, he raised a hand and simply pointed at the jeep. The driver and his passengers might have thought he was greeting them. But the result was devastating. It was as if they had hit a brick wall or as if a huge fist had punched the jeep from beneath them. With no warning at all, it rose into the air, spun forward and crashed into the ground. The bonnet and the front windscreen crumpled and both the driver and the man next to him were killed instantly. Another was thrown out and lay still. The last was buried underneath the jeep, which had ended up on its back with its wheels, still spinning, in the air. There was a brief pause and it burst into flames. Matt lowered his hand and looked away.

The soldiers who had come out of the forest had seen what had happened. They stopped in their tracks and began to chatter excitedly among themselves. It was impossible to hear what they were saying but their eyes stared in fear and disbelief. Then they simply turned round and fled. They had decided they weren't going to take on this devil boy, who could destroy a vehicle and kill four men simply by gesturing with one hand. They vanished into the rainforest. Once more Matt and Lohan were alone.

"Get me a shirt," Matt said.

Lohan nodded, then hurried forward, approaching the burning jeep. The man who had been thrown clear was dead. He had broken his neck when he hit the ground and Lohan wasn't going to waste any tears. He dragged off his shirt and carried it back to Matt. He had also grabbed a water bottle and a gun.

"How far do you think it is to the airstrip?" Matt asked. He had made the destruction of the jeep look simple, effortless. But it had taken a huge effort. He was swaying on his feet. Lohan handed him the water bottle and he drank greedily, only remembering at the last moment to hand it back while it was still half full.

"It can't be too far," Lohan said. He drank the rest of the water and threw the bottle aside. "Let's just hope the plane's still there."

"Yes. Be careful..."

It was all Matt could manage. Lohan took his weight once again and they followed the tyre tracks back into the rainforest, glad to leave the empty space, the great scar, behind them. The jeep had cut across diagonally towards them and the path it had taken led back to the airstrip. After a few minutes, they saw the wire fence through the undergrowth – only the narrowest strip of vegetation had separated it from the wasteland. And the plane was still there. Lohan felt a huge surge of relief when he saw it sitting in its place beside the control tower.

There were four armed soldiers on guard.

Matt couldn't deal with them. He was finished, the sweat trickling off his face. His eyes were glazed, out of focus. Lohan helped him sit down and rested him against a tree.

"Wait for me here," he said.

Matt nodded. But as Lohan straightened up, he grabbed hold of his arm. "Thank you, Lohan," he said.

"You don't have to say that."

"Yes. I do. Only because of you..."

Matt's voice trailed away and it was then that Lohan made his decision. There could be no other way. His father would have approved.

From the very start, Lohan had helped Matt because it was to his own advantage but things were different now. Matt was finished – and even if he'd had the strength to reach the plane, Lohan had come to a decision. There was no way he was flying to Antarctica. It was a crazy idea! His time in Serra Morte had taught him that he had no part in this adventure. If he could reach the Legacy 600, he would fly north to America, as he had always planned. Somehow he would survive and make enough money to begin the journey east. He wanted to go home, back to the Triad, his family and his friends. The Old Ones didn't matter. Nor did the Gatekeepers. They could look after themselves.

Lohan slipped round the perimeter fence, keeping close to the edge of the forest. Matt was already forgotten. He could see the four soldiers ahead of him and despite everything that had happened – the destruction of part of the mine, the escape, the jeep that had just crashed and exploded – they looked remarkably relaxed. It was always possible that they had no idea what was going on, but as Lohan drew closer, he saw the true reason. They had been smoking ganja, the mind-altering drug that was cultivated all over Brazil. Lohan smiled to himself. It was the first stroke of luck he'd had all week. The next time they looked, they'd be dead.

Lohan had learned many martial arts in his time with the Triads, some of them handed down by the ninjas, the famous secret agents of feudal Japan. One of these was stealth walking, the ability to approach an enemy without being seen. Lohan knew that he was barely more than a novice. He had once sent an assassin across a crowded restaurant to kill a man who was surrounded by friends and bodyguards, and nobody had seen him approach. It was only when the shot had been fired that they realized he was there.

Even so, Lohan had had been taught the rudiments of stealth walking and he applied them now. From the gate to the aircraft was a matter of some thirty steps and, with flat rubble and grass all around, there was nowhere to hide. The secret of stealth walking is mental, not physical. It is finding a oneness with your surroundings so that you blend into them, become them. He knew that time was short. More soldiers would be on the way. But he made himself slow down, searching for the necessary concentration. Only when he was sure that he was ready did he step forward.

He passed through the gates and walked over to the men.

They were talking among themselves, telling obscene jokes and laughing. Not one of them so much as glanced his way. Lohan was carrying the gun he had taken from the jeep. Step by step he approached, standing in plain sight and yet invisible. Suddenly he was there, in front of them. The soldiers scrabbled for their weapons but it was far too late. He shot all four of them at close range, watching the bodies slump. And there he was, alone with the aircraft. It was hard to believe he had got away with it.

A flight of steps led to the plane. The cabin door was open. Lohan climbed up quickly, not looking back, already going over the various procedures for taxiing and take-off. But even as he reached the top he heard the grinding of metal, and before he could do anything, the door slammed shut like the entrance to a tomb. His first thought was that someone inside had closed it but that was impossible. There had been no one there. He reached out and tried to open it, but the door was stuck fast. Slowly, with a sense of foreboding, he turned round.

Matt had managed to drag himself to the perimeter fence and he was clinging onto it, his eyes fixed on the plane. Even at this distance, Lohan could see his anger, his sense of betrayal. He also knew that if Matt wanted to, he could sweep the Legacy 600 aside … or cause it to shatter into a thousand pieces.

"Open the door!" he shouted. "I just want to go in and check the controls."

Matt didn't reply.

Lohan stood there, waiting for him to speak, the two of them about thirty metres apart. Stalemate. Matt couldn't fly the plane without Lohan. But Lohan wasn't leaving here without Matt. The rainforest was still, the sun beating down. Nothing moved. It was as if they were the last two people in the world.

Then Lohan swore silently and ran back down the steps, past the dead bodies and through the gate to reach him. Matt couldn't move. If he had let go of the fence he would have collapsed. All his strength was focused on the plane.

"I was coming back for you," Lohan insisted.

Still Matt didn't speak. He didn't need to. It was all in his eyes.

It seemed to take for ever to get back to the plane and all the time Lohan was expecting more soldiers to arrive. He thought he saw a movement in the control tower, but if there was anyone there, they had decided to leave them alone. They climbed the steps together – Lohan was more or less carrying Matt again – and this time the door swung open as they approached. He set Matt down in one of the seats at the front of the plane, closed the door and went into the cockpit. It took him a few more minutes to familiarize himself with the controls, but he had been right when he had first seen the plane, more than a week ago. It was all very similar to what he had been used to.

Jet aircrafts do not have keys. This one was ready to fly.

Lohan went through all the start-up procedures, firing up the engines and waiting the agonzing length of time that it took for them to reach full velocity. Finally, he turned the plane and steered it into position. It was only now that he saw that the runway was much too short. Briefly, he wished that he hadn't shot the four men quite so thoughtlessly. One of them might have been the pilot. He checked the controls. At least the plane was full of fuel.

He pushed against the joystick, at the same time controlling the rudder, and they rolled down the runway, picking up speed. Now Lohan was the one who was sweating. This was a deadly business. The ground was uneven and full of potholes and if a wheel caught, the plane would be spun round and sent careering into the trees. The entire cockpit was vibrating like a spin dryer and his vision was blurred. He was aware of the end of the track getting closer and closer, and wondered if he had even reached V2, the correct speed for take-off. He had no choice but to find out. He pulled back. For a moment nothing happened, but then he felt a burst of sheer exhilaration as the vibrations stopped and he realized he had left the ground. Even so, it was close. The wheels hit the first of the trees. He heard the impact and the whole plane shook. But he was in the air. Looking out of the window, over to starboard, he saw the dark hole that was the Serra Morte.

Lohan muttered a short prayer in Mandarin. With a sense of relief, he banked away, checking the compass on the dashboard in front of him.

He was heading north. In a few hours he would be in the United States.

But the plane would not go north. All the computer systems were on and seemed to be working properly. Lohan flicked a few switches, tugged at the controls. Nothing happened. He couldn't make the plane turn. He could almost hear the engines screaming their refusal. The Legacy 600 simply wouldn't fly in the direction he wanted. Finally, at six thousand metres, he flicked on the autopilot and left his seat. The cockpit door was still open. Matt was still in the front seat, his legs stretched out.

"Who is flying this plane?" Lohan demanded. "Me or you?"

"How long until we get there?" Matt asked.

"There? You mean Oblivion? Is that where we're going? Antarctica?"

Matt said nothing.

Lohan gave in. "I don't know how long it will take," he said. He didn't even try to keep the bitterness out of his voice. "You tell me."

"I don't know either." Matt was sounding sleepy again. "Just let me know when we arrive."

Matt closed his eyes. Lohan watched him for a moment, then climbed back into the cockpit. The plane was still on autopilot but it occurred to him that it wasn't following the computer instructions. It was doing whatever Matt told it to. And suddenly, for reasons he couldn't quite understand, he found himself smiling. A minute later, he began to laugh.

The plane continued its journey over South America. Oblivion lay ahead.

DARK WATER

THIRTY-FIVE

They came across the fields just as the sun was rising, a line of policemen that was as long as the horizon itself. Nothing would get past them. If anything moved ahead, it would be seen. They continued forward slowly, at walking pace, and perhaps it was this – and the fact that there were so many of them – that made them seem so nightmarish. They were like robots. In their dark uniforms, clutching their weapons, there was nothing individual about them. Their faces were too far away to be seen, but even close to they would have been blank and emotionless, focused on what they were doing. They were simply a pack. They would not stop until they had found what they were looking for and they would allow nothing to get in their way.

Three hundred of them had been deployed to find their target: a thin, pale, fifteen-year-old boy with dark hair. If questioned, he would speak with an American accent. He was thought to be travelling with an older man and a girl of his own age. If possible, the boy had to be taken alive. The other two could be killed without a second thought.

They had spread out from the village in every direction, using it as if it were the centre point of a giant compass. According to the latest information they had received, the boy – Jamie Tyler – was trying to find his way through the thick woodland to the east, but it was always possible that he had doubled back or even reached the perimeter. The wood was being searched by men with dogs, and reinforcements were on the way. A platoon of fly-soldiers had already left London. One thing was certain. The boy couldn't possibly have travelled far in the night. He must be somewhere nearby.

Every building they came to, they searched. There were isolated churches and a few farms dotted around – empty now – with rotting haystacks, clumps of trees and pigsties. The county had once been famous for its pigs. Any houses that were still standing, they simply set on fire. It was easier than searching them room by room. The whole countryside was wreathed in smoke. The day had dawned a miserable, choking grey.

The village itself, where the boy had taken refuge, no longer existed. Every single home had been destroyed. The villagers were dead. They had provided shelter for one of the Gatekeepers, whether they had known it or not, and this was their punishment. The streets and the village square were littered with corpses. Already the crows had descended and were picking at the dead flesh. More columns of grey smoke rose softly into the air and would have been smelled five miles away if there had been anyone left to smell it. The police had taken everything of value. All the food had gone. The apple trees in the orchard had been picked clean for the last time.

In the middle of all this desolation, a single figure walked along the main road that sloped down from the village square, her black leather coat flapping around her, her ginger hair pulling slightly in the breeze. There was no colour in her face. Her cheeks were pinched, her eyes narrow and guarded. She knew that she had arrived at the defining moment in her life, her greatest challenge. She hoped she hadn't already failed.

Her name was Eleanor Strake and she was ... well, it was difficult to say what she was exactly. She was in charge of the police, but since the police were now in charge of the country, that made her, what, the commander? That was how she thought of herself, and with the power of the Old Ones behind her, nobody was going to disagree. The prolonged series of terrorist attacks hitting almost every major city in the United Kingdom had long ago wiped away anything that vaguely resembled government. And that had only been the start. In the years that had followed, it was as if a curse had fallen on the land and everything that everyone depended on had been taken away, one item at a time. Security, communications, healthcare, employment, law and order. And at the end of it, food and water had gone too. The pathetic rabble that had managed to survive needed someone to look after them, to save them from starvation, even if it meant putting them into the labour camps that had sprung up in the north and the south – and that someone was her. Commander Strake. Sometimes it made her giddy to think of the amount of power she had at her fingertips.

And yet all that could be at risk. She had been thrilled when she had heard that one of the five Gatekeepers had actually turned up in England. When the teacher had made the telephone call (the dead teacher now), she had been delighted. Finally, she would prove herself to be worthy of the trust the Old Ones had placed in her. She would deliver the boy to them and she would be rewarded with a life of comfort and luxury away from the stink-hole that the country had become. It had never occurred to her that Jamie would slip through her fingers. She knew that the doors were no longer working. She didn't think he had anywhere to go.

Eleanor Strake had reached the end of the road and walked onto the quay. There had been a vicious gunfight here. Nine or ten police officers had been killed – it would seem by one person; a plump, fair-haired boy in his late teens. He was lying on his side, cradling a machine gun. He looked strangely at peace. Briefly she wondered who or what he had been defending. She continued forward and stood on the edge of the black, ugly sewer that had once been a river. There was no movement either way. The water was so dead that it didn't look like water at all. It must have been years since anyone had seen a fish.

Could the boy have come this way? Some old woman in the village had said he was in the woods, heading east, and it was always possible that she could have lied. But no sailing boat could have gone far on this oily sludge. If he had tried to leave that way, the police would have already picked him up. For just a moment, Strake felt a frisson of fear. If she failed, if she didn't find him, what would happen to her? No need to answer that question. It was obvious.

She turned round and began to walk back into the village, where her private helicopter was waiting. It was still early in the day. She was confident that she would have the boy by lunch.

But in her haste and in her desire for blood, Commander Strake had made one mistake. Her officers had left no one alive to answer their questions and so she had never learnt that a man who called himself the Traveller had once arrived in the village on a canal boat. Of course, none of them had known that the *Lady Jane* was still fuelled and working, but even so, had the police asked, they might have noticed that the boat had now gone and that, following the banks of the river with a single, dim light glowing softly at the prow, it had been able to continue all night. It was already sixty miles away, heading south towards London.

Dead woman walking. As Strake made her way back through the carnage, she waited for the squawk over her radio to say that the mission had been accomplished, that Jamie Tyler had been found. But part of her already knew that it had gone wrong and that the voice would never come.

* * *

Jamie gazed ahead of him, watching the banks of the river as they slid past.

It had been twelve hours since the escape from the village and for much of the night he had been too wired up, too traumatized even to think about going to bed. He had thought he was safe, at least for a time, but in a matter of hours everything had been turned on its head. First Miss Keyland sneaking into the forest, then the telephone box, the sudden arrival of the police, the flame-throwers and the machine guns – and finally George, standing between them and their attackers even as his own life ebbed away … it had all been too much and it had happened too quickly.

And then there was the *Lady Jane*. Jamie had never been on a canal boat before. He'd never even been on a canal, and apart from the Truckee River, flowing in its concrete channel through the city of Reno in Nevada in America, any waterway was a mystery to him. For the first hour he had stood at the stern with Holly while the Traveller stood hunched over the tiller, guiding them through the night. The boat had a single lamp at the front, covered over so as to give as little light as possible, just enough to allow them to see the edges of the river. The engine hardly made any noise, just a deep throbbing, and Jamie wondered if it had been treated in some way too, to muffle the sound. He had found himself transfixed, staring at the dark water. It was like his own thoughts. Better left behind.

Nobody had said anything for the first few hours after they had left. There was still a chance that the police would overtake them and block their way. It was only when the river had carried them round a hillside, putting a mass of land between them and the village that the Traveller had finally broken the silence.

"You should get some rest," he said. "It's going to be a long day tomorrow."

"I can't rest," Jamie said. He turned back. The village was on fire. Even on the other side of the hill, he could see the red glow, spreading through the sky. He glanced at Holly, wondering how she must be feeling. He had only been there for a few weeks. For her, it had been her entire life.

But Holly's face was empty. Perhaps she was unable to accept what had happened. More likely, she was in shock. She was standing with one hand resting on the railing, the other on the roof of the cabin, oblivious to the cold of the night. Was she thinking about George? Well, that was all over now. The three of them were lucky to have got away. They had slipped through the net even as it closed all around them.

"One of you had better make some coffee." The Traveller nodded in the direction of the kitchen. The galley. Somewhere in the back of his mind, Jamie remembered that was what a kitchen was called when it was on a boat. "We have to keep going. God help us if they notice that the *Lady Jane* has gone. But if they don't, we can put fifty miles between us before it gets light."

Holly didn't move so Jamie pushed open the little door and went down the three steps into the living quarters.

The boat was long and barely six feet from side to side. That was what they were called. Narrow boats. Jamie thought that "cramped boats" would have been a good name too. All the furniture was packed in on top of itself: the cupboards, the fridge, the worktop, the two main beds and the table and benches that converted into a third. A corridor stretched from one end to the other with dim electric bulbs lighting the way, and Jamie found himself stooping as he made his way around the obstacle course that was the living accommodation. Everything was in its right place – plates, mugs, pots and pans, knives, tools, books and maps, gas canisters for the cooker – but somehow it still looked jumbled and untidy. The *Lady Jane* might have been attractive once. It was painted green and red and the floors and walls were all polished wood. But it was old. The Traveller had lived on it for too long. There was no longer any fresh water to keep it clean and although the toilet and shower were still in place, the one virtually on top of the other in a tiny compartment, it had been years since either of them had worked.

Jamie filled the kettle from a plastic bottle by the sink and made coffee as he had been instructed. It was only as he opened the jar of granules that he realized that the Traveller was giving Holly a rare luxury. There had never been any coffee in the village. Rita and John had drunk an unpleasant, bitter tea made out of acorns. The Calor gas for the cooker was also remarkable – as was the fuel that was propelling them along the canal. He wondered what other secrets the *Lady Jane* concealed.

And who *was* the Traveller? Matt had said he could be trusted. But Jamie still didn't know his name, where he had come from ... anything about him.

It was going to take a while for the kettle to boil. The flame was tiny, the gas reserves low. Jamie left the kettle on the cooker and wandered through the boat, opening cupboards and drawers. He knew he was snooping but he didn't feel guilty. The Traveller seemed to be on his side but even so he had to be sure. He knew that his job was to reach London, to find St Meredith's and hope that the door would work. Nothing else mattered.

The *Lady Jane* was packed with supplies of one sort or another. Every cupboard was filled with tinned food, medicine, spare parts for the engine and for different sorts of machines. There were maps covering the entire country on the shelves. One wardrobe contained fresh clothes – in the village nobody had owned anything more than what they were dressed in. As Jamie went from one section to the next, he realized that this was more than a canal boat. The Traveller might have spent seven years living in the village but all the time he had been secretly concealed in a world of his own.

He wasn't certain what drew him to the two benches on either side of the dining table but as he went past he noticed a hinge and realized that they were actually storage facilities and must open. He pulled the cushions back and, sure enough, there were handles underneath. The seat bottoms opened like trapdoors. Jamie looked inside.

There were guns. Rows of them. Also bullets, still in their original boxes, wrapped in waxed paper. There were two clips to one side holding a sword – Jamie assumed it was the same sword that the Traveller had been carrying when he had come to the rescue.

"I think the kettle's boiled."

Jamie spun round. The Traveller had appeared behind him, coming down through the galley without being heard. He was standing there, looking down at Jamie with a half-smile on his face.

"Are you looking for something?" he asked.

"I've already found it," Jamie replied. He glanced in the direction of the stern. "Is Holly steering the boat?"

"Yes. She's taken to it very easily. And it may help her ... take her mind off things. She and that boy were very close."

"I know." Jamie nodded at the weapons. "Where did you get all these? How did you manage to keep them?"

"I was supplied with them," the Traveller said. "Before I arrived in the village all those years ago, I buried them in a field about a mile upstream. I guessed they'd want to search the *Lady Jane* and I was right. I left a certain amount of stuff for them to find ... food, medicine, whisky. Seven years ago things weren't quite as desperate and they were happy enough with that. They never imagined there might be more. They even ate my horse. Poor old Bree! But they never looked for the rest of it and once I'd been accepted, I went back to the hiding place and dug it all up again. Lucky I did. I think we're going to need them."

"Who are you?" Jamie asked. "Why don't you have a name?"

"I do have a name," the Traveller replied. "It's Graham Fletcher." He smiled to himself. "Do you realize that's the first time I've actually spoken those words in more than seven years?"

"Why did you never tell anyone?" Jamie asked.

The Traveller was serious again. "Because I never wanted to be their friend," he said. "I had to remind myself that I wasn't part of their community, that I would never be one of them. I knew that one day I would have to leave."

"You know who I am, don't you?"

"That's right, Jamie. I know all about you ... and Matt and the others. The Gatekeepers."

"You're with the Nexus."

Jamie remembered the organization he had met when he was with Matt in London ... the men and women who had been waiting for them in the secret room in Farringdon. Graham Fletcher hadn't been there. Jamie was sure of it. But on the other hand, ten years had passed since that meeting – at least, for him. The Nexus would have changed since then. It was surprising that it still existed at all.

The Traveller nodded. "That's right."

"So it wasn't a coincidence that you were in the village. You were waiting for me."

"Waiting for you for seven years, Jamie. Away from my friends and family. You have no idea how glad I am to see you."

So he had friends. A family! And he had been prepared to abandon them for all this time, simply to help him. Jamie suddenly saw the Traveller in a completely different light and tried to imagine what it must have been like for him. He wondered briefly if it was right to leave Holly outside. Shouldn't she be hearing this? But it was probably better that way. After all she had been through, she needed time on her own.

The Traveller must have been thinking the same thing. He lifted the kettle off the gas, then made three mugs of coffee. He took one up to Holly, returning almost immediately. Once again the two of them were on their own.

"She's doing a good job," he said. "You'd have thought she'd been steering boats all her life."

"So are you going to tell me about yourself?" Jamie asked.

"Of course." The Traveller brought a second mug of coffee over to Jamie. "I work for a remarkable person," he said. "I think you know her. Her name is Susan Ashwood."

Jamie recognized the name at once. Susan Ashwood was the woman who had once helped Matt. She was a clairvoyant, with the ability to see into the spirit world. She was also blind. She wasn't the sort of woman it would be easy to forget.

"She sent me to the village," the Traveller went on. "She knew about the door in the church – and she also knew that the Old Ones hadn't found it. She believed there was a chance that one of you would show up and she told me to go there and wait for you. I can tell you, there have been times when I've cursed her and cursed myself for believing in her. But now I'm glad. She was right all along."

"So the Nexus still exists," Jamie said.

"What's happened in Britain – all over the world – it's the reason why the Nexus was created in the first place. We're here to help you and the other Gatekeepers. It's what we've been waiting for."

"Can you help me get to London? To Saint Meredith's?"

"We're on our way there now. We're going to enter the canal system, Jamie. It's the best way to travel. There are no trains or planes. The roads are too dangerous, too exposed. But the canals have always been hidden. They twist their way round the edge of towns, through fields and old industrial estates, and people have forgotten they're there. They belong to another age. If we can keep going, we can get to the very heart of London."

"If?" Jamie had picked up on the word.

The Traveller sipped his coffee. He had been cradling the mug between his hands. "It's not going to be easy, he admitted. "Right now we're on the river. To get into the canal system, we have to get to Four Ways lock. I came through it on the way up from London but that was a while ago. If it isn't working, we'll be continuing on foot. Then we have to pass through a couple of towns. They may still be inhabited and anyone who sees or hears us could be a threat. Finally, the police are going to be looking for us. Fortunately, they have no idea we're on a working boat. If they knew that, we'd already be dead."

"What about London itself?"

"I don't want to talk about it, to be honest with you. In a few days, you'll see it for yourself."

Jamie yawned. Suddenly it all seemed too much for him – everything that had happened during the day, everything that lay ahead.

The Traveller noticed. "You should get some rest. You must be worn out. Why not take the forward bunk? It's quieter there."

"What about Holly?"

"I'll stay with her. After tomorrow, we'll take it in turns at the tiller. The *Lady Jane*'s not difficult to steer."

"Do you have enough fuel to get to London?"

"So many questions, Jamie! Get this in your head. I've been preparing for this journey. I've been waiting for it for seven years. Now go to sleep!"

Jamie slept.

Almost at once, he found himself back in the dreamworld, a short distance from the library, as if he had never left it but had simply closed his eyes the last time he was there and then opened them again. His first thought was to look for Scott, his twin brother, but there was no sign of him and that worried Jamie. He knew something was wrong. It had been obvious the last time they had seen each other and right now he would have given anything to spend a few minutes with him – in this world or anywhere. Matt and the others seemed to have gone too. Jamie wondered how long it had really been since the last time the five of them had met and talked, but he knew it was impossible to say. Time worked differently in the dreamworld. It might feel as if only a few seconds had passed, but it could be a week or even a month.

Jamie hated and feared the dreamworld, even though he knew that it was somehow on his side. He remembered the strange figure of the gold prospector who had approached him at the ocean's edge and who had tried to give him a warning. "*They're going to kill him*." Why had he appeared to be a threat? Why couldn't he have just walked up and explained what he meant? And, for that matter, why was this world so grey and desolate? He looked across the empty landscape and shivered. Being here was like being dead.

He heard a soft footfall on the dust and twisted round, fearing the worst, then relaxed. It was Matt, on his own, walking towards him. Jamie was happy to see him. It wasn't just that the two of them had become close during their time in London and later, on the way to Hong Kong. Matt was the undisputed leader of the Gatekeepers and Jamie was confident that he knew how this would end and that somehow he would get them all out alive.

The two of them stood facing each other.

"Hi, Jamie," Matt said.

"Hi." There was a pause. Jamie wasn't sure what to say. How much did Matt know? "I got out of the village," Jamie continued. "Someone from the Nexus has found me."

"I know. Everything is happening the way it should. But there's something I have to tell you. To warn you about."

It was strange. Was that what Matt had become? Just another warning to be thrown at him by the dreamworld?

"Your journey's not going to be easy, Jamie. And London's going to be worse. The Old Ones know about St Meredith's and they have it surrounded."

"Is the door working?"

"Not yet. All the doors are locked."

"Then what's the point of going there?"

"They'll open … in time. And that's why I had to see you. You have to know the right moment to get into the church and break through. You can't delay. You must do it at exactly the right time."

"How will I know?"

Matthew smiled but there wasn't a shred of happiness in his face. Jamie had never seen him so old, so defeated. "You'll know. There'll be a sign. When you see it, go for it, and if everything works out like I hope, you'll reach Antarctica."

"Will you be there?" he asked. "Will Scott?"

"Jamie, I can't answer your questions. All I can tell you is that it will happen the way it's meant to happen."

"But I have a right to know!" Jamie felt something rising in him. He wasn't sure if it was anger or sadness. "What's wrong with Scott? The last time we met, he hardly talked to me. And those clothes he was wearing…" Jamie broke off. "And what about you, Matt? How do you know so much about everything all of a sudden? What's happened to you?"

Matt smiled. "I've been to the library." He paused again. "This is the last time we'll talk before the end," he said. "I'll think of you on the *Lady Jane*. And in London. Just remember – wait for the sign. Don't try anything until then. And when you see it … don't hang around!"

"Hold on, Matt…"

But then Jamie opened his eyes and found himself back on the boat. Holly was asleep on the bunk opposite him and they were still chugging slowly down the river. Matt had gone and another day had begun.

THIRTY-SIX

I felt terrible about George's death. I was sick and miserable and at the same time guilty because even though so many other people had died, he was the only one I really cared about. I had actually seen Tom Connor and Mr Christopher and Reverend Johnstone killed and I knew that nobody was going to be left alive, not even Rita and John, who had been like parents to me and who had looked after me since I was small. Maybe there was just too much grief for me to cope with.

I wasn't much good for anything when we tumbled aboard the *Lady Jane* and set off down the river. This was the first time that I had been on anything with an engine since I was about six. For that matter, I had never seen a helicopter before either. Both these things should have been a source of wonderment for me, but all I could think about was ... well, nothing. I didn't really have any thoughts. If my life were a strip of ribbon, it was as if someone had just cut off the entire length right up to where I was now, so that looking back there was nothing and I couldn't imagine anything very much ahead either. Part of me wished that I had died in the village. It would have been easier.

I wanted to hate Jamie. After all, it was his appearance that had brought the Old Ones to us. But I couldn't do it. If anyone was to blame, it was Miss Keyland for going against the wishes of the Assembly and making the telephone call in the forest. At the same time, I wondered if we hadn't been kidding ourselves all along. We hadn't been living in the village. We'd been surviving – and it couldn't really have gone on much longer. Rita had practically said as much when we parted company. The crops had been failing, the water supply dwindling. Whichever way you looked at it, we had been running out of time. I didn't think it then but maybe in some way the arrival of the police, the sudden end, had been a mercy.

I don't remember very much about the race to the river, scrambling down the bank in the darkness, somehow finding the boat and clambering on board. I was probably in shock. I think Jamie untied the ropes, or maybe it was me, but the next thing we were pulling away with the engine under my feet and a sense of total disbelief. How had the Traveller kept the boat in working condition without anyone finding out? Where had he got the fuel? I was standing there in the pitch-darkness when he asked me to take the tiller so that he could go inside and talk to Jamie, and I nearly fell overboard. How could I possibly steer a huge boat like the *Lady Jane* when I had never been on or in the river, not so much as to get my feet wet? I wanted to refuse but he didn't give me a chance and suddenly I found myself standing there, my eyes fixed on the water ahead.

"The secret is not to do too much," he said. "Small turns! Don't push too hard. I'll be right back."

And then he was gone and I was on my own. At first, I was angry. How could he just leave me like that? But almost at once I understood what had really been in his mind. I was so focused on what I was doing, so desperate not to crash into either of the banks, that I had to leave all my other emotions behind. It was exactly what I needed and I found a kind of peace, feeling the vibrations of the engine running through my hands and with the deep throb of the engine in my ears. There was something quite awesome about being in control of so much power. Even the electric light, skimming over the water, always a few feet ahead of me, was something wonderful.

I don't suppose I was there for much more than twenty minutes, although it felt longer. Then the Traveller reappeared and told me to get some rest. I didn't think I'd sleep. I might have been worn out but I didn't feel tired. I started to argue but the Traveller wasn't having any of it. "Go to bed, Holly," he said. "You can crawl into the bunk opposite Jamie. He's already out like a light. And you're going to need all the sleep you can get."

He was right. My head touched the pillow and that was that. I didn't so much fall asleep as plummet.

When I opened my eyes, Jamie was already up and grey light was streaming in through the windows. I looked out and saw the riverbank moving slowly past, drab and muddy with just a few tufts of grass. It might once have been beautiful, only it wasn't now. The weather was bad and the water was so very black. I didn't have any idea what time it was. If I'd been in the village, I'd have been in the orchard by now or else I'd have heard it from Mr Bantoft, and that was my first thought that morning. I'd never hear a word from the farm manager again. Not from any of them. That was over.

I got up and made my way through the boat, making sure not to hit my head on the pots and pans that hung down from the ceiling. Everything was very low and very narrow – like a miniature house, where everything has been squeezed together. Jamie was on deck with the Traveller, the two of them standing together by the tiller.

"So you've finally made it!" the Traveller muttered. "You've missed breakfast but you're just in time for lunch."

Lunch? Had I really slept that long? I looked around me at the unfamiliar surroundings – fields stretching out on one side, with a thick mist hanging over the grass and a few stunted trees twisting up, and a scrubby hillside on the other. It wasn't much of a view but for me it was new – the first time my eyes had had something new to see in fifteen years. I imagined that people coming out of prison would feel the same.

"What is for lunch?" I asked.

"Tinned salmon. Tinned tomatoes. Tinned beans. Tinned stew. It's really whatever tin you want to open."

We'd run out of tins in the village ages ago so the Traveller could have been describing a whole banquet as far as I was concerned.

"Are you OK, Holly?" Jamie asked.

I nodded. I should have been feeling worse but the sleep had helped – that and the distance we had come. I had managed to leave some of the nightmares behind me.

We came to a humpback bridge with a lane crossing the river and the Traveller lowered our speed and pulled in so that the old brickwork covered our heads. He seemed to know what he was doing, which was just as well because I had no idea where we were heading or what we would do when we got there.

"Take the ropes, Jamie..."

We tied up under the bridge so that if one of the helicopters happened to pass, we would be out of sight. The Traveller turned off the engine and we all went down to the galley, crowding around the table – me and Jamie on one side, the Traveller on the other. He opened various tins and also boiled the kettle and made real coffee out of a jar, which was only the second time I had ever drunk it, although I'm sorry to say I didn't much like the taste. The salmon was amazing though; soft and juicy and filling. It made my head spin to think that the river might once have been teeming with fish like this.

So there we were, the three of us, sitting in that cramped but cosy living space, hidden under the bridge, perhaps forty or fifty miles from the village. I waited for the Traveller to speak and eventually he did.

"My name is Graham," he said. "You can call me that, if you like. I was talking to Jamie last night. I'm with an organization – you might call it a secret society – that wants to help him." That made sense. I had never met anyone who looked more secretive than the Traveller. Those dark eyes of his had never given anything away. "The society is called the Nexus. Jamie knows about it and he knows he can trust me."

I was sensible enough not to say anything just yet. Anyway, my mouth was full. It had been full more or less from the moment I had sat down.

"The Nexus are waiting for us," he said. "We just have to get to the Sheerwall Tunnel, which is on the edge of London – and this is the best way. As I said to Jamie last night, the canals have always been hidden away. They were almost forgotten, even ten years ago. And the good news is that the police don't know we're on a boat ... otherwise, they'd have been after us already."

"So what's the bad news?" I asked.

"It'll still take us three days to get there. Three days and three nights, travelling non-stop. We're going to have to take turns at the tiller. You did a good job last night, Holly. First we have to get off the river and into the canal system. We're about a mile from the Four Ways lock."

"How do you know?" I asked.

"I came this way seven years ago. Of course, it was all very different then. Things were bad but they quickly got a lot worse as the food stocks ran out and the seeds stopped growing. The lock may have been vandalized. It may not be working. If that's the case, we'll have to abandon the boat and continue on foot."

He reached down and to my surprise he produced two guns – heavy pistols – which he laid down on the table with a clunk. They looked completely bizarre, sitting there, next to the plates of food. One was for Jamie, one for me.

"We can't let anybody stop us," the Traveller continued. "If anyone sees the boat moving or hears the engine, they'll know we have fuel. There was a time when people might have helped us. Not any more. We have to assume that everybody is our enemy and that they'll kill us for what we have. So if I tell you to shoot, you mustn't hesitate. Holly, you know I wanted to leave you behind and I'm not going to apologize for that. My job is to get Jamie to London and that's all that matters."

He'd certainly made that clear the night before. I remembered him turning to me in the village with all the police running amok, killing anyone they came across, and saying, "Find somewhere to hide." Until someone came and cut my head off or set me on fire. That was as much as he cared about me.

"Where are we going in London?" Jamie asked.

I wanted to know too. Part of me had always wanted to see the capital but at the same time I dreaded it. Miss Keyland had occasionally talked about London. She had shown us pictures of red buses and Piccadilly Circus and the Houses of Parliament. We all knew about the ninth of May, when the terror came. But she had never shown us what had happened next. It was as if she didn't want us to know what remained.

"You'll see when you get there," the Traveller replied. "Don't expect me to talk about it."

"St Meredith's is surrounded," Jamie said. "And the door isn't even working."

"How do you know that?"

"Matt told me. Can the Nexus get me there?"

"Yes."

"All right. But I'm the one who's going to tell you when we break in."

The Traveller looked at Jamie with something close to a scowl. "And how will you know when's the right time?" he asked.

"I just will."

The Traveller was going to argue but then he thought better of it. "All right. You're the boss."

Was he? I wasn't actually sure who was in charge. It was the Traveller's boat. He was the one who had made all the calls so far. He had decided where to stop and even what we were going to eat. But there was something about Jamie that I hadn't noticed before. Somehow, he seemed stronger than ever. The Traveller was twice his size and probably twice his age. But he was only here for Jamie. We both were, really. He and the Five ... that was all that mattered.

We cleared the stuff away and set off again. The Traveller turned a key to start the *Lady Jane*'s engine and he must have looked after it well during all those years as it kicked in at once. Jamie and I untied the ropes. We had to push the boat out and then jump on without falling into the river – not as easy as it sounded what with the banks being so uneven.

The landscape opened out on the other side of the bridge, which wasn't such good news because suddenly the *Lady Jane* stuck out ... you could have seen it for miles. The fog had lifted too. I could see a few scattered buildings, old barns and sheds that might once have belonged to farms but there was nothing moving; no animals, no people. We passed a tractor, rusting, with grass sprouting out of the wheels, then a tangle of barbed wire, then a wall of old tyres. In the books that I had read when I was growing up, the English countryside was somewhere beautiful to visit and to have adventures. You got the impression that the sun was always shining. Well, it wasn't now. Everything looked hostile and abandoned.

"There it is!" the Traveller called out and pointed and, about a quarter of a mile away, I saw the lock that would take us off the river and into the canals that would in turn lead to London. Again, I'd seen locks in books but I never thought I'd go through one. The canal led between two narrow walls. There was a gate at each end, which had to be opened and closed. The one on our side was open so we would be able to cruise in to what was effectively a deep, rectangular box. Close the gate, fill the inside with water and we would slowly float up. There was a flat surface with a dilapidated house that must have once belonged to the lock keeper, and once we were level with it and the gates were opened we would be able to motor out again, heading south. I did wonder why the lock was called Four Ways, though. You could go left or right along the river or you could head off up the canal. But there was also a track leading across the fields, so maybe that was the fourth direction they had in mind.

The Traveller had wondered whether the lock would still be working. I hoped so. I didn't like the idea of walking all the way to London. Shouldn't this secret society, the Nexus, have been looking after the canals? After all, it had always been part of the plan to use them.

"Look...!" This time it was Jamie who had spoken and there was an edge to his voice that told me straight away that he wasn't going to point out a pretty tree or flowers. He was looking up and, with a sense of unease, I tried to work out what it was that he had seen.

There was nothing. I certainly couldn't see any helicopters heading our way – anyway, I'd have heard them first. The sky was empty except for a dark cloud, which made me think it was going to rain. But Jamie had definitely seen something. As we cruised down the river with the lock still a good hundred metres away, he stared up and his face was filled with fear.

"What is it?" I asked.

He said nothing. And then I noticed something strange. There was hardly any breeze but the storm cloud was moving very quickly, heading our way. In fact, as I stared at it, I realized it wasn't a cloud at all. It was changing shape, one minute flat and oblong like a huge pancake, the next twisting itself so that it resembled a snake.

"What is it?" I asked a second time.

"Fly-soldiers," Jamie replied.

Jamie had talked about fly-soldiers when he was describing the first battle with the Old Ones, ten thousand years before. I knew what they were but I couldn't believe that I was actually seeing them for myself, in my own world, now. What I was looking at was thousands, maybe millions of insects, making their way towards us in a vast swarm. In the air, they were separate. But when they landed, they would mould themselves into human form and at that moment they would become solid. Fly-soldiers could kill you with a sword made up of flies – yet strike out at them and they would separate and your own weapon would pass through them. Jamie had told me all this. And here they were!

"The lock," Jamie said. "We have to get into the lock. Maybe they won't see us..."

"We can't go any faster," the Traveller said.

I guessed that the cloud of fly-soldiers was about half a mile away but getting closer all the time. Were they searching for us – or were they simply heading for the village that we had left the day before? And did they have ears? Could they hear us? Suddenly it seemed to me that the *Lady Jane*'s engines were making far too much noise. With the countryside so empty, they would be heard as far away as the horizon and the red and green paint simply screamed out: "Here I am!" Why had the Traveller never thought to have the boat camouflaged?

We were still moving painfully slowly. At the same time, the flies seemed to have spread out, filling the sky. The Traveller was standing in front of me, his face set, his hands gripping the tiller. Jamie and I were next to him. I resisted the temptation to crawl back inside the cabin and hide, even though the three of us were obvious targets, standing on the flat platform with the bulk of the boat stretching out in front of us. I could see the entrance to the lock. The high walls would hem us in, concealing us … if only we could reach them in time. The fly-cloud had become an arrow. In a few seconds it would be directly overhead.

The Traveller pulled the tiller. The *Lady Jane* twisted round and entered the lock. Suddenly there were tall, slimy walls on both sides. I could smell damp and decay. In front of us, water splattered through the gap where the gates met. I heard the engine roar and realized that the Traveller had pulled the throttle into reverse. Even so, we were moving too quickly. There was a loud crash and I was almost thrown off my feet as the bow of the boat hit the gate. Without being asked, Jamie reached forward and twisted the key, turning the engine off.

It seemed like we were in an oversized grave. Water splashed and trickled down all around us. The walls, with their dark brickwork, rose up nine or ten metres and I was sure they would conceal us from anything … provided it didn't come too close. None of us spoke, not so much as a whisper. I could feel my heart pounding in my chest and knew that this was a different sort of fear from anything I had ever felt. My world had been invaded by something that couldn't possibly exist. I took a deep breath, then looked up. The little slot of sky that I could see was clear. The fly-soldiers seemed to have wheeled off in another direction. We hadn't been seen.

We didn't move for a few minutes. Then Jamie climbed onto the roof and up a ladder set in the side of the lock. I followed him. We had to close the gates behind us, fill the lock with water, then open the gates ahead. I looked back in the direction we had come and saw the cloud of flies, already half a mile or more away, disappearing into the distance.

"That was close," I said.

Jamie nodded. "They'll be back."

And London was still miles away.

THIRTY-SEVEN

WELCOME TO
LITTLE MOULSFORD

There was no way round the village. The sign was placed right next to the canal and we could see the houses behind it, neatly arranged around a green that was so well tended that it didn't look real. The houses themselves were all beautiful too. Shrink them down and you would be able to buy them in the expensive toyshops I'd once seen in magazines. They were pink and mauve and lilac, with names like Bide A While and Well Barn. And there was a shop selling antiques, a public house and a little gem of a church, not like the one I'd been used to but perfect in every way, with the stained-glass windows intact and the stonework bright and clean. Look at the church and you would imagine the vicar, smiling and benevolent. He would greet everyone every Sunday. And he would know all their names.

It helped that this was a pleasant day. We had arrived in the afternoon and as always it was cloudy but the sun was doing its best to break through and there was a gentle, warm breeze.

The Traveller didn't like it. We were forty or fifty miles from London and this wasn't the sort of scene he had been expecting. He hadn't said very much but I got the impression that if Little

Moulsford had been a flyblown dump with dead bodies lying at the roadside and weeds everywhere, he would have been able to relax more. It was just too perfect. Nowhere in England was like this any more. And we had to pass right through the middle of it. Worse than that, there were three locks in a row that we had to manoeuvre, meaning that we couldn't even stay in the *Lady Jane*. As we opened and closed the sluices, we would be horribly exposed.

There were people living here. They had heard us coming and a small crowd of them had gathered at the first lock as we approached. There was nothing really we could do except motor forward, trying to pretend that the three of us were on holiday having a lovely time rather than trying to escape from fly-soldiers, violent death and the end of the world. The villagers looked friendly enough. They were all smiling at us and were dressed as smartly as possible, with neatly cut hair. They also seemed well fed ... something I noticed immediately because in my village everyone had always been waiting for the next proper meal.

"Have you got your guns?" the Traveller muttered.

I didn't really know what he was worried about. These people looked harmless enough. I was actually quite excited to see them – to discover that my village wasn't the only community that had managed to survive for ten years. But I did have my gun with me, tucked into my waistband. It was an uncomfortable feeling, having it pressing into my flesh. Part of me was afraid that it would go off and shoot me in the thigh but the Traveller had shown me how to put the safety catch on and had assured me the gun couldn't fire until it was released.

Jamie nodded.

"I've got mine," I said.

"Let's see what these people want. Don't trust anyone. Don't do anything unless I say so."

We stopped in front of the first lock. The people were standing over us, looking down. A smart, military-looking man in his fifties stepped forward. He seemed to be their leader. He had short grey hair and a moustache. There was a woman standing next to him, exactly the same height, with curly hair. She was wearing a flower-patterned dress and carrying a handbag, and even had a string of pearls and earrings. I had never seen anyone wearing jewellery, except in pictures.

"Good day to you," the man said. "My name is Michael Higham. Major Michael Higham, as a matter of fact, although heaven knows we don't stand on ceremony. And may I present my wife, Dorothy? Welcome to Little Moulsford!"

"Thank you," the Traveller replied.

"It's not very often we see a boat come this way," he went on. "The last one was a couple of years ago."

"It was more like three," his wife corrected him. She seemed to polish every word before she spoke it. "It was called *The Horizon*. A very nice boat – on the way to London. Of course, we advised them not to continue."

"They never came back," the major added, nodding his head in agreement. He ran his eye over the *Lady Jane*. "A fine vessel. Forty foot?"

"Forty-five."

"I can't believe you managed to find any fuel for her. Where have you come from?"

The Traveller looked back down the canal. "We were in a village about forty miles away. Unfortunately, the water supply failed so we thought we'd try our luck further south." I realized he was being deliberately vague and he wasn't telling them the whole truth.

"I wouldn't go much further south if I were you," the major said. "The land's contaminated. As far as we know, we're the last community between here and the city. But you must join us for supper – you and your two young friends. We're fortunate. We have our own reservoir for water and our food supplies are holding up pretty well. We see so few people these days! You'll be very welcome."

"That's very kind of you." I could see that the Traveller didn't want to accept the invitation, but at the same time there was something about the crowd of people looking down at us that told us that they might turn nasty if we refused. I don't know what made me think that. There was just something in the air. "We'll make our way through the locks and moor up on the other side." He made it sound casual, as if it didn't really matter very much. "Maybe you can help us with the gates?"

From the way that the Traveller looked at me, out of the corner of his eye, I knew that the only reason he wanted to climb the locks now was so that he could make a quick getaway if needed – not that you could move particularly quickly on a canal boat. But at least if push came to shove, we wouldn't be too exposed – which is to say, we wouldn't be up there with our backs turned, pushing and shoving the gate. The major and his wife didn't seem to mind. Indeed, they took our lock key and handed it to a ten-year-old boy, who ran off and did all the work for us. There was something quite unnerving about the boy – and the way he looked at us with large eyes staring out of a colourless face. He was friendly enough but I got the feeling there was something he knew that we didn't. After he had opened the gates he took a bone out of his pocket and gnawed it as we motored through.

Twenty minutes later, we were at the top end of the flight. Jamie and I moored the boat and we all stepped off.

The villagers had watched us as we made our progress and I was able to examine them a little more closely. They were all a bit like the major and his wife – very polite and civilized. They didn't look like survivors at all. Forget the fact that the world had more or less come to an end … they'd be delighted if you'd join them for a drink on the terrace or maybe a game of cards. There were about fifteen of them. The youngest was the boy – his name was Cosmo – who'd helped open the locks. There was a couple who must have been in their eighties. The rest were all middle-aged, and although my first impression had been that they looked healthy, I now decided there was something off-putting about the whole lot of them. It was in their eyes. They were red-rimmed and had a sort of glaze to them. The colour of their skin was odd too. It was waxy. But then, I had to remind myself, even I probably didn't look too good myself. Nobody did.

"We'll eat in the pub," the major told us. "Everyone's going to want to meet you and hear how you got here. Shall we say six o'clock? With no electricity, we all tend to go to bed early." He turned to the Traveller. "There are a few things I'd like to talk about alone, if you don't mind. *Pas devant les enfants!*" Not in front of the children. I'd learnt enough French to understand that. "Suppose you come over at five thirty? And they join us later?"

"As you like."

"Good! Well, I'll give you a chance to tidy up and whatever, and I'll see you later. Splendid boat. Tomorrow you must show me around…"

The major and his wife drifted off and the rest of the villagers followed. Only Cosmo remained behind, sitting on one of the lock gates, swinging his legs. He looked innocent, but at the same time I wondered if he was watching us, making sure we didn't leave.

The Traveller was wary too. "Listen," he said to us, once we were alone. "It may be that these people mean well. Maybe all they want to do is give us dinner. We have to go along with them, at least to begin with. But just be careful. They seem to be well-fed and they've managed to survive – which means they must be smarter than they look. Be on your guard the whole time."

"Are you going over to meet them?" Jamie asked. He looked, and sounded, unhappy.

"I don't think I have any choice. I'll go and see if I can find out what's going on. Holly, keep your gun with you. And be prepared to use it."

"They were keeping something from you," Jamie said. That was exactly what I'd thought, but with him it was more than a hunch. He had used his power to see into their minds. "I wanted to know what they were thinking," he went on. "There was definitely something there but they managed to conceal it. It was almost as if they didn't *want* to think about it. Like they were too ashamed."

"Let's hope I can find out," the Traveller said. "And if I do, I'll let you know."

He left about an hour later, setting off for his appointment with the major. The boy was still there, still swinging his legs, chewing on that bone of his again. There was something about him that got on my nerves. Jamie and I stayed on the boat, hoping that the Traveller would get back – but twenty minutes later there was no sign of him. We waited until five to six. Then Jamie made the decision.

"We'd better go."

We left together, taking care to fasten the main door. That's something I should have mentioned about the *Lady Jane*. Although you wouldn't have known to look at it, the boat had all sorts of locks and bolts. I'm not saying it was impossible to break into, but it would take a while and you'd need a good-sized hammer or crowbar. The drawers and cupboards were also fastened. All that was missing was a self-destruct mechanism if anyone tried to tamper with anything – and I wouldn't have been surprised if the Traveller hadn't managed to rig one of those up too.

It was already growing dark and without meaning to we quickened our pace, keeping close together. The canal looked darker and more dead than ever. The *Lady Jane* was wrapped in shadow.

I felt more uncomfortable with every step I took. I hated leaving it behind.

We walked across the green with the houses spread out in front of us and I remembered Miss Keyland telling us how, before the terror, there had been people who kept second homes – one in London, one in the countryside. I imagined that this was exactly the sort of place they would have come. Everything was so neat, so ordered, that it was hard to believe that any real country folk had ever lived here. We came to the pub, which reminded me a bit of the Queen's Head, except it was smaller and prettier with a thatched roof and bow windows. It had a low door with a sign reading MIND YOUR HEAD and next to it, in chalk, the single word – OUCH! The pub was called the Punch Tavern. There was a sign hanging outside showing a horse pulling a plough. Somebody was playing the violin. We opened the door and went in.

A fire burned inside, which was nice, and half a dozen tables arranged with candles, making everything warm and snug. There were all sorts of bottles arranged behind the bar, but I could see at a glance that they were empty. I wondered if the villagers produced their own beer like we had. By the end, they were making ours out of turnips, I think. I had never tasted it but George said it was disgusting. On the plus side, I could smell meat cooking in the kitchen and, I have to say, it made my mouth water. The food on the *Lady Jane* had been amazing in its own way. I wasn't even sure how it had kept fresh locked up inside those tins but that didn't stop me wolfing it down. Hot, fresh meat, though, was something else again. It must have been three months since I'd tasted a rabbit, and that had been scrawny and tough, and as for squirrels ... you don't want to know. This meat smelled like pork, for me a distant memory. I could hardly wait.

All the villagers were there – apart from the major. There was no sign of the Traveller either. The violin was being played by a man standing beside the fire. He was missing an eye but hadn't bothered to cover it with a patch. The socket was bunched up and ugly, like a tightly closed mouth.

Everyone seemed pleased to see us as Jamie and I walked in. The major's wife, Dorothy, showed us to a table. "How lovely to see you. Now, you must let me introduce you. This is Alfie and Amanda Bussell. Angus Withers-Green, who does all our building for us. Everything would fall down if it wasn't for him! Mr Weeks, who runs the pub. I think you met Cosmo out at the lock and that's his sister, Christabel (she was a girl about two years younger than him, pale and hungry-looking, clutching a stuffed polar bear). "Mrs Fielding and Mrs Hamilton. The Osmonds." She laughed. "I'm sure there are far too many names to take on board all at once. I'll let everyone introduce themselves. In the meantime, would you like some orange juice?"

I had only ever drunk orange juice on special holidays – at Christmas and on my birthday. The publican, Mr Weeks, was a big, round-faced man with curling black hair almost bursting out of his head. He brought over two glasses and although the liquid inside them was barely orange at all, it did at least smell vaguely of fruit.

"Here you go, my dear," he said. He smiled at me but not in a particularly pleasant way. His face was too close to mine.

"Thank you." I backed away.

He gave Jamie a second glass and the two of us sat there for a minute with nobody talking but everybody looking at us. I raised my drink to my lips.

Don't drink it!

It was Jamie, inside my head. It always unnerved me, that power of his. I remembered the first time it had happened, at the church, in front of the Assembly. It felt as if he was whispering into my ear, but inside not outside ... if you get what I mean. I glanced at him. His face wasn't giving anything away but I somehow knew that he wasn't himself, that he was wishing he was anywhere but here.

I put the glass down.

"Where is our friend?" Jamie asked.

"Mr Fletcher?" It was the major's wife who had answered. She was sipping a glass of a dark-coloured liquid that the publican had just served her. "He's with Michael. The two of them are having a good old chat. It's very rare for us to have strangers in Little Moulsford and we want to know all about you, where you've come from, how you managed to get your hands on that fine boat. But we can start dinner without them. I'm sure there'll be here soon enough." She lowered her glass. It had left a stain on her lips.

"And here it is!" someone exclaimed.

A very short woman had walked into the room, carrying a plate of roast meat and vegetables. She was so short that for a moment I got the impression that the food was somehow floating in by itself. I had never seen so much meat, not since the time when I'd managed to bag the deer in the forest. It looked like boiled gammon and I guessed that the village bred pigs ... which was more than we'd ever managed to do. The vegetables were turnips and parsnips, and there were fewer of them to go round. The woman set the plate down with a little grunt of pleasure. The man with the violin stopped playing. All the others leant in as if to sniff the aroma that was rising from the food.

Don't eat anything, Holly.

They were the last words I wanted to hear and I didn't hear them anyway – once again they were inside my head and I knew that Jamie was responsible. I glared at him. I knew there were a lot of things that didn't add up about Little Moulsford but couldn't we find out what they were after we'd eaten?

Say you want to go to the toilet.

"I'm really sorry," I said. "It looks absolutely delicious, but I'm afraid I need to use the toilet."

The major's wife looked at me disapprovingly. It was probably bad manners to say something like that after the food had been served.

"We don't have any toilets," one of the villagers said. "None of them work. You have to use the latrine."

"And where's the latrine?" I asked.

"It's at the other end of the car park. Behind the pub."

Tell them you're scared of the dark.

It was almost too much. But I'd already invested everything in Jamie. From the moment I'd met him, I'd allowed him to rip my life apart. Why should I stop now? "I know this is going to sound really stupid," I said. "But actually I'm quite scared of the dark."

And that was Jamie's cue. "That's all right," he said. "Actually, I need to use it too. I'll come with you."

The major's wife was clearly disappointed. She thought for a moment, then shrugged. "Well, you'd better go together," she said. She turned to the boy. "Cosmo. You go with them. Make sure they don't get lost."

She didn't trust us. Cosmo lurched to his feet and grabbed a twenty-bore shotgun, which he slung over his shoulder. It seemed very strange that someone so young should be armed, but Cosmo held it like he'd been born with it. Together the three of us left the room. It was much colder now that the sun had set but there was still a glow in the sky, enough to see by. Cosmo pointed at a gravel path leading down the side of the pub. "It's this way," he said.

"We've already gone ahead of you," Jamie said. "You'd better hurry if you don't want to lose us."

What he had said made no sense at all. We weren't moving. We were standing right in front of him. For a moment, Cosmo looked confused. But then he nodded and set off into the darkness, disappearing out of sight, and I realized that this was down to Jamie, that he had somehow made Cosmo believe what he said, even though he could clearly see that it wasn't true. In a way it made me shiver. Jamie was so ordinary in many ways. I mean, he was just another fifteen-year-old, like me. But at the same time, he was like some sort of superhuman. He was one of the Five. He had this amazing power.

As soon as the boy had gone, Jamie began to move in the opposite direction. "Stay close to me," he said. His voice was a whisper and he sounded afraid. "We've got very little time."

"Where are we going?"

"I have to show you something. You're not going to like it. But I have to see..."

We went round the side of the Punch Tavern and came to a window that was illuminated by candlelight from within. I realized this must be the kitchen ... where the meat had come from. I think I knew what I was going to see before I saw it. All my nerves were tingling and there was a sort of dread deep in my stomach. We tiptoed forward and looked through the glass. And there it was. I will never forget it.

There was a chef in a white apron with a white hat on. In Little Moulsford they had to do everything properly, didn't they. I bet he washed his hands before he began cooking. There was a huge slab of meat on a wooden board in front of him – except it wasn't meat. It was a human being ... or the remains of one. I could clearly make out an arm, a shoulder, and part of a torso, some of it wrapped in silver foil. So this was what we had just been served. This was what I had been about to eat. I turned round and spewed up on the grass. I couldn't help myself.

Jamie was angry. He was afraid the noise would give us away. But fortunately the pub had old walls and thick glass. The chef didn't hear me. I wiped my sleeve across my mouth and took a deep breath. I didn't know if it was a man or a woman on the board. It was too horrible to think about. But that was how these people had survived. They were cannibals. They had taken to eating each other.

"We have to find the Traveller," Jamie whispered.

"Where is he?" For a dreadful moment I wondered if I had just seen him. But that wouldn't have been possible. The dead person in the kitchen must have taken hours to prepare, while the Traveller had only been away for a few minutes.

Jamie stared into the darkness as if listening for something – and in his own way that was exactly what he was doing. He was picking up thoughts as if they were radio signals. "There's a barn..."

We ran in that direction. I was glad to put distance between myself and the Punch Tavern. I couldn't wait to get away. But we weren't going anywhere without the Traveller. We wouldn't have been able to manage the boat without him, and anyway, there was no way we were going to leave him behind. We reached the barn. There was just enough light to see that it was painted white, with a pond outside and a well. The barn had huge wooden doors but fortunately they were open. We went in.

There was a single oil lamp burning on a table and a man sitting next to it in what otherwise seemed to be an empty space. He had a rifle across his lap and he snatched it up the moment we came in. I found myself reaching for the gun which was still tucked into my waistband. Of course, he'd have shot us both before I'd even found the safety catch and remembered how to release it, but Jamie simply looked at him and said, "You're very tired. You need to sleep." And the man did just that, laying his rifle down again and closing his eyes.

"Where is the Traveller?" I asked.

Jamie looked around him, then pointed to a grid in the floor.

"Down there," he said.

The grid was like a trapdoor, solid metal, partly covered in straw. It must have opened into some sort of underground storage area. We hurried over to it but it was locked with a heavy padlock. My heart sank when I saw that. How many more problems would we have to overcome? And how long would it be before the people in the Punch Tavern realized we were missing and came after us?

"See if you can find the key," Jamie said.

I went towards the guard, who was now sound asleep, the rifle loose in his hands. At the same time, Jamie knelt beside the grid.

"Jamie – is that you?" The voice was hoarse. It came from below. It was the Traveller.

"We're looking for the key," Jamie said.

"They knocked me out. We have to get out of this place."

"I know."

"I've got it!" I'd found a key on a chain in the guard's jacket pocket. I pulled it out and threw it to Jamie, who fitted it into the padlock. I was relieved when I heard the click and the lock sprang open. Together, we heaved the grid up and the Traveller climbed out. He nodded his thanks at us but I could see that he was embarrassed. He was meant to be looking after us – the Nexus had trusted him – but without us he would have been dead meat. Quite literally. He turned back and that was when I saw something else that made my skin crawl.

He hadn't been alone.

Looking down, I saw that there were two more men in the pit below the church. They were both stark naked, with shaved heads and wide, blank eyes. I don't know how long they had been there but they had been caged like animals. That was all they were to the people of Little Moulsford. I expected them to climb up, but they just sat there, staring at us, saying nothing.

"There's nothing we can do for them," the Traveller said. "They're both mad. God knows what they've done to them." He snatched the rifle from the sleeping guard. "Is there anyone near the *Lady Jane*?"

"Not that I saw," Jamie said. "But we need to hurry. They must already be wondering where we've gone."

The three of us scrambled out of the barn. We left the trapdoor open so if the poor men who were down there wanted to, at least they could get away.

The Traveller checked the rifle. It had a clip of ammunition and the clip was full. "They took my gun," he explained.

I drew out my pistol. When the Traveller had given it to me, I'd doubted that I'd ever be able to use it. But if Major Higham or his charming wife had come anywhere near me just then, I'd have gladly blown their heads off. I saw that Jamie had his gun too. I did wonder if he couldn't just tell the entire village to drop dead, but I wasn't sure if that was how his power worked and this probably wasn't the time to ask.

We ran across the village green, keeping our heads low. We could see lights behind the windows of the Punch Tavern but there didn't seem to be anyone around. The canal was right ahead of us – and there was the *Lady Jane*, waiting quietly, moored to the side. I was doubly glad now that we had gone through the locks. Opening and closing gates in the darkness would have been impossible.

Jamie had the key to the boat door. He took it out and handed it to the Traveller.

"As soon as I start the engine, they'll hear us," the Traveller warned. "Be ready with your guns."

"Will they be able to follow us?" I asked.

It was probably a stupid question and I never got the answer because at that exact moment the entire scene lit up. We hadn't seen them in the darkness and I'll never know why we hadn't heard them. Maybe it was because they were parked in the distance, on the other side of the locks.

There was a ring of police cars. The headlamps had been turned on and they were focused on us, hemming us in, blinding us. As I stared – completely shocked – a woman walked forward, crossing the canal and continuing right up to us. At first she was silhouetted against the light and I could only make out her long hair and her coat flapping around her legs. But then she reached us and I recognized the woman who had come out of the helicopter and who had given the orders for first Miss Keyland and then everyone else in my village to be killed.

"Well, well, well," she said. "A canal boat. Who would have thought it?"

Jamie opened his mouth to speak and I knew he was going to use his power to make her go away. But before he could say anything, she hit him with her fist. She was surprisingly strong. Jamie was knocked to the ground, dazed. At the same time, a whole crowd of police officers closed in. They were all carrying weapons. There were more than a dozen of them. We had nowhere to run.

"Kill the man and the girl," the woman said. "And then let's take the boy."

I still couldn't see. The light was dancing in my eyes. The Traveller reached out and took hold of me and together we waited for the end.

THIRTY-EIGHT

There was a burst of gunfire, a thousand bullets being fired at the same time. But it wasn't the police firing at us. The shots were coming from behind us and as I turned round I saw the crowd from the Punch Tavern; a whole line of them, firing at the police. They had finally figured out that we'd slipped away and they had come slithering into the night, carrying weapons that they must have collected from their houses. I don't know why they had chosen the police as their targets instead of us. Maybe they were protecting themselves. After all, the police had completely destroyed my own village and perhaps word had got round. Alternatively, given that the major and his friends were both horrible and sick, it could be that they saw a year's supply of prime steak inside those blue uniforms. In any event, they had decided that the police were their main enemy and so that was who they were taking out first.

The police had no time to react. They had been aiming at us and hadn't seen the figures rising out of the darkness. There was a crowd of villagers firing at them simultaneously and at least half of them were blown off their feet in the opening salvo. At the same time, the headlights were blinking out, one by one, as they were hit, which was good for us because darkness would be the one thing we would have on our side. I glanced at Jamie, who was still lying on the grass, half-hidden in shadow and to some extent out of harm's way. Maybe he was making everyone fire in the wrong direction because, miraculously, neither the Traveller nor I had been killed.

Not yet, anyway.

"Get down, Holly!" the Traveller shouted at me and although I hardly heard his words above the roar of the gunfire, I pitched myself forward onto my stomach even as bullets streamed over my head. I was lucky. There was a trench in the ground, barely more than a few inches deep, but the sloping sides gave me a little cover. The villagers were still blasting at the police and more of them were falling, but then the Traveller twisted round with his gun and began firing himself. I saw the man called Withers-Green ("who does all the building for us") crumple in on himself, clutching his stomach, and thought, he won't be doing any building any more. Major Higham had finally reappeared as well. He started to shout something but suddenly the bottom of his face disappeared, turning into a smudge of red. More lights blinked out. Some of the police were returning fire. Three more villagers died.

Bullets in front of us. Bullets behind. It was like being in the middle of a war. All I could do was lie there, hugging the ground. I still had my gun in my hand but I was too scared to use it. I wouldn't have known who to aim at anyway.

The police weren't firing at us because they were afraid they'd hit Jamie, and the ginger-haired woman had told them that he had to be taken alive. The villagers were ignoring us because they had to defend themselves against the police. Caught between the two of them, I managed to crawl over to Jamie and shook his arm, trying to wake him up. This couldn't go on much longer. If were going to have any chance of reaching the *Lady Jane*, we were going to need his help.

The Traveller squeezed off a couple more shots then jerked sideways and I saw the shock and the pain in his face. He had been wounded – how badly I couldn't tell. It was impossible to say how many of the villagers and how many of the police had been killed – or even who was winning. Only one headlight remained and as I grabbed Jamie, there was a tinkle of glass and that went out too. I just had time to see Jamie's eyes open.

"You've got to stop them!" I shouted.

"What...?" He was still dazed.

"They're killing each other and if we don't stop them, they're going to kill us too!"

"Where's the Traveller?"

"I'm here!" He was still alive but he wasn't shooting any more. Either he was in too much pain or he'd run out of bullets.

Jamie sat up.

It was the worst thing he could have done. He had been protected, at least partly, by the fold in the ground but now he was deliberately making himself a target. Bullets were still flying in all directions, although there were fewer of them now as there had been so many casualties. And it was pitch-dark. The policewoman wanted Jamie alive but he could easily have been shot by accident.

"We're not here!" he shouted. "We were never here."

I realized that once again he was using his power – and in a way that was more extraordinary than anything I'd yet witnessed. Jamie could control one person. He had sent Cosmo stumbling off to the latrine. But now he was pushing his thoughts out to the whole bunch of them, interrupting a bloody battle to plant the lie in their heads. I wondered if it could possibly work. There must have been twelve or more people still alive ... from both sides. Could he really fool the whole lot of them at once?

It was time to find out.

"Let's get to the boat," Jamie said.

We crawled across the ground in the direction of the canal, moving diagonally, away from the line of fire. The Traveller came with us. I still didn't know how badly he had been hit. It was very, very dark. The *Lady Jane* was little more than one shade of black against another and the only lights were the blazes of red coming from the guns as the shoot-out continued. We reached the boat. Jamie passed me the key and I unlocked the door. The people of Little Moulsford hadn't tried to force their way in yet. Presumably they had been leaving that for the break of day. The three of us piled on board. The ignition key was hidden on a shelf inside. I found it and handed it to the Traveller.

He turned to Jamie. "Can we start the engine? Will they hear it?"

Jamie looked back. The shooting had become very sporadic. Someone – a woman – was shouting in pain. I think it was the major's wife. "They'll hear it but they won't care. They've forgotten about us. But you have to hurry. It won't last for long."

The Traveller started the engine. Our own lamp broke through the darkness, illuminating the water ahead. I wanted to go into the cabin, find my bed and hide in it – but I forced myself back onto the towpath, untying the ropes, casting off. The Traveller pressed down on the throttle and as the *Lady Jane* pulled away I jumped back on board. The noise of the engine drowned out a little of the gunfire and even now I couldn't believe that they wouldn't hear, that they wouldn't come after us. But if we had never been there, as Jamie had told them, how could we possibly be getting away?

The canal turned a corner and suddenly we had left Little Moulsford behind us. Jamie was steering. The Traveller had slumped onto the deck, holding his shoulder in pain. But I knew we hadn't escaped yet.

"How long will it be before they realize?" I asked.

"I don't know," Jamie said. "I've never done anything like that before. If it had been one person it would have been easier."

He shrugged. "Maybe an hour. Maybe two. You'd better see to the Traveller."

"I'm OK."

I found a torch and turned it on him. He wasn't OK. He'd been hit in the shoulder and there was blood spreading through his shirt. "What can I do?" I asked.

"Get me a cloth and some water." He must have heard the panic in my voice. "Seriously, Holly. It's not too bad."

I hurried into the galley and did as he asked. He poured water onto the cloth and pressed it against the wound, then he drank the rest. Finally, he looked back in the direction we had come. There was absolutely no sound now, even though the fighting was probably still going on. That was the thing about the canal. You only had to travel a short distance and you would be in a completely different world.

"How do you think they found us?" I asked.

"The police? Who knows? Maybe it was one of the villagers. Or the fly-soldiers. Or they could have worked out that we had a boat."

"They'll come after us, won't they?"

The Traveller nodded. "Jamie bought us time and he got us out of there. But sooner or later they're going to follow." He forced himself to his feet. "I'll call the Nexus and tell them to be ready for us."

"Call them?"

"I have a radio, Holly. They already know we're on our way."

"How far is it?" Jamie asked.

"Five or six hours. If we can get to the Sheerwall Tunnel, we'll be safe. I still have a couple of surprises up my sleeve." He went into the galley and I wanted to follow him. I'd never seen a working radio. I thought the technology had vanished years ago. But I stayed with Jamie.

"Five or six hours," I muttered.

"If we're lucky..."

Our single light picked out the way ahead. The darkness was pressing in all around.

That night seemed endless. The canal continued in a dead straight line, penning us in with nowhere to hide. We couldn't turn left or right. We couldn't reverse without a lot of manoeuvring. I found myself staring at the dim circle of light as it slid across the oily water, wishing it would move faster, wondering who else might be seeing it. All the time I imagined someone jumping out of the darkness. It wouldn't have been difficult because the canal had become so narrow that we were never far away from the bank. Would it be one of the policemen or perhaps Mrs Higham and some of her cannibal friends, clawing at us with snapping teeth and bloodshot eyes? I wasn't even sure which of the two possibilities would have been worse.

I had my gun and I was keeping it close. The Traveller was also on the aft deck. He might still have had a bullet in him but he had bandaged himself up, taken a shot of something – pills or alcohol – and if he was in pain he was doing his best not to show it. There was an automatic rifle cradled in his arms and I wondered just how many more weapons there were concealed on board the *Lady Jane*. He'd mentioned he had a surprise or two in store. I hoped it was a box of hand grenades or, better still, a long-range guided missile system.

And so we stood there, the three of us, drifting through the night like statues or upright ghosts. It had become very chilly. Our breath was fogging ... I could see mine against the reflecting light. A few tendrils of mist were reaching out over the water and the branches of the trees looked like steel. In a strange way it was the silence that scared me most. Of course there was the rumble of the engine beneath our feet, the one constant sound, travelling with us. But at the same time I was aware of the vast, empty countryside, the faint shadows of bushes and trees gliding past. It was like being trapped in a nightmare, unable to wake up.

We didn't speak. Although we were cold, none of us went down to the galley to make a hot drink, as if we couldn't tear ourselves away from the deck where we were standing. There were lots of things I wanted to ask. What was so important about the Sheerwall Tunnel? Did we have enough fuel to get there? Were there any more locks on the way? But I kept my mouth shut. I would find out soon enough.

And slowly, slowly the night faded and the dawn arrived, streaks of pale grey spreading through the sky. Had I somehow fallen asleep on my feet? The landscape had completely changed. We were on the edge of a city. There were buildings all around us, the remains of factories with smokestacks and loading bays. I could see at once that they were deserted. The doors were hanging open, showing dank interiors. Most of the windows were smashed. There was debris everywhere: bits of old machinery, oil tanks, tyres and industrial bins lying on their side. The ground rose up ahead of us and I could see houses, squeezed together like some of the cottages in my village, sharing a front gate. But there were rows and rows of them, more houses than I'd seen in my life. I got the feeling that they were all empty. I don't know why. I suppose there could have been people inside, asleep, but they just felt deserted.

"We're less than a mile away," the Traveller said. He sounded exhausted. The bleeding had stopped but he had been up all night, wrapped in pain.

"How much less?" Jamie was still steering. I don't know how he found the strength. He too had had no sleep.

"The Nexus will be waiting for us. They know we're here."

They know we're here.

The words had no sooner left his mouth than I saw them. Three police helicopters were coming at us out of a sky that had gone from grey to white. They were flying in an arrow formation, still some distance away but closing in on us so fast that when I looked at them a second time, they seemed to have doubled in size. At the same time, Jamie cried out and pointed straight ahead. I followed his finger to a patch of empty land on the other side of the houses. At first I thought it was raining. Thousands of tiny black objects seemed to be falling to the ground. But then I realized that before they hit, they were slowing down. They were actually controlling their descent. They were living things.

Flies. A gigantic swarm of flies was pouring down and even as I watched, it began to form itself, like black smoke, breaking up and taking on the shape of men on horses. I had never seen anything like it. It was like black wax being poured into a mould. The separate figures were forming themselves in front of my eyes. In a minute they would be complete and then they would ride forward, passing through the streets and down the hill to the canal.

But there was the tunnel! It was right ahead of us, a circular entrance with a dark passageway leading into the hill, beneath the houses. Suddenly the *Lady Jane*, which had carried us steadily through the night, seemed to have slowed down to a crawl. The helicopters were getting closer and closer. I could hear the whirring of the blades. The horsemen were almost complete. We were trapped between them and no matter how hard I looked, the tunnel refused to get closer.

"We're going to make it. We're going to make it." For a brief moment I didn't know who was saying that. Then I realized it was me.

But was I right? And what difference would it make, anyway? I suddenly saw that putting any faith in the Sheerwall Tunnel was a waste of time. It was only about twenty metres long. I could see the circle of light on the other side. The helicopters could simply park beside the canal and wait for us to come out. Or the flies could break up again and come in after us. Even if the Traveller stopped the engine right in the middle, we couldn't hide in there for ever. Why had he brought us here?

The helicopters flew overhead, so close that I could see the screws underneath the cockpit, and the scream of the rotors and the blast of air almost knocked me off the boat. There was a flat area beside the factory – perhaps it had once been a car park – and one after another they hit the ground, rocking briefly in the air before touching down. Almost at once the doors slid open and uniformed men burst out – so many of them that I wondered how they had all fitted in. Not all men. The woman who was in charge of them was there too, her ginger hair blowing wildly around her face. Meanwhile, the fly-soldiers were ready. They were further away but they began to gallop forward, following the road that would lead them through the rows of houses and eventually down to the canal path.

The tunnel was opening up in front of us. Jamie was standing absolutely still, with one hand on the steering wheel and the other clenching the throttle as if he could somehow will the *Lady Jane* to go faster. The Traveller brought up his gun and fired off several shots, aiming at the police. I saw one man go down but they surged forward without hesitating. They had already let us slip through their fingers twice. It didn't matter how many of them died. They weren't going to let it happen a third time.

Someone fired a shot and the handrail right next to me splintered, wood fragments flying up.

"Get down, Holly!"

It was the Traveller, shouting at me, and I saw that one of the policemen had been aiming at me, had come within inches of killing me. How could I be so slow and useless? I crouched down and fired six shots at the helicopter, the gun bucking in my hand. I smelled the cordite as it rose into my nostrils but I'm not sure I actually hit anyone. The police returned fire. But once again they must have been ordered not to hit Jamie and I was so close to him now that I was more or less safe. The bullets smashed into the side of the *Lady Jane*. Two of the windows shattered.

I looked up. There was a fly-soldier right above us, over the entrance to the tunnel. He drew back a spear. And just as the soldier was made up of flies, so was the spear. I swear I could hear it buzzing and briefly wondered what it would be like to be hit by it, to have it go right through me. Because he was aiming at me. There could be no doubt of it. Would the flies separate again when they were in my blood? Would they destroy me from inside? I cried out, but at that exact moment we plunged into the tunnel and a great tube of darkness and damp slid over us and the police and the fly-soldiers were cut off. There was no towpath. The police would be unable to follow us unless they decided to swim, and although the insects might break up again and fly after us, perhaps the darkness and the confined space might put them off.

Not that it mattered. We could stop and try to hide inside the tunnel. Or we could go on, in which case we'd be out the other end in about one minute. That was all the breathing space we had. The police would already be on their way to cut us off. We had come so far! We had managed to escape from Little Moulsford and we had travelled through the night. But it had all been for nothing.

And then I saw that the Traveller was already moving. He went over to Jamie and pushed up the throttle, cutting our speed by half. Then he flipped open a panel next to the tiller. I hadn't even noticed it before. Inside there was a dial and a red button.

"We've got to move fast!" he shouted. "Leave everything behind. Go to the front of the boat. Get onto the roof."

"What about the steering?" Jamie asked.

"It's OK. It's locked." The Traveller turned the dial and pressed the red button. At once, a light began to flash inside the boat. I wondered what he had done. Was this a secret weapon, the surprise he had been talking about? "Move!" he shouted again. "We have to be on the roof!"

The canal boat was still moving – but at half the speed, so we had a little more time. Nobody had followed us into the tunnel. Everything was going black–white, black–white, so I could just make out what I was doing. We dropped our weapons, dashed through the galley and the sleeping area and scrambled up. The Traveller went first, then Jamie, then me, and there we were on our feet, not moving ourselves but still gliding forward with the curved ceiling of the tunnel so close to our heads that we could reach up and touch it. I felt moisture dripping onto my neck. It was very cold in the tunnel. We were already about halfway through.

"There's a ladder!" the Traveller shouted. "Grab hold of it and swing yourself along. I'll go first. Follow me!"

I saw it almost immediately. It was attached to the ceiling, running horizontally above the water. All we had to do was grab hold of it and wait while the top of the boat moved forward underneath our feet. As the *Lady Jane* continued, the steering locked, the speed constant, we would be left dangling in the darkness. What was the big idea? Were we supposed to hang there until everyone went away?

I transferred my weight to my hands and arms and began to walk forward along the roof of the boat, remaining in the same place. And then the *Lady Jane* had gone. My feet bumped over the edge and suddenly I was dangling there with only the dark water below me. The others were in front of me and I wondered how the Traveller could possibly find the strength to hang on after everything he had been through.

But he was grimly determined. "This way!" he shouted. He had his back to me of course but I saw him swing himself forward, moving from one rung to the next. It reminded me of when I was small, in the playground in my village. There had been a climbing frame and I'd often done exactly this. First the Traveller, then Jamie, then me ... we clambered along the ladder and all the time the *Lady Jane* was getting further and further away in front of us. I reckoned it would be out in the light in about ten seconds.

And what would the policewoman do then, when she saw that nobody was on board? Would she assume that we had somehow drowned?

"Up!" the Traveller shouted.

I didn't know what he meant by that but even as he spoke, I saw him disappear from sight and realized that there was a vertical shaft inside the tunnel, directly above his head. He'd swung himself as far as the opening and then across onto a second ladder that had taken him up. Jamie did the same. One minute he was in front of me, Then it was just his feet. Then he had gone altogether. I was the last. Suddenly I was alone in the tunnel, dangling in space with my arms outstretched. I saw the second ladder in front of me. Jamie's feet were above my head. But I couldn't follow him. The *Lady Jane* had reached the tunnel exit and I had to see what happened next.

I watched as it slid into the open. I could actually see the tiller, the deck where we had just been standing, the name of the boat written in gold letters on the stern. There was no sign of the police or the fly-soldiers but I could imagine them, waiting to pounce. The boat was completely out of the tunnel now, framed by an O of light. I thought of the button that the Traveller had pressed and it was only then that I realized what was about to happen.

The *Lady Jane* blew up. The explosion was massive, not just tearing it apart but devouring it in a blazing red fireball. And as I stared, the flames rushed towards me, back through the tunnel. If the bomb had gone off a second earlier, I would have been killed instantly. I had about half a second to get out of there. Desperately, I threw myself onto the second ladder and pulled myself up even as a torpedo of burning air raced past. It must have missed me by less than an inch. I felt the heat on the soles of my feet and, looking down, everything was a dense, brilliant red. I looked up and saw Jamie's face, also reflecting red, staring in horror. He was already climbing and I followed, putting as much space as I could between myself and the inferno below.

Ten rungs. Then we came to another opening and a horizontal passageway leading into inky blackness. We were above the water, still far underground. But I didn't have the faintest idea what was going on.

THIRTY-NINE

"This way."

The Traveller's voice, barely more than a whisper, came out of the darkness ahead of me and I shuffled forward on my hands and knees because there wasn't enough room to stand up. I was in a narrow, dark tube, buried underground and suddenly I found myself on the edge of panic, fighting for breath. But then, about ten metres away, a square of electric light appeared and I realized that a door had been opened. A door into what? I didn't care. Jamie was already on his way towards it and I followed.

The door opened into a square room, with a light bulb dangling from the ceiling and breezeblock walls. I thought I could hear the distant hum of machinery. There had to be a generator powering the light. Jamie and the Traveller were being greeted by two people, a man and a woman dressed in grey overalls, both of them in their forties. The woman had fair hair tied in a knot. Her face was filled with concern as she tried to examine the Traveller's wound.

"You've been shot," she was saying. "You should have told us. We have to get you to the doctor."

"Not yet." The Traveller shook his head. "I need to see that it worked."

"Graham..." the man began. He looked remarkably like the Traveller, with black, curly hair, a lean face and lots of stubble.

Like the woman, he was quite pale, like two prisoners who hadn't seen much of the sun.

"I'm all right, Will. Honestly, I am." The two of them stood facing each other for a moment, then suddenly embraced, and in that moment I guessed that they were actually brothers, that Will had been part of the family the Traveller had mentioned, and that they hadn't seen or spoken to each other for a long time. "It's good to see you," the Traveller said.

"I've missed you."

"Are you OK?"

"Yeah."

They broke apart. The Traveller gestured at the two of us. "This is Jamie. And Holly – who was looking after him. I'll tell you about it later. But now I want to get inside..."

There was a second door leading out. By now there were about a million questions I wanted to ask, starting with who these people were, what this place was and what we were doing here. But I was able to work out some of it for myself. The police would have seen the *Lady Jane* explode and hopefully they'd assume that we had still been on board, that we'd killed ourselves rather than fall into their hands. They'd look in the tunnel but they might not notice a ladder in the darkness above their heads and surely they would never suspect that there had been people waiting to meet us. At least, that was what I hoped.

We followed a long passageway with bare concrete walls and somehow I got the sense that we were being led further and further into the hillside. I could feel the weight of it pressing down on us. Then there was another doorway – all the light was coming from here – and as I turned the corner, I froze. I just stood there, gaping in astonishment.

We were standing on a raised metal platform above a huge room with at least twenty people looking up at us, applauding.

They were all dressed in the same grey overalls as the two people who had met us, but they were every age – from twenty to about seventy. They were surrounded by equipment that I could vaguely remember from my childhood but that I had never seen working since then: electric lights, for a start, but also television screens, computers and telephones. There were other machines, too, banked up against the walls with cables everywhere. Even the air in the room was coming in through some sort of ventilation system. There were no windows.

The room was circular with a domed ceiling. A number of workstations had been arranged in a horseshoe shape in the middle and there was a proper kitchen with cupboards, fridges, ovens and a sink (did they really have running water?) to one side. Two wooden tables stretched out next to each other with different-coloured plastic chairs for meals and a short distance away, sofas had been arranged facing a widescreen TV. There were plants and flowers everywhere … in pots, vases and terracotta urns. Maybe that made them feel at home. Because this was definitely where they worked, ate and rested. I noticed more doors leading out, presumably to where they slept.

They were still applauding – but not me, of course. Jamie was the one they had all been waiting for and the Traveller had brought him here. They were the two heroes. I was just someone who had tagged along for the ride. But I still couldn't help smiling. They were so glad to see us and, at the end of the day, if I hadn't stood up for Jamie back in the village, he might never have made it. And even if the Traveller had wanted to leave me behind, I was part of the adventure too.

The Traveller held up a hand. The applause died away.

"My friends!" he exclaimed. "It's been so long since I've seen you all. I can't believe I'm back. I'm so glad to see you … especially Sophie and Will." He nodded at the man, who, I was sure, was his brother. "But the main thing is, all our work, everything we've suffered, hasn't been in vain. I found the village and the door and finally it opened and one of the Five came through. This is Jamie Tyler. If there is any hope left in the world, it rests with him. He is here and we can help him take on the Old Ones and give mankind a second chance."

At that, they all began to clap again. If I'd been in Jamie's shoes, I wouldn't have known whether to bow or make a speech or wave or what to do. But he just stood there, as if he had expected this sort of reception, and it seemed to me that in some ways I was seeing him for the first time. He wasn't just another fifteen-year-old like me. He was a Gatekeeper. He was here to save the world.

The Traveller must have decided that this had gone on long enough because suddenly he was bounding down the stairs, making for the nearest workstation, where a TV monitor was flickering with a black-and-white image. Jamie and I followed. There was a young woman there, only a few years older than me. She was quite small with shaven hair.

"How are you, Linda?" the Traveller asked. "I hardly recognize you. You were only twelve when I left." His eyes flickered to the screen. "Has it worked?"

She nodded. "I think so. They're in the water but they're looking in the wrong place."

I looked at the television, fascinated to see the canal and the moving figures. The last time I had seen a TV I had been six years old, and that had been a long time ago. There must have been cameras concealed close to the canal because we could see everything. The fly-soldiers seemed to have gone but the police were still there, standing on the bank on the other side of the tunnel or wading through the water. The image changed and I saw what was left of the *Lady Jane*. Only the front section had survived in one piece and smoke was still billowing out. The rest was either floating on the water or scattered over the ground. The image changed again and I saw the policewoman in her long coat, watching pensively, her elbow resting on her hand. In front of her, one of the policemen was slipping into the canal.

"They're going back into the tunnel," Jamie said. "What happens if they find the ladder?"

"There's nothing unusual about a ladder set in the ceiling," the Traveller replied. "When the canals were built, there were no engines and the horses that pulled the barges couldn't go through the tunnels. So the crew would lie on their backs on the roof of the boat and use their feet to propel it forward."

"What about the shaft?"

"It's already locked," the girl – Linda – said. She gestured at a set of controls in front of her. "As soon as you climbed up, a panel slid across behind you. The second door is locked too. Even if they light up the entire tunnel, they're not going to see anything."

"You knew we were coming," I said.

"We've been watching you for the last few miles."

Watching us? How? There must have been more cameras concealed along the way. "Why didn't you come and help us when we were being chased?" I asked.

"I can explain that, Holly."

Another woman had appeared, this one older, with white hair, holding a thin cane. Her eyes were covered with black glasses and because I had never met anyone who was blind before, it took me a few seconds to realize that was exactly what she was.

Next to me, Jamie started. "Miss Ashwood!" he exclaimed.

"Jamie..."

"You know each other?" I asked.

"We met once, ten years ago." The blind woman smiled. "At least, it was ten years for me. We're safe, I think. The police won't find anything and they'll assume that you died in the boat.

Don't worry. We'll keep an eye on things. What matters now is that the three of you get some breakfast. You need a shower, a change of clothes and some sleep. Then we can talk."

"Miss Ashwood…" Jamie wasn't moving. "What is this place? Is this the Nexus? Have you really done all this for me?"

"Yes, Jamie. We've been waiting for you for an awfully long time so another few hours won't hurt. Eat something and get some rest. It isn't over yet." She turned and walked away, tapping her cane on the concrete floor ahead of her.

"Something to eat," I said. "That sounds like a good idea." I yawned. "Then bed. Then a shower. I don't care which comes first."

The next twelve hours were among the most blissful in my life. First we ate … real food. Meat and fresh vegetables, then chocolate pudding and custard. Chocolate! For me it was just a faint memory, but even smelling the warm, brown sludge in my bowl was like opening a treasure chest. I don't think I'd ever felt full before. Every meal I'd eaten in the village had just taunted me, leaving me almost as hungry as when I'd sat down. But I was completely stuffed when I made my way to the sleeping quarters, where a room had been specially prepared for me.

I had a bed with clean sheets and a decent pillow. But first came the total luxury of a warm shower. Not hot but not icy cold either – and strong enough to cover my head and shoulders without me having to move around. They even supplied shampoo, which was a lovely golden colour and smelled of apples. My room was small and plain. It had no windows – but that didn't matter. I was asleep in less than five seconds and it was another nine hours before I woke up.

Jamie had the room next door – identical to mine, I noticed – and that evening (if it was evening … it was hard to say) we had supper together in the main room with the other Nexus people, who seemed like a nice bunch and looked normal, even if they were all dressed the same. Of course, there was nothing normal about this underground complex but after Little Moulsford it was nice to be introduced to people who smiled and chatted and didn't stare at you like they were imagining you served up as the Sunday roast.

Then the Traveller appeared, not just washed but shaved for the first time, which made him look ten years younger. He was dressed, like all of us, in grey overalls and his arm was in a sling. I could just make out fresh bandages wrapped around his shoulder, so I guessed they must have taken out the bullet and given him painkillers or whatever because he looked completely refreshed.

I still didn't know very much about the other members of the Nexus. We'd eaten with Will and Sophie, who had wanted to know all about the end of the village and our flight down the canal but annoyingly told us very little about themselves. Perhaps they'd been instructed not to. Will admitted to being the Traveller's brother, older by two years – so at least I'd been right about that. Sophie was just a friend, although a close one. It couldn't have been easy for her either, being apart from him all this time.

The Traveller led us away from the dining area and through a door next to the kitchen. It led to a conference room with a glass table, comfortable leather chairs and maps of the UK pinned to the walls. Susan Ashwood was waiting for us. Sophie and Will had come too, so that made six of us sitting with the door shut in this private space.

"I'm sure you have a lot of questions," the Traveller said. "So I'll begin by answering some of them. Jamie ... you met Susan Ashwood just before you went to Hong Kong. She's in charge here. You could say she's our boss. She was the one who sent me to the village to find you, although I have no idea how she knew that you'd show up. That doesn't matter. The important thing is that you're safe. And in case you're wondering, you're about ten miles from St Meredith's, to the north of London. Miss Ashwood will tell you the rest. Then we've got to decide what we're going to do."

The blind woman had been waiting for her turn to speak. It was interesting how all three of them seemed to be in awe of her, even though they had known her all this time. Nobody called her "Susan", for example. She was always "Miss Ashwood". She turned her head so that she could address Jamie directly.

"Jamie, you know that the Nexus existed only to help you and the other Gatekeepers," she began. "We were always aware that the world would come to these terrible times – it had been predicted by Joseph of Cordoba, for a start. So when we met you in Farringdon all those years ago, we had already made preparations. We had millions of pounds at our disposal. Our members were enormously wealthy ... industrialists, statesmen. We were effectively able to plan for the end of the world.

"We built survival pods. That's what you're in now. You may think it a little extreme but let me assure you that back in the Sixties – when I was a young girl – there were many places just like this in existence. The world was afraid of nuclear war and the British government built a series of bunkers deep underground. This was one of them. We bought it and adapted it to our own needs. There were six other pods. The one in Tokyo was destroyed and Istanbul was discovered by the Old Ones and overrun. But the Nexus still has people around the world. We have sent our agents to Mecca, Buenos Aires, Cairo and Delhi. It was fortunate that Matt and Richard Cole were able to bring us a copy of the monk's diary. It gave us the locations of many of the gates and we have tried to maintain a presence near every one of them. In addition, we have planes. We have food and weapons. We are here to serve you.

"I last met you ten years ago, when you and Matthew Freeman left for Hong Kong. Shortly after that, much of Hong Kong was destroyed by a typhoon and many of us believed that all five of you had been killed, particularly when we failed to hear from any of you. I knew otherwise. The spirits kept me informed. There is no time in the spirit world. They knew that you had been sent forward ten years and that if we could simply survive that long, you would be back."

"Excuse me," I said. I hadn't meant to interrupt but I had to challenge what I had just heard. "Are you saying that you talk to ghosts?"

Miss Ashwood nodded slightly, as if the question was of no importance and the answer completely obvious. Then she went on. "A year after you had gone, on the ninth of May, the UK was hit by a series of dirty bombs – part nuclear, part biochemical. To this day we do not know who was behind the atrocity. It could have been religious extremists. It could have been anybody. It hardly makes much difference to the survivors. The government was completely wiped out. Any form of infrastructure disappeared. At the same time, the world was experiencing a series of catastrophes. Massive volcano eruptions in Japan. Floods in Europe and Australia. Famine in America. Plague in China. It was as if the four horsemen of the Apocalypse had finally arrived, only there were four hundred of them, riding in a stampede. We were left on our own. Nobody came to our aid.

"I was brought here originally by Sir James Tarrant. You may remember him, Jamie. He was the assistant commissioner of the London police and a good man. He died two years ago … a heart attack. There were a dozen of us to start with but more people joined. Over the years, we've had seven casualties – mainly on expeditions above ground.

"We have kept a long vigil here, watching the Old Ones tear

apart what was left of our country. In some ways, we have been fortunate. We began with a vast depot of provisions and unlimited water ... we have our own purification system. We have fuel and electricity. We are able to grow our own food both underground and on the surface. We even have books, DVDs and computer games!

"Even so, it has not been easy. You could go mad living like this ... so many of us, thrown together, buried alive. But we have had a common cause. Very occasionally we have heard from the other pods. We have had to be careful as there is always the chance that our radio signals will be intercepted. But above all, we have had hope. We always knew that one day the Five would return.

"Seven years ago, once things had become a little more settled, I sent Graham Fletcher out to look for the door which I knew existed in the east of England, in the church of St Botolph's. He had everything he needed on the *Lady Jane* and the river and canal system would allow him to slip unseen through the country. It was a great deal to ask of him but there was no other way. He had to find the door and wait there for one of the Five to appear and then to bring them here. He has succeeded. Although he has been separated from his friends and his brother for all these years, he has never wavered. We have much to be grateful for."

"St Meredith's is still standing," Jamie said.

I was amazed how confident he was. He'd just taken all this on board but he hadn't even blinked. I was freaking out and he was totally in control. But then this entire operation, these people, the nuclear bunker or whatever it was ... all of it was only there for him. So perhaps it was natural that he should take command.

"Yes," Miss Ashworth replied. "But there's a difference, Jamie. The Old Ones know about it. They may have even left it intact on purpose, as a trap to draw you in. It looks abandoned but we have sent out spies and know that it is permanently surrounded. There are shape-changers in London … and worse. They were always waiting in the hope that you would emerge there from Hong Kong. And they will certainly be waiting for you now."

"They think Jamie is dead," the Traveller said.

"That's true, Graham. And it may help us. Maybe they'll relax their guard. But we still have to be very careful before we try to go in." She turned back to Jamie. "The doors aren't working, are they?"

"No," Jamie admitted. "But that's going to change." Suddenly he was the centre of attention. It was as if Miss Ashwood had passed over her authority to him. "Matt and the others are alive," he continued. "I've seen them in the dreamworld, which is a place we can go when we're asleep. Matt is in Brazil. The last time I saw her, Scarlett was heading for Dubai. She's with Richard Cole. Pedro is in Italy. And Scott…" He hesitated. "Scott is already in Oblivion, in Antarctica. That's where this is all going to end, and if you have people who are ready to fight, that's where they should be heading."

"We could fly you there," Will said. "Heathrow and Gatwick are both out of use but there's a landing strip at Elstree we can use…"

"No." Jamie shook his head. "The doors are going to open again. Matt is going to send me a signal. I have to get to St Meredith's as soon as possible and then, when the moment comes, I'll join him in Oblivion."

Nobody argued. Whatever Jamie wanted, that was what was going to happen.

"Can you get me there?" he asked.

"Yes." Miss Ashwood nodded. "But London is terribly dangerous. Parts of it are still radioactive. And there was some sort of virus we know nothing about. Conditions change daily, depending on how the wind blows. Incredibly, there are still people living there but they're barely recognizable as human beings. You were in Little Moulsford. You've seen what can happen. We have a safe house near St Meredith's but you can't stay there more than three or four days."

"I want to go there straight away," Jamie said. "And I'm going to need as many people as you can spare. When the time comes, we're going to have to fight our way inside. And I don't know why I'm saying this but once Matt gives the signal, I don't think we're going to have much time."

"All right. Graham will make all the arrangements."

"I'm coming too," I said. The words had come out all by themselves. Once again, I hadn't meant to speak. I also thought that someone would try to talk me out of it, that they would make me see sense. But to my surprise, nobody did.

And that was how I came to be part of it. That was why I was there at the end.

FORTY

We left at six o'clock in the evening. I only knew it because the clocks told me. In this underground world, I wondered how anyone had any sense of time. The Traveller said that it would be safer to cross London in the dark. Despite his wound, he insisted on coming with us, but this time it would be his brother, Will Fletcher, who would be in charge. Will knew the city better – but the two of them didn't want to spend any more time apart. There were another four men who had changed out of the grey overalls they always wore in the pod and were now in army camouflage, bristling with guns and other equipment. I felt a little safer having them around me, but then I had no idea what we were heading into. London. For years it had been a name – and one that you didn't mention too often. It had been destroyed, along with another eight cities in the UK, and that had been enough to tip the whole country into chaos. It was as if I was about to travel into the very broken heart.

We ate another meal before we left, which suited me. Once we were in the city we would be surviving on only what we could carry. I noticed Graham and Will Fletcher sitting next to each other, deep in conversation. They obviously had a lot of catching up to do but not much time. Finally, we stood up and got ready to leave. We had all been given backpacks. I don't know what was in mine but it weighed a ton.

I looked for Jamie and saw him perching on one of the sofas

near the TV. I went over to join him, then realized that he was talking to Susan Ashwood, the blind woman who was sitting opposite him. I didn't want to burst in on them but at the same time I was close enough to hear their conversation. He had his back to me and she, of course, couldn't see, so neither of them was aware of me. She was saying goodbye.

"I won't see you again, Jamie," she was saying. "I have very little time left now."

"You can't know that, Miss Ashwood."

"I do know that. The spirits have told me. But please don't be upset on my account. There's nothing to fear about death, once you understand it. I'll merely be passing from one place to another ... a little like you when you go to your dreamworld. But I want you to know that I am so glad to have met you. And Matt. A lot of people spend their whole lives without achieving very much but I am proud that I was able to help you a little. When this story is written, I'll have a place in it. A few lines, anyway. That's important to me."

"Do you know what happens?" Jamie asked. "Do you know how it ends?"

She shook her head. "Only one person knows that and I don't envy him. To know the future is to carry a terrible weight. But I will tell you this, Jamie. None of it is going to be easy. There will be a lot of pain and a lot of death. You'll need all your strength."

"What about Scott? Can you tell me anything about him?"

"Scott has a part to play. Like all of you."

"I really miss him."

"I'm sure. But the two of you will find each other again. In time..."

I must have moved or something because suddenly Miss Ashwood called out to me. "Holly...?"

I wondered how she could possibly have known it was me and

I felt guilty about being found eavesdropping on them and moved forward hurriedly. "I came to say goodbye," I said.

"It's very brave of you to make the journey into London, Holly," Miss Ashwood said. "And I have to say that I am quite jealous. You are now a companion of one of the Gatekeepers. Who knows where that will take you? Look after Jamie. And yourself."

The Traveller came over with his brother. "Time to go…" he said. He had a huge backpack strapped to his shoulders and I wondered how he could manage it with his wound.

The other four men joined us. Their names were Blake, Simon, Ryan and Amir and they were all in their mid-twenties. Sophie also came to say goodbye, holding the Traveller close to her and trying (I could tell) not to show how worried she was. I think she'd asked to come with us, but someone – Susan Ashwood perhaps – had told her she had to stay behind. And then we were off. There was another door that I hadn't noticed, this one with a huge handle and an airtight lock, like something on a rocket or a plane. Will opened it for us and we stepped through. I heard it close behind us and that was it. We were on our own.

There were no lights here. We were carrying our own torches and straight away I saw the answer to at least one question that had been puzzling me. The Traveller had said we were ten miles from St Meredith's, which had struck me as an awful long way to walk, but now I saw that my legs were going to be spared. There were two vehicles waiting for us; electric cars, still plugged into the wall, recharging. I sat in one with Jamie and the two brothers. The rest got into the other. Someone unplugged us and we were off, shooting down the tunnel at about twenty miles per hour, the engines whirring softly but making no other noise.

The tunnel was new. The floor was cement and the walls were tiled and I wondered if the Nexus had actually constructed it themselves. It must have cost them millions. Each of the cars had headlamps which lit the way ahead and, despite everything, I enjoyed the ride, watching the walls flash by, with the breeze – cool and musty – blowing in my hair. It had been years since I'd been in a car of any sort. The only thing with wheels that had worked in the village had been my wheelbarrow. I was sorry when, after about forty minutes, we came to a solid wall, slowed down and stopped.

"We go the rest of the way on foot," the Traveller said.

We all climbed out. Ryan and Amir turned on their torches and I saw a small, jagged opening set in the wall. We climbed through and found ourselves in another tunnel, quite different from the one we had left. It was much older, for a start. The walls were blackened with soot and as the two men swung the beams across, I made out long lines of cable, stapled together, running into the distance.

"Take care," Ryan said. He was softly spoken with an Irish accent, I think, and I didn't need to be told to know that from this moment on we were always going to be close to danger. He lowered the torch to show a series of metal tracks bolted to the metal floor. "There's no current but you can still trip over and hurt yourself. Try to stay close."

We set off again. And with a sense of excitement I realized where we were. This was the Tube – the underground train system that had run through London. I tried to imagine commuters rushing along in the darkness from Oxford Street to Piccadilly Circus and Knightsbridge. These were just names to me. And yet here I was, following one of the tunnels; a maze of tunnels, in fact, that would eventually bring me to whichever part of the city we wanted. They'd had moving staircases too. Escalators. I remembered Miss Keyland telling me about them and that made me think of how she had died and reminded me that if I wasn't careful, I'd end up dead too. This wasn't a fun expedition to a forgotten city. London was dangerous.

We walked for about fifteen minutes before the tunnel suddenly opened out and I found myself in what must have once been a station. It was called Highgate. The torchlight picked out the name printed on a blue band, surrounded by a red circle. We were low down. There was a platform above us to one side and white tiles that curved over our head. On the other side, the walls were covered with advertisements. Holidays in Israel. The *Financial Times* newspaper. Some church group promising the secret of life. The paper was damp and tatty. And nobody was going on holiday any more, money was no use, and the church hadn't saved any-one, so it was all a waste of time.

Something moved and we all froze. A gun appeared in Blake's hand so quickly that he could have been a magician, performing a trick. We looked around us, expecting to see someone appear on the platform. But it was only a rat, running along the tracks. It was a fat, bloated thing with matted fur and shiny eyes and, seeing it picked out in the flashlight, I couldn't help wondering what it had found to eat. It was probably better not to know. We continued through the station and into the tunnel at the other end. Once again, total darkness closed in on us, swallowing us up.

We walked and walked. After the comfort and speed of the electric cars, our journey into London was an ordeal. There was nothing to look at, except for the glint of light showing the rails ahead and the lines of cables which snaked along, follow-ing us all the way. I could feel the backpack dragging down on my shoulders, and my last meal and that luxurious warm shower had already become a memory. We walked through three more stations: Archway, Tufnell Park, Kentish Town. I found myself wondering about the names, about what they represented. Had there been an arch at Archway? What was so Kentish about Kentish Town? And what would I find if I climbed the escalator and exited? There might be people still living in parts of London but somehow I doubted that they'd be pleased to see us.

There was a hideous sight waiting for us at Camden Town. A train had been parked on a rail parallel to the one we were following – a huge red thing that fitted into the tunnel like toothpaste in a tube. Suddenly I was aware of a dreadful smell and someone – Amir, I think – passed me a cloth to cover my face. "Try not to look," he said.

Of course, that only made me more curious and as we walked past I peered through the curving windows, wondering what the reflected torchlight would reveal. I wished I hadn't. The carriages were packed with dead bodies. They must have been standing shoulder to shoulder, with no room to move, when they died. It was impossible to say what had killed them. The bodies had partly rotted away. I glimpsed empty, staring eye sockets and teeth grinning where the cheeks had once been. The corpses were dressed in rags, the remains of dresses and suits ... otherwise it would have been impossible to tell the men from the women. I think the most horrible thing was that so many of them were still on their feet, with what was left of their arms and hands connected to straps that ran along the ceiling. Death must have hit them like a whirlwind, blown down the tunnel. Some were sitting. Some were on the floor. But the rest of them had been caught there, jammed against each other, and that was where, for all eternity, they would remain.

I couldn't wait to get past it and, trying to speed up, I bumped into Jamie. I couldn't see very much of anything. There were still only two torches lighting our way. Anyway, in my hurry, I almost tripped both of us over.

"I'm sorry," I whispered.

"It's OK," he said. And then I felt him take my hand, just for a moment. It was quite unexpected. He and I had been through so much together but we hadn't exactly been close. Not like him and his brother. "I'm glad you came," he said.

"Are you?"

"Yes." He fell silent for a moment. "I wouldn't have got this far without you, Holly," he went on. "Back in your village ... I'm so sorry about what happened. But I'm glad you were on my side."

That was the end of it. He didn't say anything more. But it meant a lot to me and when I think about Jamie now, about the way things might have gone between us, that's the moment that I always remember most.

We stopped for a rest at King's Cross (which king and why was he cross?) and had something to eat and drink – dried fruit, nuts and water. We sat on the platform, on benches facing the rails.

"It's not much further," Will Fletcher told us. "Maybe only half an hour. Are you two all right?"

We both nodded.

"We'll have to move quickly when we get to the surface. It'll still be dark but that won't stop them watching the streets. We'll go straight to the house and get some sleep. Try not to touch anything if you can help it. The contamination isn't as bad as it was but you still have to be careful."

I wondered why he was whispering. In fact we'd been tiptoeing throughout the journey, even though we were far underground and, apart from the rats and dead people, on our own. But after King's Cross the track sloped upwards and without any warning we emerged in the open air. I might not have even realized as there was no moon and the light, or lack of it, stayed more or less the same. But the air smelled different and I got a sense of buildings, rising up above us. There was another Tube train parked behind some girders, over on our left, but this time I was careful not to look.

And then we came to Farringdon and everything changed. There were people on the platform, alive, shuffling about, muttering to each other. Suddenly everyone had their guns out and we were moving forward in a pack, looking in every direction at once. The people didn't seem to want to hurt us. In fact they were more scared of us than we were of them. But it was still strange to stumble upon them and all sorts of questions went through my mind. Where had they come from? How long had they been here? How could they have possibly survived?

Blake or Ryan swung a torch and I saw some of them, picked out in the beam. There was a woman and a man. They were both bald and almost completely naked. She was badly deformed. One half of her face simply wasn't there and the other half seemed to be frozen in an expression of pure terror, the eye on that side bulging like a ping-pong ball. The man, wearing filthy boxer shorts, was enormously fat with sagging breasts and a stomach that hung almost to his knees. I think they were both probably mad because as the light hovered over them, they cowered away, making strange animal noises. There was a group of children further along the platform. They were only about seven or eight years old so they must have been born here, after London was destroyed. They were clutching each other, pressing together like monkeys in a cage. I wondered what sort of life they'd had. They had never been to school. They probably had no parents. They might not even know how to speak.

"Survivors," Ryan whispered. "Don't worry. They won't come near us."

Even so, we hurried forward. It had been good to be out in the open air for a few minutes. But it was better to be back in the tunnel.

I never completely understood what had happened in London. It had been destroyed by a dirty bomb but what exactly did that mean? Was it nuclear or biochemical or both? And how much of the city was left untouched? I don't know how the people I saw had managed to support themselves. What had the man been eating to make himself so fat? Like the rat that I'd seen at Highgate, it was probably best not to ask. All I can say is that everything felt poisoned: the walls, the ground, the very air. I felt that I was walking through a gigantic cemetery and that somehow it was almost an insult to be there and to be alive. There will come a time, I suppose, when historians and scientists will try to make sense of the ninth of May and what happened to Britain on that terrible day. I can only describe what I saw.

We finally left the Tube system at Moorgate Station and, sure enough, there was an escalator just as Miss Keyland had described – a long, silver staircase with strange teeth at each end. It wasn't working, of course, and we had to climb up. We passed through an archway, then took a second staircase up to the entrance hall, where a row of barriers stood waiting, all of them open. Amir and Ryan guided us through with their torches and I glimpsed ticket machines, glass booths, and a kiosk selling newspapers and magazines, which were still neatly arranged in rows. If I had looked at their covers, I know I would have seen the date, ninth of May, printed on each one. The exit was closed with a metal grid but Blake had a key and I realized that we were close to the safe house that Miss Ashwood had mentioned and that the Nexus must use this route quite often.

I was exhausted by now. My legs were aching and I longed to be in bed. The streets that we followed seemed to be filled with rubble. There were cars everywhere – not just parked at the sides but stuck in a traffic jam that would never move again. I saw a bus. A red London bus. I got the impression of shops and restaurants but they were little more than shadows – and empty and broken ones at that. The breeze had dropped and nothing was moving. I think it was the stillness rather than the darkness that made the biggest impression of all.

And finally we reached the house. It loomed up in front of us, tall and narrow with a solid-looking door with the number 13 and boarded-up windows. Once again, Blake had the key and he let us into a hall with a door on one side and a staircase leading up. He didn't turn on the lights, if the lights even worked. In fact Amir and Ryan had kept their hands cupped over their torches as we hurried through the London streets. They'd found their way here through memory and instinct as much as anything else.

"We'll get some sleep," Will said. He turned to Jamie. "You and Holly will share a room. I'll be with Graham next door. The others will be downstairs. Once it's light, you'll be able to get your bearings. When you wake up, try not to leave the room. And – I probably don't need to say this – the toilets don't flush. There's a chemical toilet in the basement. Do either of you need to use it?"

Thankfully, I didn't. I shook my head.

"Then I'll show you upstairs."

Amir, Ryan, Blake and Simon went into the downstairs room. Will had a torch of his own and led us upstairs. He took us into a room that was empty apart from two mattresses on the floor. There was a pile of blankets next to them. We grabbed one each and without taking our clothes off, stretched out.

I meant to say goodnight to Jamie. I meant to thank him for the nice thing he'd said in the tunnel. But in about two seconds, I was asleep.

Daylight, when it came, was harsh and grey, as if the sun had completely forgotten about such things as warmth and colour. It filtered through the window to reveal a room that had once belonged to a child. The wallpaper was striped – yellow and blue – and although there was no electricity, a lampshade still hung down, shaped like a teddy bear. The room was carpeted and there was a fireplace. It might have been quite cosy at one time. But it made me sad just to think of the child who had once slept here, to wonder what had happened to him or her and to accept that there was little chance that he or she was still alive.

Jamie was already awake. I wondered if he had visited the dreamworld. I knew that he always hoped to find his brother, Scott, and the best chance was when he was asleep. And I thought about what it must be like to meet someone, to have conversations in your dreams and to remember them all when you woke up. But he said nothing and a moment later the Traveller and his brother arrived, knocking before coming into the room.

"Did you sleep all right?" the Traveller asked. We both nodded and he went on. "Nobody saw us arrive last night so we're safe here for the time being. We're in East London. Do you want to take a look before we have breakfast?"

"Are we going out?" Jamie asked.

"Not out in the street. It's too dangerous. We can go on the roof."

"You may be a bit shocked," Will added. "I think you'll find it's not quite the same as when you were last here."

"Let's go," Jamie said.

We left the room and walked along a short corridor. The house must have been a nice place to live once. There was an antique mirror on one wall, a chandelier, and thick carpets. But there was a mustiness everywhere. The Nexus might have used it from time to time, but the house had been abandoned for too long. It was almost as if it knew that it was no longer wanted.

We climbed another staircase to a single door, which led onto a roof with a slate floor, a low wall and a chimney stack right in front of us. There was a TV aerial still plugged in and even a couple of deckchairs, although the material looked mouldy and I wouldn't have trusted them with my weight. We didn't step outside. We didn't want to show ourselves. We stood in the shadow of the doorway, looking out.

And there was London.

We were only three floors up but it felt as if we were higher. London was all around us; the terrible wreckage of what had once been a great city. It was like looking at a million oversized matchsticks, all dropped out of the box, one on top of the other. Almost nothing tall was left … just the broken remains of what had once been offices and flats, battered and corroded, sticking up as if they had somehow grown out of the mess. I'd seen photographs of the city … St Paul's, the Millennium Wheel, the British Telecom Tower. But they'd all gone, reduced to this hopeless sprawl that stretched as far as the horizon. No. Here and there, whole buildings had survived. I picked out an office, a bank, the tube station we had come out of the night before. There was the yellow M of a McDonald's. I'd read about those too. There were vehicles everywhere – cars, taxis, lorries and buses … hundreds of them, all of them rusted and broken, many of them lying upside down or on their sides. A bit shocked? Will hadn't begun to express what I felt. I had never lived here. I had never known what it meant to be a Londoner. But thinking about them, and what they had been through, I felt sickened.

"Over there…" the Traveller was pointing around the side of the house.

A single building stood in front of us, and although it was surrounded by debris, it had hardly been damaged at all. It reminded me almost of a ship, moored in a port after a particularly vicious storm. It was a church, almost the size of a cathedral, made of dark red bricks with a steeple that looked as if it had been built at a different time to the rest of it, slightly crooked and reaching up into the sky. Only the windows had been smashed. I could make out the jagged outlines of what remained of the stained glass.

The church was barely a hundred metres away.

St Meredith's. It had to be.

"There it is," the Traveller said.

Jamie stared at it. He seemed to be dazed. "The door..."

"Scarlett Adams went through it. It took her to the monastery of the Cry for Mercy in Ukraine. Maybe it's working again. It can take you anywhere you want to go."

Jamie was still examining the church. "There doesn't seem to be anyone around."

"Believe me, they're here," Will said. "Inside the church and in the wreckage. Look...!"

Even as he spoke, I saw it. I was so shocked, I almost fell back down the stairs. A spider had appeared, coming round the side of the church. It was monstrous, enormous, and about half the size of the church itself. Its eyes were hideous ... as black as oil pools. It had two tentacle-things, protruding out of its head, twitching at the air in front of it. I could see every hair on its body and legs. And as huge as it was, the spider seemed strangely light, moving across the rubble without disturbing it. When I say it was like something out of my worst nightmares, I'm not telling the truth. I had never had nightmares like this.

I could feel Jamie standing beside me. His whole body was rigid. But what he said next really surprised me. "I have seen it before."

"When?" I had no control of myself. The word was like a scream but also a whisper.

"A long time ago. At the first battle. The spider. The monkey. The condor. They were all there. They belong to the Old Ones."

"You see what we are up against," Will muttered.

"How long can we stay here?"

"Three or four days. No more than that. It's too dangerous ... and if we stay here too long we'll get sick."

"Matt said he'd send me a sign. We have to wait for it. Then we go in."

"Well, I hope he sends it soon, Jamie. Four days maximum. Then we have to leave."

"You leave. I'll stay."

The two brothers looked at each other but there was nothing either of them could say. The spider had disappeared round the back of the church. I had seen enough. I reeled back into the house feeling sick, my heart pounding. I was glad when they closed the door.

THE GOOD PRIEST

FORTY-ONE

Pedro was coughing up water, litres of it. The water was streaming out of his mouth and over his chin and he could feel his lungs bursting inside him as they strained to push the rest out. He opened his eyes and saw only a blur but gradually his vision cleared and he was able to make out a dark-haired, bearded man, leaning over him. At the same time, he felt the man's hands pressing into his stomach and with a groan he spewed up what felt like another few litres.

He was lying on his back on the deck of the *Medusa*. The boat was still afloat. And he was still alive. He wasn't sure which of the two facts was more surprising. The last thing he remembered was a roaring, thundering mountain of water, which had fallen on him and smashed him off his feet. The eruption of the volcano had caused a tsunami and they had sailed right into it as they tried to escape from the port of Naples. The boat should have been torn to pieces, or turned upside down at the very least. But the engines were still running. Pedro could feel them vibrating underneath him. They were moving at speed, skimming across the surface of the sea. Somehow, they had survived.

The man – Pedro remembered that his name was Angelo – called out in Italian and suddenly the other members of the crew were gathered around him, grinning and reaching out to pat him on the shoulder. Giovanni was among them, soaking wet and as white as a sheet, but still smiling.

"What happened?" Pedro asked, but although he formed the words, no sound came out. His throat was burning from the salt water, and anyway, he had spoken in Spanish so nobody would have understood him. Angelo spoke again and one of the men came over and knelt down.

"You speak English?" he asked.

"Yes." Pedro nodded.

"My name is Emmanuel." He was young, about nineteen or twenty, with tangled fair hair and blue eyes. He didn't look Italian and spoke perfect English, with no trace of an accent. He was wearing jeans and a thick-knit jersey so waterlogged that it had lost all its shape. "You are very lucky to be alive," he went on. "Angelo steered the ship through the wave. He hit it straight on and he was able to climb over the crest. It was the only way to escape. Otherwise we would all have been killed. As it was, you were swept overboard and if you hadn't tied yourself with the rope, you would have been killed. We were able to drag you back ... but not before you had drunk a lot of the ocean. For a minute, we thought you had drowned. But you are OK now."

"Where are we?" Pedro asked. This time, the words managed to come out.

"About a kilometre out and following the coast."

"The volcano...?"

Pedro allowed Emmanuel to help him to his feet. The *Medusa* seemed to have come through the tsunami intact. There was water all over the deck and the bilge pumps were already working, pumping out the main cabin. The crew – there were three men along with Pedro and Giovanni – looked washed out in every sense. But at least the sea was more manageable, the waves huge and choppy but no longer lethal.

Pedro turned back to the mainland, searching for the port they had just left. He couldn't see it. The entire coast around Naples was wreathed in impenetrable black smoke. The waves simply rolled into it and disappeared. The sea, the land and the sky had all bled into each other. And yet Vesuvius was still making itself known with a hellish red glow that seemed to flicker on and off as the clouds passed in front of it. Balls of lava were still streaking down and more shafts of orange and scarlet glimmered briefly in the haze as the city burned.

He stood watching this, feeling utterly drained. If he could have imagined the end of the world, it would have looked much like this: the dead sea, the dying land. Suddenly he felt very alone, far from his home, separated from the other Gatekeepers. He barely knew Giovanni, Angelo or the others. He didn't speak their language. His broken finger was throbbing painfully. His stomach was empty. He thought back to the moment when he had first met Matt in Lima – and had tried to steal his watch. He wished now that he had made a different decision and gone another way. How could he have known that the meeting between the two of them would one day bring him to this?

Angelo and Emmanuel spoke together for a while. Then Emmanuel turned to Pedro.

"We know who you are," he said. "We know that you are important. Francesco Amati, Giovanni's uncle, told us about you. Our job is to get you to Rome, to the home of Carla Rivera. I know where she can be found and I will come with you and Giovanni because the others speak only Italian."

"How do you speak such good English?"

"My father was English. We will be in Anzio in six or seven hours. From there we can get a train directly into Rome. I would suggest that you get some sleep but that won't be easy. We have no dry clothes ... and no hot food either. I'm sorry."

"I'm very glad to be here," Pedro said. "Please thank Angelo for saving my life. And tell Giovanni that I'm sorry he had to separate from his family." Pedro thought of Francesco and the others, huddled together in the three rooms. If the police hadn't killed them, Vesuvius probably would. He fought back a great wave of tiredness. Where was this all going to end?

It was one of the most miserable nights of Pedro's life. As the light failed – apart from the endless glow of red in the sky behind them – the *Medusa* ploughed through the inky water, following the coast of Italy, heading north. Still wearing his sodden clothes, there was no chance of sleep, no relief from the cold. He could only stand shivering as Angelo turned the wheel and Giovanni crouched in a corner. Eventually, and despite himself, he did manage to drift into a light doze, although he wasn't aware of it at first. He only realized what had happened when he found himself back where he most wanted to be, in the dreamworld, at the bottom of the hill that led down from the library. He was sure that no time had passed. It was as if he had been arguing with Jamie, and Scarlett only seconds before, refusing to tell them the truth about Scott.

He wished now that he hadn't walked away in such a hurry. He wanted to be with the others, especially with Matt, who always had the answers. He still remembered the moment in the desert in Paracas, when Matt had worked out the location of the second gate and had set off to face the King of the Old Ones on his own. And later, when they had been making their plans after the death of Professor Chambers, the woman who had looked after them in Nazca. It seemed to Pedro that command came easily to Matthew Freeman. It was as if he had been born to lead them.

He wanted to ask what he was supposed to do in Rome. Carla Rivera might have connections but how exactly could she help him? How was he meant to reach Oblivion, far away at the southernmost tip of the world? He thought of going back to the library and was both pleased and surprised when Matt suddenly appeared, walking over the crest of the hill and towards him.

"Matteo…!" In the real world he was cold and exhausted. But in the dreamworld he was smiling. There was nobody he would have been happier to see.

"You're doing the right thing," Matt said. "You've had a worse time than any of us. I know that. But there's the door in Rome that will take you to Antarctica. Just be careful who you trust, Pedro. We'll see each other soon."

Pedro examined his friend with concern. Matt was talking as if everything was all right. But he himself looked broken, defeated. Pedro had never seen anyone who looked so sad.

"I don't understand, Matteo. Why don't you tell me what's wrong? What did you see in the library?

"Pedro…"

But there was nothing more. With a sense of despair, Pedro felt himself being sucked away and opened his eyes. He was swaying on his feet, next to the steering wheel. He had barely been asleep at all. If Matt had been about to tell him something more, he was doomed never to hear it.

Somehow the next day arrived and although the smoke from Vesuvius had followed them even a hundred and fifty kilometres up the coast, the sun managed to break through and Pedro did his best to dry himself in the early rays. He heard the tone of the engine rise and saw Angelo spin the wheel. The *Medusa* changed course and began to head for the coast and Pedro saw Anzio spread out in front of them and, high up on a cliff, a single white tower, a lighthouse, sticking up like a finger.

They drew closer, heading for a fishing harbour, which on a bright day might have been somewhere pretty and peaceful to stop for lunch. But now it was a tangle, a mass of boats of every size, bringing refugees from Naples and perhaps from other parts of Italy, more and more of them drawing in from every direction. It was lucky that the huge wave that had nearly crushed the *Medusa* seemed to have missed this part of the coast. The town, with its solid line of five- and six-storey buildings, many of them right up against the waterfront, looked untouched.

Angelo expertly steered them between two trawlers, each so weighed down with passengers that their bowlines were barely above the water, and they were able to moor at the edge of the port. Pedro saw hordes of people fighting against each other as they tried to make their way along the streets, many of them bowing under the weight of oversized bundles and suitcases. The sky was grey and overcast and still smelled of burning.

Emmanuel came over to Pedro. "You must say goodbye to Giovanni here," he said. "He will stay on the *Medusa*." Before Pedro could protest, he went on. "You need an ID card to travel into Rome and he is giving you his. The two of you do not look very similar but you are the same age and hopefully, because you are young, nobody will look too closely. I will accompany you to the home of Carla Rivera and ensure that you arrive safely. Then I must also return."

"Where will you all go?" Pedro asked.

"We have friends further in the north, in the mountains near Spoleto. We are safer if we stick together and they will look after us. We are doing exactly what Franceso Amati told us to. Say goodbye quickly. The train leaves soon and we do not want to miss it."

Pedro barely knew Giovanni. Not being able to speak his language had made it impossible for the two of them to become friends. But he embraced the other boy warmly and felt genuinely sorry that the two of them were being separated. Giovanni nodded and tried to smile but he was clearly as cold, wet and exhausted as Pedro.

"*Buona fortuna!*" he said.

"Good luck." Pedro smiled back. And then Pedro and Emmanuel were gone, the two of them, slipping onto the quay and making their way hurriedly inland.

Almost immediately they came upon a crush of people, filling the Riviera Zanardelli, a wide thoroughfare that crossed the entire town, running parallel with the shoreline. Anzio was a neat, elegant place with open squares, fountains and palm trees – but it hadn't been prepared for this invasion. If it had once had cafés and restaurants, they were all closed. The shutters were down, the terraces empty, the canopies rolled back. Pedro was aware of many different languages being spoken around him. These weren't just Italians pouring out of the boats. They must have come from all over Europe, maybe even from Africa. Once again, the streets were lined with policemen, barking orders, occasionally pulling people out of the line, slapping them for no good reason and sending them spinning into the gutter.

Somehow Pedro and Emmanuel fought their way through. The station at Anzio was just as crowded, with every inch of the platform taken up by people, parcels and even animals ... chickens in cages and sheep. It reminded Pedro of a war film. Sometimes he'd managed to sneak into the cinemas in Lima and would watch the latest American releases until he was discovered and thrown out. *Saving Private Ryan*, *Pearl Harbor*, *Schindler's List* ... apart from the modern clothes, everything he was seeing could have been a throwback to the Second World War. Even the light made everything look black and white. There was a train waiting, with uniformed guards at every door.

"Give me your ID card," Emmanuel said. Pedro handed it over. "I need it to buy tickets. Wait for me here. I won't be long."

Pedro did as he was told. Emmanuel pushed his way to the front of the crowd that surrounded the station office and returned with the tickets a few minutes later. Pedro was surprised that he had been so quick, but then nobody actually seemed to be going anywhere. Perhaps they couldn't afford the fare.

They chose the busiest carriage, where a tired and flustered guard was already being overwhelmed by the number of passengers. As Emmanuel had guessed, he barely looked at their ID but allowed them to climb on board.

And then, almost at once, the train pulled away and they were heading down the line, slowly picking up speed, on their way to Rome. The thought made Pedro dizzy. He had never visited Rome. He had never even seen a picture of it but he remembered that it was the capital of Italy. And it was in Rome that he would find the church of St Peter's that Matteo had mentioned to him in his dream. Pedro was certain that somewhere inside, he would find the door that would reunite him with his friends. But first he would have to find this woman ... Carla Rivera. How could he be sure that he could trust her when all he knew about her was her name? And what about Emmanuel, for that matter? He could hand Pedro back to the police, to the same people who had kept him prisoner in the Castel Nuovo. The Old Ones. They would surely pay a great deal for the return of one of the Five. He examined the young man, half-Italian, half-English, who had brought him this far. Emmanuel was almost asleep, exhausted by the long journey from Naples. Pedro decided that he had to believe in him. Emmanuel seemed genuine enough. And, alone in a foreign country, unable even to speak its language, what choice did he have?

He felt the same drowsiness stealing over him and rested his head against the window. He and Emmanuel had been lucky to get seats. Every bit of space inside the carriage was taken by people standing, sitting or crouching on the floor. They were moving much faster now. Emmanuel had said this was a direct train. Rome couldn't be more than an hour away.

But twenty minutes later, they slowed down and stopped, held up at a red light. It was raining, the grey water travelling horizontally across the windows, splattering down hard on the stony ground. They were in the middle of the countryside with a few houses dotted around them, and as they waited a second train pulled into a siding next to them, so that for a moment the two of them were side by side and quite close. It looked like a cattle train. Half asleep, his head against the window, Pedro saw wooden carriages with heavy padlocks and chains fastening the doors, and tiny windows, barred but without glass. Curiously, there were armed soldiers with capes protecting them from the weather, sitting on the roof, their legs dangling down. That couldn't be right, could it? Why would you need to guard animals?

But as he looked, he saw a hand and an arm stretching out of the window exactly opposite him, as if trying to touch his train. The hand opened, the fingers reaching out. And there, on the wrist, he saw what looked like a number, tattooed in black ink.

Maybe he had imagined it. Maybe it was just a bad dream. Because when he looked a second time, the other train had gone and they were moving once again. But even so, an hour later, when they reached the outskirts of Rome, he still couldn't put the image out of his mind.

FORTY-TWO

St Peter's Square, in the very heart of Rome, was huge, magnificent and anything but square. Pedro had never seen anywhere like it: a great expanse of cobbles with hundreds of columns curving round the edges and two stone fountains on either side of a twenty-metre-tall Egyptian obelisk. Dominating everything – St Peter's Basilica itself, the most famous cathedral in the world, stood there with more columns, statues and balconies, all crowned by the magnificent dome designed by Michelangelo. Every Easter, the Pope would step out of a window at the front of the cathedral to bless the hundred thousand people who gathered in the square … and there would be room for all of them. Pedro wondered how big this city could be to have so much space in its centre.

Emmanuel had brought him here because Carla Rivera, the woman who could supposedly help him, lived nearby. They crossed the square together and Pedro found himself gazing at the cathedral, as if his whole life had built up to this moment. He had never seen it before. He had only heard its name for the first time when Matt had told him about it in the dreamworld. And now it was here, right in front of him. He noticed a long line of policemen and soldiers, all dressed in black, stretched out in front of it, and realized that although the square was as crowded as the rest of the city, nobody was being allowed in or out of the building.

He grabbed hold of Emmanuel. "I want to get closer," he said.

"Why?" Emmanuel was in a hurry. He wanted to see Pedro safely delivered so that he could return to Giovanni and the others.

"Please..."

The two of them crossed the square, stopping in front of the wide, marble steps that led up to the front entrance. Pedro was right. The doors were bolted. There were two lines of guards preventing anyone from getting close. What was the point of having a holy place if people weren't allowed to pray there ...

Perhaps they knew about the magical doors spread all over the planet. This cathedral was at the very centre of the the Roman Catholic religion: pilgrims came here from all over the world. So the door had to be here. The guards had found it and they were determined he wouldn't get anywhere near.

He would have liked to have explored more but Emmanuel was already getting nervous. "We should move," he said.

Pedro nodded. It would be easy enough to find his way back here. The two of them set off together.

They walked back to the edge of the square, through the lines of columns and out the other side. Like Naples and Anzio, Rome was full of people carrying bundles and suitcases that might contain everything they owned, and the atmosphere of fear and desperation had followed them north. It had stopped raining but the sky was overcast and the air had the same faint smell of burning. Pedro's clothes were still damp and he was feeling filthy and exhausted. He was also starving. He couldn't actually remember the last time he'd had a decent meal.

They came to a long, narrow street with tall, very grand buildings on both sides. It was impossible to see inside any of them. All the windows at ground level were shuttered and barred, and many of the doors were twice as big as they needed to be with carvings of knights and angels who seemed to stare defiantly at passers-by, daring them to come in. There were fewer people here, and although there were cars and motorbikes parked in neat rows, none of them was moving.

Emmanuel took a sheet of paper out of his pocket and studied it. He pointed at a building that stood on its own, surrounded by an ornate metal fence with a solid-looking gate. To Pedro, it could have been a miniature palace. He had seen similar places in Lima and had learnt that the very richest people – with their own bodyguards – had lived there, and heaven help you if you were found rummaging in their dustbins or begging for food. They would beat you and leave you bleeding and broken in the street. This *palazzo*, if that was what it was, looked abandoned. The shutters were down and there were several tiles missing from the roof. And yet it had its own walled garden, with palm trees and shrubs still growing around yet another ornamental fountain. The house was pink and white and four storeys high. Some of the windows were square, others were arched. A long terrace ran down one side and Pedro glimpsed a conservatory filled with more plants at the end.

"This is it," Emmanuel said.

He pressed a bell button beside the gate. It made no sound and nobody came. At least a minute passed – maybe two – and Pedro was beginning to wonder if they'd actually come to the right place. Perhaps there was no one at home. Then, suddenly, he heard a woman's voice coming from a little speaker above the button.

"Si. Chi è?"

She spoke in Italian and Emmanuel answered in the same language. The conversation went on for quite a while and Pedro understood none of it, although he heard his name mentioned a couple of times. The woman sounded nervous. She spoke so quickly that it was impossible to tell where one word ended and the next began. For his part, Emmanuel was soft, reasonable.

He was talking with his face pressed against the gate and Pedro realized that he was watching the street at the same time. They weren't safe here. They needed to be inside.

The woman stopped speaking. Emmanuel turned to Pedro. "I am leaving you now," he said. "This is the home of Signora Rivera and she has agreed to accept you."

"What about you?"

"She does not wish to meet me. Good luck, Pedro. I do not know who you are or why you are here, but I am glad that I met you and was able to help you a little. I think it is important. I hope it all works out for you." And then, before Pedro could say anything, Emmanuel moved away, following the path that had brought them here.

He had only been gone a moment when there was a click and the gate opened automatically. Pedro went through, closing it behind him. The garden was very neat, with little pebbles forming geometrical shapes between the paths. A statue of a winged child with a finger touching his lips knelt on a pedestal. It seemed to warn Pedro of something secret. Was it telling him to stay away?

The front door of the house opened and a woman appeared, dressed entirely in black, waving him towards her. This had to be Carla Rivera! She must have been in her late sixties ... it was hard to be sure because her face was so lined with worry. She had grey hair, swept back, and although everything about her suggested an old, defeated woman, her eyes were still alert and full of fight. She had a simple gold cross around her neck. It was her only jewellery.

"Come in! Come in!" she rasped and Pedro relaxed a little, hearing his own language.

He followed her into a hallway with black-and-white tiles, a gold mirror and solid oak furniture. There were doors opening into rooms in every direction and a wide, marble staircase, leading up. Classical paintings, mainly portraits, hung on the walls. As soon as the woman had closed the front door, she turned and looked at him.

"Your name is Pedro," she said.

"Yes, *signora*."

"You were with Francesco Amati in Naples?"

"Yes."

"Is it true that the entire city has gone?"

"The volcano erupted. I don't think there can be very much of it left."

"Dear God!" The woman crossed herself. "Where will this end? What is expected of us?" She examined him. "You're wet. You look worn out. Have you eaten?"

"I'm very hungry," Pedro admitted.

"Then come with me. We do not have much but you are welcome to what we have."

She led him into a gloomy kitchen with a high ceiling, a wooden table, and pots and pans hanging from hooks. There were no lights on anywhere but Pedro knew the house must have electricity. Both the doorbell and the front gate had worked. The woman gestured and he sat down at the table while she opened various cupboards and produced some rough brown bread, ham and salami, cheese and salad. Finally, she uncorked a bottle and gave him a glass of wine. The food looked meagre, spread out on the empty table, but Pedro wolfed it down as if it were a banquet. The wine was the best of all. The liquid was dark red, almost black, and warmed him inside, at the same time making him sleepy.

The woman examined him intently while he ate. It was only when he had nearly finished that she continued with her questions. "My name is Carla," she said. "Emmanuel told me you were a prisoner in Naples. What did they want with you?"

"I don't know." As always, Pedro wasn't sure how much to say. "I think they wanted to kill me."

"You are one of the Five."

Pedro said nothing.

"You must tell me! I have a son in the Vatican ... he is a priest, with high office. With his help, I have been given access to books in the Vatican library and I know about the Five, the Gatekeepers, the Old Ones. So you have nothing to hide from me. Are you one of the Gatekeepers?"

"Yes, *signora*." Pedro nodded. He saw no point in lying.

"It is unbelievable. It is extraordinary to have you here in my house. All my prayers have been answered. My son, Silvio, will be home in a few hours. He will wish to speak to you at length. For now, I thank God for sending you to us."

Pedro was becoming uneasy. Carla Rivera was gazing at him with a sort of fervency he had never experienced before. He was also very tired. The events of the past twenty-four hours had finally caught up with him and the wine had helped to knock him out.

She saw this. "You need to change your clothes," she said. "You're soaking wet. And you must sleep. I do not know what you have been through and you will tell us everything when Silvio arrives. I cannot imagine how much you must have suffered. But that is over now."

"Am I safe here?" Pedro asked.

"You are not safe in Rome. I do not think anyone is safe anywhere in Italy. But while you are in this house, you are protected."

Pedro yawned and as if taking this as her cue, Carla rose to her feet. "We have a spare room where you can rest," she said. "Please, follow me."

She led him out of the kitchen and up two flights of stairs, passing a long line of gloomy-looking portraits, hanging in gold frames. The house was empty and silent, the carpet threadbare, but Pedro got the impression that this had been a wealthy family once. They arrived at a hallway with an antique cabinet in front of them and a chandelier above. Two doors stood facing each other. Carla led him to the one on the left, but even as he went, for reasons he couldn't understand, his eye was drawn to the door opposite.

She noticed this. "Do not go in there," she said. "It is my daughter's room. She is resting. She is not well." She opened the other door. "Here you are."

Pedro found himself in a small, square room dominated by a brass bed and with a double window looking over the garden where he had entered. There was a chair and a wardrobe but no other furniture. A wooden cross hung on the wall. A second door led into a bathroom and toilet.

"The water is warm," Carla said. "Leave your clothes outside the door and I will wash them for you. Silvio will arrive after dark, at eight. The Pontifical Commission is meeting today so he will be kept busy. You do not need to worry about anything, Pedro. We will look after you and we will help you get to where you want to go." That puzzled Pedro. How could they know where he was going when he wasn't even sure about that himself? But the woman seemed kindly enough and, although he hated to admit it, he was almost her prisoner. He had nowhere else to go. "Sleep well," she said. "If there is anything you want, I will be downstairs. Do not call out. I don't want to wake Maria."

She took one last look at him, then bustled out, closing the door softly behind her.

Pedro was desperate to lie down but first he peeled off the wet clothes, dropping them on the floor outside the door. He went into the bathroom, his bare feet slapping against the floorboards. The bath was old-fashioned with heavy, golden taps and a brown stain leading down to the plug-hole where water had dripped for perhaps a hundred years. He turned the tap. The water coughed then came spitting out in a steady stream and, as Carla had said, it was warm. Pedro got in and washed himself. He even had a block of soap, hard and gritty but effective nonetheless. All around him, the water turned dark brown and he realized that even after everything he had been through, despite the tons of water that had fallen on him when he was on the *Medusa*, he was still filthy from the Naples sewers. What must Carla Rivera have thought when he turned up in her home?

He used the soap twice, lathering himself all over and then washing it off. He held his head under the tap, letting the water stream through his hair and over his neck. Finally, he got out and dried himself. He caught sight of his reflection in the mirror. Although he had been well fed when he was staying with the Incas, he had gone back to being thin to the point of scrawny. His black hair was long and unkempt. His eyes had sunk into his face. He examined the hand with the broken finger. Despite everything, it had finally begun to heal. At least that was something to be grateful for.

Finally, he climbed into the bed. The mattress was hard but the sheets were clean and the blankets warm. Somewhere, in the back of his mind, it occurred to him that he could still be in danger. What did he know about Carla Rivera or her family? Almost nothing. But it didn't matter. He couldn't have run any more, even if he'd wanted to.

Downstairs, the woman waited for her son to return. Upstairs, on the second floor, Pedro slept.

The meeting for the Pontifical Commission for the Vatican City state had come to an end. The seven cardinals who were its members took their leave of the Holy Father, bowing but saying nothing. Pope Pius XIII was a very old man, well into his nineties, and it was quite possible that he had been asleep for the last half-hour. These days, it was impossible to tell. He seldom spoke and when he did mutter something, his words often made no sense at all. "Dogs! Magicians! Murderers!" He repeated the words endlessly. It was possible he was thinking of the Bible ... some said the Book of Revelations. Nobody knew for sure.

The cardinals all looked very grand in their bright scarlet cloaks and berrette – the square caps with four peaks and tufts that hey were entitled to wear. The room where they had met was equally magnificent, with pillars and tapestries, thick velvet curtains, a swirling marble floor and a ceiling covered in gold leaf. The curtains were closed. The Holy Father could no longer bear to look outside. He spent much of the day in bed with his eyes closed and a young priest reading to him in Latin from the Old or New Testament.

Cardinal Silvio Rivera left the meeting with a sense of dismay. The country was crumbling. There were people starving in the streets ... and there were too many of them. It seemed as if the whole world had chosen Italy as a final refuge, and with all the overcrowding, crime and violence were everywhere. The government had responded with a ferocity that he preferred not to think about. He had heard the stories about the transportations, about the prison camps outside Arezzo. How could it have come to this? Could the world really be as evil as it seemed?

The cardinal returned to his office, where his secretary was waiting for him, to help him disrobe. But Silvio shushed him away. He wanted to be on his own. There was a heavy crucifix made of solid gold around his neck – he could always feel it dragging him down – and he clutched it in both hands, dropping to his knees. The crucifix had a precious stone, an amethyst, in the middle, and as was his habit, he stroked it with his thumb, trying to find comfort there.

He knelt beside the desk and prayed.

"Our Father who art in Heaven, hallowed be Thy name, Thy kingdom come..."

The words came out in a soft whisper. The priest had tears in his eyes and as he thought about the state of the world, the tears trickled down his cheeks. He felt the pain of the world as if it were his own. He hoped that he was a good man. It horrified him that there was so little good around him.

He knelt there, praying intently, for two hours. Then, finally, he went home.

FORTY-THREE

Pedro woke up feeling a lot better. He was clean, he had eaten and he had slept for a solid five hours. His only disappointment was that he hadn't returned to the dreamworld. He was still very much on his own. But as he sat up, throwing back the covers, he noticed that Carla had come into the room while he was asleep. There were new clothes, folded on the floor next to the door; jeans, a jersey, a belt and trainers. Pedro tried them on. The trousers were a little loose and he had to tighten them using the last hole of the belt, but otherwise he looked – and felt – human again. What now? Carla had said that her son would be home soon. She had said that the two of them would talk. Once again, Pedro wondered how much he could safely tell them, how much they already knew.

He heard movement in the house. Somebody had arrived. Softly, Pedro opened the door and stepped out onto the upper landing. Yes, there was a man here. He could hear voices a long way away, perhaps in the kitchen, talking in Italian. He was about to go down when he noticed that the door opposite his was ajar. He remembered Carla telling him to keep his voice down. She had a daughter, Maria, who was sick.

Acting on an impulse, Pedro crossed the landing and pushed open the other door. He found himself looking into a room identical to the one he had just left, except that this one contained a hospital bed surrounded by medical paraphernalia that he recognized at once. There was a saline bag with a drip hanging from a metal frame, a heart and pulse monitor, bleeping softly, an oxygen tank, a tray with various pills and liquids. In the middle of all this, a young woman lay on her back, breathing so faintly that it would be hard to tell when she stopped breathing at all. She was wearing a white nightgown with a silver cross around her neck. There was a cross on the wall opposite her too. Her long hair was brushed back and rested on her pillow, forming a crown around her head and shoulders. Her face was very thin and pale. Pedro knew at once that she was close to death. She had been ill for a very long time and she had stopped fighting. And now she was patiently waiting for the end.

She was too young to die, Pedro thought. She couldn't have been more than twenty-five or twenty-six. She must have been a late arrival, given her mother's age. He thought for a moment, then stepped quietly forward. There was a wooden chair beside the bed. He could imagine Carla Rivera spending many hours sitting here. He sat down himself. Then he reached out and rested a hand on the unconscious woman.

This was Pedro's gift, his power. He was a healer. For much of his life in Lima, he had looked after his friends – the other thieves, pickpockets and street urchins who surrounded him – without even knowing that it was his power that was keeping them well. It was only when Matt had been hurt in the Nazca Desert that he had begun to understand what he could do. He had deliberately set out to save Matt, to bring him back from the brink of death. He would do the same now to heal this woman he had never met.

It was a strange feeling … as if he was allowing some sort of heat or energy to flow out of himself, through his hand and into the woman. At the same time, it could have been the other way round. He could have been drawing something out of her. The truth was that he had no idea how it worked. The two of them were together, in a sort of vacuum, and nothing else mattered. Pedro no longer had any idea of the passing of time. He was only aware of his own hand and arm, stretched out with the palm facing down, and the soft rise and fall of the woman's stomach. Without even knowing it, his heart was beating at the same pace as hers. The two of them had become one. The young woman's illness was sharing itself with him.

"Pedro!" It was Carla Rivera, calling him from downstairs.

Pedro opened his eyes. He had done everything he could and he knew that it would be enough. Already there was more colour in the young woman's face. She was breathing more easily. He had no idea at all what had been wrong with her in the first place. Pedro had barely been to school. He couldn't read or write. People were sick or people were well ... that was as much as he knew and all that mattered to him was that he could turn one into the other.

He left the room, closing the door behind him, and went downstairs. Carla was waiting for him in the hall and it seemed to Pedro that something had upset her. She smiled when she saw him in his new clothes, but the strain still showed behind her eyes.

"How are you feeling, Pedro?" she asked.

"I'm much better, thank you. And thank you for these clothes."

"I went out and bought them for you. I didn't know if I would get the right size." She smiled, but a little nervously. "Silvio is here. I have told him about you. He wants to meet you."

"OK."

Pedro followed Carla back into the kitchen, where a man in his mid-thirties was sitting at the table with a mug of hot liquid; judging from the smell of it, some sort of herbal tea. He was wearing a dark suit and a black shirt with a clerical collar – Carla had already told him that her son was a priest. His hair was thick and wavy but it was turning grey. He had a face that looked tired and lined, and the eyes of a man who spent too much time thinking about things but never found a happy answer. The two of them did not look like each other, Pedro thought. There was nothing at all, not even the way they sat, that suggested a mother and son.

"Good evening, Pedro," the man said. He also spoke Spanish.

"Good evening, sir."

"Please come and sit down. And you can call me Silvio. Would you like some tea?"

"Yes, please."

Silvio nodded slightly and Carla went over to the kettle. "You may be wondering how it is that we speak your language," he went on, "My mother and I lived for many years in the city of Barcelona when I was choirmaster at the Cathedral of the Holy Cross and Saint Eulalia. That is why we are both fluent in Spanish. But that is not where you come from..."

"I am from Lima."

"When did you come to Italy?"

"A few weeks ago."

The priest nodded very slightly as if Pedro had just told him a lie, that he knew it was a lie, but was prepared to accept it anyway. "You flew?"

There was no point in lying. Pedro made the decision even as he began to speak. "No. I was in Hong Kong. I came through a door. It brought me to a church but I don't know where that was. I was taken prisoner and locked up in a place called Castel Nuovo in Naples." He hadn't said anything about Scott. Pedro didn't want to think about him.

"That is what Emmanuel told me," Carla muttered. She had made a second mug of tea and set it down in front of Pedro.

The priest nodded again, but this time there was a crease of annoyance across his brow. "Are you saying to me, Pedro, that you entered a door in one city and came out of another door here?"

"Yes."

"You know what you are telling me is impossible?"

"I am answering your questions, Signor Rivera. I am telling you what happened."

"Describe the door to me."

"I can't really. I only saw it for a moment. There was a typhoon in Hong Kong. The temple was being destroyed..."

"The door was in a temple?"

"All the doors are in sacred places. There was another one in Coricancha, which is where the Incas worship, in Cuzco."

"There are no Incas any more, my child. And when they did exist, they had no true religion. They were pagans."

Pedro knew full well that the descendants of the Incas had survived to the twenty-first century. He was one of them. And as to their religion, he had personally seen one of their most sacred objects, a gold disc with a portrait of Manco Cápac, son of the sun god, Inti. The face that he had been shown looked remarkably like his own. Nonetheless, he thought it better not to argue with what the priest had just said. "The doors all look the same," he went on. They're quite small, made of wood." Pedro thought for a moment and suddenly remembered. "They have a star printed on them. A five-pointed star."

The woman turned excitedly to her son and spoke quickly to him in Italian. He listened to her for a moment, then held up a hand for silence. It seemed strange to Pedro and somehow wrong that she should do what her son told her, rather than the other way round.

Silvio turned back to Pedro. "I will tell you what I know," he began. "I know who you are. I have read some of the pages from the diary of Joseph of Cordoba. There was a copy made many years ago and it is kept locked up in the Vatican. It is a forbidden text … and with good reason. What this man writes is impossible. It is blasphemy.

"He writes about the Old Ones. This is the name that he gives to creatures … what shall we call them, demons? … who have come into the world simply to cause evil, to destroy mankind."

"They are here now," Pedro said.

"I do not believe that is true."

Pedro stared at the priest. "Of course they are here. They kept me prisoner in Naples. They took my friend Scott and made him bad. They caused the volcano to erupt…"

"All these things may have happened. But have you seen the Old Ones?"

"They tried to kill me twice. The first time it was condors that came out of the sky in the desert. And then they sent people who were dead, who came out of the grave."

"I asked you if you had seen the Old Ones themselves."

"No." Pedro couldn't lie. "But we have to fight them," he went on. "The five of us must be together. That's why I have to find my friends."

"Now you are talking about the Gatekeepers. Is that what you mean?"

"Yes. Matteo, Scarlett, Scott and Jamie. And me." Pedro was ignoring his tea, which was getting cold in front of him. "Why is nobody allowed into St Peter's Basilica?" he asked.

Silvio spread his hands. "There are too many people in Rome," he explained. "The authorities are afraid that it will become overrun. A few pilgrims are still allowed in and out but they have to have special permission and must show their identity papers first."

"Is it because there is a door inside? Is it because they want to stop me?"

Silvio looked as if he was about to deny what Pedro had just said but before he could speak, his mother leant forward and there was an excitement in her eyes that he had not seen before. "There *is* a door," she said.

Silvio glowered at his mother but she wasn't backing down. He shrugged. "It is true that there is a door such as the one you describe," he admitted. "It is beneath the tabernacle, in the grotto. But I have opened and closed it myself. It leads nowhere: a short corridor and a solid brick wall."

"It only works for us," Pedro said. For the first time in many weeks he felt a surge of hope. "If you can get me inside the church, I can leave Rome. I can go anywhere I like."

"We can do that for you, Pedro," Carla said. She continued quickly, before her son could interrupt. "There is a secret passage that runs from the Vatican to St Peter's. Very few people know it is there. You are right when you say they are waiting for you. The basilica has never been closed but now there are soldiers, twenty-four hours a day. Silvio may not agree with me but I am certain they are only there to stop you."

"I do not believe in this door!" Silvio brought his fist crashing onto the table. He turned angrily on his mother. "St Peter's is at the very centre of our faith. It has existed in one form or another since the fourth century and today it is unquestionably the greatest church in Christendom. Saint Peter himself is buried beneath the altar. Are you going to tell me that it also houses a magic trick ... a door that opens into a Buddhist temple in Hong Kong or a ruin in Cuzco?" He forced himself to calm down, then turned back to Pedro. "I am sorry," he said. "I am sure you have been through many troubles. You are not alone. Sometimes even I find it hard to understand what has happened in the world. But I find the answer in my prayers. It is not the Old Ones who cause volcanoes to erupt, Pedro. It is part of a greater purpose, a testing time for humanity, but in the end, if we have faith, we will be better and stronger. That, I believe with all my heart."

"But you don't believe what I say," Pedro muttered. "You don't care who I am or why I'm here."

The priest fell silent and looked away.

"What is wrong with Maria?" Pedro asked.

At that, Carla started in her chair. "Why do you ask?" she demanded.

"Please, Signora Rivera. You told me that she was your daughter." He glanced at Silvio. "Your sister. She is in the opposite room next to mine. Why is she ill?"

Neither of the adults spoke, as if they didn't dare to put it into words. Then Carla nodded. "She has cancer," she said. "It is in her pancreas. It is the very worst kind. She has been slipping away from us for many months. We have tried everything but the doctors say there is nothing more they can do. Fortunately, she has little pain ..."

"That is God's mercy," Silvio muttered.

"... but she has only weeks left to her. She is much younger than Silvio. Only twenty-four. She was the joy of my life." Carla bowed her head.

"She's not dying," Pedro said. "She's better."

"That is not true."

"It is true, *signora*. I have healed her. I'm only telling you because I need you to believe what I am saying. All five of the Gatekeepers have powers. If you have read the diary, you must know this. We can read minds. We can change the weather. But my gift is the power of healing and before I came down here, I went into Maria's bedroom and I took her illness away. Go upstairs and see for yourself."

Silvio had gone very pale. He looked at Pedro with something close to anger. "You are wrong to say this," he rasped.

"Please, *signore*..."

"No!"

"I will go!" Before anyone could stop her, Carla Rivera pushed her seat back and stood up, then strode out of the room. Pedro watched the priest. For a brief moment, he struggled with himself, then rose and followed. Pedro came last. The three of them went back into the hallway and up two flights of stairs. The door to the sick woman's room was still closed, as Pedro had left it. Carla stopped outside, as if gathering strength, then opened it and went in, with Silvio and Pedro right behind.

"Maria...!" Pedro heard the mother gasp her daughter's name.

Maria was sitting up in bed. Her eyes were open. She still looked weak and tired but there was absolutely no doubt that the illness had passed, just as a shadow will move on as the sun rises. She was still attached to the various pipes and tubes and was examining them as if she was trying to work out why they were there. As the door opened, she looked round and saw the three of them.

"Mama..." she said.

Carla rushed over to her and took her in her arms. There were tears streaming down her cheeks. She took hold of Maria and buried her head in her shoulder. At the same time, she looked back at Pedro. "It is a miracle!" she said. "She has not spoken a word in three weeks!"

Silvio looked stunned, rooted to the spot. He had seen his sister that morning, before he went to church. He went in every morning and spent an hour with her, praying beside the bed. And now...? His mother was right. All the doctors had said the same. There was no hope for her. What he was seeing was a miracle indeed.

"You must take Pedro to the door," Carla said. "You must do everything you can to help him." She was still embracing her daughter, smoothing her hair with one hand.

Silvio nodded. All the blood had drained from his face. "Yes," he muttered. "Of course we must help him. We will leave tonight."

FORTY-FOUR

They slipped out of the house just before midnight. Carla was waiting at the front door with a coat, which she handed to Pedro. She had spent the past two hours with her daughter. Maria had spoken a little. She had managed to eat some soup, the first food she had tasted in weeks. Now she was asleep – and her breathing, which had been ragged and painful, came easily.

"Where will you go?" Carla asked Pedro.

Pedro had already thought about this. He knew that the doors would only work properly if you decided on your destination before you went through them. "I'm going to Antarctica," he said. "That is where Matt is waiting for me. That's where I'll find my friends."

Carla helped him put on the coat, then took him in her arms. "I will never forget you," she said. "And I will never be able to thank you for what you have done in this house. You have given my daughter back to me!"

"I'm glad I was able to help you," Pedro said.

"We should leave," Silvio muttered. "The guards are going to be suspicious. They will want to know why we're entering the Vatican at this hour. The later we leave it, the more suspicious they will become."

"Take care, Pedro." Carla hugged him again. "Maybe one day in happier times we will meet again."

She opened the door for them and they left together. For a

moment, Silvio stood next to his mother and he gently kissed her on the cheek. "Don't wait for me," he said, in Italian.

"Of course I will wait for you. I won't be able to sleep until you're home. Look after Pedro."

The priest was wearing a dark coat over his suit and as he hurried through the garden he was suddenly shrouded in night. He and Pedro reached the gate on the other side of the fountain and passed through into the street. This part of the city had been quiet when Pedro first reached it, and it was practically deserted now. A single man, wearing too many clothes, limped down the pavement, looking hopefully in the dustbins. A family lay curled up together in the doorway of a block of flats. Otherwise there was nobody to see them as they hurried away from the house, turning down one of the many streets that led them to St Peter's Square.

Their destination was not the church, even though it was part of the Vatican City state which surrounded it. Vatican City itself was a huge walled area inside Rome with its own police and government. It contained churches, museums, offices and official residences set within a beautifully landscaped garden. Silvio Rivera could have chosen to live inside the walls but had preferred to share a house with his mother and sister – even so, he was no more than ten minutes away from the entrance that he used every day. This was an archway with a small sentry box. It was guarded by two men wearing the most bizarre costumes Pedro had ever seen: orange and blue striped tunics with trousers that were tight at the ankles but ballooned out around the legs, black berets, slashes of red in their sleeves and around their cuffs.

"They are the Swiss Guard," Silvio explained. "It is their job to guard the Holy Father. Do not say anything, even if they try to talk to you. I will explain to them that I am looking after you and hopefully they will let us through."

As he approached them, Silvio took out a badge with his

photograph and identification number. It was almost half past twelve at night but he walked confidently, as if he was simply on his way to work. Even so, the Swiss Guards were suspicious. Despite the fanciful costumes, they were hard-edged, well-disciplined men. One of them examined the badge carefully, while the other snapped out a series of questions, which Silvio answered quietly and with complete confidence. Now the guard was examining Pedro. He asked something but Pedro didn't speak, as he had been instructed. Silvio continued with a torrent of words in Italian, waving one hand at Pedro while resting the other on his shoulder. Eventually, the guards seemed to be satisfied. The badge was handed back. They were allowed through.

Pedro waited until they were out of earshot. "What did you tell them?" he asked.

"I said that you were a chorister and that you were singing a solo at tomorrow's mass but that you had forgotten your words. I said I was giving you a lesson."

"After midnight?"

"It is not so unusual for the choirmasters to come here with boys at strange times of the day and night. The mass has to be perfect."

It was too dark to see very much. Pedro was aware of the lawns and shrubbery opening up around them. He heard the tinkle of water and smelled recently mown grass. It occurred to him that even if the rest of Rome was overcrowded and grimy, this garden must be a beautiful place – if only he could see it. A building loomed up ahead of them, handsome and solid. It did look like somewhere a choir might have practised, something between a school and a small museum. A flight of about ten white marble steps led up to the front door but Silvio took them another way, using a key to open a door at the back.

A long corridor stretched out in front of them, with low-voltage electric bulbs hanging above. Pedro could tell at once that the building was empty. Everything was silent apart from their own footsteps on the tiled floor. The walls were lined with black-and-white photographs of people – all of them men, many of them in clerical dress. They passed a series of doors, marked with numbers but not names. They could have led into classrooms, but when Silvio finally opened the door at the very end, Pedro found himself in a comfortable, cluttered office and guessed that this was where the priest worked.

There was an antique desk with a chair and, behind it, two windows that might have looked out onto the garden but were closed off with shutters. One whole wall was given over to books ... heavy volumes bound in red and gold leather and with titles mainly in Latin. On one side stood a table with a vase of flowers. The desk itself was groaning under the weight of papers and files, and there were more of them piled high all over the carpet. An ornate gold mirror with old, speckled glass hung between the windows. The remaining walls were covered with oil paintings. There was an image of the Virgin Mary, looking down with a great halo behind her head, another of the Three Wise Men on their way to Bethlehem. Pedro knew the stories. When he had lived in Lima, he had gone to church occasionally, if only to steal from the congregation.

Silvio closed the door. The two of them were alone.

"Is this your office?" Pedro asked.

"Yes. No one will disturb us here."

"Why are we here? Where is the secret passage?"

"It's not in this building, Pedro. It leads from the *Cortile Borgia*..."

"What is that?"

"It is a courtyard, part of the Vatican Museums. But we can't go there until eight o'clock in the morning, just before it opens."

"I don't understand." The guards hadn't stopped them. They had made it safely inside. But even so, Pedro was feeling uneasy. "Why have we come here?"

"It would be too dangerous to come here in the day. It's better for us to wait here until sunrise. When we cross the gardens tomorrow, nobody will stop us. I'm sure you're tired, but trust me. It is safer this way. I will get us both something to drink..."

Silvio walked over to an elaborate wooden sideboard inlaid with mother-of-pearl, opened it and took out a bottle of wine and two glasses. He stood with his back to Pedro, talking all the while. "You have made my mother very happy," he said. "Maria was a very late arrival in her life but she has always adored her."

"What happened to her father?" Pedro asked.

"Our father died." Silvio turned round. He carried two glasses of wine over to the desk. "Please, sit down, Pedro. I want to talk to you."

Pedro did as he was asked. He was aware of the various saints in their gold frames, watching the two of them.

Silvio passed him a glass and raised his own. "I want to drink to the miracle that you have performed. I want to thank you for giving me back my sister."

He raised his glass. Pedro did the same. There wasn't a lot of wine in the glass and he drained it in one gulp. He felt its warmth immediately. It had a deep, heavy taste – not just of grapes but of every other summer fruit. He wondered if he was doing the right thing. He would need all his wits about him when the morning came and he made his way to the courtyard. The *Cortile Borgia*, that was what it was called. From there he would find the door that would take him just a few short steps to Antarctica. The thought would have made his head spin if it hadn't been spinning already. He couldn't believe how much the wine had affected him. He already wished he hadn't drunk it.

He lowered his glass. Silvio had also drunk his wine. He was looking at Pedro very strangely. His face was filled with sadness.

"I must explain something to you," Silvio said. "I want you to understand what I have done. I am a good man. At least, I try to be a good man. I have been a priest since I was twenty years old. I have given my entire life to the Church."

Pedro was sitting opposite him, the two of them facing each other across the desk. His arms and legs were feeling very heavy. It was almost as if they had become part of the chair on which he sat.

"As I told you when you were in our house, I have read the diary of Joseph of Cordoba. For a long time I have known about the Old Ones, about the five Gatekeepers and the fight that will take place for the survival of the world. But I never believed it." He gestured at the bookshelves. "The library here is full of the writings of prophets and visionaries across the ages. They have been visited by devils and demons and have given them many names. Some have claimed they have seen into the future. Many of these texts are ridiculous. Others are frankly blasphemous. We do not let the public read them because, in the wrong hands, they might even be dangerous. At the same time, we study them because they are instructive. They give us an illustration of what can happen when people take a wrong turn in their faith.

"St Joseph was exactly that … deluded, ignorant, wrong! At least that was what I believed. So I wonder if you can begin to imagine how I felt when I returned home this evening to be told by my own mother that one of the Gatekeepers had come to Rome and that he was upstairs, staying with us. My mother believed in you completely, Pedro. She once studied theology at the University of Rome and, like me, she had come across the stories about the Old Ones. When she told me about you – you were still asleep upstairs – I felt emotions towards her that I had never felt before. I think I actually hated her for believing you. I must ask forgiveness for that, Pedro. A man should never hate his mother."

"What have you done?" Pedro asked. The words only came out with difficulty. He wanted to get up and run out of the room but he was suddenly very tired. He could still taste the wine on his lips, but now there was something else – a bitterness that the fruit had disguised. His eyes were getting heavy. The room was shifting slowly, losing its focus.

"If only I had been right. If only you had been a street beggar trying to get food and shelter by tricking his way into our house. That was what I first thought. But then, in front of my eyes, you performed a miracle. My sister had been seen by the very best doctors in Rome. We had talked about surgery and different sorts of therapy, but in the end we were forced to accept that there was nothing more we could do and that she would die. The cancer was too far advanced. She had not spoken or eaten for weeks before you arrived. We knew that the end was very near.

"And yet tonight, thanks to you, she was sitting up in her bed. She spoke to us. I can see in her eyes that she is well again."

"I saved her." It was an effort speaking the three words. Pedro was aware of time slowing down. He felt as if there were a huge hole in the room and he was slipping into it. The priest was watching him intently.

"Yes. You saved her. You have an extraordinary power and I am grateful to you. I hope that God will have mercy on you. I hope He will have mercy on both of us."

"What have you done?" Pedro demanded a second time. He didn't try to disguise the anger and contempt in his voice.

"The wine you drank was poisoned, Pedro. I have poisoned you. You have only three or four minutes left." He raised a hand, the jewelled rings on his fingers sparkling in the light. "Do not be afraid. I have taken the same poison myself. I could not commit the sin of murder and allow myself to live. We will make this last journey together." He paused to catch his breath and Pedro saw the dreadful pallor in his face and knew that he must look the same. "I have done evil," Silvio went on. "But I had no choice. I hope you will forgive me. I hope God will forgive me. He will understand."

No.

Pedro refused to die. He had been fighting all his life – in the village where he had been born, in the shanty town where he had lived. He was furious with himself for having sat here and taken the wine in his own hand. He remembered now that Matt had tried to warn him when they were together in the dreamworld. How could he have trusted this man who was still talking to him so reasonably, trying to make sense of what he had done?

"These are terrible times, Pedro. It seems that the world is coming to an end. The whole of the south of Italy has flooded and now Vesuvius has erupted, causing more death and destruction further north. The cities are overrun with refugees escaping from war and famine in eastern Europe and there is no longer any room to feed or house them. The government has responded with measures that we cannot think about. They are being killed … tens of thousands of them. Even the Holy Father has been forced to turn a blind eye. What can we do?

"And there are worse things happening all over the planet. In India, in China, in America, in Africa. Whole countries have disappeared. Some of them have retreated into the Dark Ages. Terrorists and fanatics have killed millions. Have you ever read the Bible? The kings of the earth and the great ones and the rich and the strong hid themselves in the caves and the rocks of the hills and said: 'Fall on us and hide us from the wrath of the Lamb because the great day of wrath has come and who can stand?' That's from the Revelation of St John. The end of the world. That's what's happening now."

Pedro had to move quickly. He could actually feel his strength draining away as the heavy hand of sleep, endless sleep, weighed down on him. The priest refused to stop talking but the words were coming with difficulty. Some of them were slurred. He was sitting with his hands resting on his lap. Only his lips were moving. Very soon he would be dead.

But Pedro had one advantage over him. He was a healer. For years he had lived in a slum that was filled with poison … that had even been its name. Poison Town. But he had never fallen ill. Without knowing it, his power had kept him safe. It could do the same now. He could turn it on himself.

"Maybe you and the other Gatekeepers could save us, just as you saved Maria," the priest continued. "But don't you see? *I could not let that happen*. We have to accept all the things that occur in the world as the will of the Almighty and it is only through our faith that we will survive them. If five children suddenly turn up and use ungodly powers to save humanity, what do you think will be the result? It will be the end of the Christian church. We will have failed! All the faith, everything that we have constructed over the last two thousand years, will come tumbling down. Do you understand? There can only be one Saviour and it is not you."

First, Pedro had to get some of the poison out of himself. That was the important thing. He needed water but there was no tap in the room. Then he remembered. There it was, right in front of him … the vase of flowers. It took all his strength to reach out and grab hold of it. With one hand he dragged out the flowers. They were already dying. Like him! The water inside the vase was green and slimy. That was good. Pedro tilted it back and poured the contents down his throat. It tasted revolting. A few pieces of slime caught between his teeth.

"What are you doing, Pedro?" the priest demanded. His voice was a whisper.

Pedro ignored him. The filthy water had done exactly what he wanted. He felt nauseous and a moment later he twisted round in his chair and was violently sick. He actually felt all the contents of his stomach empty themselves. Surely they must have taken at least some of the poison with them.

"No!" Silvio was looking at him in dismay.

Pedro ignored him. Perhaps he was imagining it but he was sure that some of the taste of the poison had already left him. He jerked forward, propelling himself out of the chair and onto his knees. Now he was right in front of the antique mirror. He could see his own reflection. He looked terrible, completely white, sweating, his eyes staring back at him. He focused on the reflection, imagining that it wasn't him but Matt after the Nazca Desert, Scott in Vilcabamba, just another sick person that he had to heal. He tried to feel the power flowing through him, rebounding on himself.

"You cannot save yourself!"

"I will save myself!"

And Pedro knew that it was working, that there was something inside him fighting back and winning. It was an extraordinary sensation, his own power curing him.

"God help me...!" They were the last words spoken by the priest. He slumped back in his chair, his eyes closed.

Pedro didn't dare move. He remained on his knees, his hands pressed against the glass of the mirror. He was still there many hours later when the sun began to rise.

OBLIVION

FORTY-FIVE

There was nowhere in the world that was anything like it.

The ice shelf was as flat and as desolate as it was possible to be. It was almost two kilometres long and half a kilometre wide, narrowing to a point, with a range of mountains rising up, black and impenetrable, at the far end. It was from these mountains that the ice had come, part of a glacier that had oozed and crawled its way forward a few centimetres at a time over hundreds of years. The ice shelf widened out until it reached the edge of a cliff, which formed a straight line, as if it were the end of the world. From here, there was a hundred-metre drop down to a thin strip of beach, hammered endlessly by the icy-grey water of the Southern Ocean.

The cliff face had been sliced and sculpted by the weather. It might once have been nothing more than a solid wall. But the wind and the sea-spray had worked with infinite care, turning it into a frozen firework display of strangely shaped hollows, knotted outcrops and bending pillars that seemed unable to support the weight of the rock and the ice up above. From a distance it almost seemed to be writhing in pain, but apart from the waves and flurries of snow, nothing moved. The seabirds, whales, penguins and seals had long gone, as if some instinct had warned them to keep away from this place.

The fortress was situated above the sea, at the other end, two kilometres inland, standing in front of the mountains … part of them, in fact, as it was impossible to say if the structure had been built or if it had grown out of the rocks. No two walls were alike. Some were straight and some were curved; some cut out of ice and some out of stone, the two fused into each other, stark white and iron grey.

A massive gatehouse and barbican stood at the very front. This was the first line of defence, with ramparts and battlements slanting back on both sides. Then came two circular towers, one to the west and one to the east. These were the far edges of the fortress. The walls then turned towards each other, meeting in front of the vertical face of the mountain behind which loomed over the entire place.

Two more towers stood at the back of the fortress, but they hadn't been built separately. They were also carved out of the mountain, with caverns and corridors running far underground. A narrow bridge led from one to the other, forming an arch behind – and slightly higher than – the barbican. There was an open area, a courtyard or perhaps a parade ground, with a few very ugly buildings, like Second World War bunkers, placed almost haphazardly. These were kitchens, dormitories, storage huts and prisons.

This was Oblivion. This was where Chaos, the King of the Old Ones, had chosen to make his last stand against humanity.

He had brought the greater part of his army here and it was monstrous, all-powerful, running into thousands. Some of them had chosen to be here, selling themselves to the Old Ones' cause in the belief that when the struggle was over, they would be allowed to live in comfort. But as they had quickly discovered, Chaos didn't care if they lived or died. They slept in freezing rooms and ate what scraps they were given. They marched or stood guard in the cold for such long hours that most of them were being eaten away by frostbite, their fingers and noses turning black and rotting away. They looked hideous. They carried weapons that they had been forced to manufacture themselves and wore scraps of rags, patches of fur and odd pieces of armour. Anyone who complained was whipped or hanged. There was no such thing as an easy death in Oblivion. And yet even so they were glad to be here. They had persuaded themselves that whatever happened, they were on the winning side.

They were commanded by the wretches who had been "adjusted", mutilated to make them more frightening and less human. Among them were the politicians and businessmen who had attended the Endgame conference in New York. They were unrecognizable now. Some of them had had their arms or hands sawn off and replaced with metal rods and spikes. Some had been put into iron masks, which completely enclosed their heads and which could never be removed. Some had jagged iron teeth or horns welded into their skulls. A few had lost their legs and had been put on wheels, turning them into half-machines. Those that could be seen had faces distorted with pain ... grimacing mouths, bulging eyes. They had long ago gone mad and were prepared to fight more savagely than anyone because they no longer had any fear of death.

Shape-changers moved among them, keeping order. Half man and half alligator, half man and half snake, pigs with human heads, humans with wings ... every sick and nightmarish combination seemed to be there, armed with swords, arrows, clubs and whips. They could kill anyone they wanted to and often did, just to set an example, lashing out without warning. A man or a woman might be walking past and would cry out, falling face down with blood spraying across the ice. And everyone else would continue what they were doing but more quickly, more attentively, not wanting to be next.

There were knights on horseback, both man and beast covered

in poison-tipped needles that seemed to ripple as they moved. Fly-soldiers, thick clouds of buzzing black insects, had descended and taken solid form. Just once, a giant monster had appeared. A hummingbird the size of a plane had suddenly launched itself into the air and soared over the mountain tops, the snow exploding beneath its beating wings. There were said to be other monsters too: a condor, a monkey, even a spider. Nobody had seen them. But they would come out when they were needed and nothing could stand in their way.

And what of Chaos himself? He was nowhere and he was everywhere. He never appeared but there was no doubt that the fortress was his creation and that he was aware of everything that took place within its walls. Some said that he lived deep within the mountain itself and that he was injured. At night, they heard the cracking of the ice and the deep rumble as the glaciers disintegrated and collapsed into the sea. But there was another, uglier sound. A tortured breathing, the rasp of breath drawn in pain.

Long ago, Chaos had been hurt by one of the Five. And all this – the fortress, the walls, the ice shelf, the gathered forces, the monsters – existed only to draw him in. The King of the Old Ones had no further interest in the world. All he wanted was revenge. That was what people said.

In the last few weeks, an army had come together to fight him.

There were only a few thousand of them, a ragtag assembly of survivors who had somehow been drawn together from all over the world. They had come by plane and by boat, making their crossings from South America, South Africa and Australia. Somehow the word had spread. The Internet had disappeared a long time ago but there was still rumour, whispers, even dreams. The last surviving Incas had come down from Peru. The Society of the White Lotus had sent representatives from the East. Native Americans from different tribes had come together and made the journey south. Even in the twenty-first century there were secret societies and organizations that remembered the Old Ones and who knew what had to be done.

And the Nexus had been busy, recruiting volunteers, arming them, helping them on their way. They'd had ten years to prepare. They knew they would only have one chance for success.

There were more than sixty aircraft scattered across the ice at the edge of Oblivion, close to the sea, most of them commercial, a few private or military. They had landed, skidded, spun and stopped, ice spitting from beneath their wheels. Now they looked like discarded toys, facing in every direction, their wings almost touching. They would never take off again, but at least they could be used as living and sleeping quarters. It was summer in Antarctica. The sun never set. But still the temperature was close to zero and the wind howled across the ice shelf, bringing with it blizzards and snow that travelled horizontally, rattling against the metal and the glass.

Down below, just off the beach, a whole fleet had assembled and lay at anchor. It looked like some sort of marine scrapyard. There were cruise ships, container ships, luxury yachts, hydrofoils, trawlers, fishing boats, even an oil tanker. The remains of different navies had found their way here: two battleships – one from Argentina, the other from France – a US aircraft carrier, a British submarine. They were spread out along the coast, being tossed up and down by the waves, waiting for the call to action. The sailors had been busy. They had cut pathways and steps all the way up the ice cliff so that they could make their way up to land, joining the pilots and the passengers who had already arrived. And up on the surface they had constructed tents and bivouacs close to the planes. This was where they met, made their plans, prepared their weapons.

They called themselves the World Army.

It was a brave title but everyone knew that it disguised an unpleasant truth. They were little more than a rabble, outnumbered and ill-equipped; short on weapons, ammunition, medicine and food. There was a limit to the amount of time they could stay here. Every hour was a constant struggle against the cold, and the danger was that they would begin to die even before the fight began.

They were waiting for the five Gatekeepers. Without them they had no chance. Five children. It seemed incredible that four boys and one girl were all that stood between them and complete destruction. Between them and Oblivion, they might say.

For several days now, the fortress had stood silent. More planes had landed, touching down on the ice and slithering to a halt. One, the most recent, was an Emirates airline Airbus that had come all the way from Dubai. Every day, more ships appeared on the horizon, joining the growing flotilla.

One last battle. It would come soon enough.

The snow fell and the wind blew and the sun hung low over the ice shelf, and everyone wondered when Chaos would make his move.

FORTY-SIX

Scott woke up late with that deep, heavy feeling that told him he had slept for a long time. He twisted sideways and reached out for his watch – the brand-new watch that he had been given in Italy. It was eleven o'clock ... although it could have been morning or night. He still hadn't quite got used to the fact that while he was in Antartica, the sun never set, hovering over the horizon as if it were afraid to go any further. There was no sign of it today, however. The sky outside was a dirty white, the clouds solid and unbroken. He yawned and stretched. He was naked underneath the sheets and furs that covered him and he had never felt quite as warm or as cosy in his life.

He was in an extraordinary room – a suite of rooms – like something out of a science-fiction film. He was lying in what was effectively a cave, scooped into the side of the mountain, with the walls and ceiling – living rock – curving round him. His bed was also a flat piece of stone – a giant piece of flint – and it should have been hard and uncomfortable. But he was lying on a thick mattress that seemed to mould itself to his shape, and the sheets, changed every day, were soft and luxurious. The bed was huge and piled with pillows of different shapes and sizes. Three people could have slept in it without touching each other.

There were no doors. An opening led into a private bathroom with a bath the size of a small swimming pool, permanently filled by a thermal spring that gushed out of a crevice in the wall. The water would also explain why the room was so warm. There was a wide open fireplace with a fire lit for him every evening, but even when the flames died down the temperature never dropped. There had to be some sort of natural heating system – perhaps it was volcanic – at work.

Nor was there any electricity. The entire fortress, the inner passageways and dungeons, were illuminated by a natural blue light that seemed to emanate from the rocks themselves. Scott's room had plenty of daylight. He had worked out that he was three storeys up in the right-hand tower, one of the two built into the rock face. He had no idea how far the passageways penetrated into the mountain itself. There could be rooms – possibly prison cells – that were little more than tombs. But the point was, he was right at the front. An entire wall of his room had been given over to an oval-shaped window looking out over the courtyard and the barbican. Scott had run his finger down the glass, only to discover that it wasn't glass at all but a sheet of ice, perfectly clear and cold. He was astonished that it didn't melt.

There was always some sort of activity going on outside. Lying in bed, he could watch soldiers marching past, wrapped in their rags and armour. They were always being made to practise ... left turn, right turn, day and night. Sometimes there were sword fights, training sessions that often ended with someone losing an arm and being rushed off, screaming, to the infirmary. He had no idea how many thousands of men and women had been recruited into the army of the Old Ones but he was very glad that he wasn't one of them. He had made all the right decisions. He was going to be OK.

Matt had known what Scott was planning. He had almost said as much back in the dreamworld. The two of them had spent five minutes together and Scott had been expecting anger, recriminations, an attempt to make him change his mind. But in fact Matt had been completely relaxed. He hadn't said anything about Pedro or what had happened back at Castel Nuovo. He knew that Scott was flying to Antarctica with Jonas Mortlake. And he accepted it.

Scott almost wondered if Matt had given up. Perhaps he had seen the odds that were stacked against him and realized that the whole thing was hopeless. Matt, Pedro, Scarlett and Jamie could travel back in time or perhaps they could go to the dreamworld. They'd be all right. That was what Scott believed, anyway. The one thing that worried him was that Matt would tell Jamie what he had done, but as far as he knew that hadn't happened either.

"We all have to make our choices, Scott." Those were the last words Matt had spoken to him. *"You've made yours."*

Scott still hoped that he and Jamie would be reunited when this was all over. The Old Ones owed him that. After all, thanks to him, they were safe. The five Gatekeepers would never come together now that he had chosen to be on the other side. Very soon there would be a fight and the last human resistance would be wiped out. What would be left would be a planet of slaves, living and dying simply for the Old Ones' pleasure. Jamie would be among them but Scott would find him and the two of them would be together, finally enjoying the sort of life that had always been denied them. Jamie would understand what he had done and that he had done it for both of them. And that would make it all worthwhile.

There was a movement at the entrance and a girl appeared. She could only have been a year or two older than Scott with fair hair, a pale face, downturned eyes. She was wearing a simple dress and carried a tray with fresh bread and butter, fruit, boiled eggs, cheese and coffee. Scott didn't know her name. She was forbidden to talk to him. She wasn't even permitted to meet his eyes. She was

Scott's personal servant and he could treat her any way he liked.

She set the tray down on a table in front of the window, picked up Scott's clothes from the night before, bowed and left. Later she would return to make the bed, sweep out the fire and clean the room. Scott waited until she had gone, then slid out from beneath the covers and put on a pair of undershorts and a T-shirt. He sat down and began to eat. He often wondered how the kitchen managed to get hold of fresh food in the middle of nowhere, literally at the end of the world. But ultimately, it didn't really matter. All that was important was that it was here.

It was snowing heavily outside. Thick flakes seemed to hang in front of the window before being swept aside by the wind. A man hung from a scaffold near the gate, his eyes frozen, his flesh turning blue. It was a soldier, hanged for stealing extra food. Several were killed every day and Scott had watched this latest execution. He looked up at the sky. Just before the man died, he had seen a plane coming in to land and he had wondered if Jamie had been on it. Or Matt.

And Pedro? He was probably still in Italy. Scott had given him money, but not enough to buy his way out. He thought back to their last meeting at the Piazza Dante, Pedro so thin and scrawny, with his hand wrapped in a filthy bandage. Suddenly Scott wasn't so hungry and just for a minute, glancing at his food, it seemed to change. It wasn't bread or cheese on the plate. It was a scrap of rotting meat with white maggots crawling around it. And across the room, the fire had gone out. He shut his eyes as tight as he could. When he opened them again, a few moments later, everything was all right. He took a deep breath. Then he turned away from the window and went to get dressed.

A little while later, Scott left the room. As far as he knew, he was allowed to go anywhere he wanted. Certainly Jonas Mortlake hadn't told him otherwise. Scott was wearing jeans and a padded jacket complete with a white fur collar and hood that had been provided for him. He didn't know which animal it had been made from but it was obvious to him that the fur was real. He had already explored the fortress a little. Parts of it reminded him of a medieval castle. He had seen dining rooms with flagstones, long wooden tables and minstrels' galleries. Other parts – his own room, for example – were more modern.

He emerged into the courtyard with the massive gatehouse in front of him and the twisted figure dangling from his scaffold. A boy, twelve or thirteen, staggered past with two pails of water hanging from a wooden rod over his shoulders. The boy was careful to avoid his eyes. A team of men and women, bundled up in rags, were shovelling snow into wheelbarrows. There didn't seem to be any point as more was falling even as they worked. A few shape-changers were patrolling the battlements, some with legs, some with scales and claws. It was intensely cold outside but they were lightly dressed and didn't seem to feel it.

Scott turned right and walked into the other tower, which was both wider and taller than the one where he was staying. Both towers seemed to be made of rock or maybe coral. They had no obvious man-made decoration. There wasn't even any visible brickwork. He wondered vaguely if this was where Chaos lived. And what of Jonas Mortlake? He hadn't seen the chief executive officer of Nightrise since he had arrived. Not that he cared. There was certainly no love lost between them.

Nobody stopped him as he had made his way through the open door and along a short corridor that sloped down into the ground, the strange blue glimmer showing him the way. The walls were once again natural stone with some sort of ingrained crystal, sparkling and cold to the touch. After about ten paces, the corridor suddenly opened and Scott found himself in a huge chamber with rock walls and ledges, a sort of conference hall with seating for at least a thousand people. Stalactites hung down from the ceiling. It was empty now but looked very much like a sports auditorium. Scott could imagine a fight taking place here. There actually was a sort of boxing ring in the middle with a white plastic floor, although it was surrounded by thin silver wire instead of rope. A wooden frame had been constructed inside it, a single, vertical plank with two rings stretched out on either side. It reminded Scott of a crude Totem pole and seeing it made him shudder. He took one last look around, then quickly left again.

On the other side of the auditorium, further inside the mountain, he came across a workshop filled with shaven-headed, half-naked men, sitting at long tables, chained to benches. They were hammering at swords, spears, pieces of armour and shields that had just come out of the forge. The entire room was filled with a deep red glow and the heat was so intense that Scott could feel it burning his cheeks.

He wondered what it must be like to slave away in there twenty hours out of twenty-four, finally sleeping, still chained in the same place. Scott watched as a man pulled a helmet out of the flames and plunged it into a pool of water. Steam hissed. The room was being patrolled by yet more shape-changers. He saw one of them with the head and single wing of a vulture. With his human arm he trailed a whip, which followed him like an ugly, brown snake that could strike at any time. The hammering continued, the clank of stone against metal suddenly a little faster. Scott moved on.

A short while later he found a fissure in the rock that led outside and he made his way to the gatehouse and the massive wooden doors that were bolted shut, keeping the enemy out and perhaps the slave workers in. The walls stretched out on either side. He turned round. The bridge between the two towers was ahead of him. Scott examined the mountain that veered up behind. It was completely vertical, sheer and glistening, with no obvious footholds. It would have been impossible to climb. It was just like a solid wall with no visible way through.

And yet there was an opening, a cave that ran in several metres before disappearing into shadow. The mountain was black granite but water had trickled down, forming icicles. It gave the entrance the look of a snarling mouth. Scott walked over to it. There was a chain hanging across the cave entrance. Why had someone decided to bar the way? He looked more closely and saw a sign carved into the rock, a five-pointed star. He recognized it at once. He had seen exactly the same at Lake Tahoe, at the church in Cuzco and even in Hong Kong. He knew exactly what he was looking at. This was the twenty-fifth door.

Now he understood why Chaos had built his fortress in this place. Locking the doors hadn't been enough. He had made sure that he ruled over them. If Matt or Pedro or any of them tried to travel to Antarctica, they would find themselves surrounded, locked in. They would be captured at once.

He moved closer. The chain was made out of some sort of dark silver metal, the links surprisingly thin. He imagined they would snap quite easily. The lock itself was actually made up of two human hands, beautifully carved out of white ivory and clasping each other, the palms interlocked, slender fingers bending round. As Scott approached, he heard a strange buzzing sound. He looked into the cave. He had no idea how far it went but guessed that eventually it would stop at a solid wall. Unless, that was, the hands were unclasped. Surely that was the point? Then it might take him to London, to Italy, to anywhere he wanted to go. He reached out to touch the chain.

"I wouldn't do that if I were you."

The voice came from behind him. Scott wheeled round to find himself facing two men, both of them wrapped up in hooded anoraks, padded trousers and boots. One of them was Jonas

Mortlake – but it was the other man, much older with watery eyes and grey, unhealthy skin, who had spoken.

"You hear that buzzing sound?" he went on. "There are thousands of volts running through that chain. It's not electricity … not exactly. But you touch it and it'll kill you just the same." Scott said nothing so the man went on. "You don't believe me? I could get someone to demonstrate, if you like. That kid with the buckets. You want to see him frazzle?"

"This is one of the doors," Scott said.

"That's right, son. And it's out of service. The funny thing is, locking this one has locked all the others too, so don't expect any of your friends to come tumbling through. I hope you weren't thinking of leaving us?" Suddenly the eyes were full of suspicion as the old man waited for Scott to respond.

Scott shook his head. "No. I like it here. Why would I want to leave?"

"I'm glad to hear it." The man extended a hand wrapped in a thick glove. "I'm the chairman of Nightrise," he explained. "You've already met Jonas, of course."

Scott couldn't see much of Jonas, with his hood and high collar, but his eyes gazed at him with undisguised hatred.

"I need to talk to you, Scott," the chairman continued. "Why don't you step into my office?"

Scott did as he was told, following the two men back into the tower he had just left. The chairman had a suite of rooms similar to his own but higher up, with a view overlooking Oblivion … the great expanse of unbroken snow with the scattering of planes at the end. The walls of his office were covered in fabric, making it feel less like a cave. The windows were more regularly shaped. There was a round, wooden table and four chairs. The chairman took off his outer garments, revealing a suit and an open shirt underneath. The three of them sat down.

"So let me explain things to you," the chairman began. "Any day now there's going to be a fight and there can be no doubt that the Old Ones are going to win. Have you seen the rabble out on the ice? Pretty pathetic, really. You'd have thought mankind would have been able to come up with a little more than that. As for the so-called Five, the Gatekeepers, they've been split up. You're with us. We don't know where your brother is. He slipped through our fingers just outside London but we're sure he'll turn up soon enough. Pedro is somewhere in northern Italy. But you might like to know that Matt Freeman and Scarlett Adams are here in Oblivion. At least, that's what we believe."

Scott started when he heard this. So two of them had actually made it all the way to Antarctica, even with the doors no longer working!

"Matt Freeman is the one that matters to us," the chairman went on. "He's the leader of your little group and he did something very bad indeed, out in the Nazca Desert. He wounded Chaos. Do you have any idea how serious that is? The simple fact is that the boy has to be punished. That's more important than anything. And you're going to help us find him."

"Me?" Scott's eyes flickered.

"That's right, Scott. We've taken a lot of time and trouble getting you here and I hope you don't think we did it because we like you! We need you to make contact with him and draw him into a situation when he's on his own. Despite everything that's happened, Matt trusts you. If you tell him it's safe, he'll believe you."

"Why do you need me? You've got a whole army. Why don't you just go out and get him?"

"Because we want to be certain we get him alive."

"What are you going to do with him?"

The chairman glanced at him sadly. "Do you really want to know?"

"No." Scott turned away, looking at the surface of the table.

Jonas Mortlake had said nothing but now he leant forward with an ugly smile on his face. Behind his glasses, his eyes had come alive. "You can always refuse to help us," he whispered.

Scott knew what Jonas wanted. If he didn't do what he was being asked, he would lose everything. He'd probably end up in a cell himself ... or chained to a table beating out pieces of armour. There was no way he was going to let that happen. "How will I reach him?" he asked.

"You can leave that to us," the chairman replied. "We'll make all the arrangements. You just have to turn up and lead him into the trap."

The interview was over. Outside the window, fifty soldiers were dragging some sort of catapult into place, straining at the end of ropes, their feet sliding in the snow. As ever, there were shape-changers whipping them on.

Scott looked past the walls, out to the ice shelf itself. So Matt and Scarlett were there! He tried to imagine them walking among the aircraft. Or maybe they had arrived by boat. Had the two of them met? And did they know that he was here? Maybe they were watching him even now, with binoculars trained on the window, a tiny figure sitting behind the glass.

Just for a minute he wished he could see them again. But he knew that wasn't possible. He was on his own.

"*We all have to make our choices, Scott.*"

That was what Matt had said to him – and he was right. Scott had chosen. There could be no going back.

FORTY-SEVEN

They used the emergency chute to leave the plane, sliding down into the snow. Matt had seen the extraordinary flotilla of different-sized ships as they had flown in. The other aircraft were all around them, sitting, seemingly abandoned, at the far end of the ice shelf. He knew that he had arrived at the place where the last battle against the Old Ones would be fought. Lohan had brought them down expertly, the two of them sitting next to each other, strapped into their seats in the cockpit – but even so Matt had felt a twinge of nervousness. Could the ice support the weight of the Legacy 600? Would they be able to stop before they skidded head first into the nearest mountain? He had no need to worry. One moment they were in the air, circling the area with the fortress at one end and the sea at the other. Then they were sliding along with snow blasted by the wheels and the turbines forming a blizzard around them. They could see nothing out of the windows. Everything was white. Finally, Lohan slammed on the reverse thrust. The engines screamed. They slowed down and stopped.

They had arrived.

Matt reached the bottom of the slide and stood up, taking his first step onto the Antarctic continent with the snow crunching beneath his feet. He had managed to find extra clothes on the plane but he was still aware of the intense cold slicing through him. At least his fever seemed to have burned itself out during the flight. He was tired and hungry and desperately needed something to drink. But he could walk without help. He could feel his strength returning.

He became aware of Lohan, who was just getting to his feet, having slid down behind him. There was an uncomfortable silence. Lohan was angry – not just because Matt had somehow fixed the plane's controls, forcing them to fly here, but because Matt knew what he had been intending to do. Lohan had tried to leave the gold mine at Serra Morte without him. If he had been given a choice, he would have flown north to the United States. Lohan was a man who was used to giving orders and having them obeyed without question. It was not part of his nature to serve the wishes of a fifteen-year-old boy. But it was more than that. He was ashamed. He had behaved dishonourably. If anyone had attempted to betray him in that way while he was a leader in the Triad, he would have had them put to death.

"How are you feeling?" he asked. It was almost the first time he had spoken since they had left Brazil.

"I'm feeling better," Matt said. "Thank you for flying us here."

"I wasn't going to leave you behind," Lohan said. The words came tumbling out and he couldn't stop them. "I didn't think it was a good idea coming here. That's all. I need to find my own people. So do you."

"Maybe they've arrived ahead of us."

"Do you think so?"

Lohan turned and looked at the fortress in the far distance, half obstructed by the falling snow. It was built on the very edge of the mountain, the barbican jutting out, the four towers all around. It looked small from the distance, almost two kilometres away, but he knew it must be huge. There were figures moving around in front of it ... guards or soldiers, some of them constructing some sort of machinery. Lohan had seen all this from the air as they prepared to come in. But it was somehow more ominous, more real now that they were down on the ground.

"The Old Ones," he said.

"Yes." Matt nodded.

"Do they know you're here?"

"I don't know. Probably."

"I still think we were wrong to come..."

"You don't need to worry about what happened at Serra Morte," Matt said. "That's all over now and we don't need to talk about it any more. What matters is that we arrived and you brought me here. I wouldn't have made it without you."

The two of them stood facing each other, their breath frosting in the air..

"There are people coming..." Lohan said.

It was true. There were half a dozen of them, identically dressed in white padded anoraks and trousers with balaclavas and goggles, carrying rifles. The clothes camouflaged them against the snow. They took up positions a few metres away, circling them. Their weapons hung over their shoulders but they were poised and watchful, ready to bring them round at any time.

"Where have you come from?" one of them shouted. He hadn't taken off his face covering and his voice was muffled. He spoke English with an American accent.

"From South America," Lohan replied.

"Why are you here?"

"To fight the Old Ones."

The leader examined them briefly. What must he be thinking – an Asian man and a Western teenager, emerging alone from a Brazilian plane? "Do you have ID?"

Lohan looked at him scornfully. "What use is ID any more? We escaped from a prison camp in Brazil. We're here to fight with you. Maybe you could make us feel a little more welcome."

The man nodded slowly, then gestured at the plane. "Have you got any supplies with you? Food? Weapons? How are you for fuel?"

"We stole the plane," Lohan said. "We have about a quarter of a tank but there wasn't much on board. We found a few clothes. There are a couple of crates of brandy. But that's all."

"We'll appreciate the fuel. And the brandy. We can take a look later." He came to a decision. "My name's Greyson. Welcome to Oblivion. Right now you need to meet the commander. Come with us."

The commander. Matt wasn't sure he liked the sound of that but he had no choice but to follow the group back towards the encampment that stood close to the cliff edge. At the same time, it occurred to him that he had no idea who these people were. The man who called himself Greyson could have been a shape-changer and the others could be … anything. They could have flown straight into a trap. But there wasn't really anything he could do and at least, if they were being led into danger, they weren't completely helpless. Lohan had his gun and Matt could feel his own powers returning.

They walked about fifty metres, following the tracks they had just made in the snow and leaving the Legacy behind them. They were heading for the largest tent at the centre of what was almost a makeshift city. The tent was like something out of a circus, tall and round, a sturdy affair with thick white canvas secured by about forty ropes, pegged into the ice. Dozens of smaller tents and wooden bivouacs huddled all around it and as they drew closer, Matt was aware of faces watching them nervously from behind the flaps. A few fires had been lit on the ice and people were standing over them, boiling kettles or cooking meals in tins. They were wearing a variety of protective gear.

Some had fur gloves and hats. There were men as well as women of every age. They nodded in his direction but said nothing as he went past.

Two armed guards were standing at the entrance but they recognized Greyson and stood aside. Matt and Lohan followed him in, glad to be out of the cold. They saw at once that there were stoves burning in the tent. The air was warm and smelled of aviation fuel, which must have been used to keep the fires alight. The ground was carpeted. Trestle tables had been set up in long lines ... a hundred people or more could have met here at any one time, and there were blackboards and white screens set up for presentations. As they entered, Matt saw a group of about twenty men and women, the majority of them in uniform, sitting together, deep in discussion. Their heads turned as Matt and Lohan walked towards them. At the same time, the white-suited men were removing their headgear. "We have two new arrivals," Greyson said.

"Matt!"

Matt heard his name called and looked in astonishment and delight as Richard Cole leapt up from the table and hurried towards him. Richard was dressed in a thick jersey and trousers, which he must have borrowed – they looked too neat for him – and his hair had been cut shorter. He was grinning from ear to ear, ignoring everyone around him. There was a moment of awkwardness as the two of them faced each other, then they fell into each other's arms.

"I can't believe you've made it," he said. "Scarlett told me you were in Brazil."

"I was."

"Nice place?"

Matt shook his head. "I'm not going back."

They were still standing close to each other. Richard lowered his voice and spoke quickly. "Man in charge. Cain. American. Means well but watch out for him. Planning an attack with the World Army. I think he's crazy but he won't listen." He moved away and continued in a normal voice. "I'm so glad you're here, Matt. I've missed you. It's so good to see you again."

A second person was moving towards them and Matt recognized Scarlett. Her hair was shorter too and he could see the scar where she had been wounded. Both she and Richard had red streaks on their cheeks and noses from their time in the Middle East sun. She grabbed hold of Lohan first and kissed him on the cheek. Then she did the same for Matt.

"It's great you've arrived at last," she exclaimed. "I've been waiting every day for you to show up."

"How long have you been here?" Lohan asked.

"Almost a week. We were in Egypt and Dubai and so many things have happened. We were helped by the Nexus and there was this sheikh..." She broke off. "I don't want to talk about it with everyone here. All I can say is, I'm glad Richard was with me. I don't know what I'd have done if I'd been on my own."

"You know these people, Mr Cole?"

Another man had left the table and was walking towards them, and even before he introduced himself Matt knew that he must be the commander that Greyson had mentioned and Richard had just warned him about. He was a big man, physically fit, with broad shoulders, a solid neck and silver hair, cut very precisely. He had the sort of face that demanded to be taken seriously, with a square jaw and ice-blue eyes. Matt guessed he must be about fifty. He was dressed in the uniform of the United States Navy: a khaki jacket and trousers, button-up shirt, black tie, epaulettes and gold belt buckle. There were two rows of coloured ribbons across his chest and although he was in the middle of Antarctica, his shoes were polished and every crease was in place.

"Yes, Commander," Richard said, in reply to his question. "It's the best thing that could have happened to us. This is Lohan. I told you about him. He helped us in Hong Kong..."

"And the young man?"

Richard hesitated a moment, wondering if Matt would want to tell these people who he was, but Matt caught his eye and nodded slightly. "He's Matthew Freeman," Richard said. "He's one of the Gatekeepers."

This caused a stir among the other people who had left the table and were grouped around them. Matt saw that they were all naval people, lieutenants and commanders – but from different navies. One looked South American. Another pair were obviously British, with their navy blue jackets trimmed with gold on the cuffs and crowns displayed prominently on their caps. There were two serious-looking women and an older man in a suit who might have been a university professor.

The commander had heard what Richard said and shook his head slowly, weighing up his words. He showed no emotion at all. Matt could see that he was being careful not to be impressed. "Did they bring in any supplies?" he asked. It was an odd question, almost irrelevant. And he hadn't even addressed it to Matt, as if he would be unable to answer for himself.

"No, sir," Greyson replied. He had removed his hood to reveal a short, naval haircut, blue eyes and freckles. He didn't look much older than Matt himself. "They have a little fuel and alcohol, nothing more. We haven't had a chance to look over the aircraft, though."

Matt was growing increasingly uncomfortable. What right did these men have to walk onto their plane – and who had put them in charge? But perhaps he was being unfair. The so-called World Army might have two or three thousand people in it, but someone had to give the orders. A military or naval commander would be the obvious choice. And this wasn't the time for an argument.

Matt wanted to be alone with Richard and Scarlett. He needed to know what was going on.

"It was a Legacy Shuttle, wasn't it?" the commander asked.

"A Legacy 600, sir."

"Well, that's good. We can move some more folk out of tents and put them on board. This weather is too cold to be sleeping outside and we've still got women and children with no proper place to go. You can see to it, Greyson."

"Yes, sir."

The commander turned back to Matt and although he still wasn't smiling, at least he seemed to have become a little more friendly. He extended a hand. "It's very good to meet you, Matthew. Mr Cole has told me a lot about you. You too, Mr Lohan. I guess you and I wouldn't normally have much to say to each other but that's the way it is. My name is David Cain, commanding officer on the US *Pole Star,* and the way things have worked out I'm pretty much in command of the World Army too. We have a lot to talk about, but I imagine you people would like to be together for a while. We were just wrapping up this meeting anyhow."

He looked at his watch, a chunk of stainless steel on an oversized wrist.

"It's fifteen hundred hours, almost time for dinner. We don't eat together but we make sure there's enough food to go round. And we go to bed early here. It's hard enough to get any sleep with this permanent daylight. Have you arranged the patrol, Lieutenant?"

"Yes, sir," Greyson snapped back.

"Right. I suggest we get together for the morning briefing at zero six hundred hours. Obviously, the fact that you're here changes things – and I have to say, it couldn't be better timing. My men will escort you back to the Airbus while we check out the Legacy. Does that sound all right to you?"

"Whatever you say," Matt said. He wasn't sure whether to add "sir" or not but decided against it.

"I'm glad you've come," Cain said.

He turned away, walked back to the table and began to examine the documents he had been reading when Matt arrived. The other officers and staff were reluctant to leave Matt, but eventually went back and joined him. Lieutenant Greyson and his men waited to one side.

"Let's go," Richard muttered.

They went.

Richard and Scarlett had agreed to share the Airbus, giving over the whole lower floor to people who had found it too cramped and the sea too rough on the boats. There were about a hundred of them, sleeping on camp beds that had been set out the entire length of the fuselage. They were mainly Europeans – French, German and Italian – and all ages. As Cain had said, there were even some very young children. The plane was already covered in snow but that helped insulate it and someone had set up a heating system using the aviation fuel that remained. A pyramid of packed ice led up to the main door and steps had been hacked into it to stop people slipping. The door itself was kept open much of the time, although with a thick curtain to keep out the cold.

Matt was glad to get inside. Walking here from the commander's tent, he had been unable to keep his eyes away from the fortress of the Old Ones at the far end of the ice shelf. He could feel the muscles in his chest tightening. He knew that Chaos was somewhere inside. He was waiting for him. And Chaos would know that he had arrived. The end, the final reckoning between the two of them, was very close.

The people on the plane were already preparing their evening meal, cooking tins of food over Primus stoves. Condensation was running down the windows and the air was warm and fuggy, smelling of tinned soup.

"We're upstairs," Richard said, taking Matt through the galley and up the spiral staircase that led to the first class cabin. Like the rest of the plane, most of the seats had been taken out and replaced with camp beds. There was also a table and four chairs. Two men, fair-haired and dressed in pilot uniforms, were sitting there, playing cards with a battered deck. They looked round slowly as Matt and Lohan came in.

"Matt, this is Larry and Zack," Richard said. "They flew us here."

"You're Matt Freeman?" Larry asked. He set down his cards. "I'm glad you've arrived, mate. Richard here hasn't stopped going on about you. So maybe you can do whatever it is you're supposed to do and get us the hell out of here."

Matt shook hands with the two Australians. They nodded at him, then promptly went back to their game, as if it was the only thing that mattered in the world. They hadn't been exactly welcoming but they were so laid-back that he couldn't help liking them. A few minutes later they finished, Zack spreading out a hand of aces, then they made their excuses and went downstairs. Maybe they realized that Matt and Richard needed time together.

Matt, Richard, Scarlett and Lohan sat at the table. Richard rummaged around and pulled out a bottle of water, some processed cheese and biscuits and a couple of tins of fruit. Matt saw at once that there wasn't a lot of food but, as hungry as he was, he didn't complain. There were thousands of people camped out here and no way of getting fresh supplies. How long had the World Army been here? Days maybe, or weeks. But with the cold, the unrelenting wind and snow, it was clear they were already running out of time.

"I can't believe we're together again," Scarlett said. "Now all we need are Scott, Jamie and Pedro. Do you have any idea where they are?"

"Jamie is in London and Pedro is in Rome," Matt said. He paused. "Scott is here in Antarctica."

"Where?" Richard was amazed to hear it. "Are you saying he's with the World Army? Why haven't we heard from him?"

"He's not with us, Richard." Matt's voice faltered. "He's joined the Old Ones."

"No..." Scarlett couldn't believe what she'd just heard. "That can't be true, Matt. He'd never do that."

"He's with them now, Scarlett. Just two kilometres away on the other side of Oblivion. I know you don't want to hear it – but it's true. He decided to join them when he was in Italy and they flew him here."

"But that means we can't win!" Scarlett looked horrified. "There have to be five of us."

Matt sighed. "I know. But you have to understand. Scott has been through a lot and he doesn't really know what he's doing. At least he's here, close to us. He could still change his mind."

"Can we reach him?"

"Not yet."

"If only Jamie was here," Richard said. "He was closer to Scott than any of us." He turned to Matt. "Where have you been? What were you doing in Brazil?" He nodded at Lohan. "I'm glad you were there to look after him."

"I'd never have got out without him," Matt said and Lohan cast his eyes down, remembering how he had behaved.

"I want to hear everything," Richard said. "When I came out of that door in Giza and found that you weren't with me..." His voice trailed away. "I thought I'd never see you again," he said.

"We'll have time for that later," Matt said. "But first of all I need to know more about what's happening here. Tell me about the commander. You said you were worried about him…"

"David Cain!" Richard shook his head. "I suppose we're lucky to have him. He's a good man – but the trouble is, he insists on doing things his own way. I don't know if you saw when you came in, but we've got quite a few naval vessels. There's an Argentinian destroyer, the *Pintada*. Then there's the *Duc d'Orléans,* which is a French surveillance frigate and not much use. There's even a British submarine, armed with Polaris missiles. Funnily enough, they're the most stand-offish. They won't have anything to do with Scarlett or me.

"Cain came off the US *Pole Star*, like he told you. It's a Nimitz-class supercarrier. But it's difficult for him. You have to remember that all these people are basically deserters. They've set off on their own to fight the Old Ones. Cain was given the all-clear by Senator Trelawny. Remember him?"

Trelawny was the American politician who had helped Scott and Jamie when they were on the run and who had almost been assassinated in the town of Auburn, California. He had lost the race to become president but he had been helping the Nexus ever since.

"The Nexus have been busy," Richard went on. "Nobody could rely on government any more. Most of the politicians are either working for the Old Ones or too busy looking out for themselves. But the Nexus have been there with money, supplies, communications. A big part of this army is only here because of them."

"What's Cain planning?" Matt asked.

"He was one of the first to arrive and he more or less appointed himself leader of the entire World Army. Maybe it's no bad thing. He's decent enough. But you have to watch out for him. I saw his face when you walked in and I don't think he's exactly overjoyed you're here. Anyway, he's already decided. He's going to attack the fortress. He was drawing up the plans when you arrived. A military bombardment followed by a full-on assault."

"That won't work."

"I'm sure you're right. I've already said the same. But Commander Cain has no idea what he's up against. He's been to military academy and all the rest of it. He fought in Iraq in Operation Iraq Freedom, but that didn't quite prepare him for shape-changers and demons. He still thinks this is a conventional war."

"How many people are there here?"

"At the last count, there were two thousand nine hundred and there are more arriving every day. I don't think there's a country in the world that isn't represented. Russia, China, Japan, Australia ... you name it. In a way, it's quite amazing."

"How long have they been here?"

"The longest ... a couple of weeks. And that's the main problem. We can make our own water but there isn't enough food to go round, particularly for the people who came on ordinary boats. Two or three more weeks. That's all we can manage. People are already cold and hungry and they're beginning to get weak. We can't let that happen."

"Has Cain said when he wants to attack?"

"Yes. Tomorrow. If you'd come twenty-four hours after you did, it would have been too late. Scarlett's going to raise a blizzard and we're going to use it as cover when we cross Oblivion."

Matt glanced at Scarlett.

"I'm not sure if he believes me or not," she said. "I've been trying to make it warmer here, to get the sun to break through, but I don't think I've been able to make much of a difference. It's too much for me. I told the commander I could give him a snowstorm for the attack but he probably just thinks that there was one on the way anyway." She sighed. "I'm fifteen years old and I'm a girl. Commander Cain doesn't really like having me around."

"I'll talk to him in the morning," Matt said. He had eaten the fruit and cheese and quickly drained his glass. "Right now, I'm tired. I need to sleep."

"We've got more camp beds set up in premium economy," Richard said. "Larry and Zack prefer to sleep in first class … but I suppose it's their plane. I'll show you."

He led Matt out of the front cabin. Lohan stayed behind with Scarlett. The two pilots still hadn't returned but there was guitar music coming from below, soft and strangely comforting in the pale grey night. There were half a dozen bunks spread out with blankets and pillows. Richard took Matt to the one at the very end.

"You can go next to me," he said.

"Thanks, Richard."

Matt lay down on the bunk and pulled the cover over himself.

"Tell me about Scott," Richard said. "You knew it was going to happen, didn't you?"

Matt wasn't sure how to answer. "I had an idea. Yes."

"Couldn't you have stopped him?"

"I don't think so." Matt propped himself up on one elbow. "I never thought it would end this way," he said. "Everything seems so different now. When you and I first met, in Yorkshire … did you have any idea?"

"If I'd had any idea, I wouldn't have spoken to you. I wouldn't even have opened the door."

"Do you remember Jayne Deverill?

"I'm hardly likely to forget her."

"That was ten years ago," Matt said. "That's what I have to keep reminding myself. Ten whole years have gone by since then … at least for everyone else. And nothing's the same any more."

"But we'll win in the end," Richard said. "Won't we?"

"It'll all work out the way it's meant to." Matt sank back onto the bunk, curling his body with his head against the pillow. He smiled tiredly. "I'm glad to see you again. You're my closest friend. At least that hasn't changed."

"You still haven't told me about Brazil," Richard said.

But Matt was already asleep.

FORTY-EIGHT

Commander David Cain, senior officer on the US sixth fleet aircraft carrier *Pole Star*, holder of the Legion of Merit and the Bronze Star Medal, acting chief executive of the World Army, stood on a raised dais, addressing the one hundred and fifty servicemen and resistance leaders who had been invited into the tent. This was his moment. There was nothing left to discuss. As far as he was concerned, all the decisions had been made.

"Ladies and gentlemen," he began. "We have arrived at the day of Oblivion. This is the day we bring the fight to the Old Ones and take the world back into our own hands. I'm not pretending it's going to be easy. Only a fraction of the people here have been combat trained and the great majority of them have never seen action before. We have done our best to equip them. Since we have been here, we have tried to show them how to fight. But I would be the first to admit to you that we're a poor excuse for an army and we can expect many casualties.

"And yet, at the same time, never underestimate what is possible if you have right on your side. There have been revolutions in France and America, in Russia and South Africa. History is full of moments when the people have come together and taken what is rightfully theirs. This is our world. We never invited the Old Ones into it. And with God's help, we will drive them out. We will prevail."

Perhaps Cain was waiting for applause. Perhaps he saw himself as the lead actor in a Hollywood film. But what he had said was greeted only by a respectful silence and when he continued, his voice was quieter, his words more considered.

"We cannot wait any longer. Food supplies are already running low and you all know we can't spend very much more time out on the ice. The Old Ones are waiting for us to make our move but there's always a chance that they will take the initiative and launch a surprise attack. That would be disastrous. They have superior manpower. They have ... creatures. I wasn't brought up or trained to face anything like this. I'll be honest. To me, frankly, they're like comic-book nightmares. But the fact is that they have us with our backs to the sea. That's not a good position to be in and I will not wait for them to come out of their hidey-hole and drive us back. We must hit them before they hit us. We must do it now.

"And so I am putting Operation First Strike into action, the details of which we have discussed in this room. Starting at twelve hundred hours today, our six Super Hornet aircraft will launch an attack on the fortress, firing infrared, homing surface-to-air missiles. Their aim is to breach the outer walls and to cause major casualties within. They will be supported by cruise missiles from the British and the Argentinians and Sea Darts from the French.

"This will be followed by an armed assault by our ground forces. We will move across the ice shelf in five groups. I will be leading the group code-named Hawk. Captain Allenby will lead Bear. Colonel General Shubniakov will be in charge of Lynx. General Sabato will lead Panther. And Lieutenant Greyson will head up Wolf. Field hospitals will be in place at Sectors Nine and Seventeen. We had earlier agreed that no children under the age of eighteen would be allowed to participate, but in view of the presence of two Gatekeepers among us, I intend to amend that rule. Scarlett Adams has told me that she can produce weather cover in the form of a blizzard commencing immediately after the initial bombardment. My guess is that smoke and snow disruption caused by the Super Hornets will provide much the same, but in any event, our troops have every chance of crossing Oblivion unseen.

"Just so that we are quite clear about this, let me say with the very greatest regret that a nuclear strike is still not an option today. Our friends in the British Royal Navy carry Trident missiles on board the submarine HMS *Percival*, each of which has twelve independently targetable nuclear warheads. That's more than enough to vaporize the fortress and everything inside it. But the computers have crashed and they're unable to implement launch procedures. I don't have to tell you that this situation is unprecedented and we can only assume that somehow, impossibly, the enemy have managed to hack into the system. Our people are still looking into it but we have to accept that the missiles are not operational and we can no longer wait for that situation to change. We have to fight with what we have. And that fight will begin just under six hours from now. Any questions?"

The commander's bright blue eyes swept across the assembly, almost challenging them. Richard waited for someone to speak. As far as he could see, the plan was suicidal whichever way he looked at it. But nobody said anything. Maybe they had spent too long sitting on the ice. They just wanted it to be over. They didn't care how.

"All right," Cain said. "Go and prepare your people. I want everyone in position by eleven hundred hours. Captain Johnson, you will be executive officer on board the *Pole Star* in my absence. In the event of my death, command passes to Captain Allenby. Good luck, everyone, and may God be with you."

The tent began to empty but Richard saw that Matt hadn't moved. Just looking at him, he guessed that Matt had decided to challenge the commander but hadn't wanted to do so in front of the crowd. Eventually, only Cain and a couple of his personal staff were left. Matt moved forward. Richard, Scarlett and Lohan went with him.

Cain was studying a map full of arrows and troop formations. He looked up as Matt approached. "Yes?"

"Your plan won't work, Commander," Matt said. The other members of Cain's staff stared at him, shocked. He went on quickly, before they could interrupt. "If you launch this attack, a lot of people are going to be killed – for no good reason. I'm not sure that planes and missiles will do any damage at all to the fortress. The same goes for nuclear bombs. With respect, sir, I don't think you know what you're dealing with. You don't know how powerful the Old Ones are."

"And you do?"

"Yes, sir. I saw them in the Nazca Desert. That was when they came back into the world. I tried to stop them."

"You failed."

Matt shrugged. "That's what I'm trying to tell you. You can't stop them. Even this briefing this morning ... that was probably a mistake. They could have been listening in. They could have heard every word."

"I know every single person who came into this tent. There wasn't a single man or woman here I don't trust with my life."

"They have shape-changers. I could be one of them. So could you. So could any of your advisors. But it doesn't matter anyway." Matt sighed. "Why do you think they're here in Antarctica, Commander? And why haven't they come out and attacked you? Why aren't they attacking you right now?"

"You tell me."

"It's because they're toying with you. They're waiting for you to come to them. You're doing exactly what they want."

"How do you know that?"

"Because I know them. I've fought them before."

Cain considered what Matt had said. His advisors stood around him, doing their best to avoid his eye. His face was as grave and as composed as ever, but Richard noticed that two red spots of anger had appeared on his forehead. At last he spoke. "Do you have a better idea?"

"You should wait for the Gatekeepers," Matt said. "All five of us have to be here. Then we'll have the strength to defeat them. The power of Five. That's how it works."

"There are only two of you here now. Where are the other three?"

"On their way."

"And how long do you think we'll have to wait? A week? A month?"

"I can't answer that, Commander."

Once again, Cain fell silent. Matt was standing next to Scarlett, looking very small in comparison to the military personnel who were so much older, smarter and physically larger than them. And yet there was something impressive about him. Richard had already noticed the change. The Matt he had met in Antarctica was very different from the one he had left in Hong Kong. He had been here for less than twenty-four hours and yet he had somehow taken command of the situation and was holding his own. The true authority in the tent belonged to him, and all of them knew it.

"We can't wait a week or a month," the commander said. He had made up his mind. He spoke very deliberately. "You weren't listening to what I said, Matthew. We can't survive out here on the ice. We have to take action while we can." He paused as if expecting Matt to interrupt but Matt said nothing. "And let me tell you something else," he went on. "You may be special. You may be one of these Gatekeepers that seem to mean so much. I don't know. But you're only fifteen years old. I have a son as young as you. I wouldn't take orders from him and I won't take them from you either. Do I make myself clear?"

"I'm not giving orders," Matt said. "It's just advice."

"I don't think you quite understand the situation here. You only got in yesterday. And as for these powers of yours, I haven't actually seen anything yet. This young lady says she can control the weather. Well, it's been pretty cold these last few days. I can't say I've been too impressed. What's your party trick?"

Matt didn't reply. He looked quickly around him and saw a bottle of water on the table where the commander had been sitting. Matt barely moved. He flicked a hand in its direction and the bottle exploded instantly, spraying glass and water over the surface. The commander blinked. His officers glanced uncomfortably at each other.

"All right," he drawled. "I'll admit that's quite impressive." Cain nodded slowly. "But it's just a bottle. It's just a magic trick. Could you do the same to the fortress? How about those walls? Could you blow them apart?"

"No, sir. I'm not strong enough. That's exactly the point I'm trying to make. I need Pedro, Jamie and Scott. Once they're with me, I can do anything."

"And I've already told you. We can't wait."

"You're not changing your plans," Scarlett said.

"That's right." Cain drew a hand across his brow and for just a second Scarlett saw the strain he was under. "There may be something in what you've said," he continued. "But I can't be sure, and anyway, it's too late. I've made my decision. I've given the command. And now, if you don't mind, I have work to do."

He marched out of the tent, followed by the other officers. Once again, Matt and the others were alone.

"The man is an idiot," Lohan snarled. His face was full of contempt.

"No," Matt said. "He's scared – and he doesn't want to show it. And he has no idea what he's up against. Six months ago he wouldn't have believed in any of this. Now he's looking across the ice and seeing giant creatures and soldiers made out of flies. He's only doing what he thinks best."

"So what do we do?" Richard asked. "Do we join the battle?"

Matt glanced at the pages left on the table, the folded maps, the white board with its scribbled lines and arrows. For a moment his eyes were far away, as if he were searching through his memory for something that had been lost. Finally, he turned to Richard.

"Yes," he said. "We fight."

FORTY-NINE

The Super Hornets streaked low across the ice shelf in arrow formation, moving so fast that by the time they were seen they had already gone, flashing past with their payload delivered and already gaining altitude, climbing up into the clouds. They had fired Sidewinder and Harpoon missiles, which had been guided into their targets, hitting the fortress with pinpoint accuracy.

The explosions were spectacular, huge plumes of orange and red leaping up directly out of the snow. The flames looked all the more intense as they were reflected against the brilliant white, and it seemed incredible that they could burn so long when they were only able to feed on stone and ice. Again and again the fortress was hit, the mountain shaking, the black rock disintegrating, sheets of ice cascading down. The barbican, with its huge gate, took the first strike and was blown into a thousand pieces, leaving a gaping hole in the wall. The west tower, hit three times, trembled and then collapsed. The wall itself was smashed in half in a dozen places, exploding the courtyard and the other buildings behind.

Nearly two kilometres away, watching from the other side of Oblivion, Matt and Richard could feel the heat against their cheeks. It was extraordinary to be so cold and yet to feel warmth at the same time. Three of the four towers were wrapped in flames that seemed to be spreading over the stonework, as if searching hungrily for anything that would burn. The very ice seemed to be on fire.

The planes returned a second time, wheeling out of the sky and slanting down for another attack, this time with their own twenty-two-millimetre nose-mounted Gatling guns firing thousands of rounds a minute. Lohan was watching from beside the commander's tent. He hadn't volunteered to take part in the fight and certainly he wasn't going to run across the ice as part of any ragtag army. He had persuaded himself that it was his job to protect Scarlett, who was standing next to him. Besides, he was no foot soldier. Was he not an Incense Master, a commander in his own right?

He watched the bombardment continue and tried to imagine what it must be like to be inside the fortress, trying to find somewhere to hide. It didn't matter what they were – men or monsters – they would be deafened by the scream of the jet engines, shaken by the endless blasts, blinded by the spinning, whirling mass of debris. If they hadn't managed to burrow deep down, they would have simply been ripped apart, and even those that survived the assault would never forget it. He wondered if there would be any need for a land attack. The Old Ones had relied on the tactics of medieval warfare, which might have worked for them ten thousand years ago, but now they were facing a twenty-first-century air force. They had underrated their enemy and this time their powers had failed to protect them.

The planes were strafing the courtyard, tearing it apart. Lohan saw tiny figures attempting to run over the humpback bridge that connected the two towers. Suddenly, without warning, it shattered beneath them, sending them plunging down. More missiles exploded. If the planes returned a third time, they might smash through the very ice shelf itself. And why not? Somewhere deep beneath the ice was the sea. Another couple of attacks and the fortress might sink into it and disappear, carried down by its own weight.

But the Super Hornets had finished their work. There had been no air defences, no counter-attack. Not a single one of them had been hit. The pilots would have been happy to continue the bombardment but, obeying orders, they peeled away, heading back to the US *Polar Star*. Moments later, a bombardment from the various destroyers had followed, missiles streaking down with ferocious accuracy. When the smoke finally cleared, it seemed to be all over. The walls were breached, the fortress in ruins. There were dead bodies everywhere, lying on the ice, surrounded by fragments of stone and broken bricks. Nobody was moving. Any soldiers who had been guarding the fortress on the battlements or standing outside, when the onslaught began, would have been killed at once. Many of the corpses were on fire, the flames tugging at their clothes. Others were so smashed up that they were hardly more than red smears on the ice. It really did look as if the battle had already been won.

Standing on the platform that had been raised outside his tent, waiting to make his next move, Commander David Cain lowered his binoculars and resisted the urge to smile. Less than half the fortress remained standing. Casualties must have been enormous. And this was just the work of six aircraft! For all the talk of creatures from another world, of strange gates and children with special powers, he had relied on old-fashioned American firepower – and he had been right in his judgement. He wondered now if he had been unwise to commit land troops but he was interested to see what he would find inside the fortress and the clean-up operation would end this once and for all. At least his troops would be in no danger. He could see for himself. All resistance had been shattered. The air attack simply couldn't have gone better.

He was holding a radio transmitter. He raised it to his face, pressed a button and spoke a single word.

"Amber."

It was the agreed signal. At once, the entire World Army, divided into five squadrons, began to move across the two kilometres of ice that separated them from the fortress. Cain knew that they weren't much to look at. The great majority of them were on foot, already picking up speed. Few of them were in uniform and some of them didn't even have guns. But he had done what he could for them. Every man and woman had received some training in hand-to-hand combat. And, he reminded himself, this was their choice. They wanted to be here. He was proud of every last one of them.

The advancing troops were accompanied by around forty armoured vehicles and jeeps, American, French and Argentinian, offloaded from the boats. These were being driven by professional marines equipped with rocket and grenade launchers, heavy-duty artillery and automatic machine guns. They were moving at a steady sixteen kilometres per hour. It would take them just six minutes to reach what was left of the walls. As he watched them dwindle into the distance, moving in the exact formation that he had prescribed for them, David Cain decided that command could be a pretty lonely place. With all his heart, he wished that he could be with them too.

Scarlett was just a few metres away from him but her thoughts were very different. She had been watching the devastation with a mixture of horror and excitement. The fireballs and great columns of flame that had erupted one after another certainly had a degree of majesty. It had been like watching the most spectacular firework show on earth. And she didn't care how many of the Old Ones died. In fact, she hoped every shape-changer and fly-soldier in the fortress had been torn apart by the bombardment.

But at the same time, she couldn't forget that there were men and women inside there too, even if they had chosen to fight for the other side. Scott was one of them. She remembered seeing images of war on television, the smooth commentary of the newscasters telling of allied victories and heavy casualties among the insurgents. It was all too easy to forget that "insurgents" was another name for human beings and right now, she was actually watching hundreds of them die. Was that really something to be pleased about?

She also had a part to play and had been preparing herself before the first plane had begun its attack. Despite her misgivings, she was confident she would not fail. Sure enough, she felt the power flowing through her and saw with relief that the snow had begun not just to fall but to swirl around with such intensity that it formed a perfect barrier between the World Army and the fortress. Of course, Commander Cain would say it was just a coincidence. He would persuade himself that the blizzard had been caused by the bombardment. But Scarlett knew differently. She was actually moving it, keeping it a few steps ahead of the advancing army so that it would remain hidden all the way to the walls.

There were more than two thousand people out on the ice. Only the children had been left behind, along with the doctors and nurses, who were preparing for casualties. Some of the tents had been turned into field hospitals complete with fully functioning theatres. Scarlett had seen the operating tables being wheeled into place. A skeleton crew had also remained behind on the warships – just in case there was the need for an emergency evacuation. But that looked unlikely now. The World Army had advanced more than halfway across Oblivion and nobody had so much as taken a shot at them. There wasn't a sound or any sign of movement from the fortress.

Matt had gone with them. He and Richard had joined Wolf Squadron, thinking it right that they should attack with people from their own country. Their leader, a man they knew only as Captain Johnson, was riding ahead of them in a jeep, a tiny Union Jack fluttering from the window, the wheels spinning on the ice. At the moment, Matt could see almost nothing beyond the backs of the people in front of him. He was out of breath, his feet tramping through the snow. They had just ten minutes to cross Oblivion. The air attack would have devastated the enemy. The blizzard would confuse them. Even so, they still had to use their advantage, to make sure they didn't arrive too late.

But as they drew closer, Richard grabbed hold of him. "That's far enough, Matt," he said.

Matt shook himself free. "I'm going all the way, Richard. I haven't come here just to stand here and watch."

"You're not armed."

"I don't need guns. You know that." They were already being left behind, the other soldiers disappearing in the spinning snow.

"They don't need you," Richard insisted.

"I think they do!" Matt wasn't prepared to have this argument now. "There's something wrong," he went on. "Everything is wrong. Why did they just let the planes attack them? Why didn't they even try to defend themselves?"

"They were taken by surprise."

"No. I know them, Richard. This is what they want."

Matt was already moving forward again, his breath freezing in the air. He was dressed in outdoor gear and he had a balaclava over his face. That had been Lohan's idea. He had persuaded Matt that it would protect him from the cold but they both knew the real reason was to stop him being recognized. Richard swore briefly to himself, then hurried forward to catch up with him. He drew a gun out of his pocket, thinking to himself how mad this all was. He was a journalist. He had a little flat in York. Less than six months ago, he had been writing stories about weddings. But suddenly he was steps away from taking part in a war.

People were streaming past him on both sides and it was just then that something happened that he would remember later on. A man turned towards him, just a couple of metres away, and smiled.

Richard couldn't see very much of the other person ... he had a hood and goggles. But instinctively he knew who it was. His name was Atoc. He was an Inca who had been with them in the hidden city of Vilcabamba ... indeed, he had brought Matt there. Richard wanted to call out to him, to greet him, but everything was happening very quickly as the army continued its advance. He was gone as suddenly as he had appeared. Richard didn't see him again.

He caught up with Matt. "All right," he said. "But you can't get hurt. You can't let yourself fall into their hands. You're too important..."

Matt nodded. "I know..."

Scarlett had steered the blizzard all the way up to the edge of the fortress, hiding the army behind it. She let it fall away as they covered the last few metres ... they had crossed the full length of Oblivion with amazing speed. The wind died down. The snow seemed to fall aside like a curtain. And it was only then, when it was far too late, that the truth was revealed.

The moment before, the fortress had been in ruins, burning, blasted by the air strike. Now it was intact again, the four towers and the barbican still standing, the walls unbroken. At the same time, the gates had opened and the forces of the Old Ones came pouring out in their hundreds. And that wasn't the worst of it. There were thousands more of them. They had been lying flat on their stomachs, buried under the snow. But just as the World Army reached them, when it was far too late to turn round, they rose up, seeming to appear like ghosts or zombies, and suddenly they were everywhere, six rows deep, screaming and, surging forward with weapons raised.

First came the ordinary soldiers with axes, swords, spears and pitchforks, then their hideous and deformed commanders, the men and women who had been "adjusted". They were followed by shape-changers, scrambling over the ice, a blur of half-human and half-animal constructions, screeching and howling. Fly-soldiers poured down from the battlements, solidified, and joined the others. It was a tidal wave of death. The World Army had walked right into it.

Scarlett couldn't believe what was happening. From where she stood it had been like a mirage in the desert – as if what she was seeing had evaporated in a single shimmer of heat haze. She turned to Lohan. "How…?" she began.

"It's a trick!" he snapped.

The fighting began at once, but for the World Army it was no longer an attack – it was a desperate struggle for survival. They had the guns, but even so they found themselves being stabbed and hacked at by a surging mob that had no interest in its own life or safety. Many of the Old Ones' recruits were longing to die and they took out all the anger and the pain that they had suffered on the soldiers who had been sent to fight them, lunging out with arms that had been made into swords or biting with teeth made of jagged tin, moaning with pleasure when they themselves were shot down. Meanwhile, the fly-soldiers cut and slashed their way forward more slowly, deliberately. Bullets couldn't hurt them. The insects simply separated to let them pass through. But when they congealed back together they were solid, their swords and spears razor-sharp. One after another, men and women from the World Army fighters died, with a buzzing horde of black insects in the shape of a spear plunged into their chests or throats.

There was blood everywhere, enough to turn the snow bright red. It was as if the shock of seeing the fortress undamaged had paralysed the World Army and many of them barely moved, allowing themselves to be cut down. A few turned and ran, dying with arrows fired into their backs. Others held their ground, even though it was hopeless, shooting again and again until their guns clicked empty and they were grabbed and torn apart.

The massacre had reached its height when Chaos sent out the forces that were closest to him. Thirteen black figures on horseback rode out of the fortress, hooded and shrouded like monks or friars, their faces hidden apart from their eyes, which glowed as specks of red in the shadows. Matt recognized the fire-riders. They had only to reach out and whatever they touched shrivelled and burnt. As he looked desperately around him, trying to work out what to do, he saw one of the British marines, a man in his twenties, firing with a machine gun. The man didn't notice as one of the riders stretched out a single finger. He barely had time to scream. Instantly he was dead, blackened and disintegrating like a scrap of paper in a furnace.

Almost alone, Matt held them back. Just like Scarlett, he could feel the energy as it surged through him and he directed it at the enemy, simply gesturing with an outstretched arm. The fire rider who had just killed the marine was flung backwards, the black robes crumpling around him, his horse rearing up in terror. A shape-changer with two snake heads who had been scything through the squadron was hurled ten metres into the air and sent crashing into the fortress wall. With a single movement Matt scattered a long line of enemy soldiers, sweeping them off their feet and toppling them onto the ice. Next to him, Richard was firing wildly. It was impossible to be sure what was going on. Everywhere they looked, there was carnage – flailing arms, distorted faces, splattering blood.

The blizzard had sprung up again. Seeing what was happening from one and half kilometres away, Scarlett had done the only thing she could. She had sent the wind and snow whipping into the enemy lines, hoping to blind them and drive them back. She, better than anyone, understood what had happened. She had spent time in Hong Kong with the Old Ones in power and knew how easily they could twist reality, to make you see whatever they wanted. She knew that not a single missile fired by the Super Hornets had really found its target. There must have been some sort of shield in place. The buildings hadn't been touched. Nobody had been hurt or injured. But the Old Ones had created a mass illusion and they had foolishly believed it.

Commander David Cain had also realized that he had been tricked. His hands were locked onto the binoculars, holding them as if he could crush them. What he was watching was no battle. It was mindless slaughter. He knew that this was his fault. The boy, Matt, had tried to warn him.

"They're toying with you. They're waiting for you to come to them. You're doing exactly what they want."

He remembered the words but he hadn't believed them at the time. Why should he have? He'd thought he had the advantage. A classic air strike followed by an infantry attack. It was what he had been taught decades ago, back at the US Naval Academy in Annapolis. Nothing he had learnt there could ever have prepared him for this.

Once again, he lifted the transmitter to his lips.

"Red-seven."

It was the signal for the retreat: not that he thought it would make any difference now. The Old Ones, these ... things ... would follow the World Army across the ice. They would hack them down as they ran. None of them would actually make it back to the tents and the tents would probably be destroyed too, the doctors and nurses, the children and civilians butchered. Was there anything he could do? Perhaps the Super Hornets could come back in. He could order a bombardment from the frigate. No. That would just kill his own people. He could only stand there and watch.

The World Army had already fallen back, separating itself from the enemy, and for a few seconds there was a gap between them. Cain could see the white space, even with the snow falling. At the same time, he heard an explosion like nothing that had gone before. It was a hollow boom that seemed to start from inside the very earth. It was ten times louder and lasted ten times longer than any of the missile strikes he had commanded. And suddenly he saw. The entire ice shelf was shaking. People were running towards him – there were hundreds of them – but for some reason the Old Ones had pulled back. Some sort of black line had appeared in front of them. It was acting like a barrier. They were slowing down, afraid to cross.

Cain raised the binoculars to his eyes and stared in disbelief. There was a crack in the surface of the ice that ran the entire width of Oblivion. The glacier had split in half! He was looking at a chasm which must have been hundreds of metres deep. The World Army was on one side. The Old Ones were trapped on the other. Dozens of the enemy soldiers nearest to it, the ones who had been closest to it when it opened, were falling into the void. He saw them tumbling like black crumbs swept off the edge of a table. Of course, there were creatures who could fly. The fighters made out of insects. Some of the shape-changers. But they seemed confused by what had just happened. They were holding back.

The remnants of the World Army drew closer. Almost half of them – perhaps as many as a thousand people – had been killed. The battle was lost. But thanks to some miracle, a freak of nature, the massacre hadn't been total.

Ten paces away, Scarlett knew exactly what had happened. It was Matt. Only he could have done this. He must have grown stronger than ever to split an entire ice shelf in two! She wondered if there was any limit to his power. Maybe, given time, he could take on the fortress itself.

"Commander…? One of the staff officers approached Cain, waiting for further orders.

Cain shook his head and walked back into the tent.

FIFTY

It had been a disaster. The list of the dead was endless and the field hospitals had been working without pause to help the living. All through the afternoon, they had been performing operations, amputations – and by the time the clocks showed that night had arrived, they had run out of anaesthetic, bandages, basic supplies. But still they worked on in the Antarctic light, using alcohol and torn strips of sheet, doing what they could. The doctors were faced with horrible injuries, all the worse because they had been deliberately inflicted to wound, not to kill outright. The tents were crammed with men and women, lying in shock, stretched out on camp beds. The nurses and stretcher-bearers were in and out constantly, checking on who was still living and who had died, quietly removing the bodies and burying them out of sight, beneath the snow.

Those who were still able to walk had left the ice shelf, returning to the boats. There was talk of a mass evacuation. Certainly, a second attack on the fortress was out of the question. The World Army had been outnumbered to begin with. Now there were just a thousand of them left and the great fear was that the Old Ones would press home their advantage and launch a counter-attack. If that happened, they would be wiped out. Ammunition was running low. Few people had the strength or the resolve to fight. All they wanted to do was to leave this dreadful place. Most of them wished they had never come to begin with.

Matt, Scarlett, Richard and Lohan had returned to the Airbus just in time to meet the pilot, climbing down the ice steps. He was carrying a suitcase and looked pale and worn out.

"Good luck to you," he said and they noted the bitterness in his voice. "I'm getting a berth on the *Polar Star*. There's no point in hanging around here."

"Where's Zack?" Scarlett asked.

"He's already gone."

There was nothing else to say. Larry brushed past them and hurried towards the edge of the cliff and the pathway leading down.

The four of them made their way back to the upper cabin. The lower section of the plane was empty, abandoned, the metal framework, with its snow-covered windows, stretching into darkness. At least some food had been left behind and Richard was able to make them a meal of hot soup, tinned fruit, cheese and biscuits. None of them talked very much as they ate. Richard was coldly furious. Why hadn't the commander listened to Matt? Why did he have to be so pig-headed? Lohan wanted to leave. As far as he was concerned, there was no further reason to stay. Scarlett was exhausted. Zack and Larry had gone. Everyone was abandoning them. Matt kept his thoughts to himself.

When the hours of night arrived, they were still sitting together in silence. Lohan had managed to retrieve a bottle of brandy and he and Richard were sipping from it. Outside, it was snowing softly. Although it was eight o'clock, the light was unchanged, a pale silver-grey without a shred of warmth. Lohan wiped some of the condensation from the window and looked across the ice shelf.

"Why don't they come?" he asked. "They know we're weak, defenceless. They could come over here and finish us off, one by one."

Richard turned to Matt. "So what happens now? Do we leave?"

"We can't leave without Scott," Matt said.

"Scott?" Richard sighed. "Do you know, I'd forgotten all about him." He shook his head. "Even if you could reach him, do you really think he'd want to come? And what about Jamie and Pedro? Maybe we should try to find them."

There was a movement at the cabin entrance and one of the American officers appeared, dressed in a greatcoat and cap. For a moment, Richard struggled to remember his name. Of course ... Greyson. That was it. With his straw-coloured hair and upturned nose he looked like he should still be in college. He had driven in with Wolf Squadron and had been in the thick of the fighting but it seemed that he hadn't been hurt.

"Good evening," he said. "I'm sorry to break in. But Commander Cain very much wants to see you. Something's happened that you should know about. He asked if you would accompany me back to command HQ."

Command HQ. That was just another name for the big tent. Richard glanced at Matt wearily, wondering if he would want to go out in the cold again. They'd all had more than enough of Commander David Cain. But Matt was already getting to his feet, reaching for his weatherproofs that he had taken off when he came in. Scarlett did the same. Lohan shook his head, an ugly look on his face, but he wasn't going to be left behind on his own. He muttered something in Mandarin and dragged on his jacket.

The four of them followed Greyson out of the plane and back across the ice shelf. Even now, the doctors were still working. Matt saw movement behind some of the tents and he could smell blood and antiseptic in the air. Two stretcher-bearers walked past, carrying a body covered in a sheet. He glimpsed a hand hanging down streaked with blood. From somewhere, they heard a man groaning. Outside one of the wooden shacks, a group of uniformed soldiers stood together, sucking on cigarettes, the smoke and their own misting breath indistinguishable from one another. They glanced at Matt as he went by but said nothing. They were probably waiting for orders, even if they didn't fully trust the people who were giving them. Their eyes were haunted. None of them was speaking.

Eight officers were waiting for Matt and the others inside the tent. Cain was one of them and Matt recognized most of the others. The Russian, Shubniakov, and the Argentinian, Sabato, had both died. But some of the other military men who had attended the morning briefing were there. The British commander, Johnson, was supporting himself on a crutch. Others were bandaged. Almost nobody from the day's assault had escaped completely unscathed. The mood in the tent was quiet and subdued. It was as if they all knew that they were responsible for what had happened but none of them wanted to blame themselves.

There was a stranger sitting in a chair, the centre of attention. He was West African, muscular, dressed in rags with a gash in the side of his head and dried blood running all the way down his cheek. He had short hair, in dreadlocks, and a tattoo of some sort of animal around his neck. He had recently been in shackles. His wrists were raw and there was more blood on his arms. He looked up quickly as Matt came in. His eyes were large and staring. Matt saw a spark of hope and yet, he thought, at the same time, fear.

"What's happening?" Richard asked.

David Cain stepped forward. Something had gone out of him since he had made his speech that morning. There was a waxy quality to his face, a sense that he was only holding himself together, being himself, with an effort. And the men around him knew it too. They were uneasy in his presence. They probably weren't even aware they were doing it but they were avoiding each other's eyes.

"We took this man prisoner," Cain said. "That is, he came back with our forces after the attack. It's not clear how he made it across the ice before it cracked but the point is he came here deliberately, of his own free will. He says his name is Omar and he's originally from Senegal. He was working for the Nightrise Corporation in New York and they brought him down here. He says he's a Christian and that he has no loyalty to the Old Ones. He fought with them because he had no choice but he took the first opportunity he could to desert. According to Omar, a lot of the people in the fortress wanted to do the same but they're too afraid."

"What does he want?" Matt asked.

"He wants to talk to you."

"I bring you a message," Omar said. "It comes from a friend of yours. He told me to find you. His name is Scott."

"Scott!" Scarlett muttered the single word.

"That's right." The commander was holding a scrap of paper. He turned it in his hands as if unwilling to part with it. "Scott wants to meet with you. At least, that's what he says."

He handed the note to Matt, who unfolded it. There was a brief message, handwritten presumably by Scott, although Matt had never seen his writing before. He read it out loud:

"Matt – I hope this reaches you. I've made a bad mistake. I know that now. But if it's not too late, if you'll trust me, we can beat the Old Ones. I've learnt things about this place and I know its weaknesses. Will you at least meet with me and let me explain? There's a place called Skua Bay, about a kilometre down the coast. I'll be there alone at midnight tonight. Come alone ... just you and me. We can work this out, I promise you, and we can win. Whatever you may think, I'm still one of the Five. Scott."

Matt lowered the page.

"It's a trap," Richard said. His voice was heavy.

"I agree," Scarlett said. "Why would Scott want to meet with you now? If he really wanted to talk to you, he could have come to the dreamworld. Or he could have escaped himself. He didn't need to send a note."

"We've interrogated the prisoner," Cain muttered. "There may be a little more he can add."

"I spoke to Scott!" Omar had a high-pitched, nervous voice. "He is very scared. The Old Ones watch him all the time. This place that he speaks of, Skua Bay, it is safe. It is near to your ships, away from the fort. He will be alone. You will be alone. You will see that. Scott is your friend. He wants to help you."

There was a brief silence. Then Lohan stepped forward. "Give me five minutes alone with this man," he said. "Give me fire and give me a knife. I will tell you very quickly if he is lying to us. But let me say right now that I do not believe a word of this. They want Matt. That is all they want. And this is their way to draw him in."

"We're not going to torture him," Matt said. He was still holding the note, weighing it in his hand. He approached Omar. "You saw Scott?"

"Yes."

"Describe him to me."

"He is thin with dark hair. Pale skin. Brown eyes. He told me to say something when we met, so that you would know it was really him."

"And what was that?"

"He said that he was sorry about Professor Chambers. He made a mistake and he knows you were angry with him."

Both Matt and Richard knew what Omar was talking about. Scott had blamed himself for the death of the professor at her home in Nazca. Nobody else in the fortress could have known about that. At the very least it proved that the message really must have come from Scott.

But then Richard put into words what both of them were thinking. "It could still be a trap," he said. "If Scott's working with the Old Ones, they could be using him to get at you."

Matt glanced at Greyson, the man who had collected him. "Do you know Skua Bay?" he asked.

"Yes. It's where he says. About a kilometre to the west."

"Could you drop me there?"

"Sure. We could take you down there on a Zodiac."

"Wait a minute!" Richard cut in. "You're not seriously thinking of taking Scott up on his little invitation, are you? That's crazy! Think about it for just one minute. What Scarlett said is right. If Scott really wanted to, he could just walk out of the fortress and see you. He could use his powers. Can't he control people's minds? He could get one of the shape-changers to give him a lift! Or the dreamworld! Scott was turning bad even when we were in Peru. I'm sorry to say it, but it's true. You can't trust him, Matt. The Old Ones are looking for you. This is a trick."

Matt turned to Cain. "What do you think, Commander?"

Cain shrugged. "I don't know, Matthew," he said. "I suppose I tend to agree with Mr Cole. The whole thing seems more than a little suspicious. But at the same time, I will add this." He paused. "We've been beaten. I suppose I need to shoulder most of the blame but today was a disaster. We have only half the men we started out with. Our aerial forces have been shown to be useless. Right now I would say that the future of the world hangs by a thread.

"So what does that mean? It means that if there's even a whisker of a chance that this man is telling the truth and that Scott can help us, we don't have any choice but to go for it. God knows, I realize I've lost the right to advise you. But that's what I think."

Matt nodded. "I agree."

Richard went over to him. "Don't do it, Matt," he pleaded.

"There is no other way," Matt said. "You know that, Richard. The Five have to come together. If we're separated, we have no choice at all."

"But you're nowhere near each other," Richard said. "You and Scarlett are here. Pedro is in Italy. Jamie is in England. And the doors are closed. You're not going to come together any time soon." He took a breath, then continued more slowly. "We've lost, Matt. The attack today was a monumental gamble and it didn't pay off. The best thing right now would be to get out of this hellish place as soon as we can. Regroup somewhere else. Live to fight another day."

Everyone turned to Matt, waiting for him to answer.

"You're right, Richard," he admitted. There was a tiredness in his voice that Richard had never heard before. "Everything has gone wrong. But that's why I've got to do this. If we run away and hide, what then? We're on a dying planet. The Old Ones have ruined everything." He glanced one last time at the letter. "Right now, this is the only hope we have left. Scott may be lying, in which case it's all over. They've won. But you know him. Do you really think he would deliver me to them? Isn't there just a tiny chance that he has changed his mind and wants to help? I don't think we can ignore him. I think I have to hear what he has to say."

"No," Scarlett said. There were tears in her eyes. "You can't go, Matt. What if he's lying? What if they manage to capture you?"

"Fight another day," Lohan said. "Do not go to this place. Do not put yourself in the lion's den."

Cain was the only person in the tent who seemed to think differently. "We can give you full support," he said. "You can stay in radio contact the whole time and I can have a rapid response team standing by in skimmers."

"I think it's worth a chance," Matt said. He had decided. "I'm going."

Scarlett groaned and Lohan looked away but Matt ignored them. Cain walked over to the table and pulled out a map showing the coastline around Oblivion. The man called Omar sat in his chair, his expression blank.

"Wait a minute," Richard said. He turned to Matt. "I don't understand why you're making this decision but I'm not going to let you go there alone. If you're heading off to this Skua Bay or whatever it's called, I'm coming with you."

"Richard..."

"No. There's no argument. I started this adventure with you and I'm going to finish it with you, however it turns out."

"Scott wanted me to come alone."

"Scott knows me. If he sees me with you, he's not going to be surprised. But just for once I'm putting my foot down, Matt. Either you let me come with you or you don't go at all."

"Then we'll go together," Matt said, and at that moment Richard got the impression that he had known it would happen this way all along and that he had actually been waiting for him to make his stand. He already knew that Matt had changed. But right then he felt as if the two of them were complete strangers. It was as if everything they had been through together had somehow been left behind.

"I'm going to assign Lieutenant Greyson to ferry you to the beach," Cain said. "If you want to be there by midnight, you should leave now. It's going to take a while to get down the cliff and onto the Zodiac."

Matt nodded. Richard was standing next to him, silent and pale. Scarlett looked shocked.

"OK," Matt said. "Let's go."

FIFTY-ONE

The Zodiac was a high-performance Rigid Inflatable Boat, or RIB, made of black rubber with a powerful 110 horsepower engine. It was waiting for Matt and Richard as they climbed down to the beach, following the intricate network of paths and staircases that had been cut into the side of the ice cliff. A handful of marines were waiting for them at the bottom. The beach was a thin strip of black shingle carried there by the movement of the glacier. The water was calm tonight, the waves lapping tamely at their feet.

They climbed in and set off, Matt sitting at the front, Richard in the middle, Lieutenant Greyson standing at the back. It was a quarter to twelve but the sun was still out behind the cloud, hovering somewhere over the horizon, and the surface of the water was more steel-like than ever. As Richard looked up towards the ice field of Oblivion, it occurred to him, almost for the first time, that he was in one of the most extraordinary places on earth: Antarctica. Travellers – explorers – had been drawn here for hundreds of years, losing themselves in the endless reaches of this vast, unspoilt wilderness. Even the light was like nothing he had seen before. And yet he looked on it with dread. He hated being here and would rather have been anywhere else.

They motored gently between two icebergs; huge, irregular blocks drifting silently, without purpose. In the distance, Richard could see the frigate, lying at anchor, surrounded by a ragtag collection of vessels that seemed to cling together as if afraid of the water around them. It was intensely cold. Although there was no wind, he could feel the chill cutting into him, reaching to his very bones. Apart from the splutter of the engine, everything was silent. He looked for any sign of wildlife – even a single bird – but nothing appeared.

"There it is," Greyson muttered. "Straight ahead of us now..."

The young lieutenant was pointing at a small cove, an indentation on the edge of the water with solid black rock behind. The cliff face loomed high above them and Richard guessed that it was in some way connected to the mountains that surrounded the Old Ones' fortress at the far end of Oblivion. As the Zodiac headed towards land, he looked out for Scott but there was no sign of him. It occurred to him that Scott might have been telling the truth all along. He could have been captured as he tried to leave the fortress. In a way that would be for the best. They could turn round and leave.

He looked back. There was no sign of the back-up that Cain had promised either, but Richard was confident that there were men with binoculars watching them as they made their progress towards the shore. Cain had said it would take just two minutes for the skimmers to reach the cove if they needed help.

The Zodiac hit the beach, the rubber grinding against the shingle. Greyson cut the engine and lifted the propeller clear. They sat there for a few seconds in complete silence. This was a bad idea. Richard was quite certain of it. There was a sick feeling in his stomach. But it was already too late. They had arrived.

The two of them climbed out and stood once again on land. Richard hadn't told Matt but in the end he had brought a gun with him. It was concealed in his jacket pocket. He reached down and felt the weight of it through the material. He knew that it was ridiculous, small and insignificant compared with the danger that was immense and all around them. But it still gave him a certain comfort.

And it wasn't the only weapon he had brought.

Greyson was crouching at the back of the Zodiac, watching them. "Are you OK?" he asked.

"Yeah. Sure," Richard muttered.

"There's no one around. The beach is empty. Your friend doesn't seem to be here either."

"He'll come," Matt said.

"OK. Well, good luck to you." He threw the engine into reverse and the Zodiac backed out into the ocean, then spun round and drove away.

They were alone.

"I know it's a bit late, but are you sure you want to go through with this?" Richard asked.

"Much too late," Matt said. He took a step forward and his foot came down on a piece of loose shingle. He lost his balance and put a hand out to steady himself, holding onto Richard's arm. It was a moment Richard would never forget. "It's all going to work out in the end, Richard. Remember that. But I'm glad you're with me. I wouldn't have wanted to be here with anyone else. I know I can trust you. When the time comes, you'll do what's right."

What did he mean by that? But there was no time.

Scott had appeared.

He had been standing well back in the shadows, a solitary figure wearing a black padded jacket with a fur collar. It was impossible to say how he had got here but he was already walking towards them, his feet crunching on the shingle. Richard felt a mixture of emotions seeing him. How long had it been since they had all been together? He remembered the garden at Nazca after the death of Professor Chambers. Scott had stormed off angrily, believing they were all against him. He had always been the outsider, identical to his brother in appearance but different in every other way. Matt had had his doubts about him even then. But none of them could have guessed that he would change sides and join the Old Ones.

So what had changed his mind and brought him here tonight? Richard glanced over his shoulder and saw that the Zodiac was already far away, heading back towards the boats. As Scott drew nearer, Richard became increasingly uneasy. This was a grim, lonely place. Everything about it – the beach, the cliff face, the sea – seemed harsh and inhospitable. If Scott really had been able to escape from the fortress, why hadn't he simply walked into the camp?

Scott had come about halfway across the beach but now he stopped, waiting for them to climb up to him. Matt and Richard moved away from the water's edge, every step taking them further away from safety. At last they were face-to-face.

"Hello, Scott," Matt said.

"Hi, Matt." Scott nodded in the direction of Richard. "I thought I told you to come alone."

"You know Richard. I didn't think you'd mind if he came along."

"Of course I don't mind. I'm glad he came." Scott tried to smile. "It's good to see you again, Richard."

"It's good to see you, Scott." Richard tried to sound as if he meant it.

"So here we are again." Scott made a gesture. He was wearing gloves. All his clothes looked brand new and expensive.

"You said you could help us," Matt said.

"That's right, Matt. That's what I said."

At that moment, Richard knew with absolute certainty that they shouldn't have come. The boy who was talking wasn't the Scott they had known. He seemed to have aged ten years – not in appearance but in the way he stood there, the way he talked. Skua Bay was a cold, arid place but it suited him well. Scott had been touched by evil and it had contaminated him. The boy he had once been was already dead.

"How many people were there camped out on the ice?" Scott went on. "Two thousand? Three? I guess quite a lot of them died this morning. What a waste of time that was! Who persuaded them that they had the slightest chance of winning the battle? I hope it wasn't you, Matt. Because if it was, you have an awful lot of blood on your hands."

Matt didn't reply.

"You do realize that the whole lot of them could have been killed," Scott went on. "By the way, that was a neat trick you pulled, breaking the ice. That was you, I suppose?"

"Yes."

"It still wouldn't have stopped them. The Old Ones could have jumped right over if they'd wanted, and kept coming. In fact, right now they could be out there, destroying the boats one by one. But that's not going to happen. That's the good news, Matt. Nobody else has to die."

"And why is that, Scott?" Matt asked.

"Because that's not what they want. What's the point of ruling the world if there's nobody left in it? They didn't set up Oblivion and all the rest of it because they wanted to fight the World Army. They set it up because they wanted you."

"And how are they going to get me?"

"They already have."

The words could have been a signal. At that moment the beach came alive, suddenly exploding out and taking shape around them. They had been there all along, in front of their eyes. They had seen them without seeing them. Flies, in their millions. The entire cliff face peeled away. It wasn't black at all. It was white.

The whole surface, every last inch, had been made up of more flies, clinging to the snow. Richard hardly dared to breathe. The air darkened as the insects poured down on them, cutting off the sea and the sky, blocking out the light.

Scott had betrayed them after all. Richard saw the flies beginning to take the shape of fifty men, an entire platoon. Already he was pulling out his gun. He knew it would be useless against the soldiers. Even when they were solid, a bullet would pass right through them ... he had seen as much in the battle, earlier that day. But they weren't his target. He would kill Scott for what he had done. It didn't matter that he was a Gatekeeper. He deserved to die.

You can't shoot me, Richard. You can't move.

Scott hadn't spoken the words. He had thought them. Richard felt him inside his head and instantly his arm came to a halt with the gun only half-raised, still pointing at the ground. He tried to step forward but his legs wouldn't obey him. He couldn't even shout. He was locked into place, forced to watch the trap close in.

Fifty metres out at sea, Lieutenant Greyson saw the ambush and swung the Zodiac round, hitting the throttle. At the same time, he shouted into his radio transmitter. "Mayday! Mayday!"

Five rapid-response skimmers were already being launched, just as Cain had promised. But the Old Ones had been prepared for this too. In an instant, a creature appeared, plummeting out of the sky. It was a bird – but not one that belonged in this part of the world and it was a hundred sizes too big. Black feathers, a white collar around its neck, a curving beak ... the bird was a South American condor. It swooped down over the Zodiac. One moment Greyson was there, leaning forward with his hand on the outboard motor, the next he had gone and the Zodiac was spinning in circles with nobody to guide it. It was impossible to say if he had been knocked into the sea or devoured. The condor let out an ear-splitting screech and soared back into the clouds. The other marines held back, knowing that if they tried to cross the water they would only die.

Matt was still standing opposite Scott, not moving as the soldiers formed. There was very little time left. Once they had solidified, they would take him.

"I'm sorry, Matt," Scott said. "They told me what to do. I didn't have any choice."

"You don't have to blame yourself," Matt said. "I knew you were going to betray me."

"You couldn't have known." Scott stared at Matt, suddenly angry. The soldiers were forming a circle around the two boys, arms and legs, swords and shields all defining themselves, being drawn out of the black haze. "If you knew, why did you come?"

"I told you in the dreamworld. We all have a part to play. This is yours."

"To betray you?"

"Yes."

The soldiers were ready. Matt wasn't even trying to use his power. He simply stood there as they closed in.

"It was never my role to save the world," Matt said.

"Then whose was it?"

"Yours."

The nearest soldiers fell on Matt and on Richard, clubbing them down with shields that were as hard as steel. A kilometre away at sea, the commanders and marines watched helplessly through binoculars as the drama was played out, knowing there was nothing they could do.

Matt was stretched out on the shingle, unconscious. Richard was next to him. The fly-soldiers picked them up by their feet and dragged them away, disappearing in the haze. Scott stood utterly still, watching them go. He felt sick. He had known what he was doing but he had never thought it would be as bad as this.

"I knew you were going to betray me..."

Matt had known but he had still come.

The waves rolled in, breaking against the shoreline. Scott stood there for a long time, deep in thought. Then, finally, he sighed and, with heavy steps, set off back towards the fortress.

FIFTY-TWO

The cell was like an animal's lair, deep underground and with no window, no electric light. It would have been pitch-dark but for the strange blue glow that hung in the air. The floor was covered with straw. Three of the walls were natural rock. The fourth contained a solid metal plate, which must have been the door but which seemed to have been welded into place.

Richard Cole had woken up here and had found himself alone. That was his first and his greatest fear. Scott had betrayed them after all and they had taken Matt. What were they doing with him? For the first time since this whole adventure had begun, Richard felt a sense of grief and hopelessness that threatened to tear him apart. He had flown all the way from Dubai, halfway round the world, to come to this evil place ... and to what end? He had simply delivered Matt into the hands of the Old Ones. The two of them should never have gone to the meeting at Skua Bay. They should never have come to Antarctica at all.

Slowly, his thoughts turned to his own situation. He hadn't been killed yet. The fly-soldiers had taken him alive. Could it be that they needed him for something? Or was this to be his end? As far as he could tell, he had been here for about twelve hours and nobody had brought him food or water. Maybe he had been sealed in here. This was his tomb and he had simply been left here to die. When he had first opened his eyes, he had slammed the heels of his hands against the door, shouting for attention. He had soon given up. Even if anyone could hear him, they weren't going to come. And he could hear nothing. He had to fight against the sudden panic; the knowledge that he had been buried alive.

Why had Matt insisted on meeting Scott? It was obvious that this was going to happen. Lying on the straw, Richard felt a wave of fury that made him want to scream. How could Matt have been so stupid? How could *he* have been so stupid to let him have his way? Why hadn't anyone – Cain, Lohan or Scarlett – done more to stop them? The questions were futile but they still tormented him. Once again he went over to the door and kicked out at it, shouting, making as much noise as he could.

Nobody came.

Richard forced himself to calm down. There was a danger he could lose his mind in here and then he would be no use to anybody. Perhaps that was what the Old Ones intended. But even now, even when everything had gone so wrong, he still had one tiny spark of hope. He had been aware of it the moment he had opened his eyes.

They had searched him when they had brought him here. They had taken the gun that he had been carrying. But, as impossible as it seemed, they had overlooked the other weapon he had brought, the knife that the Incas had given him – the gold *tumi*. It was still tucked into his belt, underneath his jacket, where he had been carrying it. He drew it out now and turned it over in his hands, examining his own reflection in the blade. It was a beautiful thing, carved with an Inca deity and a scattering of semi-precious stones inlaid in the hilt. And of course it was no accident that neither the fly-soldiers nor the prison guards had managed to find it. That was the knife's power. It could never be found. It seemed so long ago since the Incas had given it to him. And yet he had it still. He remembered glimpsing Atoc as they launched the attack on the ice. The two of them hadn't spoken but perhaps Atoc had been there for a reason, to remind Richard of what he had been given. One thing was certain. Richard needed the knife more than ever.

The knife was all he had left. Even as he slid it back into place, he knew that his sanity depended on it. The Old Ones might have written him off but in fact they had made their first mistake – and that told him they weren't quite as powerful as they thought. Sooner or later, someone would come into the cell and when they did, they would be in for a surprise. Richard would go down fighting. He would feel better if he took one or two of them with him.

And if they didn't come, if they left him to rot, the knife would give him a swifter end than the one they had planned. There was some comfort in that thought too.

Richard sat with his legs stretched out, watching the door. He wasn't beaten yet. He was certain his moment would come.

Sitting behind his desk on the US *Pole Star*, Commander David Cain thought about his family, his career, his country and his religion ... anything to stop him thinking about the events of the last twenty-four hours. He was on his own, seated in a room which looked more like a suite in a smart hotel than a cabin on a United States aircraft carrier. The walls were covered in green paper, the lights and furniture were antique. The portholes were concealed behind plush red velvet curtains that hung from the ceiling to the floor. A door led to a comfortably sized bedroom. The commander even had a private bathroom. But for the constant rocking movement beneath his feet, it would have been easy for him to forget that he was at sea.

He shouldn't have come to Antarctica. At the time, based in Pensacola, Florida, he had been a man on a mission – saving not just his country but the world. It didn't matter that he had received no official orders. As far as he could tell, there had been nobody left in a position to give them. While his ship had been idly docked there, a quarter of his men had abandoned ship, simply getting up and going home. With every day that passed, more had followed. The United States of America was falling apart, driven by catastrophic food shortages and riots. The politicians had spent years blaming each other but doing nothing and in the end they had simply disappeared, no longer relevant. It was men like David Cain who had to take command. At least, that was what he had persuaded himself on the day he had lifted anchor and made his way south. Now he wasn't so sure.

He hadn't been prepared – but then nothing on this earth could have prepared him for what he had found at Oblivion. The strange thing was that Cain didn't think he had made any mistakes. He had launched an attack that had lost almost half his army. He had met the one person who might have helped him – the leader of the Gatekeepers – and had delivered him straight into a trap. But neither of these things had been his fault – that is to say, anyone else would have done the same. He was convinced of that. The Old Ones were more powerful than anyone could have guessed. David Cain had been going to church for fifty years, but it was only now that he had actually learnt what the Devil really was.

There was a knock at the door.

"Come!" he called out.

The door opened and three men walked in. One was a fairly junior officer on the *Pole Star*, an ensign by the name of Paxton. The other two were dressed in the dark blue uniforms of the Royal Navy – a captain and a sub lieutenant. The captain, Johnson, had been hurt in the fighting. He was still leaning on a crutch.

"Gentlemen…?" Cain came out from behind his desk. There was no small talk, no pleasantries between them. They were all exhausted. There was nothing left to say.

"We're leaving, Commander," Johnson said. "There doesn't

seem to be any point in staying here, so I've come to say goodbye."

"I understand that, Captain." Cain extended a hand. "It's been a privilege serving with you."

"There is just one thing before we go," Johnson went on. "We've managed to effect repairs on board the *Percival*. My men have been working 24/7 and they've done a terrific job. What it boils down to is that we now have limited nuclear capability restored to us."

"You can fire your missiles?

"We can deploy five Trident missiles, sir, with twelve nuclear warheads. We could hit the fortress of the Old Ones in a little under six hours. There are still a few people camped out on the ice … mainly the medical staff and their patients. But it would be possible to order an immediate evacuation. The *Percival*, the *Pole Star*, the *Pintada* and the *Duc d'Orléans* can easily cope with the extra passengers. Of course, there are a few casualties who are too sick to be moved…"

"And there's Matthew Freeman," Cain added.

"If the Old Ones have him, my view is he's probably dead," Johnson said. He paused. "There's every chance that a nuclear strike will do no good. After all, as it turned out, your aircraft were ineffective. But we're leaving here anyway and I thought we might as well leave a calling card. And you never know. We'll vaporize the mountains and melt the entire ice shelf. Even the Old Ones may not be able to survive that."

"Why are you telling me this, Captain?" Cain asked.

"You're still in command of this operation, sir. I don't think I'm telling you. I think I'm requesting your authorization."

Cain considered. The last two decisions he had made had both had disastrous consequences. And here he was, facing a crisis for the third time in a single day. The nuclear option. If Matt Freeman was still alive, he would certainly die. And the journalist with him.

The girl, Scarlett Adams, was still on the ice. Would she even agree to withdraw while the other Gatekeeper was held captive? And then there were the wounded to consider, the survivors. Even if all the ships left immediately, not all of them would get far enough away…

But they had nothing left.

This was it.

"We'll evacuate Oblivion as quickly as we can," Cain said. "As to the timing of the missile launch, that's entirely up to you. But if you want my authorization, you have it, Captain. Let's give it one last shot and see if we can't send the Old Ones back to hell."

"Everyone is leaving," Lohan said.

"I've seen."

Scarlett had been numb with shock and disbelief ever since she had heard that Matt had been captured. She was sitting with her legs curled up and half-covered by a blanket in the upper cabin of the airbus. The temperature inside the plane had dropped several degrees but even if she could have done anything about it, she no longer cared. For the last few minutes her face had been pressed against the window, watching the last passengers make their way across the ice shelf before climbing down to the waiting ships. She still found it hard to accept that everything could have gone so wrong. When she had seen Matt in the dreamworld, it had all seemed so easy. The five of them would come together at Oblivion. They would form a gate. The Old Ones would be banished. End of story.

Except that must have been a different story. Scott really had turned against them and Matt had been taken … for a second time. He and Scarlett had been prisoners together in Hong Kong but then it had been different. They had known all along that Lohan and his men were on the way to get them out. This time there was no one. Richard, who had been such a friend to her in

Egypt and Dubai, had also been captured and he was probably dead. Apart from the bodies, buried underneath a thin coating of snow, the ice shelf would soon be empty. Nobody cared about the survivors any more. Despite its grand name, the World Army was scurrying away like a dog with its tail between its legs.

"We should go," Lohan said.

"What do you mean?" Scarlett stared at him.

"We can't fly out of here, even if we had enough fuel. But there's plenty of room on the boats. If we can get to Australia..."

"I'm not leaving here, Lohan," Scarlett said. "Not without Matt."

"Matt is dead."

"He isn't."

"How can you know?"

Very briefly, Scarlett hated Lohan for the way he had asked that. He reminded her of a sulky child. "I can't explain it to you," she said. "He's one of the Gatekeepers. So am I. If he had been killed, I think I'd know."

"Then maybe it's worse than that." Lohan's face was hard. "If they're keeping him alive, try to think what they might be doing to him. They're certainly not going to let you get anywhere near him. Either way he's finished. You might as well leave."

Scarlett's temper flared. "You go if you want to," she said. "It'll only be the second time you've walked out on him. You go and save your precious skin, Lohan. You can go to Australia, or what's left of it. I'm sure you'll manage to survive quite a long time before the Old Ones find you. Thanks for your help. It was great knowing you."

There was a long silence. Lohan seemed to be examining the floor in front of him. Then he looked up. "Matt told you about Serra Morte."

"Yes."

"It's not how you think. I wasn't going to leave him behind."

"Really?" Scarlett didn't hide her contempt. She looked out of the window again. There were fewer people on the ice, the last of them moving steadily towards the edge. "Well, you're leaving him behind now. And me. You'd better hurry up and get down the cliff face. You'll miss the last boat."

"What will you do?"

"Why should you care?"

"Tell me."

Scarlett shrugged. "I'm going to find my way into the fortress."

"That's not possible." When Scarlett didn't reply, Lohan went on. "The doors are locked. The walls weren't even cracked by the air bombardment. And you saw that other trick they played. There could still be hundreds of them camped out on the ice."

"Who says I'm going in that way?" Scarlett stood up and let the blanket slide onto the floor. She was still wearing her outdoor gear. "From what I understand, Scott appeared on the beach – at Skua Bay – on his own. And the fly-soldiers dragged Matt and Richard away."

"What about it?"

"Well, unless Scott has learnt how to fly, he must have walked there. There must be a path that nobody saw, leading from the beach through the cliff face. Maybe it goes right into the fortress. I'm going to get a Zodiac and go round and find out for myself."

"That's madness, Scarlett. If there is a path, it will be guarded. And if it leads into the fortress what good will it do? You'll be walking into a death trap."

"You're right, Lohan." Scarlett pulled on her gloves. "But I'm too tired to argue with you, and anyway, I don't want to waste any more time. Thank you for helping me get out of Hong Kong. I hope you get back there and find your dad and all the rest of it. Maybe I'll see you again one day. Maybe not."

She brushed past him and took the spiral staircase down to

the lower deck. The plane door was open, a few flakes of snow spinning round outside. She climbed out and crossed the ice shelf, following the last stragglers, suddenly one of them. She took one look back at the distant fortress ... the great walls, the barbican, the four towers. In her heart, she knew that Lohan was right. She had no hope of saving Matt and if she was discovered that would probably make everything worse. But at the same time she was certain that if she simply left without trying, she would never forgive herself. The Old Ones might have defeated the world. But she wasn't going to give up and let them beat her too.

It took her an hour to reach the beach. There were officers from the various navies ferrying passengers out from the edge, many of them being lifted in on stretchers. Most of the smaller boats had already gone, motoring or sailing towards the horizon, disappearing into the Antarctic mist. Eventually she managed to find an American marine who had just pulled up in a patrol boat. There were already a dozen or more people on board and there was little space left. The water, freezing cold and silvery grey, lapped close to her feet as she waved across the shingle.

The marine saw her. "I'm with the *Pole Star*," he shouted. "Climb on board and we'll get you out of here."

"I'm not coming!" Scarlett shouted back. "I need a Zodiac."

"There are no Zodiacs! And you can't stay here, miss. We're pulling out."

"You don't understand. I'm with Matt. I have to go to Skua Bay. Please, can you help me...!"

"You have to come with me," the marine insisted. "This is my last run. If I leave you behind, you're on your own."

"Get in the boat, girl!" one of the passengers called out. It was a woman who had been hurt in the fighting. Her face was streaked with blood and she was shivering. Scarlett was keeping them waiting.

"Where can I find a Zodiac?" she cried.

"You can't. Are you coming?"

"No."

"Then – good luck!" The marine pressed down on the throttle. The water foamed behind the boat and then it was away, rapidly dwindling into the distance.

Scarlett looked around her. In a few minutes, she would be alone on the beach. Already, the cliff face, with its twisting ice columns and pathways, was empty. With a feeling of complete misery, she realized that Lohan had been right. For all her fine words, there was nothing she could do. There were no spare boats. If she tried to swim to Skua Bay, she would freeze to death before she had completed a dozen strokes. She couldn't walk across the ice shelf. She had no choice but to abandon Matt. She couldn't help him. It was time to go.

And then she saw a boat – a Zodiac – skimming across the surface towards her. It had appeared from nowhere and, unlike all the other vessels, it was empty, with just a single driver hunched over the outboard motor. She couldn't recognize him – like everyone else, he was wrapped up in weatherproof clothes – but as he pulled in he looked up and she saw (she had already guessed … at least, she had hoped she had guessed) that it was Lohan. He must have found a faster way down the cliff, somehow arriving well ahead of her. She had no idea where he had got the Zodiac from. Knowing Lohan, it was probably better not to ask.

He brought the boat up onto the shingle and for a moment the two of them stood facing each other.

"I have behaved dishonourably," he said. "Always, from the earliest age, it was my father's teaching that I should consider myself and my own safety to be of paramount importance. But that is not the same thing as acting like a coward. I tried to leave Matt at Serra Morte. It was a bad thing to do. And I almost did the same thing with you today. I will take you to Skua Bay and we will go together to the fortress. I am certain we will die there. But better that than to die like a rat, hiding in Australia."

"Thank you, Lohan," Scarlett said. "I was about to give up. I didn't think there was any way."

"We must hurry. I think we have very little time."

Scarlett climbed into the Zodiac and the two of them pulled away.

Scott was ashamed of himself.

No. It was worse than that. He felt himself being sucked into a pool of guilt and self-hatred like nothing he'd ever known. He remembered the day following the death of his foster father. Scott had blamed himself – and rightly – for the man's death. He had actually ordered him to kill himself and he had been horrified and sickened by what he had done. It was true that Ed had been an alcoholic, violent and abusive, but even so Scott hadn't meant to do him harm. But in the end he had lived through it. Part of him had even been glad that things had turned out the way they did.

This was different. He must have been mad, throwing in his lot with the Old Ones. He thought of Pedro in the Castel Nuovo. He saw now that he had taken out all his anger on the Peruvian boy just because the two of them had been left behind in Peru. Pedro was smaller and weaker than him but he had never complained, he had never shown any fear. In his own way, he had tried to help. It was true that Jonas Mortlake had played tricks on Scott's mind, using drugs, magic, hallucinations to break down his defences. But he had stood back and cold-bloodedly decided that Pedro could have one of his fingers broken simply so that he, Scott, could have a decent night's sleep.

And what he had done with Matt had been far, far worse. Matt was the first of the Gatekeepers, their leader. He was also the only one of them who had stood, single-handed, against Chaos. He had become their target and Scott had delivered him to them. How could he have done that? What would Jamie say? When Jonas had told him what he had to do, Scott hadn't even tried to argue. He hadn't wanted to lose what he had here. A comfortable room. Warmth. A sense of safety. And what would they have done to him if he had turned against them? He had been too scared even to think about it.

But once he had handed Matt over, from the moment he had seen him taken by the fly-soldiers, Scott had begun to wonder exactly what he had gained. It was true that he was still alive. But the fortress, his suite of rooms, the food he was given, even the people around him, seemed to be changing. It was like a broken television with a flickering image. One moment there would be a fire blazing in the hearth. Then it would go out and he would realize that he was freezing and that the walls around him were dripping with some sort of oil or slime. He had spent the night tucked under the fur covers on his bed only to wake up and see – for just a few seconds – that they were filthy and matted in blood. Just a few minutes ago, he had been eating his lunch, a steak cooked specially for him. But even as he raised the fork to his mouth, the meat had changed and suddenly it was cold and green and crawling with maggots. It had changed back again just before he swallowed it.

And everything stank. It was a smell like nothing Scott had ever encountered ... dead and rotting and utterly filthy. He wanted to be sick all the time. It was like having some horrible disease inside his nostrils, reaching all the way to his lungs.

The Old Ones were tricking him just as they had done with the World Army by making it appear that the fortress had been destroyed. They had lied to him. He knew that now. And Matt had never doubted what would happen if he came to Skua Bay. Scott thought back to their last moments together. He hadn't even tried to fight back as the fly-soldiers closed in. He had been expecting them.

"It was never my role to save the world."

"Then whose was it?"

"Yours."

Scott hadn't done anything. His brother, Jamie, had gone with Matt to London and to Hong Kong. He had always thought of Jamie as the younger of the two of them – but it was Jamie who had escaped from prison, who had travelled back in time and fought against the Old Ones ten thousand years ago. For his part, Scott had just allowed himself to be used. He wondered what was happening to Matt right now. He had a good idea. Almost everyone in the fortress had been summoned into the conference hall that he had visited in the opposite tower. For the last six hours, Scott had been hearing laughter, shouting applause. Part of him wanted to go there and see for himself. But he knew that he couldn't ... that if he did, he would never sleep again.

Jamie.

The thought came to him quite suddenly. He didn't care any more if he lived or died but the one last thing that he wanted was to see his brother again. He and Jamie had been through so much together, in Salt Lake City, in Carson City, in Reno. Yet somehow they had survived. More than that. They had often been happy together, before the agents of Nightrise had come searching for them. Scott had looked after Jamie. That had been his role in life. And they had always said that no matter what happened, the two of them would never be apart.

Right now, there were thousands of kilometres between them. Jamie was in London, outside the church of St Meredith's. Matt had warned him it would turn out this way when they had all met outside the library, in the dreamworld. But the twenty-five doors, their passageways across the world, were locked. Scott remembered the cave he had seen – at the back of the courtyard. The twenty-fifth doorway. There was a chain running across it and two ivory hands clasped together in a lock. The chairman of Nightrise had warned him that if he touched the chain, it would kill him.

But what did that matter? If he could just separate the hands, open the door, then he would go to London, to Jamie. The two of them would be together again. They might only have a few minutes. Maybe less. But it would be worth it, wouldn't it?

Scott had been stretched out on his bed, alone in his room. Looking up, he saw that the ceiling was full of cobwebs. Spiders were crawling all around him. The pillows behind his head seemed to have been whipped away and replaced with filthy straw. He himself was covered in dirt. He looked as if he had been lying in his own grave.

Jamie.

It was the only thought in his mind. With something between a sob and a grunt of determination, Scott rolled off the bed and went out to do whatever was necessary to see his brother one last time.

Scarlett was right.

They discovered it soon after they had landed. Although the cliffs in front of them seemed to be solid, there was actually a crack, a tiny fissure just wide enough for two people to squeeze through. It had been hidden from the sea because of a fold in the rock, but once they had walked to the very top of the beach, they were able to see into it. There was a path snaking into the distance and the footprints the fly-soldiers had made were still visible in the snow. The walls rose up on either side, so close that they seemed to touch, blocking out the light and any sign of the sky. It was not so much a pathway as a tunnel. They had no idea how far it went but there was no reason why it shouldn't open out in the fortress itself.

"There'll be guards," Lohan whispered.

"I can deal with that," Scarlett said.

They continued forward, leaving the beach and the Zodiac behind. The thick layer of snow absorbed the sound of their feet and they didn't speak a word to each other. Both of them were fairly certain that they were going to die. In a way, with millions of tonnes of stone pressing down on them, they felt they were already dead.

Shape-changers had been positioned on rocky ledges above them, standing watch over the passageway just as Lohan had warned. It was a miserable posting. They were out on their own, in the freezing cold. They carried rusting spears in their human hands and looked about them with pig, snake and falcon eyes.

But even as they stood there, a strange fog sprang up, filling the crevice beneath them. The fog helped to muffle any sound. And so they saw and heard nothing, quite unaware of the two figures creeping past, following the twisty path far below.

FIFTY-THREE

LONDON

Jamie Tyler woke up very suddenly, with the knowledge – even before he opened his eyes – that something terrible had happened.

Matt had said he would send him a signal and it had come, as he had expected, from the dreamworld. But the strange thing was that, this time, Jamie had no memory of being there. For once there had been no library or hill, no island or sea. Indeed, he couldn't even remember seeing Matt and had no idea exactly what he had said. But as he opened his eyes and took in his surroundings, the echo of Matt's voice was still there and Jamie knew that he had to move at once, that there couldn't be a minute's delay.

Quickly, he threw back the covers and got to his feet. He had no need to dress – he slept in his clothes. Holly was stretched out on the mattress on the other side of the room with its striped wallpaper, carpet and fireplace. Her hair, tangled and dirty, was sprawled over the pillow. He shook her awake and left the room, searching for the Traveller and his brother, who slept next door. In fact, they were already out of bed. Jamie wasn't surprised. The two of them got up well before sunrise every day.

"What is it?" Will Fletcher asked. He had seen the look on Jamie's face and knew at once that something had changed.

"We have to go," Jamie said.

"You've seen Matt?"

"No. But I heard him." He tried to explain what had happened. "He didn't say anything but I think he's been hurt and he wants me to come. That's all I can tell you. We have to move right away."

Graham and Will exchanged a glance but they didn't argue. They had served the Nexus for almost ten years and the Nexus existed only to help the Gatekeepers. The Traveller might have been in charge when they were in the village and on board the *Lady Jane*, but it was inconceivable that he would question anything Jamie said here in London. By the time Holly appeared in the doorway, rubbing her eyes, he was already moving past her, on his way downstairs.

"I'll tell the others," he said. "We'll be ready in less than a minute."

"What's happening?" Holly asked.

"We're leaving."

Jamie was aware that his heart was beating more rapidly than usual and that he had left sleep far behind him. He had arrived at the end. If they could fight their way into St Meredith's, if the door finally worked, he might be in Antarctica in just a few minutes' time. He would see Scott again. And the others: Matt, Scarlett, Pedro. To be together to finally confront the Old Ones and finish them once and for all ... it was what he wanted above all else.

They couldn't leave it any longer anyway. Only the evening before, Simon – one of the men who had come with them from the survival pod – had been taking readings with the complicated equipment that had been waiting for them in the house, testing the air and the atmosphere as he did every day.

"It's suddenly got worse," he had muttered. "One more night. Maybe the morning. But we can't stay here any longer than that. By midday, we're going to have to be on our way."

Jamie didn't know what the "it" referred to. Radioactivity? Viral infection? It didn't matter. He would have stayed behind anyway. He had promised himself that he wouldn't leave until Matt contacted him, even if he became ill.

Will Fletcher had gone back into his room and when he re-emerged he was carrying the array of weapons that he had brought with him; a miniature machine gun, grenades and pistols. Dressed in his grey and brown camouflage gear, he looked like an urban soldier from a hundred news reports. Jamie and Holly followed him downstairs. The other four men were already gathered in the hall with the Traveller, clustered together in the narrow space beneath the chandelier. They looked up as Jamie descended and he knew what they were thinking. Why now? It was broad daylight, half past seven in the morning. It would have been much less dangerous if they had waited for night and the cover of darkness. For just a moment, Jamie doubted himself. Suppose he had been wrong! He could be leading them all to their death. But he remembered waking up. Matt had called him. Like everyone else, he had been given no choice.

"Jamie…?" Will checked one last time.

Jamie nodded. He had decided.

"We're going into St Meredith's," Will explained to the others. "We have to move fast. Once we step outside this door, we don't know what might hit us. We've seen the spider. There may be shape-changers. And there's always the possibility of police or other human forces. The main thing is to get Jamie into the church and through the door, which is on the right of the main aisle, close to the nave. Look out for the five-pointed star." He turned to Jamie. "Assuming we make it, do you want one of us to go through with you?"

It was something Jamie had never considered. He could take one person with him to Antarctica. That was how the doors worked. But which one of them? He knew he had to make an instant decision. It might be sensible to have an adult with him, particularly one that was fully armed. But did he have any right to ask any of them to make such a journey?

He caught the Traveller's eye and saw him nod slightly. "The Traveller," he said.

"Right." If Will was upset that he was about to be separated from his brother a second time, he didn't show it. "Graham will stay close to you the whole time and we'll keep the two of you covered. Holly—"

"I'm coming too," Holly said. She was certain that Will was going to ask her to stay behind. "I know I may not be much use but I'm not leaving Jamie. Not after all we've been through."

To her surprise, Will didn't argue. "OK. Good luck, everyone. Maybe this is going to work out all right. Graham – try not to leave it seven years this time. You'll come back as an old man." Very briefly, the two of them embraced. "And good luck to you, Jamie. I hope the others are waiting for you in Antarctica. I hope this is the end."

He took a breath. Then they went out.

ROME

The two priests were late for morning mass. They hurried across the *Cortile Borgia*, passing a cleaner who was sweeping the cobblestones. They smiled and nodded at him.

"Buongiorno, Tasso."

"Buongiorno, padri..."

The two of them disappeared round the corner. Neither of them had seen the boy, skulking in the shadows.

Pedro wondered what he must look like. He had been kept on starvation rations during his time at the Castel Nuovo and when had that ended? More than a week ago for sure but he had lost all track of time. There had been the eruption of the volcano. He had nearly drowned on the *Medusa*. The flight across Rome had been exhausting, draining all his strength. And finally, just when he thought things couldn't get any worse, there had been his encounter with Silvio Rivera … *Cardinal* Silvio Rivera. A priest who had tried to murder him.

The poison had come close to killing him. Rivera himself had been dead in minutes. Pedro knew that he had only survived because of a vase of slimy water – he could still taste the foul liquid on his lips. In the minutes that remained to him, he had done the impossible. He had used his power to save himself. Even so, the inside of his body felt not just empty but wrung dry. As he stood there, breathing in the fresh morning air, he knew he was lucky to be alive.

It sometimes seemed to Pedro that he had been alone all his life – and never more so than now. He wondered why it was that many children around the world had parents, brothers and sisters, and friends, but not him. He had been fighting from the day he had been born … for food, for friendship, for shelter, simply for survival. Why was that? It was strange that the thought had never occurred to him before. What was it that made him different from everyone else?

Was this what it meant to be one of the Five?

He wanted to rest but he knew he must keep going. He wanted to see Matteo again. Somehow when he was with Matt and the others, he understood things a little more … or at least accepted them. The thought of it gave him new strength. He could do this. There was a passage that the shape-changers and the Roman police didn't know about. It led from the Vatican Museums into

St Peter's Basilica. Inside the church he would find a doorway that would take him to Antarctica. Matt had said it was there. So it must be.

The sun had only just risen but to Pedro it seemed very hot and the light was hurting his eyes. He was aware of walls soaring above him, of tall windows and archways. In the far distance, he thought he could hear organ music but he might have been imagining it. There were several doors leading into what might be offices or state rooms but they weren't going to be any use to him.

But he had a problem. How was he meant to find a secret passage when even the name told him it was supposed to be secret? For a moment he was confused, as if the poison had seeped into his brain and made him forget what he was looking for. He remembered that he hadn't eaten or drunk anything since he had emptied his stomach. He thought he might faint.

The cleaner, pushing his trolley and sweeping his brush over the cobbled surface of the *Cortile Borgia*, saw the boy staggering towards him. His first thought that he was a refugee who had somehow broken into the Vatican. The whole city was swarming with them, many of them dying on their feet. This boy looked worse than any of them. His skin was white and drawn tight over his bones. There was a dreadful tinge of yellow in his eyes. He was clearly racked with pain.

The cleaner's name was Leonardo Emilio Tasso but everyone just called him Tasso. He was sixty years old and he knew that he was very lucky to be employed at the Vatican. How else would he be able to support himself and his family in these terrible times? As he hurried over to the boy, his first thought was to summon the Swiss Guard and to have him ejected. That was the right thing to do. But at the same time he wondered if he shouldn't call a doctor first. The boy would die if he was simply put out on the street, and Tasso, who had two grandsons of his own, would be responsible.

"Where have you come from?" he demanded as he caught hold of Pedro. "What are you doing here?"

Pedro didn't understand anything he said. All he knew was that he had failed. He had been discovered before he could find the passageway. "Please, help me," he said in English.

The choice of language took Tasso by surprise. He had been expecting Croatian, Polish or Russian. English was not often the language of the refugees. "Who are you?" he asked. He spoke a little English himself.

"My name is Pedro. I have to go into the Basilica."

"You cannot go into the church. It is not allowed."

"There's a door. I have to find the door. A door with a star. Do you know it?"

Tasso had spent almost all his adult life in the Vatican. He knew the gardens, the buildings, the priests … and he knew the stories. The door with the star was something that people sometimes talked about – but always in whispers. It was in the church, behind the altar. It was half the size of a normal door and it looked completely different from the rest of the building. It led nowhere. Behind the door, there was a short corridor and then a brick wall. And, just as the boy had said, there was a five-pointed star above it. The symbol was very strange. It had nothing to do with Christianity – so why was it there?

There were those in the Vatican who wanted to destroy the door, to break down the wall around it and then to brick the whole thing in. But for some reason that had never happened. People said that there was something special about it, that the Vatican authorities knew something that they would never share. In any event, it was still there now. Tasso knew exactly where it was. He had passed it a hundred times.

And this strange, foreign boy was asking to be taken there.

Leonardo Emilio Tassio had a choice to make. He could call

the Swiss Guard. In which case, Pedro would be dragged out and deposited on the other side of the Vatican walls. That would be the end of the matter. He would go on with his cleaning and after a while he would forget that this meeting had ever taken place. Or he could do as Pedro asked. He knew perfectly well that there was a flight of steps in the corner of the *Cortile Borgia* that led down to a dark, narrow tunnel, which ran underground for about a hundred metres before it emerged in the sanctury of St Peter's Basilica. Senior members of the Pope's office occasionally used it as a short cut. He himself sometimes went down there to smoke a secret cigarette.

"Please..." Pedro muttered.

The cleaner did not realize that he had arrived at the single most important moment of his entire life. All he knew was that he should do something to help this dying boy.

He let his broom fall to the ground.

"Come with me," he said.

ANTARCTICA

Scott followed the stairs down to the courtyard with the great doors locked on one side, the mountain behind. It was strangely quiet, the snow falling more heavily and blanketing any sound. There were no guards in sight; they were no longer needed. The pathetic rabble that called itself the World Army had gone, scurrying for ships that they thought would take them to safety, unaware that nowhere in the world would ever be safe again. And Matt Freeman had been taken. Even now he was providing entertainment for the massed ranks of the Old Ones. Only the man on the scaffold was still here. He had frozen solid. The snow was settling on his shoulders and head.

Scott was wearing only a shirt, trousers and jacket. The cold cut into him almost gleefully and in seconds his fingers, his ears and his cheekbones were both numb and hurting at the same time. He realized that if he stayed out very long the weather would kill him – but he didn't care. It was likely that quite soon he would be dead anyway.

He walked towards the cave set in the mountainside, opposite the gatehouse and the two towers. He saw the five-pointed star carved into the rock. There was the silver chain drawn across the mouth with the two pale white hands clasped together, keeping it locked. All he had to do was separate them and the way ahead would be clear. He would take ten steps and he would find himself in London. He wondered what Jamie would say. Would his brother even be glad to see him after everything that had happened? How much did he know?

There was also the question of the chain itself. The electricity or whatever deadly force ran through it. If there had been a guard or a servant around, Scott could have ordered them to pull the chain apart for him. But something inside him rebelled against the idea. Why should anyone else die because of him? Much better to do it himself.

He stepped forward, anxious to get it over with. He was very cold. His breath was coming out white and he could actually feel his lips freezing. It was time to get it over with.

But then something hot sliced across his shoulders. He yelled and spun round, just in time to see a glint of silver whip through the air, coming at him again. Instinctively, he jerked back. He had been wounded. He could feel blood trickling down his back. But the second blow had missed.

Jonas Mortlake stood opposite him.

Unlike Scott, Jonas was dressed for the weather with a padded anorak, gloves, hood, heavy boots with thick soles. He was holding a sword, one of the weapons that Scott had seen being manufactured only two days before. Somehow it looked incongruous in his hands ... the antique weapon contrasting with the modern clothes. At least, it would have done if it hadn't been so deadly.

"Are you going somewhere, Scott?" he demanded. "You're not leaving us, are you?"

He swung again. Scott fell backwards and the blade passed just above his head. Jonas smiled at him, his eyes wide and bright behind his wire-framed spectacles, his artificially whitened teeth displayed in a brilliant smile. Scott knew that everything had changed. The Old Ones had Matt. They no longer needed him. And Jonas had been given permission to kill or cripple him. A payment for his services.

But Scott still had his power.

He opened his mouth to say the command that would root Jonas to the spot or send him running into the Antarctic waste. But before he could find the words, Jonas kicked him, the toecap of his boot driving into the side of his head. He had aimed very carefully and Scott was thrown back onto the snow. White light exploded behind his eyes. He was barely conscious, aware only of the dreadful pain sapping all his strength.

"Were you about to say something?" Jonas crooned. "Or maybe you were about to think it." He lashed out a second time, hitting Scott in exactly the same place. Scott's head jerked back. He tasted blood.

Jonas laughed and walked forward. "I think that puts us on equal terms," he said. "But I'm just going to make absolutely sure." This time he used the hilt of the sword, slamming it down like a club. Scott howled. He wondered if his skull had been fractured.

"The Old Ones don't care about you any more. They've told me to finish this right here, right now." Jonas drew back his hood so that there was nothing between the two of them, so that Scott could see how much hatred there was in his face. "I wish I could spend more time with you, Scott. I'd love to pay you back for what you did to me. But we don't want you getting your head together, do we? Better get it over with..."

Scott tried to collect his thoughts, to draw on his power and direct it against his tormentor. But it was hopeless. He was in too much pain. The whole world was spinning around him.

Jonas straightened up, then brought the sword shooting down, the point aiming for Scott's stomach. It was all Scott could do to roll over, saving himself by inches. The sword plunged into the snow beside him. He tried to grab hold of it but his vision was blurred and his hand missed. Jonas plucked it free, preparing himself for the next attack. He was in no hurry. Scott was unarmed. He had nowhere to go. His power had been neutralized. Jonas clasped the sword in both hands, enjoying the feel of it. The next time he wouldn't miss.

"The Old Ones wanted Matt Freeman," he said. "They were never interested in you. You're nothing. A traitor. You don't deserve to live. Goodbye, Scott."

Jonas brought the point of the sword plunging down towards Scott's chest.

It never reached him.

Halfway down, Jonas stopped, a look of surprise on his face. He lowered the sword as if he had already forgotten it. Then he pitched forward and lay still.

There was a knife jutting out between his shoulders.

"Scott!"

Scarlett ran forward with Lohan close behind. Scott had no idea how they had got here. It didn't occur to him that they had followed exactly the same path that he had taken the night before and that it had brought them into the fortress, behind the walls. Lohan had a second blade and was looking around, waiting for a guard to come. But the snow had formed a curtain around them. They were invisible. Scarlett had seen to that.

"Scott!" she cried a second time. Everything was forgotten ... the betrayal, Matt's capture. All she cared about was the boy lying in the snow with terrible bruises around his head and blood seeping from the wound across his shoulders and along his right arm. She knelt beside him, trying to work out how badly hurt he was, if he could stand, if she could get him out of here.

"I'm sorry..." Scott muttered.

"Do you know where Matt is?" Lohan asked. "Have you seen him?"

"No. I don't know." Tears were trickling down the side of Scott's face, freezing before they could reach his chin. He was suddenly seeing what a terrible mess he had made of everything, how hopelessly he had played his hand. "I'm sorry," he said again.

"Scott, it doesn't matter. Not now."

"No. You don't understand." Scott took a deep breath.

He wasn't apologizing for what he had done but for what he was about to do.

"Stay still," he commanded.

Both Scarlett and Lohan felt him enter their minds. They had no protection. They had been completely unprepared. As he had lain in the snow, Scott had recovered enough to regain his power and had used it against them: one of the Five turning against another. For a dreadful moment, Scarlett wondered what he was going to do. Surely he wasn't going to betray them as he had Matt?

Slowly, he got to his feet. He was covered in snow. At least the extreme cold was masking some of the pain. "You have to forgive me, Scarlett," he rasped. "I know you'd stop me and I can't let you do that. Please tell Jamie, if I don't see him, that I was thinking of him..."

Scarlett wanted to move. She wanted to stop him from doing

what he was about to do … whatever it was. But her body wouldn't obey her. She couldn't even speak. Out of the corner of her eye, she saw Lohan struggling to break the spell. He was still holding the knife. Jonas Mortlake was on the ground in front of them, his eyes closed.

One step at a time, hunched over like an old man, Scott limped towards the cave. Scarlett noticed it for the first time. She saw the chain, the clasped hands, the five-pointed star and understood at once that this was one of the doors and that, somehow, it was the reason why all the other doors weren't working any more. At the same time, she heard a faint buzzing sound coming from the chain and knew that whatever they did, none of them should touch it. But it was already too late because Scott was reaching out for it, and although she screamed at him to stop, no sound would come.

Scott grabbed the ivory hands.

FIFTY-FOUR

The door of the cell had been opened without making a sound. Despite everything, Richard must have dozed off because he only nodded awake when he felt a gust of warm air blowing in from outside.

"Could you please get up, Mr Cole," a voice commanded. "There's something I want you to see."

Almost instinctively, Richard felt for the Inca knife, knowing that it was tucked into his belt, hidden from view. Nobody suspected that he had it. Perhaps this might be the moment to use it. He got to his feet. His legs and the back of his neck were stiff and he wondered how much time had passed. Minutes? Hours? The metal plate had been pulled back, revealing a corridor on the other side. Two guards dressed in black leather jackets and carrying misshapen clubs stood on either side. They looked human – with hungry, beaten-up faces – but they could just as easily have been shape-changers. Neither of them showed any emotion beyond a dull, lingering hostility. Neither of them had spoken.

A third man stood between them: old, bald, wrinkled, wearing a suit with a silk scarf around his neck. Richard suspected that he didn't have very long to live. He looked ill. His skin was an unnatural colour, as if the blood beneath it had somehow drained away, and his eyes were full of pain. He was the one who had given the order.

"Who are you?" Richard demanded. "What have you done with Matt?"

"Two very good questions," the man replied. "If you'd like to follow me, I'll answer them as we go."

Richard left the cell, passing between the two guards. They smelled bad, as did everything in the fortress ... he assumed that was where he was. It was as if people had been living here for years without washing or cleaning, as if food had been left to rot, the cells and corners had been used as toilets, and dead and decaying bodies had simply been left where they fell. All these foul odours came together and attacked Richard as he stepped through the doorway. He found it hard not to gag.

"I'm very pleased to see you," the man said. Perhaps he had got used to the smell and didn't notice it any more. "I'm chairman of the Nightrise Corporation. The new chairman. You may have met my predecessor in Hong Kong. You may even have been partly responsible for his early retirement. Let's get moving. I'm afraid we don't have a lot of time."

The chairman began to walk, wheezing a little as he went, and Richard fell in beside him with the two guards behind. Everything was bathed in the same blue glow which emanated from the walls and hung in the air. The corridor looped and began to climb upwards, then turned into a flight of stairs. It was like being inside a gigantic anthill. In the distance, Richard heard shouting, the hammering of metal against metal, then cheering and applause ... the clamour of a crowd. His outer clothing had been taken from him, leaving him in only jeans and a shirt – but he wasn't cold. There was a damp, animal heat inside the rock. He could see water, like sweat, glistening on the surface.

"Where is Matt?" Richard asked.

There was a great shout from the crowd. More metal hitting metal. Richard paused, afraid of what might lie ahead, then grunted as one of the guards punched him in the back, using his club.

"You don't want to linger," the chairman remarked. "As a matter of fact, I'm taking you to him now, although I should warn you, he's not a pretty sight. He's being punished for what he did a while ago. You're part of the punishment. You two are good buddies, aren't you?"

Richard didn't reply.

"We're almost finished with him for now, but before we stop, we want him to watch you being killed. We want him to see you die."

So they were going to kill him. Richard received the news quite calmly. The blade was pressing against his flesh, under his shirt. Well, he would use it to take the chairman with him when the moment came ... and maybe the two guards as well. But first he wanted to see Matt.

"The two of you should have a couple of minutes together," the chairman went on. "We're going to kill you as slowly and as painfully as possible. We have two professionals who are waiting for you just around the corner. I've set them to work on other prisoners and I can assure you they're very good at their job."

"Is this how you get your kicks?" Richard asked. It was hard to talk. His mouth was dry, his heart pounding. But he had to say something. It helped to hide his fear.

"Not really. No. I serve the Old Ones. I do as I'm told and I survive. Actually, people have been doing horrible things to each other for a very long time, Mr Cole. You might say it's part of being human and I'm just the same as everyone else. Kill or be killed, that's what it all comes down to. I guess you made the wrong choice."

The stairs emerged inside a vast chamber filled with people ... thousands of them. They were packed together on benches or swaying on their feet, dressed in the same bits and pieces they had worn when they attacked the World Army. Many of them were holding their swords and shields, banging one against the other. This was the noise Richard had heard. There had been an extra food ration. They were drinking wine out of skins which they passed along the rows, tearing up thick slabs of bread and meat with their bare hands.

Richard looked up. The ceiling was so high above that it was invisible and he realized that he must be in one of the towers that he had seen across the ice shelf, that this was indeed the fortress, the very heart of the Old Ones' lair. Blue light, shining with a harsh almost radioactive intensity, was pouring in through caverns and grottoes that had eaten into the walls all around. Stalactites, needle-sharp, hung down. Narrow ledges – pathways – connected the different entrances and there were crumbling, uneven staircases connecting all the levels. The crowd continued all the way to the top, disappearing into the shadows. Every step, every patch of ground was occupied by men and women with long, straggling hair and wide eyes, screaming, laughing, waving their fists or pounding their shields, all of them fixed on the spectacle below.

A boxing ring, with wire instead of rope, had been constructed in the very centre of the cavern and the crowd was arranged on all four sides of it. Richard felt a fist punch him in the small of the back and he continued forward. Grief tore at his throat and heart.

Matt was there.

He was standing up with his arms outstretched, tied to a wooden frame so that the crowd could see him. It was impossible to guess how much pain he had already endured. His clothes were in rags and his body was a mass of lacerations. Richard barely recognized him. Matt's hair had been shaved off. His face was horribly swollen. His nose had been broken. Barbed wire had been twisted around his neck.

Two men, dressed in butcher's aprons, stood close to him. One was holding a knife which he had taken from a trolley, waving it first at the audience for their approval before using it on Matt. As Richard drew closer, approaching the edge of the ring, Matt's eyes flickered open. He was still conscious, but he showed no emotion. He didn't even seem to understand what was happening any more. But he knew Richard was there. Something deep inside him – it might have been sadness or it might even have been acceptance – appeared briefly in his eyes. Yet even as Richard began to climb up, his head lolled forward and the audience jeered and booed.

"Keep going," the chairman said. "I want you to be nice and close."

Sick, hollowed out, Richard climbed the short flight of steps that led into the ring. The crowd fell silent as the chairman followed. The two guards remained below. Matt was still alive but the breath was rattling in his throat. Blood was running down into his eyes, which were dazed and out of focus.

"It's time to finish the performance right now," the chairman announced, speaking directly to Richard but loudly enough for everyone else to hear. "I'd say the boy deserves a rest. But we want him to take away some very special memories of what happened here today, so you can say goodbye to him before we kill you.

"This is where it ends for you, Mr Cole. But not for him. I think it's important for you to know this. When you're dead, we're going to take your little friend somewhere quiet and let him recover. I'd say it'll take a couple of months. There are a lot of broken bones in there. But we're going to look after him really well, and in the end, he'll heal. He'll get strong.

"And then we're going to do this again. We're going to bring him in here and we're going to tie him up and start all over again. And again, and again, and again – we're going to keep doing it for the next one hundred years. He'll be an old man and we'll still be working on him. Can you imagine that?

"So why don't you say goodbye while you still can? Then we're going to kill you in front of him. But in a way you're lucky. You only get to die once."

The chairman gestured. The crowd was still silent, hoping that Matt would speak, maybe cry for mercy. Matt's lips were cracked and swollen but they seemed to be moving slowly, trying to form words. No sound came out.

Richard glanced at the chairman with more loathing than he had felt for anyone or anything in his life. He knew now exactly what he had to do. He understood at last why he had been given the knife.

Before anyone could stop him, he took two steps forward, pulled it out of his belt and, looking Matt straight in the eyes, plunged it into his heart.

LONDON (HOLLY)

I will never forget those terrible last moments at St Meredith's church.

My heart was already pounding as we slipped out of the house where we'd been hiding ... number 13, although I never found out the name of the street. Everything was very quiet – it was still early morning – but in a way that made me even more nervous. There was so much wreckage, so many broken-down buildings and rusting cars, that I could almost feel the ghosts wandering along the pavements. And there must have been millions of those. It was incredible to think that in the space of less than ten years, a whole city could have been reduced to this wasteland. But then I suppose in other parts of the world, with earthquakes and super-volcanoes, it had happened in minutes. I can't even begin to imagine how London had been before the terrorists came. I just don't have that much imagination. What I saw that day was just the vaguest impression of a city, a few scraps blowing in the wind.

We came out into the road, or what was left of it. I could make out some of the white lines painted in the middle and the yellow lines, which used to mean you weren't allowed to park, but they were partly concealed by dust and debris, and actually it was impossible to tell where the road was or where it went. The church was very close to us, only a hundred metres or so away, and as it was just about the only building that was still standing, more or less intact. It seemed enormous. It could have been a monument to the whole dead city of London. There were bits of shops and offices on either side of us, so we weren't completely exposed. But like everyone else, I wished Jamie had chosen a time when it was darker or rainier to bring us out.

"Stay close," Will said, speaking in a whisper.

I didn't need to be told. I had Amir and Ryan in front of me. Simon and Blake were in front of them. Jamie was next to me. And the two brothers, Graham and Will, were behind. Jamie and I had each been given a gun too and I hoped that if I had to use mine, I'd be more effective than I had been on the *Lady Jane*. To be honest, I was glad to be surrounded by so many armed men, and as we moved down the street – quickly but carefully, looking in every direction – I did my best to stay right in the middle.

The attack, when it came, was completely unexpected. It didn't come from shape-changers, the evil policewoman or anything to do with the Old Ones.

It came from dogs.

It was probably quite by chance that they found themselves in this part of the city, but there were a dozen of them and they were out hunting for food.

When London was attacked, they must have been pets that had been left behind and they had banded together, just like the people we'd seen in the Tube station, forming a pack. As they came rushing towards us I saw that they certainly weren't anyone's pets any more. They were horrible. There were little fat ones, running as fast as they could on stupid stunted legs, and tall, raggedy thin ones with matted fur and blank eyes. They were all mongrels, the worst bits of every dog you ever saw thrown together to make the ugliest creatures you could possibly imagine. It was obvious that all of them had only one thought in whatever was left of their brains: food. They were howling and barking, snapping at the air with teeth that were jagged and as sharp as razors. Obviously they spent quite a bit of time attacking each other. There wasn't a single one of them that didn't have some dreadful injury … bites on the stomach and chest, throats torn open, ears and eyes missing. One of them was dragging itself after the others on two legs.

They must have been downwind of us when we came out of the house and had picked up our scent. God help any of us if we had been alone and unarmed. The dogs would have gleefully torn us apart and eaten us. From the look of them, they must have often done exactly that. Of course, we had weapons. We had plenty of time to see them coming. So although they were like something out of a nightmare, there really was no chance that they could do us harm.

But that wasn't the point. I saw Blake raise his machine gun and send a spray of bullets, which cut into them, killing four or five instantly and halting the others, as if they had run into a sheet of glass. Several of the dogs were wounded, not killed outright, and they went completely mad, snapping at their own bodies, trying to bite out the cause of the pain. One or two of them sniffed at their dead companions, realizing that there was an easier meal right in front of them … although maybe it would be better if they came back later. In any event, the attack was over. But at the same time the sound of the machine-gun fire had echoed across the city and now anyone in St Meredith's or nearby would know that we were here.

"Run!" Will ordered.

He was right. If we were going to reach St Meredith's and find Jamie's door, we had to get there as quickly as we could. We had lost the advantage of surprise but there might still be a few moments before the enemy worked out which direction we were coming from. Forgetting the dogs, we belted towards the entrance to the church. As we went, I saw Will take something from his belt and throw it. It was a grenade! It only occurred to me then that the entrance to the church was almost certainly locked, and although he might have been planning a more cautious approach – picking the lock, for example – we couldn't waste any more time. We just had to get in.

Will put up his arm to signal us to stop and we crouched down. The grenade exploded, smashing open the wooden door which had stood there for centuries, even surviving the destruction of London … until we had arrived. We were about thirty metres away now and out of the corner of my eye I saw something move and felt my legs turn to jelly as the spider scuttled round the side of the church and stood there, quivering, looking down at us with the dozens of glittering black discs that were its eyes. There was a huge, heaving sack of venom under its belly. I had seen the spider the day we first came to St Meredith's but it was even more horrible now because it had seen us. It knew we were there.

We couldn't go back. If we turned round, it would leap onto us in a second, and anyway, what would be the point? We had to get into the church. We had no choice but to continue forward, racing towards it. Twenty-five metres. Twenty metres. We weren't going to make it.

It would have killed us all. I'm sure of it. It was already tensing itself to jump right onto us. But then, before it could make its move, something else happened – so extraordinary and inexplicable that I couldn't believe it. I really did think I must be dreaming or hallucinating. Or maybe my fear had driven me insane.

The sky burst into flames.

I mean, the whole sky. If you can imagine dousing all the clouds in petrol and then putting a match to them, that was what happened. We didn't feel any heat. Perhaps there was none. But the whole of London, the church and the spider were bathed in a deep red glow. At the same time, I thought I heard a bell strike somewhere in the far distance, coming from another church or maybe from St Meredith's, and later on I realized that it must have been exactly eight o'clock – twelve o'clock in Antarctica – and if ever there was a moment of truth, this was it.

The sky blazed. The spider froze. We didn't stop. It took us less than a minute to reach the front entrance where the door was shattered and the stonework charred, wisps of smoke still rising. For just a second, Jamie and I were close to each other, our shoulders touching and I saw him turn and look back, the flames reflecting in his face. I had never seen him look so dismayed.

"What is it? I asked.

"Matt," he said. Just the one word, but I knew it meant that something dreadful had happened.

And then we were inside the church. It was a big place, five times the size of St Botolph's back in my village and a lot gloomier too, with most of the windows broken, rubble over the floor, the pews all smashed up and most of them taken away, probably for firewood. There were huge pillars holding up the ceiling and chapels leading off at the sides. Everything was very dark and red.

I didn't know what to think. Part of me thought that we'd done it, that we'd made it here and nothing was going to stop us finding the door. Jamie and the Traveller would soon be on their way … on yet another journey. I suppose I should have been glad. But I wasn't. I would never see Jamie again and without him I had no reason at all to be here. What would happen to me? The Nexus would look after me, I guessed. And if Jamie won the fight against the Old Ones, perhaps I'd be able to return to the village, or one like it. But George was dead. Rita and John were dead. Just about everybody I knew was dead. And on top of that, the world was on fire. I was in the middle of a ruined city. There was no way back.

Blake, Simon, Ryan and Amir had fanned out in front of us. I had my gun. Jamie had his. The Traveller and his brother were covering us from behind.

Blake pointed. "There it is," he said. "The door..."

There was a burst of gunfire, horribly loud, deafening in the empty space, and Blake was hurled off his feet, dead before he hit the ground. I cried out. The ginger-haired woman who had come in the helicopter to the village and followed us to Little Moulsford before she lost us at the Sheerwall Tunnel had caught up with us again. She was striding towards us in her long coat with a look of grim determination on that pale, thin face of hers. It was she who had fired the shots but she was surrounded by armed policemen and I knew at once that they weren't going to stop, that there weren't going to be any warnings or questions. They would kill us all – Jamie too, this time – and that would be the end of it.

But Jamie had his power, didn't he? I waited for him to tell the woman that he wasn't there or to order her to simply drop her gun or whatever. It never happened. A gas cylinder exploded – I didn't even see who threw it – and suddenly there was smoke everywhere, thick yellow clouds gushing out around our feet. I gasped for breath. My throat was raw. My eyes were burning and I could feel the tears streaming down my cheeks. It was some sort of tear gas. The woman knew just what Jamie could do and she'd taken no chances, disabling him and the rest of us before she closed in. How had she got to St Meredith's? It was obvious. She had known where we were heading and she had simply waited for us to turn up.

Blake was gone but the others were shooting back. Bullets exploded all around me. Once again I found myself in the middle of a gun battle, unsure what to do. I didn't dare fire myself in case I hit Jamie or the Traveller.

"Go, Jamie! Go!"

I think it was Will who shouted the order. It was impossible to be sure. There must have been hundreds of bullets being fired and I screamed as one hit my hand, going right through the palm. With what little vision I had, I saw Jamie start forward and even then the thought occurred to me that it was a shame that he hadn't had time to say goodbye properly. Maybe that was why I followed him or maybe it was simply because I didn't want to be left on my own. Either way, four of us made the sprint to the door, although Will only took a few more steps before he was shot down. I couldn't tell if he'd been wounded or killed. A second later I saw the Traveller turn round and fire off three shots: at least one of them found its target – a perfect target – because I saw the policewoman throw her head back, and when she lowered it again there was a round, red hole where her left eye had been. She fell onto her knees, but then the Traveller cried out and went sprawling, and suddenly there was just Jamie and me with the door right in front of us and there was no chance of the Traveller following so Jamie just grabbed me instead and the two of us burst through.

The church was behind us. The policemen were still firing. There was smoke everywhere. And I remember thinking that, this time, I really, really hoped the door would work.

ANTARCTICA

It was exactly like being electrocuted.

Scott felt the terrible shock running through him, and even if he had wanted to let go of the lock it would have been impossible because his own hands were fused to it. He was burning up. It seemed to him that the world was on fire ... the sky, the ice. He could barely see, his vision torn away from him. He knew that he was dying on his feet.

But this was for Jamie and he refused to black out. He refused to die. He fought back, ignoring the pain even as it shuddered through his arms, and instead he focused all his remaining strength on separating the white ivory hands, pulling them apart. He had forgotten the injuries that Jonas Mortlake had inflicted on him. He had forgotten everything that had happened since he had walked out of the door from Hong Kong and into the Abbey of San Galgano. All that mattered was that he should succeed and, sure enough, in the half-second before he collapsed, unconscious, he felt his hands come apart and knew that the chain had been unfastened, that the door was open and that Jamie could come through.

Scarlett felt herself being released from Scott's power and ran over to Scott, who was lying dead still, his hands and wrists blackened, smoke seeping out of the corner of his mouth. He looked hideous, like the victim of some terrible accident. Lohan was right behind her.

"What's happening?" Lohan shouted. "The sky!"

It was true. Scott hadn't imagined it. Flames were rippling across the Antarctic sky. It was a shocking, horrific image. The end of the world.

"I don't know!" Scarlett was next to Scott, certain he was dead, cradling him in her arms.

Lohan looked past her, at the two chains with the ivory hands, now lying apart. "He did it!" he exclaimed. "The door is open. You and I can leave! You can take us anywhere in the world!"

"We're not going anywhere," Scarlett cried.

"Wait...!"

Lohan was pointing. Scarlett looked into the cave.

There were three figures in the darkness, moving out of the shadows. They were coming towards her.

FIFTY-FIVE

In their own way, they were beautiful.

They might have been designed only to bring death and devastation but the Trident missiles, fired from the submarine twelve minutes before, had an undoubted magnificence as they grouped together and began their descent.

Not all the boats carrying the survivors of the World Army were far enough away from Oblivion and many of them would be caught up in the blast and the inevitable tsunami that would follow. But innocent people must die in every war and they would be serving a greater good. Surely even the power of the Old Ones could not stand up to the blast wave generated by twelve nuclear warheads. The fortress would be vaporized. In fact the entire ice shelf for miles around would disappear.

And there they were, silver needles in the sky. They were like a flock of birds, each one with a separate intelligence and yet coming together in a single, unified whole. The target was ahead of them. The fortress was still tiny but with every second it seemed to grow as the missiles closed in.

Nobody saw them. They were still covered by the clouds, and anyway, they were moving too fast. By the time anyone looked up, it would be too late.

* * *

Pedro was the first one to emerge from the cave, still dressed in the thin clothes he had been wearing in Rome, and he was hit at once by the full force of the Antarctic cold. Maybe the shock of it did him good because it was as if he had finally left the poison behind him, and as he continued forward his steps became stronger and more confident until he was almost running, ready for whatever else he had to face.

Scarlett saw him and was shocked by the change in his appearance. She had only seen him once, briefly in Hong Kong, and she was unsure if that had been a few weeks or ten years ago. He was so much thinner, hollow-eyed and pale. But then he recognized her and smiled, and suddenly she knew that he had survived and he was here and that everything was going to be all right.

"Pedro!" she exclaimed.

"Scarlett!" Pedro looked around him, unable to take everything in. Something had happened to the sky. There were flames stretching as far as he could see, an ocean of them reflecting in the real ocean below. He was in some kind of fortress, in the snow. A great mountain rose up behind him. To one side there was a figure hanging from a scaffold. He had thought that Naples was a terrible place but this was much, much worse.

And then he saw the broken body of Scott, with Lohan standing helplessly beside him. At once, everything that had happened in the past weeks was forgotten. It didn't matter what Scott had done. He was one of the Five and he was hurt. Pedro went over to him, stretched out his hands and prepared to do what he had always done, to bring the power of healing.

Meanwhile, Scarlett was standing in front of the cave, the broken chain resting on either side of her. Two more people had emerged. One of them was a girl she had never seen before, round-faced and pretty with freckles over her nose, and fair hair. She was cradling one hand in the other and she looked shocked.

The other was a boy. Even if he hadn't been identical to Scott, she would have known him instantly. It was Jamie.

Finally, there were four of them here together. But where was Matt? And what had happened to Richard Cole?

Jamie had escaped unhurt from St Meredith's. He didn't know if he had been right to bring Holly with him, but everything had happened so quickly and he had decided it was the only way to save her. He couldn't have left her behind. Like Pedro before him, he felt the extreme cold almost like a hammer blow. He took in the fortress walls, the towers, the mountain and the sky. So the whole world was on fire! He saw Lohan looking up at him, read the pain in his eyes and finally realized that the figure lying stretched out on the snow in front of him was his brother, Scott, and he had arrived too late.

Forgetting everything else, Jamie ran over to him, dropping onto his knees. Pedro was already with him but one glance told him that there was nothing that even a healer could do.

"Scott!" Jamie swept his brother into his arms. "I'm here, Scott!" he shouted, and for the first time since this whole thing had begun, he felt a sense of overwhelming grief that came with the knowledge that whatever had happened, it was his fault, that he should never have left Scott on his own. "I'm sorry," he continued. "I shouldn't have left you behind. I should have stayed with you. We were always together, you and me. You always looked after me. Please tell me you're not angry with me, Scott. I was only doing what I thought was best..."

Scott's eyes flickered open. He smiled.

"Jamie..." he said.

"What happened here, Scott? What have they done to you?"

"It's been bad. But it's OK now. I'm glad you're here."

"Scott..."

"Tell Matt..."

Scott's eyes closed. Jamie waited for him to say more but no more words came. He glanced at Pedro, who was staring at him with shock in his eyes. Both of them knew.

Scott had died.

Scarlett saw what had happened and all the strength drained out of her. Scott had sacrificed himself. But his death meant that the Five could never come together. The Old Ones had won.

The ground began to shake.

All of them – Jamie, Pedro, Scarlett, Lohan and Holly – felt the sudden, intense lurching, the sense that the world was tearing itself apart beneath their feet. The clouds seemed to be burning more brightly than ever and the walls were vibrating, huge cracks appearing, rock and ice beginning to tumble down. There was a rumble of what sounded like thunder, only deeper and a thousand times louder. Lohan looked up and felt pure terror as the entire mountain began to break open. The noise was deafening, pounding at his ears and eyes. Huge boulders rolled down, smashing into the ground below. A wind had sprung up, sending snow and dust whipping into his face, blinding him.

At the same time, the forces of the Old Ones began to appear, swarming out of the far tower. They poured out of the doors, over the battlements, down the stairs, across the courtyard ... shape-changers, fire-riders, fly-soldiers, slaves. They were coming from every direction, gaining speed, while outside the fortress, the giant monkey bounded across the ice, the condor and the humming bird swooping down behind. Still on his knees, cradling Scott, with the tears freezing on his cheeks, Jamie knew that the end had arrived – but he no longer cared. His brother had died in his arms. He had arrived too late. Everything he had endured had been for nothing.

Chaos, the King of the Old Ones, finally appeared, bursting into the sky, black rubble cascading around him. To Scarlett and the others, it was as if the mountain had turned into a volcano with molten lava and smoke pouring out. At first, Chaos was nothing more than an enormous fog, dark and shapeless. There was the glimpse of an eye, yellow and lizard-like. Something like a claw seemed to take hold of the edge of the crater, pushing him free, as if he were being born. He might have had horns, the skin of a snake. It was impossible to say. Chaos was too huge, too unfathomable. He could take any shape he wanted and even now he was changing…

In front of their eyes, all the different pieces were drawn together and formed the perfect figure of a man, human-sized, walking down the side of the mountain towards them. Except he wasn't a man. He was a black cut-out of a man, a silhouette. Scarlett was reminded of the paper figures she had once made as a child. But it was as if Chaos had been cut out of the very fabric of the world. He was a black hole. He was nothing. The mountain and the sky rippled around him but he was pure energy, pure evil, faceless and lifeless, sucking everything into him.

"The Five…" he whispered and his voice seemed to belong to the beginning of time, before light had first come to the world. The flames twisted and writhed above him. His army stood back, waiting for his command.

But he was going to finish this himself. He continued to walk down.

Scarlett closed her eyes and prepared to die.

Richard Cole had also expected to die.

He knew that he had cheated the chairman and the Old Ones, taking their greatest prize from them. Matt was slumped in front of him, still on his feet – the frame that he was tied to kept him upright – but Richard could see that he was at peace. His head had dropped forward, his eyes were closed and he wasn't breathing.

Richard felt as if he was being torn in half. Right then, he was consumed by more grief than he had ever known in his life. But at the same time he was glad that, at least for Matt, it was over.

He had fully expected the chairman to kill him. The entire arena had gone silent, the spectators – row after row of them – staring at him in shocked silence like children who had just had a toy snatched away. The guards who had brought him here and the two torturers whose work he had seen were holding back, waiting to be told what to do. And the chairman himself was furious and frightened at the same time. This was his fault. He had brought the journalist here and somehow, inexplicably, he had failed to see that he was carrying some sort of antique knife. He had allowed him to kill the boy – the one thing that couldn't happen. What would the Old Ones do now. What would they do to him?

All the blood had drained out of his face. There was a pulse beating at the front of his bald head and a hollow had formed in his throat as he struggled for breath. His arm shot out and he pointed a trembling finger in Richard's direction.

"Kill him!" he screamed, in a high-pitched voice. "Kill him now!"

Nobody moved. Who was the order aimed at? Richard thought of fighting back, of trying to escape, but he was too exhausted. He didn't care any more. After what he had been forced to do, it didn't matter to him if he lived or died. Matt still hung in front him, his head shaved, his almost naked body covered with injuries that would cause him no more pain. Richard just wanted to stay here with him. He wasn't going to run any more.

He was aware of something moving under his feet and fought for balance. He thought he was imagining it, until one of the guards tumbled against the other. It wasn't the platform. The entire cavern had begun to tremble. The audience was feeling it too. Some of them stood up. Panic began to spread even as the first rocks and stones came loose. The vibrations were getting worse, more severe. The blue light was flickering on and off so that there were moments when everyone was plunged into darkness. Richard's vision was blurred. He had the extraordinary sensation of being sucked into a hole that didn't exist.

"Kill him!" the chairman shouted again but the guards weren't listening, afraid that the ceiling was about to collapse in on them. The audience was panicking, staggering in every direction, making for the exits. To Richard, they were invisible one moment and then seemed frozen in panic and desperation when the light returned. Larger boulders had begun to fall. At the very back of the auditorium, one of the ledges suddenly gave way, sending twenty people plunging to their deaths in a cascade of rubble. The side wall had cracked and, impossibly, Richard saw fire on the other side. But it wasn't the building that was ablaze. It was the very sky.

The chairman didn't seem to have noticed what was happening. All he cared about was Richard. He glanced at the trolley with its array of knives and scalpels and snatched one up, then lumbered forward, meaning to do the job himself. Richard reacted instinctively. If he was going to die, it wasn't going to be at the hands of this madman. As the chairman swung the knife towards him, he reached up and caught hold of the old man's wrist, wrenching it aside. He heard the bone break. The chairman howled and reeled back, dropping the knife.

The two of them stood face-to-face. The lines of spectators had become a sprawling, fighting mass. Richard heard a cracking sound and looked up just as one of the stalactites separated from the ceiling. He saw it shoot down. The chairman looked up and at that same moment the stalactite hit him, the sharpened point piercing his throat just under his chin and continuing all the way through his body, finally pinning him to the boxing ring. The chairman's hands flailed. His legs kicked out. Then he went still.

Nobody cared about Richard any more. The walls were falling

in, the floor heaving. Everywhere, people were dying, crushed by falling rocks, or trampled, slashed and battered by other people trying to get past them. He ignored them. Somehow he managed to force all the noise out of his head and found himself alone, in a quiet place. He stepped forward and took hold of Matt, trying not to look at the golden *tumi* that still protruded from his chest. Very gently, he untangled the barbed wire from around his neck. Then he released him from the frame. Matt's body tumbled forward into his arms. Richard laid him on the ground and, reaching out with one hand, closed his eyes one final time.

Outside, he heard two words whispered. They seemed to come from the bowels of the earth.

"The Five..."

And suddenly he got the sense, without knowing how or why, that this was what Matt had wanted and indeed that he had expected it and that somehow, despite everything, they had won after all.

Pedro could only watch as the black emptiness that was Chaos walked towards them, one step at a time, the whole world shifting around him. Jamie was kneeling on the snow, holding his brother, with Lohan standing over them. Scarlett was beside the cave. And all around them the human and non-human forces of the Old Ones were poised, waiting for the order that would finally end it all.

It happened with no warning.

The two doors at the front of the fortress disintegrated. It wasn't quite an explosion. It was as if they had somehow chosen to tear themselves apart, turning in an instant from solid planks of wood into a vaporous cloud of splinters. Scarlett opened her eyes and saw a single, open-top vehicle speeding towards them across the ice shelf, one figure driving, another standing beside him.

Matt and Scott.

Except it couldn't be Scott because Scott was here. And how had Matt escaped from the fortress? But even as the jeep burst into the courtyard and skidded to a halt, she saw that it *was* them. And it seemed to her that the army of the Old Ones hesitated and drew back, and that there was suddenly a sense of uncertainty that began with Chaos and rapidly spread throughout his forces.

Jamie knew at once. He had met Flint when he had gone back in time to replace Flint's twin brother, Sapling, who had been killed at the battle of Scathack Hill. Sapling was the earlier version of himself, because – as he had learnt – he had lived twice, ten thousand years apart. Now he realized that, at the very moment Scott had died, Flint had travelled forward in time, repaying the debt. And Matt – the old Matt – had come with him.

So the Matt he knew in the modern world was dead. Jamie understood that but he wasn't sad. Perhaps it was because he was beyond sadness, that there was nothing more he could feel. At the same time, he was certain that all this was meant to happen. Impossibly, after being separated and flung all over the world, after enduring so much, the Five had come together again, here, at Oblivion. And it didn't matter that they were outnumbered by a factor of a thousand to one. There was nothing anyone could do.

Matt was driving. Both the boys were dressed in the grey tunics with the blue star that was the insignia of the first rebel army that had defeated the Old Ones. As Flint leapt down, Jamie saw that he had two swords – one in his belt, the other in his hand.

He saw Jamie and hailed him. "Jamie ... this is yours!" he shouted and, turning the first sword around, he threw it towards him, the thin blade glittering as it travelled the short distance through the air. Jamie caught it by the hilt and recognized the five-pointed star in the middle of the crosspiece, made out of precious stones. Once again he felt the weight and fine balance of the blade, tapering to a point.

It was Frost, the sword he had fought with at that first battle. It had been returned to him.

There was a series of gunshots.

Everyone had forgotten Holly. But she had been standing at the entrance to the cave, trying to make sense of the insanity around her. She had seen Chaos as he reached the foot of the mountain and swept towards her, and without knowing who he was, without understanding anything really, she had finally found the strength to use her gun and had emptied it into him.

The bullets passed straight through him. He ignored her. But it was as if the noise of the detonations were a signal for everything to happen at once.

Matt and Flint ran forward from the jeep. As they went, one of the fire-riders galloped forward, trying to intercept them. Matt swung his sword and the blade sliced through the fluttering black robes, cutting the creature in half. A great cry went up from the battlements as a tangled mass of shape-changers, fly-soldiers and hideous deformities that had once been people surged towards them. Scarlett turned and faced them and at once a blast of wind rushed into them with such force that they were thrown off their feet, sent spinning away. She had never felt like this before and knew that it was because they were all there together. Her powers had multiplied by five.

Jamie felt the same. It was wonderful having Frost in his hand again, the return of an old friend, but he almost didn't need it. Nobody could come near him. He only had to think a command and it happened. Two of the knights who were utterly covered in black spikes, fell back, their horses panicking, and collided with a fire rider. All three of them disappeared in flames. A shape-changer with two lizard heads turned its sword on itself. Jamie couldn't bring himself to look at the body of his brother. As long as he was close to Flint, it was almost as if Scott had come back to him again.

Pedro snatched up the swords dropped by the two knights that Jamie had just killed. He passed one of them to Scarlett and kept the other himself. He no longer felt the cold. He wasn't afraid of anything. Everything he had been through, the suffering of his whole life, was worth it for this moment.

"It's over!" Matt shouted. "Let's finish it."

They all knew what to do. Chaos was between them, all-powerful and powerless at the same time. He had been in total command. Scott had belonged to him. Matt had been his prisoner. Jamie and Pedro had been thousands of miles away. But somehow, in the space of just a few minutes, everything had changed. Even as he had made his way down the mountain, the Five had finally come together. The fire in the sky was going out. The light was returning.

Matt was first, plunging his sword into the King of the Old Ones so that it disappeared all the way up to the hilt. Jamie followed, crying out in exaltation as he once again tested the power of Frost. Scarlett, Pedro and finally Flint all struck together and somewhere, deep inside Chaos, the five points touched.

Chaos screamed, a sound that was heard not just all over the world but to the very end of the universe. He was pinned to the spot, his own shape distorting and breaking up as if it were a reflection on the surface of a stormy sea. Finally he turned back into smoke and was whisked away, and Matt, Pedro, Jamie, Scarlett and Flint were facing each other with their five swords extended.

The circle was complete.

Right then, they all knew that it was over, that nobody could touch them and there was no need to be afraid any more. It was like being trapped inside a glass dome, except they were the ones who had created it and it was keeping everything else outside. One of the giant birds had appeared, far too late, and tried to dive-bomb them, hurtling down, but it was bounced away again, turned into a spiralling ball of broken bone and feather. Slowly, the world began to turn around them. There was no sign of Lohan or Holly. At that moment, there were only the Five, the Gatekeepers, brought together at last.

Faster and faster the wheel turned. The fortress spun round. The Old Ones. Oblivion. The mountain. The sky. It was all becoming a blur. There was an ear-splitting crack and the ice field disappeared, replaced by a gigantic hole that revealed another world beneath, a universe of black space and glittering stars. A torrent of wind chased around it, sucking everything in. The soldiers and horses were unable to resist it. There were thousands of them and a moment before they had seemed unstoppable but suddenly they were little more than a handful of soot thrown into the breeze. All of them were dragged in. The fortress itself fell apart, turning into a vortex, a million pieces of brick and stone. The giant birds were pulled out of the sky. The giant monkey, arms outstretched, slithered backwards across the edge of the ice and disappeared into the black hole. The fire-riders were smashed into each other, exploding into flames. It was impossible to say which was man and which was horse. Every last sword and shield, every knife and gun was swept away.

And, at the very end, when every last evil thing had gone, the missiles sent by the World Army finally arrived, streaking out of the sky. They too disappeared through the great hole in the ice. There was no impact, no explosion. They had been visible for barely more than a few seconds, raining downwards, and then they were gone.

It was over. Deep inside the other world, something flickered, red and black. Then the circle closed, the ice reforming itself.

The five of them were standing together in the courtyard, holding their swords. Lohan and Holly were nearby, white-faced, unable to take in what they had just witnessed. Only a few broken pillars and walls of the fortress remained. The field of Oblivion stretched out, white and unbroken, all the way to the sea.

"Richard!" Scarlett called out his name, seeing the journalist staggering out from the remains of what had been one of the towers. But he didn't hear her. He was staring at Matt, his eyes full of wonder.

Everything was silent.

It was still snowing but the clouds had parted and a ripple of pink was already spreading across the sky.

FIFTY-SIX

It was a celebration of sorts.

Jamie couldn't help thinking about the last great confrontation, when Raven's Gate had been created. When it was all over, there had been a feast and an army to share it with. All the Gatekeepers had been there – Flint, Inti, Scar and Matt as they were then – but there had been other people to celebrate with too. Scar's friends Corian and his older brother Erin. And her great friend Finn, although he had died. Jamie remembered the wine and the music and the mood of the survivors, sharing the victory, glad to be alive but remembering all those who had been less fortunate.

This time it was different. There were so few of them left on the ice field after the World Army had packed up and left … just the eight of them. And it seemed to have taken them so long to get here. It was as if they had been fighting all their lives.

They had buried Scott and Matt's bodies side by side not far from where they had fallen, covering them with ice and snow and erecting a simple memorial – two slabs of grey granite, each one decorated with a five-pointed star that Lohan had chiselled with a knife. Jamie had spoken a few words for both of them as they stood together around the grave.

"Scott … you can't hear me and you'd probably tell me to shut up anyway, but I want you to know that, in many ways, you were the best of us. You were taken away from us right at the start and I know how much they hurt you, trying to turn you into one of them. But in the end, you were stronger than all of them put together and you came through. If it wasn't for you, we would never have got here. You opened the doors even though you knew what it meant. And I'm just so glad that I was able to see you and be with you. You were the best brother anyone could ever have. I will always think of you. I'll never forget you.

"And Matt. What can I say to you, Matt? You were my friend. You were our leader. I still don't understand how you figured it all out but I know Scott didn't betray you. Not really. He did what you wanted him to do – we all did – and you went through all that pain and death just so things would work out the way they were meant to..."

It felt strange, giving the funeral address when anyone else would have said that Scott and Matt were standing right beside him. But Jamie understood. They were the same but different. They had lived ten thousand years apart, mirror images separated by a gulf of time. He had once had to step into Sapling's place and he knew better than anyone how strange it was to have to live up to himself.

A few hours had passed since the funeral. It was late at night, although the sky was still bright. The snow had finally stopped falling and so they had lit a bonfire on the ice, not wanting to hide themselves away in the carcasses of the planes or even in the tents that had been abandoned. Lohan had brought out rugs, blankets and cushions, which he laid out around the fire, and he had managed to find a surprising amount of food, left behind during the evacuation. He and Holly were preparing a hot dinner. They had promised a feast, although it was going to be a lonely one. They were almost certainly the only people on an entire continent, utterly alone in the middle of the vast wilderness.

Of the five Gatekeepers, Pedro was the happiest. He felt a great sense of contentment just being back with the others, cradling a mug of hot soup that Holly had given him and talking animatedly to Scarlett, who was sitting beside him. He was describing his escape from the Castel Nuovo and he was clearly sparing no details. Jamie saw Scarlett gasp out loud and then rock back, holding her nose. He was sitting on the other side of the fire with Flint, the two of them sharing a bottle of red wine.

"How did you get here?" Jamie was asking.

"I'm not really sure," Flint replied. "You and I were together only yesterday. Anyway, it was yesterday for me. The battle happened. We all went to bed. And then I woke up here with Matt telling me to get into the jeep. I didn't believe I'd have to go through it all a second time!"

"I was certain I'd never see you again."

"I'm sorry you had to, Jamie. As soon as I found myself here, I knew what it meant. Scott..."

"I can't believe Scott is dead when I'm sitting here talking to you," Jamie said. He thought for a moment. "I suppose you'll have to leave quite soon, like I did." It was a gloomy thought, being on his own again.

"I don't know," Flint said. "I expect Matt will tell us."

Holly appeared, struggling with a large steel cauldron, steam rising into the air. Jamie glanced in her direction and smiled. Scarlett and Pedro liked her already. Holly had spent her whole life in the same small community and had suddenly found herself caught up in things she couldn't possibly understand, incredibly transported to the other side of the world. She had also been hurt. Her left hand was bandaged following the gunshot that had gone right through it during the ambush at St Meredith's. But she had just got on with it, doing whatever she could to help the others.

Lohan had followed her over, carrying a tray with plates, cups knives and forks. He had even found one of the bottles of brandy that he had brought with him from Serra Morte. Jamie watched as he uncorked it with his teeth and took a swig straight from the bottle. The flames of the bonfire sparked. Suddenly they were all feeling warm and close together.

"Dinner is ready," Lohan announced.

"What is it?" Flint asked.

"It's whatever we were able to find, thrown together and cooked in red wine," Lohan replied.

"Lohan did it all," Holly said. "I'm useless in the kitchen. And don't let him pretend it's just scraps. We actually found some proper meat and vegetables. It was all packed in the ice. And we've got chocolate biscuits for dessert."

"I'm starving," Pedro said. He had already drunk two mugs of soup and was lying back with his head on a pile of cushions, his feet stretched out towards the fire.

"Where's Richard?" Holly asked.

"He'll be here in a minute," Scarlett said. "He's talking with Matt."

Richard and Matt were about twenty metres away, on the other side of what had been the commander's tent. They could see the edge where the ice shelf dropped away and the sea beyond it. The water was surprisingly calm and the sun so low in the sky that it almost touched.

Richard was gazing at the boy who stood in front of him. He was the same age as Matt. He looked just like Matt, particularly now that he had set aside his sword and put on modern clothes to protect himself from the cold. He even sounded like him. But the events in the fortress were still fresh in Richard's mind and he knew that whoever this was, it wasn't his friend and companion, and that in truth the two of them had only just met for the first time.

"So what happens now?" Richard asked.

"What do you mean?"

"Well – for a start – how do we get off this ice shelf? I know Lohan can fly, but I wouldn't have thought any of these planes are up to much."

"One of the ships is coming back, Richard. It peeled off from the rest of the fleet and it'll be here in about an hour. It'll take you where you want to go."

"The captain's happy to come back here?"

"I didn't give him any choice."

So Matt had used his power. He made one of the ships turn around and there wouldn't have been anything that the captain or crew could do to prevent it. Once again, Richard examined him. He had already seen how much the Matt he knew had changed – he had almost said as much when they were re-united on the ice. The Matt Freeman of Yorkshire and Lesser Malling had become older, wiser, more confident. But this Matt was something else again. He didn't speak very much. He gave the impression of being deep in thought all the time. But Richard felt he only had to say the word and the sea would part, the sky would open ... or whatever else he had in mind.

"Who are you?" he asked.

"You know who I am."

"No. I don't."

"I'm Matt."

"I killed Matt." Richard's voice broke as he said the words and he had to fight back the tears prickling his eyes. He was seeing Matt once again as the knife pierced his heart. He was remembering what they had done to his friend before he had got there.

"You did exactly what you had to do, Richard," Matt said in a voice that was honest and yet somehow soothing. "Why do you think the Incas gave you the knife all that time ago? Didn't they warn you?"

"They couldn't possibly have known." Matt said nothing so he went on. "Did you know?"

"There was only one way to win this battle and that was the way it happened," Matt replied. "Chaos was too interested in revenge. Once he had his enemy in his hands, everything else was forgotten. He didn't care if Scott or the others lived or died." He paused. "There was no other way to beat him and although it was horrible and painful, it's over now and the world can begin again. Isn't that what matters?"

"What will you do?" Richard asked. "Will you go back to your own time?"

"No. I'm not needed there any more."

"Then what...?"

"Let's join the others. But you should be glad, Richard." Matt reached out and briefly touched Richard's arm. "You were Matt's greatest friend. My greatest friend. It's only thanks to you that we're here now."

They walked back towards the bonfire, where the others were waiting. Richard tried to force a smile onto his face. Scarlett looked happy enough, digging into a plate of hot stew with Pedro beside her. Jamie was with Flint – twin brothers, even if they had been born ten thousand years apart. Lohan and Holly were both looking pleased with themselves as they served the meal. It was a bizarre sight in a way, the cold-blooded boss of a Chinese criminal organization working hand-in-hand with a fifteen-year-old girl from an English village. Suddenly Richard found that he was actually smiling for real. Why not? They had won, hadn't they?

They spent the next hour together – eating, drinking, talking. They all had stories to tell from different parts of the world. Holly told of their escape from the village, their journey down the canal and their time with the Nexus in London. Scarlett described her bet in the casino in Dubai. Even Richard joined in with a perfect impersonation of Sheikh Rasheed. The strange thing was that, in the telling, some of the horrible details fell away and they concentrated instead on the memories that made them smile or laugh out loud. It was a perfect meal. It really didn't matter that they were alone because they were, at last, together.

Finally, Matt raised a hand.

"It's almost time for me to leave," he said. "The ship will be here soon. But before it arrives, I think we need to stop for a minute and try to understand what we've accomplished here today. We need to know that it was all worth it.

"The Old Ones have finally gone, not just here but in every country all over the world. We have made another gate here in the ice, the gate of Oblivion, and this time I think it will hold. They won't come back. They had the planet in their hands for ten years and they brought it to the edge of ruin, but we have to remember that even though they had everything on their side, even though half the world chose to support them, they still lost. Think how outnumbered we were. They had governments, police, businesses ... whole armies helping them. They had monsters and limitless power. There were just five of us and a handful of companions, but we still came through in the end. That should tell you something about the universe that the Old Ones never understood. Evil will never win entirely. It can't. It's not in its nature."

He paused. Richard felt the strength of the boy sitting next to him. He had a sense almost of being healed.

"Richard, Lohan, Holly – all three of you have been a part of this story," he went on. "And we couldn't have made it without you."

"I didn't do very much," Holly protested.

"You emptied your pistol into Chaos," Matt reminded her. "There aren't many people who can say they have shot the Devil.

But you also looked after Jamie when he most needed you, just as Lohan looked after Scarlett and Richard looked after me. It makes me sad to have to say goodbye to you. You've been true friends, but that's the way it has to be."

"You're not coming with us!" Richard sounded shocked.

"We can't, Richard. At least, not all of us. Flint and I came from the past. You know that. We were brought into your world for a purpose but that's over now. We have no reason to stay."

"You're going back where you came from?"

"No. That's finished too. We have another journey."

Richard hesitated. "What about the others?" he stammered.

"That's up to them." Matt looked across the glowing fire. "Jamie, Scarlett, Pedro. You have a choice. You can stay here and help build this world. Or you can come with us. But you have to choose now."

There was a long silence. Then Scarlett laughed nervously. "You don't make things very easy for us, Matt."

"It's easy for me," Jamie said. "I'm leaving too." He looked up and the flames, low now, reflected in his face. His eyes were very bright. "Holly, I've loved travelling with you and being your friend," he went on. "But I never really got used to not having Scott around and I guess I need him now. Or Flint. Whatever he wants to call himself, we belong together. So that's my decision."

"Of course I understand," Holly said but there was a crack in her voice.

"I want to go with Matteo," Pedro said. "What is there for me in Peru? There is nothing. You think I want to go back to Poison Town? Forget it!" He drained his glass. He had drunk a lot of wine that night. "I'm with you."

"That just leaves me," Scarlett said. She glanced at Richard. Of the five of them, she was the most torn. But finally she came to her decision. "I'm one of the Five," she said simply. "I suppose that's all it comes down to. I would like to go back to Dulwich. I had a friend called Aidan and I'd love to know what happened to him … or maybe it would be better not to find out. And I'd like to help, if I could. But if I was left on my own I'd probably regret it for ever, so provided there are no more shape-changers, evil monks or mad sheikhs, I'll stick with Matt and see where it takes me." She sighed. "So that's that."

Matt stood up. "We should leave now," he said.

They all made their goodbyes, keeping them as brief as possible. None of them trusted themselves to speak too much. Matt shook hands with Lohan and hugged Holly. Finally he came face-to-face with Richard one last time. "Goodbye, Richard," he said. "You may not believe it but I can promise you that we will see each other again one day, not so long from now, and it won't be quite as you imagine. We'll all meet again. Nothing is ever completely over."

"Goodbye, Matt. I'll miss you."

The two of them embraced. Then the five Gatekeepers gathered their things and set off. Richard still had no idea where they were going.

They walked in a group, making their way across the ice with the sea behind them, heading towards the mountains. If the fortress had still been standing, it would have been right in front of them. But it wasn't and although it might have been an illusion, it seemed as if the mountains had opened up, revealing a path that would take them further on.

That was the last Richard saw of them … five small figures in their Antarctic gear, getting smaller and smaller as they moved towards the horizon. But that wasn't what he would remember most. The weather had changed and unexpectedly Oblivion had become quite extraordinarily beautiful. The ice was sparkling, a pure and brilliant white. There was no sign of the huge crater that had been formed and so little remaining of the fortress that it simply blended into the landscape. The snow looked as if had fallen long ago and had lain there undisturbed ever since. There was a mist hanging in the air, obscuring the mountains that rose up into a sky, which was now the softest grey infused by layers of pink that shimmered through. The first birds had already returned … just a few of them. They were wheeling round and round, their wings outstretched, as if reclaiming the nesting grounds that had once been theirs.

"There's a ship coming!" Lohan said.

Richard twisted round and sure enough a single frigate was ploughing through the water, heading towards them. He turned and looked back across the ice.

It was empty. The Five had gone.

ENVOI

FIFTY-SEVEN

An envoi is a short chapter which you find at the end of a book. It's a very literary word, a sort of goodbye. I can't imagine why I should remember it now. I think Miss Keyland taught me the term a very long time ago. And there's another funny thing. I started this story with her and I'm finishing it with her too – which is more than she deserves because she was actually a pretty nasty piece of work.

There is so much to tell about what happened after Antarctica. In fact, I could write a whole book about it, and maybe one day I will, although I think I've written quite enough already. My job now is just to tie up the loose ends, as it were. And perhaps to add a little more.

After Matt and the others disappeared, we packed a few things and made our way down to the beach, not saying very much and feeling very full and tired after so much food and drink. It was also the middle of the night, not that you would have known it. We arrived at the beach just in time to be met by some French marines from the *Duc d'Orléans* and they ferried us out in an inflatable boat and that was how we finally left Oblivion behind.

The captain wanted to hear everything that had happened before he would weigh anchor again. He was particularly keen to know why the nuclear missiles hadn't gone off although it seemed quite an irrelevant detail to me. He was amazed and, I think, a little ashamed when we told him that the Old Ones had been beaten.

After all, he had gone off, and left us and, indeed, he wouldn't have come back at all if his engines and guidance systems hadn't gone haywire and forced him to turn around. He had been certain he was being drawn to his death, that the Old Ones had taken control of his ship. So he and his men were hugely relieved to find that everyone had gone and only we were left.

And then, before we left, he insisted on climbing back up to the ice shelf and examining everything for himself. Not that there was much left to look at. The fortress had gone, the ice was undisturbed, and apart from the planes and the tents and the two gravestones with their five-pointed stars, there was no evidence that anything had actually taken place. The captain could see quite easily that *something* had happened. He could tell just from looking at the sky and the sea, at the birds that had returned and the occasional penguins that appeared, jetting across the water. But when he returned to the ship, he was completely mystified and spent much of the journey home trying to make us tell him more.

As for me, I was dead to the world and if any high-level conversations took place, I didn't hear them. I was given a cabin and a bunk bed and, as far as I remember, I slept flat out for the next twenty-four hours while the *Duc d'Orléans* headed back to Europe. It must have been difficult for the captain because although he was the most senior officer, in charge of the ship, he had actually deserted the French navy, heading off under his own steam to take on the Old Ones – so he wasn't sure where to go next. A lot of his men had died and he felt responsible for them. I did talk to him a few times and he seemed a nice enough man. I hope he didn't get into trouble for what he had done but I doubt that he did. Anyone who had fought against the Old Ones was greeted as a hero ... even Commander David Cain of the US *Polar Star*. He actually became Vice President of the New United States of America. People were willing to forgive the fact that he had been completely useless.

I didn't want to talk about Oblivion – and certainly not with the captain. My cabin was next door to Matt's friend, Richard Cole, and we had an adjoining door, so in a way we were thrown together and on the journey home we became friends. He never told me exactly what had happened in the fortress but I often heard him crying out in his sleep and I know it gave him nightmares. To be honest, Lohan made me nervous and I saw much less of him. He struck me in some ways as being quite sinister, and I was glad when we docked at Brest and he announced that he wouldn't be coming with us to England. He would head east ... to find his family and friends back in Hong Kong. I don't think Richard was too sorry to see him go either, although the two of them parted amicably enough.

Lohan had a long way to go and I can't tell you if he arrived because I never heard from him again. I bet he did, though. He was a major criminal who would cheerfully kill whoever stood in his way. If anyone was able to look after themselves, it was him.

So many more adventures. Our time in Brest, our journey across northern France, crossing the Channel back to England and then finally the return to London and contact with the Nexus. But that will have to wait for another time.

We managed to find our way back to the underground survival pod but by the time we got there, the medium, Miss Ashwood, was dead. She'd warned us that she was ill and apparently she'd died peacefully in her sleep shortly after we'd left. But everyone else was there and they couldn't believe we'd made it back. Richard and I were both treated like heroes, although I felt guilty because whatever Matt might have said, I hadn't actually done very much at all. And there was more good news. I was amazed to discover that Graham Fletcher and his brother, Will, had both survived St Meredith's. It was interesting that once Jamie and I had gone through the door and the ginger-haired woman had been shot in the head, the other policemen lost interest in it all. I suppose there was nothing left to fight about.

We spent a month at the pod but in the end it was too claustrophobic, hiding out all the time, and anyway, there was less danger now that the Old Ones had gone. Of course, it was going to take the country years and years to recover. Pollution scales in London were off the map and the dogs, the rats and the gangs still hadn't gone away. Finally, there was a meeting and a whole group of us decided to leave together, following the canal out of London, heading back exactly the way we had come. This time we had to go on foot so it took a lot longer, but fortunately we didn't run into any marauding cannibals or anything like that along the way.

My own village had been destroyed, but Graham Fletcher had discovered another when he had been the Traveller, one not so far away. It still had buildings standing and fields ready for planting, and there was nobody living there so that was where we settled. And there you have it. I had been chased the whole length of the country. I had crossed the world through a mysterious door. And now I was back almost exactly where I'd started. Funny how it goes.

It was difficult at first. I know that Richard badly missed Matt. And I was surprised how much I missed Jamie ... and George as well. But very quickly things began to get better and this is the important thing.

The world was healing itself.

You could see it every day in the weather, the clear skies, the fact that you could actually see stars at night. I'd had no idea how beautiful they were. The seeds we planted quickly grew instead of withering and dying. Fish began to reappear in the rivers and animals in the woods. We still had no electricity or telephones – in fact we don't to this day, despite all the work being done on the lines. But people stopped attacking people. If there were any police around, they had decided to hang up their black uniforms and do something useful. There was no need to be afraid any more. More people started arriving, coming out of the fields and woods, looking for somewhere to settle down, and very quickly our community grew.

I am seventy years old now. I've had a pretty reasonable life, with a husband, four children and no fewer than eleven grandchildren. I still see the Traveller, who married Sophie (the woman with fair hair from the pod). I'm glad he doesn't need to travel any more. Everyone in the village asks me about Oblivion and people can't believe I was actually there. And I shot the Devil. I suppose that is something to be proud about.

Richard lives just a few doors away. He married late and had just one child, a son. I wasn't at all surprised when he christened him Matt and I sometimes think he even looks a little bit like Matt too – or what Matt would have looked like if he'd grown up – with the same dark hair and blue eyes. Richard is ten years older than me and his hair has gone quite white but he's still in pretty good shape. He never wrote a single word about his adventures, even though he had always promised to. In the end, he left that to me. I'm not sure what will happen to all these pages, but I expect in the end the Old Ones will be forgotten, just as they were forgotten after they were first defeated, ten thousand years ago. I don't really mind. Just so long as they don't come back.

And the Five?

They went back to the dreamworld, as that was what lay on the other side of the mountains of Oblivion. When we were on the *Lady Jane* together, Jamie told me something of the dreamworld and I know how he saw it, how it was when he and the others visited it before the end: black and white, like a desert, with everything dying or dead. It was a world full of frightening things ... giant swans that swooped out of the night sky, poisonous trees that turned out to be volcanic eruptions. There was a huge library in the middle of it all. Matt had visited it – but none of the others.

Jamie had told me all this, but in fact when he and the others returned, it all changed.

As they made their way forward, leaving the ice and the Antarctic night behind them, the colours came back. The sky turned blue. A bright yellow sun rose over the horizon. The hills were covered with grass and of course there were hedges and wild flowers dotted here and there like splodges of paint. The sea which had once seemed so dark and threatening was suddenly crystal clear, reflecting the sun, with waves breaking onto a white sand beach.

In front of their eyes, the dreamworld changed and became something quite different from what they had experienced. There were birds in the trees and animals – cows and sheep – in the fields. Matt saw a grey horse cantering across a field, throwing its head from side to side and kicking out with its hooves, and he had to smile because he recognized it. It was the very horse he had ridden in the first battle at Scathack Hill, all those years ago. Meanwhile, Scarlett found herself in an orchard, and not one with maggoty apples like the ones I'd spent so many years picking. There were peaches and apricots and every kind of fruit right at her fingertips. There was a bonfire burning in the distance and it added its scent to the summer air.

Flint and Jamie were walking together as though they'd never been apart. As far as Jamie was concerned, it was as if Scott had never died because really he and Flint were the same, even if they had lived centuries apart. Pedro simply stood there, wide-eyed, unable to take it all in. And gradually they were no longer alone in the dreamworld. There were other people and somehow they seemed to know them. Houses sprung up in the distance, with smoke curling from chimneys. They heard music.

And finally, right in the middle of it all, they came upon the library. It hadn't changed – at least, not in size. But the walls and the doorways, the windows and domes were all bright and colourful, and even though Matt had sworn he would never go back in there again, he didn't feel threatened any more.

The Librarian was waiting for them when they arrived and he wasn't alone. There was a woman with him. Scar – the first Scar, the one who had lived ten thousand years ago – had once said she had met a strange woman in the dream world, but none of the other Gatekeepers had seen her before. And here's the strange thing. There was only one woman but she looked different to each and every one of them. To Pedro, she was Peruvian, small and olive-skinned. To Scarlett, she was Indonesian. Flint and Jamie saw her as Native American. And Matt saw her in a pink jacket and a white linen dress, on her way to a wedding – just as she had been long ago. His mother. A mother to all of them. That was what she was and it was as if the Five had become one.

You're wondering how I know all this.

It's very simple. I dreamt it.

I have often visited the dreamworld. I have seen Matt, Jamie, Flint, Pedro and Scarlett and spoken to each of them. It's a little different for me because in the morning, when I wake up, I can't remember everything they've said, but enough of it is there for me to scribble down notes in a book and that is what I've written here. Richard has also been there, although less often, but he tells me that one day he will go there and he won't return. I have a feeling that the same thing will happen to me.

But that's still a long way away and in the meantime I have

plenty of work to do, the garden to see to, the dinner to be made.

Sometimes, in the evening, Richard strolls round to my house or I go to his and we sneak out a bottle of wine, which we make ourselves from the elderberries that just won't stop growing. We like it when there's just the two of us and the sun is beginning to set and we can smell fresh hay in the air. I open the bottle and pour two glasses and we sit down opposite each other, by the fire.

"To the Five," I say.

"To the Five," he replies.

We clink glasses and we really are as happy as we can be.

GO BACK TO THE BEGINNING, AND

Raven's Gate

He always knew he was different.
First there were the dreams.
Then the deaths began.

Evil Star

It began with Raven's Gate.
But it's not over yet.
Once again the enemy is stirring.

Nightrise

Darkness covers the earth.
The Old Ones have returned.
The battle must begin.

Author photo by Des Willie

ANTHONY HOROWITZ is the author of the number one bestselling Alex Rider books and The Power of Five series. He has enjoyed huge success as a writer for both children and adults, most recently with his highly acclaimed Sherlock Holmes novel, *The House of Silk*.

He has won numerous awards, including the Bookseller Association/Nielsen Author of the Year Award, the Children's Book of the Year Award at the British Book Awards, and the Red House Children's Book Award.

Anthony has also created and written many major television series, including *Injustice*, *Collision* and the award-winning *Foyle's War*.

WATCH THE COVER COME TO LIFE... Download The Power of Five app from the App Store or Google Play, then hold your device in front of the cover or the author photo and watch them come to life.